3/15/96

Coyne Thanks for taking the wait and getting my f... published

D0128760

THE ULTIMATE FISHING GUIDE

MARCH 1996

Tight lines,

Steve Price

THE
ULTIMATE
FISHING
GUIDE

*WHERE TO GO, WHEN TO LEAVE, WHAT TO TAKE,
WHAT TO WEAR, WHAT TO KNOW, HOW TO FIND OUT,
& OTHER INDISPENSABLE INFORMATION
FOR THE ANGLER*

STEVEN D. PRICE

COMPUTERIZED GRAPHICS BY MARK HANSEN

HarperPerennial
A Division of HarperCollinsPublishers

THE ULTIMATE FISHING GUIDE. Copyright © 1996 by Steven D. Price. All rights reserved. Printed in the United States of America. No part of this book may be used or reproduced in any manner whatsoever without written permission except in the case of brief quotations embodied in critical articles and reviews. For information address HarperCollins Publishers, Inc., 10 East 53rd Street, New York, New York 10022.

HarperCollins books may be purchased for educational, business, or sales promotional use. For information, please write to: Special Markets Department, HarperCollins Publishers, Inc., 10 East 53rd Street, New York, New York 10022.

FIRST EDITION

DESIGNED BY JOEL AVIROM AND JASON SNYDER

Library of Congress Cataloging-in-Publication Data
Price, Steven D.
    The ultimate fishing guide : where to go, when to leave, what to take, what to wear, what to know, how to find out, and other indispensable information for the angler / Steven D. Price.
        p.   cm.
    Includes bibliographical references.
    ISBN 0-06-273290-0 (pb : alk. paper)
    1. Fishing. 2. Fishing—Equipment and supplies. I. Title.
SH441.P9 1996
799.1'2—dc20   95-19028

96 97 98 99 00 ❖/RRD 10 9 8 7 6 5 4 3 2 1

*To Martin Price, who could always be counted
on to save time for, and spend time with,
his son, especially on a lake or along a stream.
This book is lovingly dedicated to his memory.*

CONTENTS

ACKNOWLEDGMENTS

Thanks to David Blinken; Kathy Burd; Kevin Dart of Shimano; Clem Dipper of *Fishing Tackle Retailer*; Arnold Falk; Alanna Fischer of the American Museum of Fly Fishing; Jim Gorman; Robin Hopp of The In-Fisherman; Nick Karas; Joe Kuti and Tony Fedler of the American Sportfishing Association; Loretta and Bill Landsman; Donald Maclean of Lac Loon Fly Fishing; Caryn, Jamie, and Jim Magid; Bruce Matthews of the New York Sportfishing and Aquatic Resources Education Program; Gail M. Morchower of the International Sport Fishing Association; Lori-Ann Murphy of Reel Women Fly Fishing Adventures; Gil Musinger; Rich Pagano; Christopher Parkening; Bruce Richards of Scientific Anglers; Sharon Rushton of the Future Fisherman Foundation; Doug Tucker-Eccher of The Bass Pond; Mary Wright of Bass Pro Shop's Product Information Department;

And to the many other manufacturers, distributors, and dealers who sent catalogs, brochures, and good wishes for this project.

Also, a heaping helping of gratitude to: Tony Ballay, for his good words on tournament fishing; Dr. Larry Burd, for forty-something years of friendship, from Lake Ashmere to the Genesee River to Lake of the Woods; Angus Cameron, mentor, friend, and inspiration: "Wherever The Cameron sits *is* the head of the table."; John Day, HarperCollins' resident computer ace (and improver of the breed); Sandy Densen, raconteur and fishing pal, whose review of the manuscript was of inestimable assistance; Jack Fragomeni, for his piece on guiding, his classroom materials on fly-fishing, and his plentiful good cheer; Joe Guglielmelli, of The Black Orchid Bookshop, for his essay on the raft of mystery novels that involve fishing; Mark Hansen, who deftly produced the book's computer-generated graphics out of cyberspace, if not thin air; Lisa and Joe Hughes of PRADCO, for pointing me in helpful directions, and for Joe's essay on lure design innovations; Gordon Kato, a very model of an agent; Richard Liebmann-Smith, for his initial help and ongoing encouragement; Joan Lipton and Norton Wolf, for their ongoing encouragement and for their cookery section; Nick Lyons, for his generosity of spirit and in sharing resources; Jerry O'Connor, for his down-home hospitality (and also to "Ernie," the most enthusiastic canine angler this side of "Norman" McKinnis); Rose Price, for maternal encouragement and the gift of a love of language and books; and Robert Wilson, a Most-Valuable-Player-caliber editor.

And to Anne L.W. Price, who maintained her composure despite cascades of catalogs, snowstorms of fly-tying feathers, hours of TV fishing shows, and the time when a fish was uncooperative enough to strike while she minded her husband's fishing rod.

INTRODUCTION

At the height of the "Whole [Fill-in-the-Category] Catalog" craze some 20 years ago, I came up with an idea for a sourcebook of equestrian products, services, and organizations. I rounded up four other book-publishing types who, as I did, spent many non-working hours on and around horses, we divvied up the known equestrian world and then set to work. The result was *The Whole Horse Catalog*, a survey of what's available for horses and riders and where to find out more about whatever subject might be of interest.

Fade out, horses; cue the fish. . .

Some five years ago, I began doing public relations work for a horse farm in northern Kentucky, an assignment that took me several days each month to its 700+-acre spread outside of Louisville. Among the fringe benefits was the chance to spend leisure hours fishing in the farm's half-dozen ponds and one large lake. Some real lunker largemouths often proved cooperative, and at least one member of the farm's staff was always available as companionable company.

As if that weren't a slice of heaven, literally five minutes down the road was a shop devoted to fly-fishing. Wooly Buggers on a fly rod became a viable alternative to Texas-rigged plastic worms on a bait-casting rod. The shop became my home-away-from-home-away-from-home, and when I wasn't spending free time wetting a line, I could be found squinting over the proprietor's shoulder as he shared the arcane mysteries of spinning deer hair into bass bugs and other skills of the fly-tying bench.

The Kentucky idyll ended just about the time *The Whole Horse Catalog* was due for an updated revision. As equestrian catalogs came pouring in, I thought back to Kentucky lakes and farm ponds. Was there a similar volume for anglers, one that covered fishing products, services, and organizations?

A few laps around bookstores and libraries revealed nothing along those lines. Although most how-to-fish manuals included information on what to use as well as how to use it, there was no sourcebook as such in print, certainly nothing that encompassed the range of fishing disciplines.

On the way to a New Jersey fly-fishing exposition, I broached the matter to a fellow writer/editor/part-time angler, Richard Liebmann-Smith. Good idea, he replied, quickly adding that the book should definitely not include how-to-catch-fish instruction.

Richard got no argument from me. My record in that area is spotty at best, certainly nothing that suggested holding myself out as a master angler. But even if my ambition to be able to catch fish like a pro remains unfulfilled, the book that I contemplated could certainly refer readers to top-of-the-line books and videos, clinics, and other sources of expert instruction.

In addition to not being a how-to-fish book, another thing that *The Ultimate Fishing Guide* would not be, nor could it be, is a fishing version of *Consumer Reports*. Even if one has the requisite expertise about and unrestricted access to all the tackle, accessories, clothing, and other items, the task of analyzing and (either expressly or by implication) rating products and services is better left to magazines.

One example will suffice to explain why. Two

years ago, a "tackle roundup" column in a major magazine criticized a reel for lacking a particular feature. A year later, the same columnist had nothing but kind words for the reel's new model with its no-longer-missing feature. It takes at least nine or ten months from the time a book is completed to when it is published. A magazine's time frame offers a flexibility to report on ever-changing and ever-improved goods and services in a way that books cannot. Moral: leave it to the mags.

As for the prices of goods and services, no one needs to be reminded how quickly they go up, to the extent that any book that cites current market prices is instantly dated. Similarly, a manufacturer's introducing new products or adding "innovations" to existing ones has an effect: older products tend to be considered less desirable and, accordingly, their cost drops. In addition, the growing number of discount tackle outlets, magazine subscription "deals," and other opportunities to pay less than list price are other dangers in a book's quoting even approximate prices as a guideline.

Someday someone will compile a "Whole Fishing Boat Catalog" that will cover all the types of vessels used for fresh- and saltwater fishing as well as inboard and outboard motors, bait-wells, depth-finders, navigation aids, and everything else used on and around boats. The subject deserves such a thorough treatment, which space constraints did not allow this author to consider doing even in the most cursory fashion.

All right, you may well be asking, if that's what *The Ultimate Fishing Guide* is not, then what *is* it?

In the best of all worlds, a tyro angler is introduced to the sport by a mentor, usually a friend or a relative who can provide expert guidance through the maze (if not minefield) of tackle, clothing, accessories, and other items. Often, however, such a person isn't available or, although a good teacher

on the water, is as equally at sea on land when it comes to "stuff." That leaves a store's salesperson or, in the case of catalog sales, a telephone order-taker. Although that person may have the best will in the world, he or she can't always be relied on to know what's appropriate and, equally relevant, what's essential. Catalog copy too is not always the most helpful, since it tends to assume expertise on the part of the prospective purchaser, and often raises more questions than answers.

Accordingly, one of the book's functions would be to guide the novice with regard to what's necessary.

A detailed analysis of each and every piece of tackle, accessory, or apparel used in all fishing disciplines would be impossible to do in anything under an encyclopedia-sized volume, and probably several of them. Moreover, such an effort is unnecessary because no one fishes in a vacuum. Whether it's someone on the lake, stream, bay, or ocean, or in a tackle shop, or via a magazine article or TV show, there are people whom a novice will find ready, willing, and able to share their knowledge about the specific needs for local fishing conditions. But the novice still needs some background, if only to understand what these experts are talking about; something of a primer to supply a working knowledge of the basics, including the right vocabulary.

That was exactly the approach: a volume that would help novice anglers with regard to basic hardware, yet contain a plethora of subjects of interest to more experienced fishermen. A book that would cast a wide net, exploring the range of products, services, and organizations that are available to help catch fish. A sourcebook. . . a guidebook.

Then too, it became clear that *The Ultimate Fishing Guide* should be as much of a reference book as possible, providing the reader with what can collectively be referred to as "for further information." Where can you find out more about rods, reels, and other tackle? Fishing vacation opportunities? Fishing shows on radio and television? Catalog shopping? Locations of tackle shops? That meant compiling lists: names and addresses of manufacturers and dealers, titles and authors of instructional and expository books, videos, magazines, and other publications. . . fishing and environmental groups. . . the list of prospective lists grew almost as fast as the lists themselves.

[A word about the lists of manufacturers, distributors, and retailers that appear in this book: the companies so listed are those that came to our attention through references in books and magazines, by word-of-mouth, and through advertisements and promotional materials. The lists are not intended to be a complete roster of a particular category, not should the failure to mention a company be necessarily considered any reflection on the quality of its goods or services.]

And on a more savory note, the book should also teem with fillers and "factoids," bits of information that delight as well as instruct.

In addition to helping to formulate the book's approach, Brer Liebmann-Smith was kind enough to recommend an agent: Gordon Kato of International Creative Management, who first smiled favorably on the idea and then cast my book proposal into publishing waters. Several houses rose to the bait, Gordon worked his magic, and the project ultimately found its home waters in the reference department of HarperCollins Publishers.

Drop a pebble in a pond, and watch the splash grow in ever-widening circles. Make an inquiry, and receive a response that leads to another source of information. And another, and another. Although the people who were involved in this way are acknowledged elsewhere, I cannot thank them

From Great Fishing Tackle Catalogs of the Golden Age.
[courtesy Nick Lyons Books]

enough for their enthusiasm, their generosity of spirit, and their more tangible contributions. Letters and phone calls to tackle manufacturers and dealers, book and magazine publishers, clubs and associations, and many other sources of information led not only to answers in their particular areas of interest and expertise, but also produced equally intriguing and fruitful suggestions about where else to look. For example, a question to a tackle manufacturer's representative about colleges and universities that offer courses in fishing drew the recommendation that I get in touch with someone at the American Museum of Fly Fishing. No, she hadn't heard of a master list either, but why didn't I put the question to a fellow who teaches a course in fly-fishing at a college in upstate New York? I did, and although he didn't know of such a list, our conversation revealed that he knows a great deal about using the services of a guide. . . as you'll see from Jack Fragomeni's essay on that subject.

That was not the only time that serendipity reared its head. A chance word to one of the proprietors of a bookshop that specializes in mystery novels about mysteries that include fishing produced the essay on that subject cajoled out of the proprietor's partner. Similarly, a question to the neighborhood video shop's resident film expert led to the list of fishing-in-films list that appears in quiz form.

What you have in your hands is what its author, contributors, and editors believe to be the ultimate fishing reference guide. The section on species of fish help you locate and identify popular sport fish. If you're the competitive type, the extensive list of International Game Fish Association world records indicates what to shoot for if you want to get your name in the record books.

The chapters on tackle might be considered "hardware." In addition to a survey of rods, reels, line, terminal tackle (including bobbers, sinkers, and swivels), hooks, and accessories, you'll have the names and addresses of manufacturers and other sources from which further information comes in the form of catalogs, brochures, and videos. This "tackle" section also contains introductions to rod-building, tackle collectibles, and ice-fishing.

The "bait" category includes live bait, a panorama of plugs, spoons, and other lures, and flies of all types. Moreover, the public relations director of a major lure company offers insights into the development and marketing of such items.

The section on clothing, intended to present the range of apparel most often used by anglers,

From Great Fishing Tackle Catalogs of the Golden Age.
[courtesy Nick Lyons Books]

ranges from footwear to hats and from underwear to outerwear (and everything in-between).

There's more to fishing that doing it only in our "home waters." The section on vacation opportunities contains a wealth of suggestions to help you plan and then make the most of your holidays. There's even an essay on selecting a guide, something that you'll find helpful wherever you go to fish.

You'll note, however, that the vacation chapter does not contain recommendations of specific resorts or even lists of them. The wisest way to choose a destination is to base the decision on the recommendations of people who have first- or even secondhand information. That's why we suggest you consult travel agents and (through books and articles) writers, who are familiar with or have access to such intelligence.

Fishing on the airwaves? Programs on TV and even the radio combine advice on tackle and techniques with vacation ideas and plain ol' wish fulfillment. *The Ultimate Fishing Guide* critiques the TV shows and gives a roster of stations that carry In-Fisherman's well-regarded radio show.

As an integral part of this book's emphasis on safe and enjoyable sport, the section on first aid emphasizes preventing outdoors medical problems as much as it does the treatment.

Tournaments have become a major aspect of sport (and of the fishing industry too). An experienced tournament fisherman describes opportunities that range from local tournaments to national "major-league" competitions. The section contains an international calendar of events and references to sources for further information, as well as an interview with Christopher Parkening, whose successes in competitive fishing rival his acclaim as a classical guitarist.

The chapter on "catch-and-release" discusses the pros and cons of this conservation approach and then recommends techniques to be used when returning fish to their home waters.

Not all fish are caught and released. . . some are caught and reheated. The chapter on fish cookery outlines the most popular methods of preparing your catch, and even offers a few recipes.

The section on organizations and associations includes a state-by-state roster of sport-fishing and environmental agencies.

Want to learn to fish? There's a listing of fishing schools, and one of colleges and universities that offer courses in fishing and related disciplines.

Sections on matters of interest to women and youngsters focus on these important segments of angling society. Another is on where to find out about fishing opportunities for the physically challenged.

Where to buy tackle and other products is answered by lists of mail-order catalog houses and a listing of tackle shops arranged by state and city or town.

Finally, just we all speak the same language, a glossary defines words and phrases from "Aberdeen" to "zinger."

Before turning you over to the text, I'm going to share my thoughts on several subjects.

Contrary to popular notion, Izaak Walton, the seventeenth-century author of *The Compleat Angler*, was not a fly-fisherman; he used balls of dough, insects, and worms. It was his fishing companion, Charles Cotton, who used artificials and who contributed the fly-fishing chapters to Walton's celebrated treatise. As with such other pursuits as cricket and riding to hounds, fly-fishing became an upper-class pastime, the technique of choice for catching trout and salmon. (The British still apply the term "coarse-fishing" to live bait and lures used for pike, perch, and other species, which shows which class controlled that portion of the language.)

Anyone attempting to take a panoramic view of the sport finds this distinction existing in this country too. Usually not in so many words, though, but in attitudes that reflect the gulf between fly-fishing and everything else. In one corner, wearing the olive vest and carrying the 6-weight bamboo rod, is the fraternity of fly-fishers who regard the use of live bait or plastic facsimiles with the same degree of horror that certain religions view a diet of pork. In the other corner, wearing a black back-brace belt and carrying two flippin' and one pitchin' rods, are guys and gals who pay no attention to strictures first promulgated along the banks of English chalk streams—they're too busy having a good time to care about such matters.

Shall the twain meet? Not to hear the fly-fishing fraternity talk about it (bait-fishermen tend to have a laissez-faire fish-and-let-fish view). However, tackle manufacturers and a growing number of tackle shops have taken a considerably more ecumenical view of things. Not too long ago Cabela's and Bass Pro Shop made no effort to attract the fly-fishing market. Then both firms devoted a few pages of their catalogs to such tackle, accessories, and clothing. The number of pages grew, until the subject warranted its own catalog.

Also from the first batch of research material, the importance of fishing as a national pastime became increasing clear. Although statistical sources differ over the precise number, between 60 and 85 million Americans fish. That works out to one in every four or five of us. Women constitute one-third of the number of license holders. As for how often we fish, one survey revealed that among anglers age seven years or older who fish more than once a year, 31% freshwater anglers admitted to fishing 110 or more days a year, 38% between 25 and 109 days, and 30% between 6 and 24 days. As for saltwater, the numbers were 23%, 39%, and 39%, respectively.[1]

As long as we're flinging industry statistics about, you may be interested to learn that 67% of tackle purchasers account for 33% of the products. The percentages for freshwater gear breaks down fairly evenly (that is, 33% apiece) among fishermen who are most interested in bass, trout, panfish, and all other species.

The financial impact of sport-fishing is staggering; a few statistics will prove this point. The annual amount of money spent by Puerto Rican residents and guests in pursuit of billfish was $26 million in 1993. Freshwater fishing in Texas contributes $2 billion to $4 billion annually to that state's economy. And despite diminishing amounts of land and water resources for outdoor recreation and the devastating increase of pollution, the U.S. Fish and Wildlife Service predicts that the number of recreational fisherman in the U.S. will increase by 90% over the next 40 years.

That's a great deal of people spending a great deal of money, with the prospect of much more being spent in the future. Legislators and other officials—in whose hands the future of sport-fishing rests through the judicious use of our land and water resources—should be made aware of this potent economic and political force, if they aren't already.

Which brings up the matter of participation. There's the political variety, as in the good work done at local, state, and national levels by environmentally-conscious clubs, federations, and other organizations. You owe it to yourself to be aware of the work being done to protect wildlife, preserve existing natural resources, and increase the amount

of land and waters that this and future generations can enjoy. Even if you don't think of yourself as a "joiner," you can still explore the rich sources of information offered by private groups and local and state agencies and networks (you'll find their names and addresses throughout the book). And don't be surprised if one day you find yourself rolling up your sleeves and pitching in.

Guides who are worth their salt direct fishermen to productive waters, but they don't do the actual fishing. That's the fisherman's responsibility. A similar sense of participation should apply to this book. *The Ultimate Fishing Guide* may not be on a CD-ROM (at least in its first incarnation), but it's meant to be just as interactive. Use it as a hands-on workbook: send for catalogs, brochures, and newsletters, add books, magazines, and videos to your library, join on-line networks, and then let these resource tools become catalysts for acquiring even more information.

An old adage tells us that "books can't make you a good fisherman, but they can make you a better one." That's the real message of *The Ultimate Fishing Guide*, and it's the intention and the wish of everyone associated with this book. The rest is up to you.

Tight lines,

STEVEN D. PRICE

P.S. And please think of the information highway as a two-way street. If you come across any products, services, or organizations that you think deserve to be included in future editions, we'd very much like to heard from you. Please send your suggestion, along with a description of the item or service and the name, address, and phone number of the manufacturer or organization, to *The Ultimate Fishing Guide*, c/o Reference Department, HarperCollins Publishers, 10 East 53 Street, New York, NY 10022.

---

[1] Apropos of women who fish, let's get a linguistic issue out of the way. As this book uses the word, "fisherman" refers to an angler of either sex. Although some may object to the sexist implications, please understand that, like "craftsman" and "horseman," the word "fisherman" has a traditional meaning that has nothing to do with gender specificity. Read "angler," "fisher," or "fisher-person" instead if you must, but please accept the usage of "fisherman" and "fishermen" in the spirit in which the words appear.

The ULTIMATE FISHING GUIDE

1

SPECIES OF FISH

The following list of selected frequently encountered game fish is divided alphabetically between freshwater and saltwater species.

For more detailed and more "scientific" descriptions of these and many other species, including reproductive and migratory patterns and fishing tips, consult the redoubtable *McClane's New Standard Fishing Encyclopedia and International Angling Guide* by A.J. McClane (Henry Holt, 1974).

Other good reference works are *The Complete Guide to North American Freshwater Game Fish* by Henry Waszczuk and Italo Labignan (Key Porter Books, 1992) and *Simon & Schuster's Guide to Saltwater Fish and Fishing* by Angelo Mojetta (Simon & Schuster/ Fireside, 1992).

A standard introductory guide for budding ichthyologists is *A History of Fishes*, 3rd edition, by J.R. Norman and P.H. Greenwood (John Wiley, 1975).

Fish Watching by C. Lavett Smith (Comstock/Cornell University Press, 1994) is a well-illustrated handbook for anyone interested in observing freshwater fish in their habitats. Among the book's many fascinating features is a guide to deciphering the classifications and the scientific names of species.

Freshwater

BASS, LARGEMOUTH

Scientific Name: Micropterus salmoides
Regional Names: largemouth; bigmouth; bucketmouth; black bass; green bass
Identifying Features: Mouth extends beyond eye; black to green back, with dark wavy band running the length of side; separated dorsal fins.
Primary Locations: weedy and mud-bottomed warm-water lakes and ponds throughout U.S. and Canada.

BASS, PEACOCK

Scientific Name: Cichla orinocensis
Regional Names: peacock; butterfly; royal *pavon*
Identifying Features: gold sides with three black vertical bands; aqua dorsal fins; protruding "bump" on head.
Primary Locations: Florida canals and northern South America.

BASS, REDEYE

Scientific Name: Micropterus coosae
Regional Names: Redeye; coosa; shoal bass; Chipola bass
Identifying Features: red eyes; black spot on gill cover; red dorsal, caudal, and anal fins, with a white tip on the caudal fin.
Primary Locations: Cold streams and ponds in southern U.S.

BASS, ROCK

Scientific Name: Ambloplites rupestris
Regional Names: black perch; goggle-eye; rock sunfish
Identifying Features: mouth extends beyond eye; dark mottled olive sides; red eye.
Primary Locations: clear rivers, ponds, and streams from New England and Canada to Gulf states.

BASS, SMALLMOUTH

Scientific Name: Micropterus dolomieui
Regional Names: smallmouth; bronzeback
Identifying Features: Bronze to brown back, with vertical bands on sides; three horizontal stripes behind eye; joined dorsal fins.
Primary Locations: rock-bottomed cool-water lakes and rivers in eastern and midwestern U.S. and throughout Canada.

BASS, SPOTTED

Scientific Name: Micropterus punctulas
Regional Names: Kentucky bass; Alabama spotted bass
Identifying Features: Olive-green back, with diamond-shaped spots above white belly.
Primary Locations: clear, deep lakes of midwestern, Gulf, and some western states.

BASS, STRIPED

Scientific Name: Morone saxatilis
Regional Name: striper
Identifying Features: black dash-like stripes along length of bright silver body.
Primary Locations: Atlantic and Pacific coastal waters; Gulf of Mexico (Louisiana to Florida); southern inland lakes and rivers.

BASS, WHITE

Scientific Name: Morone chrysops
Regional Names: whitey; silver bass; dwarf striper
Identifying Features: silver sides with black horizontal stripes; separated dorsal fins; ten unbroken narrow stripes; protruding lower jaw.
Primary Locations: large clear rivers and lakes throughout Midwest; Great Lakes, St. Lawrence River; and some southern and southwestern states.
Note: Often crossed with striped bass to produce "whiterocks."

BASS, YELLOW

Scientific Name: Morone mississippiensis
Regional Names: stripe; barfish; streaker
Identifying Features: dark olive back; six stripes running along body, the lower ones of which are broken; equal length of jaws.
Primary Locations: Shallow gravel and rocky lakes and riders of central U.S.

BLUEGILL

Scientific Name: Lepomis macrochirus
Regional Names: bream or brim; copperbelly; sunny or sunfish; sun perch
Identifying Features: round and flat body with dark vertical stripes above an orange "sun" belly; dark ear flap with no margin.
Primary Locations: quiet and weedy lakes and ponds throughout U.S. and Canada.

BOWFIN

Scientific Name: Amia calva
Regional Names: dogfish; grindle or grinnel; cypress trout; mudfish
Identifying Features: flattened bony head; olive heavily scaled body; long dorsal fin; lobe-shaped tail.
Primary Locations: Shallow lakes and slow-moving rivers in the midwestern and eastern U.S.

Burbot

BUFFALO, BIGMOUTH

Scientific Name: Ictiobus cyprinellus
Regional Names: buffalo; lake buffalo; blue buffalo
Identifying Features: round olive-brown to blue body; long dorsal fin; prominent mouth.
Primary Locations: large rivers and shallow lakes of the midwestern, Appalachian, and Gulf states.

BUFFALO, SMALLMOUTH

Scientific Name: Ictiobus bubalus
Regional Names: razorback buffalo; roachback
Identifying Features: light olive humped back over white belly; small downturned mouth.
Primary Locations: large rivers and warm lakes of the Midwest and South.

BULLHEAD, BLACK

Scientific Name: Ictalurus melas
Regional Names: bull; horned pout; yellow-belly cat
Identifying Features: black or dark green body with spine-like stripes with a light colored bar; dark facial barbels.

Primary Locations: mud bottoms of warm ponds and lakes throughout central and eastern U.S.

BULLHEAD, BROWN

Scientific Name: Ictalurus nebulosus
Regional Name: speckled cat
Identifying Features: mottled markings on yellow to light brown body; dark facial spines; strongly barbed spine.
Primary Locations: deep weedy lakes and slow-moving streams of central and eastern U.S.

BULLHEAD, YELLOW

Scientific Name: Ictalurus natalis
Regional Names: greaser; white whisker bull
Identifying Features: white barbels; no barbs on spine; rounded tail.
Primary Locations: lakes, rivers, and streams throughout U.S.
World Record: 4 lb. 4 oz.

BURBOT

Scientific Name: Lota lota
Regional Names: cusk; ling; lawyer
Identifying Features: eel-shaped

body with dark olive chain-like markings; spike on either side of nose; round tail.
Primary Locations: cold-water lakes and streams of U.S and Canada.
Note: The burbot is the only freshwater member of the cod family.

CARP

Scientific Name: Cyprinus carpio
Regional Names: German carp; European carp
Identifying Features: scaleless head with four barbels (barbules); olive-gold body with cross-hatched diamond-patterned scales.
Primary Locations: warm streams, lakes, rivers, and ponds throughout the U.S. and Canada.

CATFISH, BLUE

Scientific Name: Ictalurus furcatus
Identifying Features: Eight barbel "whiskers"; pale blue upper body above whitish lower portion.
Primary Locations: clear rivers and streams throughout U.S.

CATFISH, CHANNEL

Scientific Name: Ictalurus punctatus
Identifying Features: Eight barbel "whiskers"; olive-blue body with dark spots; deep forked tail.
Primary Locations: deep streams, rivers, and lakes in eastern and central U.S.

CATFISH, FLATHEAD

Scientific Name: Pylodictis olivaris
Regional Name: flathead
Identifying Features: Eight barbel "whiskers"; brown body with wide flat head and prominent lower jaw; square tail.
Primary Locations: slow-moving deep pools of rivers in central U.S.

CHAR, ARCTIC

Scientific Name: Salvelinus alpinus
Regional Names: blueback; silver char (when sea-run).
Identifying Features: pink, red, or cream spots on silver-green sides; white leading edges on lower fins. Reddish spots when sea-run.

Arctic Char

Primary Locations: upper U.S., Canada, and elsewhere in the world's arctic regions.

CRAPPIE, BLACK

Scientific Name: Pomoxis nigromaculatus
Regional Name: croppie
Identifying Features: olive-black back with scattered spots on sides; 7–8 spines on front dorsal fin.
Primary Locations: still ponds and lakes in central and eastern U.S. and Canada.

CRAPPIE, WHITE

Scientific Name: Pomoxis annularis
Regional Names: calico bass; papermouth
Identifying Features: olive-green back with spots arranged in vertical bars; six spines on front dorsal fin.
Primary Locations: silt-laden rivers and lakes in eastern and central U.S., as well as some western states.

GAR, ALLIGATOR

Scientific Name: Lepisosteus spatula

Identifying Features: olive-brown upper body with large black spots at rear and on rear fins. Two rows of teeth on upper jaw.
Primary Locations: central and southern U.S. and Mexico.

GAR, LONGNOSE

Scientific Name: Lepisosteus osseus
Identifying Features: slender nose; silvery body with overlapping diamond-shaped scales; spotted brown tail.
Primary Locations: Great Lakes, central and southern U.S.

GAR, SHORTNOSE

Scientific Name: Lepisosteus platostomus
Identifying Features: relatively short and slender nose (compared to longnose gar); small round spots on rear of body and fin.
Primary Locations: slow-moving rivers and streams and lakes of central U.S.

GRAYLING, ARCTIC

Scientific Name: Thymallus arcticus
Regional Names: Arctic trout; sailfin
Identifying Features: large rounded dorsal fin (its base as long as the fish's head); small dark spots on silver-violet sides.
Primary Locations: far northern streams, lakes, and rivers.

INCONNU

Scientific Name: Stenodus leucichthys
Regional Names: sheefish; connie
Identifying Features: silver body with green to pale brown back; dark-tipped dorsal and caudal fins; projecting lower jaw.
Primary Locations: Alaska and northwestern Canada.

MUSKELLUNGE

Scientific Name: Esox mesquinongy
Regional Names: muskie, 'lunge
Identifying Features: dark diamond-shaped markings on pale green back.
Primary Locations: Great Lakes and St. Lawrence River areas.

PERCH, YELLOW

Scientific Name: Perca flavescens
Regional Names: lake perch; striped perch
Identifying Features: dark vertical stripes on yellow sides; orange lower fins.
Primary Locations: lakes, ponds, and rivers throughout U.S. and Canada.

PERCH, WHITE

Scientific Name: Morone americana
Regional Names: whitey; silver perch
Identifying Features: olive to black green back, silver-green sides, connected dorsal fins.
Primary Locations: eastern coastal and tidal waters, and freshwater lakes and ponds.

PICKEREL, EASTERN CHAIN

Scientific Name: Esox niger
Regional Names: grass pickerel; chain jack
Identifying Features: elongated green-bronze body with dark chain-like markings on sides; unspotted dorsal fin.
Primary Locations: clear weeded rivers, creeks, and lakes in northeastern, midwestern, and southern U.S. and Canada.

PIKE, NORTHERN

Scientific Name: Esox lucius
Regional Names: great northern; jack or jackfish
Identifying Features: pale bars on olive-green back; scales on cheek and top of gill cover.
Primary Locations: large cold lakes in northern U.S., Canada, and other arctic regions.

REDHORSE, NORTHERN

Scientific Name: Moxostoma macrolepidotum
Regional Names: redfin; bigscale sucker
Identifying Features: short head with sucker mouth; silvery sides with red-orange fins and tail.
Primary Locations: clear rivers, streams, and lakes of north-central U.S. and Canada.

REDHORSE, SILVER

Scientific Name: Moxostoma anisurum
Identifying Features: short head with sucker mouth; silvery body with slate fins and tail.
Primary Locations: clear streams of central U.S. and Canada.

SALMON, ATLANTIC

Scientific Name: Salmo salar
Regional Name: ounaniche (in Canada)

Northern Pike

Identifying Features: small black spots on a yellow body; silver body (when sea-run); hooked lower jaw during spawning season.
Primary Locations: cold-water streams and lakes along Atlantic coast.

SALMON, CHINOOK

Scientific Name: Oncorhynchus tswawytscha
Regional Names: king; tyre; blackjaw
Identifying Features: black gums; silver body with dark spots on back and tail.
Primary Location: cold-water Pacific coastal waters.

SALMON, CHUM

Scientific Name: Oncorhynchus keta
Regional Names: dog salmon; calico salmon
Identifying Features: dark vertical bars on silver sides; black-edged fins.
Primary Location: northern Pacific.

SALMON, COHO

Scientific Name: Oncorhynchus kisutch
Regional Name: silver salmon
Identifying Features: blue-green back and silver sides; black spots on back and caudal fin.
Primary Locations: northern Pacific and freshwater rivers with access to ocean; also Great Lakes.

SALMON, LANDLOCKED ATLANTIC

Scientific Name: Salmo salar (the same as Atlantic salmon, since the Landlocked variety is considered the same fish)
Regional Name: ounaniche (in Canada)
Identifying Features: See Atlantic salmon
Primary Locations: landlocked lakes of northeastern U.S. and Canada.

Pink Salmon

SALMON, PINK

Scientific Name: Oncorhynchus gorbuscha
Regional Names: humpback; humpy; pinky
Identifying Features: silvery body with black spots on back; oval dark spots on caudal fin

(humped back in spawning males).
Primary Locations: Pacific coast and Great Lakes.

SALMON, SOCKEYE

Scientific Name: Oncorhynchus nerka
Regional Names: red salmon; kokanee
Identifying Features: tiny black spots on steel-blue back.
Primary Locations: Pacific Northwest, western Canada, and Alaska.

SHAD, AMERICAN

Scientific Name: Alosa sapidissima
Regional Name: white shad
Identifying Features: silvery body with a dark spot behind gill cover and other dark spots in one or two lateral rows along body.

Primary Locations: Atlantic and Pacific coasts and rivers with access to ocean.

STURGEON, WHITE

Scientific Name: Acipenser transmontanus

Identifying Features: elongated snout with four projections; five rows of plates on sides; upper fork of tail longer than lower fork.

Primary Locations: Pacific coast and large rivers with access to ocean; also, landlocked lakes in northern U.S.

SUNFISH, GREEN

Scientific Name: Lepomis cyanellus

Regional Names: green perch; sand bass; sunny

Identifying Features: mouth extending beyond eye; olive body with bronze belly; dark gill tab with pink rim.

Primary Locations: streams and ponds throughout central and western U.S.

SUNFISH, REDBREAST

Scientific Name: Lepomis auritus

Regional Names: yellowbelly; sun perch; sunny

Identifying Features: yellow-green sides with red belly; elongated black gill flap.

Primary Locations: creeks and rivers of eastern U.S. and Canada.

SUNFISH, REDEAR

Scientific Name: Lepomis microlophus

Regional Names: stumpknocker; shellcracker

Identifying Features: bronze to teal body with vertical bars on sides; red-edged gill flap.

Primary Locations: lakes and ponds throughout U.S., especially in the South.

TROUT, BROOK

Scientific Name: Salvelinus fontinalis

Regional Names: brookie; speckled trout; salter or sea trout (when sea-run)

Identifying Features: dark back with light worm-like markings; large pale and small red halo-like spots on side; dark and light edges on lower fins.

Primary Locations: cold streams, lakes, and rivers along eastern U.S. and Canada, often with access to sea.

TROUT, BROWN

Scientific Name: Salmo trutta
Regional Names: brownie; German brown
Identifying Features: yellowish-

brown sides with many black and fewer red/orange haloed spots; steel-gray sides on sea-run individuals.

Primary Locations: cool or relatively warm streams and rivers, with or without access to the sea.

TROUT, BULL

Scientific Name: Salvelinus confluentis

Regional Name: bull

Identifying Features: same shape and markings as Dolly Varden, but with a more prominent head.

Primary Locations: Rocky Mountain lakes and rivers.

TROUT, CUTTHROAT

Scientific Name: Salmo clarki

Regional Names: cutt; mountain trout

Identifying Features: prominent orange/red "slash" marking under lower jaw; black spots on body and tail.

Primary Locations: western U.S. mountain lakes and streams.

TROUT, DOLLY VARDEN

Scientific Name: Salvelinus malma

Dolly Varden Trout

Regional Names: Dolly; bull char
Identifying Features: cream and pink spots on silver-green sides.
Primary Locations: cool coastal waters.
Note: Named for the character in Charles Dickens' novel *Barnaby Rudge*, a woman who wore a polka-dotted green dress.

TROUT, GOLDEN

Scientific Name: Salmo aguabonita
Regional Names: goldie; mountain trout
Identifying Features: gold sides with red horizontal band and 10 dark oval marks; white edges on fins.
Primary Locations: mountain lakes and streams at high elevations.

TROUT, LAKE

Scientific Name: Salvelinus namaycush
Regional Names: laker; togue; gray trout
Identifying Features: light worm-shaped markings on dark background; deeply forked tail.
Primary Locations: lower depths of cold, clear lakes in upper Midwest and Canada.

TROUT, RAINBOW

Scientific Name: Salmo gairdneri gairdneri
Regional Name: 'bow

Identifying Features: pink lateral stripe and small black spots on silver sides.
Primary Locations: cold, well-oxygenated streams, lakes, and rivers, with or without access to salt water.

COASTAL RAINBOW TROUT (STEELHEAD)

Scientific Name: Salmo gairdneri irideus
Regional Name: steelies
Identifying Features: glowing steel-blue body with spots on upper body.
Primary Locations: Pacific Northwest and western Canada.

WALLEYE

Scientific Name: Stizostedion vitreum
Regional Name: walleye pike
Identifying Features: largest member of perch family; milky cast to eye (hence the name "walleye"); long, round olive body with dark narrow bands; white tip to lower fork of tail.
Primary Locations: large cool lakes in U.S. and Canada.

WHITEFISH, LAKE

Scientific Name: Coregonus clupeaformis
Regional Name: Otsego bass
Identifying Features: white arched body with small head; dark back in front of tail.
Primary Locations: lakes and

rivers in northern U.S. and Canada.

WHITEFISH, MOUNTAIN

Scientific Name: Prosopium williamsoni
Regional Name: Rocky Mountain whitefish
Identifying Features: round white body with brown back.
Primary Locations: lakes and streams in Rocky Mountain region of U.S. and Canada.

WHITEFISH, ROUND

Scientific Name: Prosopium cylindraceum
Regional Name: Menominee whitefish
Identifying Features: white tapered body with brown sides.
Primary Locations: Great Lakes and throughout Canada and Alaska.
World Record: 6 lb. 0 oz., Putahow River, Manitoba, Canada (1984)

Saltwater

AMBERJACK, GREATER

Scientific Name: Seriola dumerili
Regional Name: Medregal
Identifying Features: silvery body with yellow or copper stripe running from mid-eye to tail; dark band from upper jaw past eye; crescent tail.

Primary Locations: warm waters, especially the western Atlantic and particularly the West Indies.

BARRACUDA, GREAT

Scientific Name: Sphyraena barracuda
Regional Names: 'cuda; sea pike
Identifying Features: pointed head with prominent teeth; silver body with dark irregularly spaced blotches below lateral line.
Primary Locations: warm waters of western Atlantic, especially Florida Keys and Caribbean.

BASS, BLACK SEA

Scientific Name: Centropristis striata
Regional Names: humpback; pin bass
Identifying Features: flat head; high back of gray, brown, or black.
Primary Locations: bottom-feeder of northeast Atlantic coast.

STRIPED BASS

Scientific Name: Morone saxatilis
Regional Name: striper
Identifying Features: black dash-like stripes along length of bright silver body.
Primary Locations: Atlantic and Pacific coastal waters, especially New England and mid-Atlantic coasts.

BLACKFISH

See Tautog

BLUEFISH

Scientific Name: Pomatomus saltatrix
Regional Names: blue; snapper; chopper
Identifying Features: prominent lower jaw; sharp teeth (that make the fish risky to handle); pointed snout; blue-green body; tall dorsal and anal fins.
Primary Locations: Atlantic coast from New England to South America.

BONEFISH

Scientific Name: Albula vulpes
Regional Names: bone; grubber
Identifying Features: undershot jaw; long silver-green back with wide vertical bars above silvery sides.
Primary Locations: tropical coastal waters, especially Florida Keys and Bahamas "flats."

BONITO, ATLANTIC

Scientific Name: Sarda sarda
Identifying Features: blue-green back with darker oblique stripes; crescent tail.
Primary Location: Atlantic coastal waters from Newfoundland to northern Florida.

BONITO, PACIFIC

Scientific Name: Sarda chiliensis
Regional Name: California bonito
Identifying Features: virtually identical to Atlantic Bonito.
Primary Locations: Pacific Ocean, from British Columbia to Baja California, and also lower South America.

COBIA

Scientific Name: Rachycentron canadum
Regional Names: black kingfish; ling; runner; sergeantfish
Identifying Features: flat head with projected lower jaw; dark brown back with lighter brown and white horizontal stripes on sides; first dorsal fin composed of eight small spines.
Primary Locations: warm waters worldwide; Atlantic coast, especially Florida Keys.

COD, ATLANTIC

Scientific Name: Gadus morhua
Identifying Features: one barbel on chin; red or gray body with pale lateral line; three dorsal and two anal fins.
Primary Locations: cold waters in north Atlantic down to mid-Atlantic states.

COD, PACIFIC

Scientific Name: Gadus macro-cephalus
Identifying Features: virtually identical to Atlantic cod.

Primary Locations: cold waters of the north Pacific, from the Arctic Circle to Oregon.

DOLPHIN

Scientific Name: Coryphaena hippurus
Regional Names: dolphin fish; dorado; mahi-mahi
Identifying Features: flat-faced head (in males); blue-green-yellow body, with dorsal fin running length of body.
Primary Locations: warm waters worldwide, especially Florida and Hawaii; Baja California, and Gulf Stream waters.
Note: The dolphin fish should not be confused with the dolphin mammal, which is akin to the porpoise.

DRUM, BLACK

Scientific Name: Pogonias cromis
Identifying Features: barbels on chin; arched back; silver-brass body with four or five dark vertical bars.
Primary Locations: from mid-Atlantic states south along Atlantic coast.

DRUM, RED

Scientific Name: Sciaenops ocellata
Regional Names: channel bass; redfish
Identifying Features: no barbels on chin; copper-red body; one or more black spots on tail.

Primary Locations: Atlantic and Gulf coasts.

FLOUNDER, SUMMER

Scientific Name: Paralichthys dentatus
Regional Name: fluke
Identifying Features: both eyes on left side of body; olive brown back (or top side), with small dark spots.
Primary Locations: bottom-dweller along Atlantic coastal waters down to South Carolina.

FLOUNDER, WINTER

Scientific Name: Pseudopleuronectes americanus
Regional Names: flatfish; mud dab; blackback
Identifying Features: both eyes on right side of body; reddish-brown to slate body with spots.
Primary Locations: shallow waters along Atlantic coast of U.S. and Canada.

JACK, CREVELLE

Scientific Name: Caranx hippos
Regional Names: jack; cavelly; common jack
Identifying Features: domed head; black or dark green back above yellow-white belly; dark spots on gill flaps and pectoral fins.
Primary Locations: warm waters worldwide.

JACK, ATLANTIC HORSE-EYE

Scientific Name: Caranx latus
Regional Names: kingfish; cavalla
Identifying Features: prominent eyes with thick lids; blue-gray back above white or golden sides; yellow caudal fin.
Primary Locations: Atlantic coast from mid-Atlantic states through the West Indies to South America.

MACKEREL, KING

Scientific Name: Scomberomorus cavalla
Regional Names: kingfish; cavalla
Identifying Features: long blue-green body with dark stripes above light fluorescent belly; thin irregular stripe running length of body.
Primary Locations: Atlantic coast south from southern New England.

MARLIN, BLUE

Scientific Name: Makaira nigricans
Regional Name: blue
Identifying Features: dark steely blue back above yellow lateral stripe; light blue vertical bars on silver-white sides.
Primary Locations: warm Atlantic and Pacific waters, especially southern U.S. coastal waters, Hawaii, and the Bahamas.

MARLIN, BLACK

Scientific Name: Makaira indicus
Regional Name: black
Identifying Features: heavier sword than other marlins; blue-black back; non-retractable pectoral fins.
Primary Locations: warm waters of the Pacific.

MARLIN, STRIPED

Scientific Name: Tetrapturus audax
Regional Names: stripe; striper
Identifying Features: steely blue upper body with prominent vertical stripes on sides; tall pointed dorsal fin.
Primary Locations: warm waters of the Pacific, especially along North and South American coasts.

MARLIN, WHITE

Scientific Name: Tetrapturus albidus
Regional Names: whitey; spike-fish
Identifying Features: smallest of the marlins; slender blue-green upper body over white belly; long rounded dorsal fin with dark spots.
Primary Locations: warm waters of Atlantic, especially mid-Atlantic states.

PERMIT, ATLANTIC

Scientific Name: Trachinotus falcatus

Regional Name: great pompano
Identifying Features: flat diamond-shaped body with blue-gray back above silver sides; trailing ventral and dorsal fins.
Primary Locations: warm waters of western Atlantic, especially Florida and the Caribbean.

POMPANO, AFRICAN

Scientific Name: Alectis ciliaris
Regional Names: threadfin; Cuban jack
Identifying Features: blunt, vertical head; blue-green back and silver belly; bony scales (scutes) in front of tail.
Primary Locations: warm Atlantic waters, especially Florida and the Caribbean.

SAILFISH

Scientific Name: Istiophorus platypterus
Regional Name: sail
Identifying Features: long bill; long slender body of dark blue above silver sides with vertical bars; prominent blue dorsal fin with dark spots.
Primary Locations: warm waters of Atlantic and Pacific.

SNOOK

Scientific Name: Centropomus undecimalis
Identifying Features: protruding lower jaw; brownish-copper back above lighter belly; black

lateral stripe along length of body; sharp gill-cover edges.
Primary Locations: warm waters of Atlantic and Pacific, especially Florida.

TARPON

Scientific Name: Megalops atlanticus
Regional Names: sliver king; tarpum; silverfish
Identifying Features: prominent upturned lower jaw; narrow band of dark blue-green on back; silver sides with large scales; single dorsal fin with elongated last ray.
Primary Locations: warm Atlantic waters, especially Florida.

TAUTOG

Scientific Name: Tautoga onitis
Regional Name: blackfish
Identifying Features: blunt snout; dark mottled olive or gray body; rounded dorsal fin; blunt-ended tail.
Primary Locations: bottom-dweller of north Atlantic coast, especially New England and mid-Atlantic states.

TUNA, ALBACORE

Scientific Name: Thunnus alalunga
Regional Name: longfin
Identifying Features: long, curved pectoral fins; violet lateral stripe; crescent, white-edged tail.

Primary Locations: warm waters of Atlantic and Pacific, especially Mexico and southern California coasts.

TUNA, BIGEYE

Scientific Name: Thunnus obesus
Regional Name: bigeye
Identifying Features: bright yellow first dorsal fin; darker yellow or brown second dorsal fin.
Primary Locations: warm waters of Atlantic and Pacific.

TUNA, BLACKFIN

Scientific Name: Thunnus atlanticus
Regional Name: blackie
Identifying Features: dark back above bluish sides with a copper vertical band.
Primary Locations: warm waters of western Atlantic.

TUNA, BLUEFIN

Scientific Name: Thunnus thynnys
Regional Names: tunny; horse mackerel
Identifying Features: steel blue back over silver-green sides; small "finlets" in front of crescent tail.
Primary Locations: worldwide.

TUNA, YELLOWFIN

Scientific Name: Thunnus albacares
Regional Name: yellowfin
Identifying Features: yellow stripe on sides; white spots on belly; yellow fins.
Primary Locations: warm waters worldwide, especially Hawaii, Gulf of Mexico, and the West Indies.

WAHOO

Scientific Name: Acanthocybium solanderi

Regional Name: oahu
Identifying Features: beak-like nose; bright blue back above dark blue vertical bars on light blue sides; long dorsal fin.
Primary Locations: warm waters worldwide, especially Pacific coast of Central America.

WEAKFISH

Scientific Name: Cynoscion regalis
Regional Names: tide runner; sea trout
Identifying Features: projecting lower jaw with soft mouth; olive-green back with dark spots above copper sides; yellow tinge to fins.
Primary Locations: north Atlantic coast, especially mid-Atlantic states.

Books and Videos on Selected Species of Fish

Anyone interested in learning about particular species, especially with regard to techniques used to catch them, can begin with the following books and videos. The titles are arranged alphabetically by species. Those books that have been reprinted and/or revised are indicated by their most recent publisher and date of publication.

The following books and videos are by no means everything available on the species, nor is every species included. For further reading and other subjects, you might begin by browsing among the bookshelves of tackle shops, bookstores, and libraries, or among the entries in mail-order catalogs. Book review sections of

fishing magazines are another likely source of information. So is a comprehensive reference work called *Books in Print* that's available at bookstores and libraries; check the subject index under "Fish" or the particular species.

Which species holds the record for "greatest-volume-of-volumes"? The winner is trout, with books on fly-fishing representing the largest category on any angling subject.

BOOKS

The Bass Fisherman's Bible, by Erwin A. Bauer (Mark Hicks, ed.)(Doubleday, 1989).

Hannon's Big Bass Magic, by Douglas Hannon and W. Horace Carter (The In-Fisherman, 1986).

Smallmouth Bass: An In-Fisherman Handbook of Strategies, by Al Lindner et al. (The In-Fisherman, 1984).

Roland Martin's 101 Bass Catching Secrets, by Roland Martin (New Winchester Pub., 1988).

L.L. Bean Fly Fishing for Bass Handbook, by Dave Whitlock (Lyons & Burford, 1988).

Bass Fishing Fundamentals, by Ken Schultz (Viking Penguin, 1986).

Largemouth Bass in the 1990s, by the staff of *The In-Fisherman* (The In-Fisherman, 1990).

Bluefishing, by Henry Lyman (Lyons & Burford, 1987).

Fishing for Bluefish, by Al Ristori (The Fisherman Library, 1986).

Bonefishing with a Fly, by Randall Kaufmann (Damato Publications, 1992).

Fly Fishing for Bonefish, by Dick Brown (Lyons & Burford, 1994).

Channel Catfish Secrets, by the staff of *The In-Fisherman* (The In-Fisherman, 1989).

W. Horace Carter's Crappie Secrets, by W. Horace Carter (Atlantic Pub. Co., 1991).

The Masters' Secrets of Crappie Fishing, by John E. Phillips (Larsens Outdoor, 1992).

Crappie Wisdom, by the staff of *The In-Fisherman* (The In-Fisherman, 1985).

Musky Mastery, by Steve Heiting (Krause Publications, 1992).

Guide to Catching Muskelonge, by Robert A. Smith (Atlantic Pub. Co., 1987).

Panfish, by Dick Sternberg and Bill Ignazio (The Hunting and Fishing Library, 1983).

The Panfisherman's Bible, by John Weiss (The Hunting and Fishing Library, 1983).

Pike, by the staff of *The In-Fisherman* (The In-Fisherman, 1983).

The Trout and Salmon Fisherman's Bible, by Jim Bashline (Doubleday, 1991).

The Trout and Salmon Handbook, by Robin Ade (Facts on File, 1989).

Salt-water Salmon Angling, by Bob Mottram (Frank Amato Publications, 1990).

The Atlantic Salmon, by Lee Wulff (Lyons & Burford, 1988).

Salmon on a Fly, by Lee Wulff (John Merwin, ed.)(Simon & Schuster, 1992).

How to Fish for Snook, by Earl Downey (Great Outdoors, 1985).

Fishing for Sharks, by Pete Barrett (The Fisherman Library, 1988).

Sharks: A Fisherman's Point of View, by Mitchell Waite (Southwest Publications, 1992).

The Snook Book, by Frank Sargeant (Larsens Outdoor, 1991).

The Striped Bass, by Nick Karas (Lyons & Burford, 1994).

Striper, by John Cole (Lyons & Burford, 1989).

Sturgeon Fishing, by Larry Leonard (Frank Amato Publications, 1987).

The Tarpon Book, by Frank Sargeant (Larsens Outdoor, 1991).

Tarpon Quest, by John Cole (Lyons & Burford, 1991).

Trout, by Ray Bergman (Outlet Book Co., 1991).

The Trout and Salmon Handbook, by Robin Ade (Facts on File, 1989).

The Classic Guide to Fly-Fishing for Trout, by Charles Jardine (Random House, 1991).

New American Trout Fishing, by John Merwin (Macmillan, 1994).

The Way of the Trout: An Essay on Anglers, Wild Fish, and Running Water, by M.R. Montgomery (Knopf, 1991).

The Field & Stream Treasury of Trout Fishing, edited by Leonard M. Wright, Jr. (Fawcett, 1988).

Trout Magic, by Robert Traver (Simon & Schuster, 1989).

Trout on a Fly, by Lee Wulff (Lyons & Burford, 1986).

To Catch a Tuna, by Al Anderson (MT Books, 1990).

Fish the Chair If You Dare: The Ultimate Guide to Giant Bluefin Tuna Fishing, by Greg Beacher (Dawn Pub. Co., 1993).

Sport Fishing for Yellowfin Tuna, by Dave Preble (The Fisherman Library, 1988).

Walleye, by Dick Sternberg (The Hunting and Fishing Library, 1986).

Walleye Wisdom, by the staff of *The In-Fisherman* (The In-Fisherman, 1983).

VIDEOS

Even the most die-hard bookworms must admit that when it comes to learning a sport or hobby, instructional videos are no longer the wave of the future—they're the pick of the present. A well-produced tape is the equivalent of a private lesson, with the advantage of being able to be replayed over and over.

The following representative tapes have been recommended by fishermen who are knowledgeable about the particular species that the tapes cover. Be aware, however, that there are others tapes on these and other species, and that new ones are constantly being released. You'll learn about them by browsing through tackle shops' shelves and mail-order companies' catalogs.

For information on The In-Fisherman videos, phone (800) 814-8404. For information about tapes available from Bennett Marine Videos, phone (800) 733-8862.

How to Catch Amberjack, with Dr. Jim Wright [Bennett Marine Video](56 min.)

Bass Fishing Techniques, with Bill Dance (60 min.)

Bass Fishing Strategies, with Bill Dance (60 min.)

Bass Fishing Tips, with Bill Dance (60 min.)

Fly Fishing for Bass, with Dave Whitlock (92 min.)

Bassin' with a Fly Rod, with Jack Ellis (60 min.)

Larry Nixon's Tournament Tactics for Locating Spring Season Bass (45 min.)

Larry Nixon's Tournament Tactics for Locating Summer Season Bass (45 min.)

Jimmy Houston's 101 Bass Fishing Secrets, Parts 1 and 2 (55 min. each)

Doodling for Bass, with Don Iovino (55 min.)

Largemouth Bass: A Day in the Boat, with Al Lindner [The In-Fisherman video](60 min.)

Bassin' Today [The In-Fisherman video](73 min.)

Stalking Smallmouth Bass [The In-Fisherman video](44 min.)

Fly Fishing for Billfish, with Billy Pate (60 min.)

How to Catch Billfish, with Dr. Jim Wright [Bennett Marine Video](60 min.)

How to Catch Bluefish, with Dr. Jim Wright [Bennett Marine Video](60 min.)

Bluefish Blitz—"The Ultimate Surf Fishing Experience" [Bennett Marine Video](60 min.)

Bonefish, with Flip Pallot and Sandy Moret (40 min.)

Catfishing, with Bill Dance (60 min.)

Catfish Fever [The In-Fisherman video](62 min.)

The Big Catfish Connection [The In-Fisherman video](44 min.)

Crappie Fishing, with Bill Dance (60 min.)

Crappie Tactics for Lakes and Reservoirs [The In-Fisherman video](56 min.)

Dolphin: The Yellow and Green Fighting Machine [Bennett Marine Video](60 min.)

Dorado! [Bennett Marine Video](54 min.)

Trophy Fluke Fishing, with Captain Charlie Nappi [Bennett Marine Video](52 min.)

Giant Halibut of Alaska [Bennett Marine Video](30 min.)

How to Catch King Mackerel, with Dr. Jim Wright [Bennett Marine Video](36 min.)

The King Mackerel Video [Bennett Marine Video](50 min.)

Mako on Fly, with Billy Pate [Bennett Marine Video](45 min.)

Killer Mako: One More Time, with Captain Jim Tabor [Bennett Marine Video](30 min.)

Marlin Magic, with Captain Bill Hall [Bennett Marine Video](80 min.)

Marlin Mania, Part I (30 min.), Part II (60 min.), and Part III (40 min.), with the Murray Brothers [Bennett Marine Video]

Modern Muskie Methods, with Jim Saric (60 min.)

The Great Muskie Hunt [The In-Fisherman video](62 min.)

The Greatest Muskie Video Ever Made [The In-Fisherman video](56 min.)

Trolling for Muskies [The In-Fisherman video](45 min.)

Trouting Tactics for Panfish, with Jack Ellis (60 min.)

Northern Pike, The Water Wolf [The In-Fisherman video](59 min.)

Fly Fishing for Pike, with Larry Dahlberg [The In-Fisherman video](74 min.)

The Flyrodder's Guide to Pike, with Tom Smith and Barry Reynolds (60 min.)

Sailfish—Rigging to Release [Bennett Marine Video](48 min.)

Sailfish Techniques [Bennett Marine Video](60 min.)

Pacific Ocean Salmon Fishing, with Dick Pool and Barry Canevaro [Bennett Marine Video](58 min.)

Shark Fishing Made Easy [Bennett Marine Video](40 min.)

Fishing for Sharks, with Peter Barrett [Bennett Marine Video](60 min.)

How to Catch Snapper [Bennett Marine Video](40 min.)

Catching More Steelhead, with Jim Teeny (63 min.)

Fly Fishing for Pacific Steelhead, with Lani Waller (68 min.)

Advanced Fly Fishing for Pacific Steelhead, with Lani Waller (55 min.)

Fly Fishing for Trophy Steelhead, with Lani Waller (60 min.)

Cooper's Steelheading, with Gary Cooper [Bennett Marine Video](78 min.)

How to Catch Striped Bass, with Dr. Jim Wright [Bennett Marine Video](50 min.)

Stripers! with Lou Tabory (60 min.)

Fly Rodding for Tarpon, with Billy Pate (63 min.)

Challenge of the Giant Tarpon, with Bill Pate (70 min.)

The Quest for Giant Tarpon, with Stu Apte (70 min.)

Tarpon Paradise, with Rick DeVaney [Bennett Marine Video](30 min.)

How to Catch Tautog, with Dr. Jim Wright [Bennett Marine Video](40 min.)

Fly Fishing for Trout, with Gary Borger (58 min.)

Trout in Stillwaters, with Gary Borger (60 min.)

The Trout Fisherman: New Challenges, with Mike Fong (60 min.)

Strategies for Selective Trout, with Doug Swisher (75 min.)

Advanced Strategies for Selective Trout, with Doug Swisher (75 min.)

Anatomy of a Trout Stream, with Rick Hafale (60 min.)

Trophy Lake Trout Tactics [The In-Fisherman video](57 min.)

Stream Trout Tactics [The In-Fisherman video](51 min.)

New Strategies for Trout Fishermen, with Mike Fong (60 min.)

Giant Tuna, Small Boat, with Lee Wulff [Bennett Marine Video](30 min.)

Tuna Supreme [Bennett Marine Video](38 min.)

Tuna Tactics [Bennett Marine Video](30 min.)

Where the Biggest Bluefins Swim, with Lee Wulff [Bennett Marine Video](30 min.)

Basic Walleye Strategies and Techniques, with Jim Swanstrom and Jeff Howard (30 min.)

Advanced Walleye Systems, Part I (58 min.), Part II (53 min.), and Part III (67 min.)[all three are The In-Fisherman videos]

2

WORLD RECORDS

Here are the big ones that *didn't* get away: the freshwater and saltwater all-tackle world records. The list, which was compiled by the International Game Fish Association (IGFA), the organization whose responsibilities include certifying such records, is reprinted with the association's kind permission.

The scientific name of each species is in parenthesis, followed by the weight, location, and date of the catch, and the angler's name.

If you think your catch belongs on the list, contact the IGFA to learn about the regulations that govern qualifying for a record catch. And even if your "big one" got away, you might want to become a member of the IGFA and support its many good projects. The organization's address is 1301 E. Atlantic Blvd., Pompano Beach, FL 33060; phone: (305) 941-3474; fax: (305) 941-5868.

AGUJON (*Tylosurus acus*), 8 lb. 3 oz., Nags Head, North Carolina, USA, Aug. 31, 1986, Keith Tongier

ALBACORE (*Thunnus alalunga*), 88 lb. 2 oz., Gran Canaria, Canary Islands, Spain, Nov. 19, 1977, Siegfried Dickemann

AMBERJACK, GREATER (*Seriola dumerili*), 155 lb. 10 oz., Challenger Bank, Bermuda, June 24, 1981, Joseph Dawson

APAPA, YELLOW (*Pellona castelneana*), 6 lb. 6 oz., Araca River, Amazon, Brazil, Oct. 27, 1991, Gilberto Fernandes

ARAWANA (*Osteoglossum bicirrhosum*), 10 lb. 2 oz., Puraquequara Lake, Amazon, Brazil, Feb. 3, 1990, Gilberto Fernandes

ASP (*Aspius arpius*), 12 lb. 7 oz., Lake Vanern, Sweden, Sept. 25, 1993, Jan-Erik Skoglund

BARBEL (*Barbus barbus*), 5 lb. 10 oz., Rhine River, Germany, Sept. 12, 1990, Marc David Hartmann

BARRACUDA, MEXICAN (*Sphyraena ensis*), 21 lb., Phantom Isle, Costa Rica, March 27, 1987, E. Greg Kent

BARRACUDA, PACIFIC (*Sphyraena argentea*), 6 lb. 3 oz., Point Loma, San Diego, California, USA, April 4, 1992, James A. Seibert

BARRACUDA, BLACKFIN (*Sphyraena qenie*), 15 lb., Puerto Quetzal, Guatemala, Oct. 29, 1988, Alejandro Caniz

BARRACUDA, GREAT (*Sphyraena barracuda*), 85 lb., Christmas Island, Republic of Kiribati, April 11, 1992, John W. Helfrich

BARRACUDA, PICKHANDLE (*Sphyraena barracuda*), 58 lb. 6 oz., Mission Beach, Queensland, Australia, Nov. 7, 1993, Bruce Shepherd

BARRAMUNDI (*Lates calcarifer*), 63 lb. 2 oz., Normah River, Normanton, Queensland, Australia, April 28, 1991, Scott Barnsley

BARRAMUNDI, JAPANESE (akame) (*Lates japonicus*), 25 lb. 14 oz., Urado Bay, Kochi, Japan, Aug. 30, 1992, Yuji Shimasaki

BASS, GUADALUPE (*Micropterus treculi*), 3 lb. 11 oz., Lake Travis, Austin, Texas, USA, Sept. 25, 1983, Allen M. Christenson, Jr.

BASS, ROANOKE (*Ambloplites cavifrons*), 1 lb. 5 oz., Nottoway River, Southampton Co., Virginia, USA, Nov. 11, 1991, Thomas F. Elkins

BASS, SUWANNEE (*Micropterus notius*), 3 lb. 14 oz., Suwannee River, Florida, USA, March 2, 1985, Ronnie Everett

BASS, BARRED SAND (*Paralabrax nebulifer*), 13 lb. 3 oz., Huntington Beach, California, USA, Aug. 29, 1988, Robert Halal

BASS, BLACK SEA (*Centropristis striata*), 9 lb. 8 oz., Rudee Inlet, Virginia Beach, Virginia, USA, Jan. 9, 1987, Joe Mizelle, Jr.

BASS, BLACK SEA (*Centropristis striata*), 9 lb. 8 oz., Virginia Beach, Virginia, USA, Dec. 22, 1990, Jack G. Stallings, Jr.

BASS, GIANT SEA (*Stereolepis gigas*), 563 lb. 8 oz., Anacapa Island, California, USA, Aug. 20, 1968, James D. McAdam, Jr.

BASS, GOLDSPOTTED SAND (*Paralabrax aurguttatas*), 6 lb., San Frasciquito Baha, Mexico, June 13, 1993, Charles F. Ulrich

BASS, GUADALOUPE and SMALLMOUTH (*Micropterus treculi and M. dolomieui*), 3 lb. 12 oz., Staples, Texas, USA, April 11, 1993, Douglas D. Grumbles

BASS, KELP OR CALICO (*Paralabrax clathratus*), 14 lb. 7 oz., Newport Beach, California, USA, Oct. 2, 1993, Thomas Murphy

BASS, LARGEMOUTH (*Micropterus salmoides*), 22 lb. 4 oz., Montgomery Lake, Georgia, USA, June 2, 1932, George W. Perry

BASS, LEATHER (*Dermatolepis dermatolepis*), 27 lb. 8 oz., Isla Clarion, Revillagigedo Islands, Mexico, Jan. 26, 1988, Allan J. Ristori

BASS, PEACOCK, OR SPECKLED PAVON (*Cichla temensis*), 26 lb. 8 oz., Mataveni River, Orinoco, Colombia, Jan. 26, 1982, Rod Neubert, D.V.M.

BASS, PEACOCK BUTTERFLY (*Cichla ocellaris*), 9 lb. 8 oz., Kendale Lakes, Florida, USA, March 11, 1993, Jerry Gomez

BASS, REDEYE (*Micropterus coosae*), 8 lb. 3 oz., Flint River, Georgia, USA, Oct. 23, 1977, David A. Hubbard

BASS, ROCK (*Ambloplites rupestris*), 3 lb., York River, Ontario, Canada, Aug. 1, 1974, Peter Gulgin

BASS, SMALLMOUTH (*Micropterus dolomieu*), 11 lb. 15 oz., Dale Hollow Lake, Kentucky, USA, July 9, 1955, David L. Hayes

BASS, SPOTTED (*Micropterus punctulatus*), 9 lb. 7 oz., Pine Flat Lake, California, USA, Feb. 25, 1994, Bob E. Shelton

BASS, STRIPED (*Morone saxatilis*), 78 lb. 8 oz., Atlantic City, New Jersey, USA, Sept. 21, 1982, Albert R. McReynolds

BASS, STRIPED [landlocked] (*Morone saxatilis*), 67 lb. 8 oz., O'Neill Forebay, San Luis, California, USA, May 7, 1992, Hank Ferguson

BASS, WHITE (*Morone chrysops*), 6 lb. 13 oz., Lake Orange, Orange, Virginia, USA, July 31, 1989, Ronald L. Sprouse

BASS, WHITEROCK (*Morone saxatilis and Morone chrysops*), 24 lb. 3 oz., Leesville Lake, Virginia, USA, May 12, 1989, David N. Lambert

BASS, YELLOW (*Morone mississippiensis*), 2 lb. 4 oz., Lake Monroe, Indiana, USA, March 27, 1977, Donald L. Stalker

BASS, YELLOW HYBRID (*Morone mississippiensis and Morone chrysops*), 2 lb. 5 oz., Kiamichi River, Oklahoma, USA, March 26, 1991, George R. Edwards

BIARA (*Rhaphiodon vulpinus*), 3 lb. 5 oz., Cuiaba River, Mato Grosso, Brazil, June 30, 1992, Luiz Carlos Nolasco

BIGEYE (*Priacanthus arenatus*), 2 lb. 8 oz., Ocracoke, North Carolina, USA, June 25, 1988, Roberta L. Cloud

BIGEYE (*Priacanthus aurenatatus*), 2 lb. 9 oz., Charleston, South Carolina, USA, May 15, 1993, D. Edward Collins

BIGEYE, BARENOSE (*Monotaxis grandoculis*), 13 lb., Otec Beach, Kailua, Kona, Hawaii, USA, July 12, 1992, Rex C. Bigg

BIWAMASU (*Oncorhynchus masou rhodurus*), 2 lb. 12 oz., Lake Biwa, Shiga, Japan, May 21, 1993, Shoji Matsuura

BLUEFISH (*Pomatomus saltatrix*), 31 lb. 12 oz., Hatteras, North Carolina, USA, Jan. 30, 1972, James M. Hussey

BLUEGILL (*Lepomis macrochirus*), 4 lb. 12 oz., Ketona Lake, Alabama, USA, April 9, 1950, T.S. Hudson

BOCACCIO (*Sebastes paucispinis*), 21 lb. 4 oz., Swiftsure Bank, Neah Bay, Washington, USA, July 29, 1986, Terry Rudnick

BONEFISH (*Albula vulpes*), 19 lb., Zululand, South Africa, May 26, 1962, Brian W. Batchelor

BONITO, ATLANTIC (*Sarda sarda*), 18 lb. 4 oz., Faial Island, Azores, July 8, 1953, D. Gama Higgs

BONITO, AUSTRALIAN (*Sarda australis*), 20 lb. 11 oz., Montague Island, N.S.W., Australia, April 1, 1978, Bruce Conley

BONITO, PACIFIC (*Sarda chiliensis lineolatus*), 14 lb. 12 oz., San Benitos Island, Baja California, Mexico, Oct. 12, 1980, Jerome H. Rilling

BONITO, STRIPED (*Sarda orientalis*), 23 lb. 8 oz., Victoria, Mahe, Seychelles, Feb. 19, 1975, Anne Cochain

BOWFIN (*Amia calva*), 21 lb. 8 oz., Florence, South Carolina, USA, Jan. 29, 1980, Robert L. Harmon

BREAM (*Abramis brama*), 13 lb. 3 oz., Hagbyan Creek, Sweden, May 11, 1984, Luis Kilian Rasmussen

BREAM, BLACK (*Hephaestus fuliginosus*), 10 lb. 14 oz., Lake Tinaroo, Queensland, Australia, Sept. 15, 1993, Jack Leighton

BREAM, GUILTHEAD (*Chrysophrys aur*), 2 lb. 7 oz., South Mole, Gibralter Bay, Dec. 10, 1993, Joseph Anthony Triay

BREAM, HURTA (*Pagrus caeruleostictus*), 20 lb. 3 oz., Chullera, Spain, July 11, 1992, J.A. Triay

BROTULA, BEARDED (*Brotula barbata*), 15 lb. 3 oz., Destin, Florida, USA, May 7, 1989, Clint Sasser

BUFFALO, BIGMOUTH (*Ictiobus cyprinellus*), 70 lb. 5 oz., Bussey Brake, Bastrop, Louisiana, USA, April 21, 1980, Delbert Sisk

BUFFALO, BLACK (*Ictiobus niger*), 55 lb. 8 oz., Cherokee Lake, Tennessee, USA, May 3, 1984, Edward H. McLain

BUFFALO, SMALLMOUTH (*Ictiobus bubalus*), 68 lb. 8 oz., Lake Hamilton, Arkansas, USA, May 16, 1984, Jerry L. Dolezal

BULLHEAD, BLACK (*Ameiurus melas*), 8 lb., Lake Waccabuc, New York, USA, Aug. 1, 1951, Kani Evans

BULLHEAD, BROWN
(*Ameiurus nebulosus*), 5 lb. 8 oz.,
Veal Pond, Georgia, USA, May
22, 1975, Jimmy Andrews

BULLHEAD, YELLOW
(*Ameiurus natalis*), 4 lb. 4 oz.,
Mormon Lake, Arizona, USA,
May 11, 1984, Emily Williams

BURBOT (*Lota lota*), 18 lb. 4 oz.,
Pickford, Michigan, USA, Jan. 31,
1980, Thomas Courtemanche

BURRFISH, STRIPED
(*Chilomycterus schoepfi*), 1 lb. 6
oz., Delaware Bay, New Jersey,
USA, Aug. 13, 1989, Donna L.
Ludlam

CABEZON (*Scorpaenichthys
marmoratus*), 23 lb., Juan de Fuca
Strait, Washington, USA, Aug. 4,
1990, Wesley S. Hunter

CABRILLA, SPOTTED
(*Epinephelus analogus*), 49 lb. 3
oz., Cedros/Natividad Islands,
Baja California, Mexico, Nov. 18,
1990, Barry T. Morita

CARP, COMMON (*Cyprinus
carpio*), 75 lb. 11 oz., Lac de St.
Cassien, France, May 21, 1987,
Leo van der Gugten

CARP, CRUCIAN (*Carassius
carassius*), 4 lb. 7 oz.,
Ostanforsan, Falun, Sweden, June
12, 1988, Lars Jonsson

CARP, GRASS
(*Ctenopharyngodon idella*), 62 lb.,
Emerald Valley Lake, Pinson,
Alabama, USA, May 13, 1991,
Craig Bass

CARPSUCKER, RIVER
(*Carpiodes carpio*), 10 lb. 2 oz.,
Lake Michigan, Indiana, USA,
Nov. 20, 1993, Mike Berg

CATFISH, EURASIAN (*Silurus
biwaensis*), 15 lb. 10 oz.,
Katayama, Biwako, Shiga, Japan,
May 14, 1991, Manabu Koumura

CATFISH, BLUE (*Ictalurus
furcatus*), 109 lb. 4 oz., Cooper
River, Moncks Corner, South
Carolina, USA, March 14, 1991,
George A. Lijewski

CATFISH, CHANNEL (*Ictalurus
punctatus*), 58 lb., Santee-Cooper
Reservoir, South Carolina, USA,
July 7, 1964, W.B. Whaley

CATFISH, FLATHEAD
(*Pylodictis olivaris*), 91 lb. 4 oz.,
Lake Lewisville, Texas, USA,
March 28, 1982, Mike Rogers

CATFISH, FLATWHISKERED
(*Pinirampus pinirampu*), 5 lb. 13
oz., Cuiaba River, Mato Grosso,
Brazil, June 28, 1992, Sergio
Roberto Rothier

CATFISH, GAFFTOPSAIL
(*Bagre marinus*), 8 lb. 12 oz.,
Indian River, Stuart, Florida,
USA, March 30, 1991, Jack
Leadbeater

CATFISH, GILDED
(*Brachyplatystoma flavicans*), 85
lb. 8 oz., Amazon River, Amazon,
Brazil, Nov. 15, 1986, Gilberto
Fernandes

CATFISH, HARDHEAD (*Arius
felis*), 3 lb. 5 oz., Mays Marina,
Sebastion, Florida, USA, April
18, 1993, Amanda Steed

CATFISH, REDTAIL [pirarara]
(*Phractocephalus hemioliopterus*),
97 lb. 7 oz., Amazon River,
Amazon, Brazil, July 16, 1988,
Gilberto Fernandes

CATFISH, SHARPTOOTHED
(*Clarius gariepinus*), 79 lb. 5 oz.,
Orange River, Upington, Republic
of South Africa, Dec. 5, 1992,
Hennie Moller

CATFISH, WHITE (*Ameiurus
catus*), 18 lb. 14 oz.,
Withlacoochee River, Inverness,
Florida, USA, Sept. 21, 1991, Jim
Miller

CHAR, ARCTIC (*Salvelinus alpinus*), 32 lb. 9 oz., Tree River,
Manitoba, Canada, July 30, 1981,
Jeffery L. Ward

CHAR, WHITE SPOTTED
(*Salvelinus leucomaenis*), 3 lb. 11
oz., Enosimacoast, Simamaki,
Hakkaido, Japan, March 4, 1988,
Akira Kitagawa

CHINAMAN FISH (*Symphorus nematophorus*), 26 lb. 4 oz., Thevenard Island, Onslow, W.A., Australia, Aug. 18, 1988, Robert Bassett

CHUB, BERMUDA (*Kyphosus sectatrix*), 11 lb. 2 oz., Fort Pierce, Florida, USA, Jan. 18, 1993, Herman Cross

CHUB, EUROPEAN (*Leuciscus cephalus*), 5 lb. 12 oz., Helige, Gemla, Sweden, July 26, 1987, Luis Kilian Rasmussen

CISCO (*Coregonus artedi*), 7 lb. 6 oz., North Cross Bay, Cedar Lake, Manitoba, Canada, April 11, 1986, Randy K. Huff

COBIA (*Rachycentron canadum*), 135 lb. 9 oz., Shark Bay, W.A., Australia, July 9, 1985, Peter William Goulding

COD, ATLANTIC (*Gadus morhua*), 98 lb. 12 oz., Isle of Shoals, New Hampshire, USA, June 8, 1969, Alphonse J. Bielevich

COD, PACIFIC (*Gadus macrocephalus*), 30 lb., Andrew Bay, Alaska, USA, July 7, 1984, Donald R. Vaughn

CONGER (*Conger conger*), 110 lb. 8 oz., English Channel, Plymouth, England, Aug. 20, 1991, Hans Christian Clausen

CORVINA, CALIFORNIA (*Menticinrhus undulatus*), 5 lb. 15 oz., Manhattan Beach, California, USA, June 22, 1993, Dana O'Dowd

CORVINA, HYBRID (*Cynoscion xanthulus and Cynoscion nebulosus*), 10 lb. 8 oz., Calaveras Lake, San Antonio, Texas, USA, Jan. 27, 1987, Norma E. Cleary

CORVINA, ORANGEMOUTH (*Cynoscion xanthulus*), 54 lb. 3 oz., Sabana Grande, Guayaquil, Ecuador, July 29, 1992, Felipe Estrada Estrada

CRAPPIE, BLACK (*Pomoxis nigromaculatus*), 4 lb. 8 oz., Kerr Lake, Virginia, USA, March 1, 1981, L. Carl Herring, Jr.

CRAPPIE, WHITE (*Pomoxis annularis*), 5 lb. 3 oz., Enid Dam, Mississippi, USA, July 31, 1957, Fred L. Bright

CROAKER, ATLANTIC (*Micropogonias undulatus*), 3 lb. 12 oz., Escambia River, Pensacola, Florida, USA, Sept. 29, 1992, Tina Marie Jeffers

CUNNER (*Tautogolabrus adspersus*), 1 lb. 9 oz., Brielle, New Jersey, USA, March 12, 1994, Alex Gerus

CUSK (*Brosme brosme*), 32 lb. 13 oz., Sommersel, Hamaroy, Norway, July 10, 1988, Ingemar Toren

CUTLASSFISH, ATLANTIC (*Trichiurus lepturus*), 1 lb. 10 oz., Port Canaveral, Florida, USA, Aug. 26, 1992, Doug Olander

DENTEX (*Dentex dentex*), 21 lb. 11 oz., Cecina, Secche DiVada, Italy, May 21, 1993, Ermini Sergio

DOGFISH, SMOOTH (*Mustelus canis*), 17 lb. 13 oz., Great Bay, Absecon, New Jersey, USA, July 9, 1988, Christopher Smith

DOGFISH, SPINY (*Squalus acanthias*), 15 lb. 12 oz., Kenmare Bay, County Kerry, Ireland, May 26, 1989, Horst Willi Muller

DOLLY VARDEN (*Salvelius malma*), 18 lb. 9 oz., Mashutuk River, Alaska, USA, July 13, 1993, Richard B. Evans

DOLPHIN (*Coryphaena hippurus*), 87 lb., Papagallo Gulf, Costa Rica, Sept. 25, 1976, Manuel Salazar

DORADO (*Salminus maxillosus*), 51 lb. 5 oz., Toledo (Corrientes), Argentina, Sept. 27, 1984, Armando Giudice

DRUM, BLACK (*Pogonias cromis*), 113 lb. 1 oz., Lewes, Delaware, USA, Sept. 15, 1975, Gerald M. Townsend

DRUM, FRESHWATER (*Aplodinotus grunniens*), 54 lb. 8 oz., Nickajack Lake, Tennessee, USA, April 20, 1972, Benny E. Hull

DRUM, RED (*Sciaenops ocellatus*), 94 lb. 2 oz., Avon, North Carolina, USA, Nov. 7, 1984, David G. Deuel

EEL, AMERICAN (*Anguilla rostrata*), 8 lb. 8 oz., Cliff Pond, Brewster, Massachusetts, USA, May 17, 1992, Gerald G. Lapierre, Sr.

EEL, EUROPEAN (*Anguilla anguilla*), 7 lb. 14 oz., River Aare, Buren, Switzerland, July 10, 1992, Christoph Lave
and (co-record):
7 lb. 14 oz., River Lyckeby, Sweden, Aug. 8, 1988, Luis Kilian Rasmussen

EEL, MARBLED (*Anguilla marmorata*), 36 lb. 1 oz., Hazelmere Dam, Durban, South Africa, June 10, 1984, Ferdie Van Nooten

EMPEROR, BLUE (*Lethrinus nebulosus*), 8 lb. 14 oz., Arlington Reef, Cairns, Queensland, Australia, July 17, 1989, Peter R. Cooper

EMPEROR, LONGFACE (*Lethrinus elongatus*), 10 lb. 11 oz., Christmas Island, Republic of Kiribati, Oct. 16, 1988, Jeff Konn

EMPEROR, YELLOWLIP (*Lethrinus xanthochila*), 12 lb., Lifuka Island, Kingdom of Tonga, Nov. 25, 1991, Peter Dunn-Rankin

FALLFISH (*Semotilus corporalis*), 3 lb. 8 oz., Lake Winnipesaukee, Gilford, New Hampshire, USA, July 12, 1991, John Conti

FILEFISH, SCRAWLED (*Aluterus scriptus*), 1 lb. 14 oz., Kailua, Kona, Hawaii, USA, April 18, 1989, Jim Dixon

FILEFISH, UNICORN (*Aluterus monoceros*), 5 lb. 15 oz., Orange Beach, Alabama, USA, March 10, 1993, Yvonne Hanek

FLATHEAD, BAR-TAILED (*Platycephalus indicus*), 4 lb. 11 oz., Shirahama, Chiba, Japan, Sept. 27, 1992, Yukihiro Inoue

FLATHEAD, DUSKY (*Platycephalus fuscus*), 13 lb. 7 oz., Macleay River, New South Wales, Australia, Dec. 15, 1992, Wayne Colling

FLIER (*Centrarchus macropterus*), 1 lb. 4 oz., Little River, Spring Lake, North Carolina, USA, Aug. 24, 1988, Dr. R.D. Snipes

FLOUNDER, EUROPEAN (*Plaricthys flesus*), 2 lb. 10 oz., Bua Harbor, Halland County, Sweden, Sept. 3, 1993, Henning Madsen

FLOUNDER, GULF (*Paralichthys albigutta*), 5 lb., Sebastian Inlet, Florida, USA, Dec. 8, 1993, Ben H. Howard

FLOUNDER, SOUTHERN (*Paralichthys lethostigma*), 20 lb. 9 oz., Nassau Sound, Florida, USA, Dec. 23, 1983, Larenza W. Mungin

FLOUNDER, SUMMER (*Paralichthys dentatus*), 22 lb. 7 oz., Montauk, New York, USA, Sept. 15, 1975, Charles Nappi

FLOUNDER, WINTER (*Pleuronectes americanus*), 7 lb., Fire Island, New York, USA, May 8, 1986, Einar F. Grell

GAR, FLORIDA (*Lepisosteus platyrhincus*), 21 lb. 3 oz., Boca Raton, Florida, USA, June 3, 1981, Jeff Sabol

GAR, ALLIGATOR (*Lepisosteus spatula*), 279 lb., Rio Grande, Texas, USA, Dec. 2, 1951, Bill Valverde

GAR, LONGNOSE (*Lepisosteus osseus*), 50 lb. 5 oz., Trinity River, Texas, USA, July 30, 1954, Townsend Miller

GAR, SHORTNOSE (*Lepisosteus platostomus*), 5 lb., Sally Jones Lake, Vian, Oklahoma, USA, April 26, 1985, Buddy Croslin

GAR, SPOTTED (*Lepisosteus oculatus*), 8 lb. 12 oz., Tennessee River, Alabama, USA, Aug. 26, 1987, Winston H. Baker

GEELBEK (*Atractoscion aeguidens*), 26 lb. 14 oz., Noorhoek, Port Elizabeth, Republic of South Africa, April 17, 1993, Gerard Wessels

GLOBEFISH (*Ephippion quttiferum*), 9 lb. 7 oz., Nouadhibou, Mauritania, March 10, 1986, Raphael Levy

GOLDEYE (*Hiodon alosoides*), 3 lb. 13 oz., Pierre, South Dakota, USA, Aug. 9, 1987, Gary Wayne Heuer

GOLDFISH (*Carassius auratus*), 3 lb., Southland Park, Livingston, Texas, USA, May 8, 1988, Kenneth R. Kinsey

GOLDFISH/CARP HYBRID (*Carassius auratus and Cyprinus carpio*), 3 lb. 8 oz., Cermak Quarry, Lyons, Illinois, USA, Aug. 22, 1990, Donald A. Czyzewski

GOOSEFISH (*Lophius americanus*), 49 lb. 12 oz., Perkins Cove, Ogunquit, Maine, USA, July 9, 1991, Nancy Lee Regimbald

GRAYLING, ARCTIC (*Thymallus arcticus*), 5 lb. 15 oz., Katseyedie River, N.W.T., Canada, Aug. 16, 1967, Jeanne P. Branson

GREENLING, KELP (*Hexagrammos decagrammus*), 3 lb. 2 oz., Rivers Inlet, B.C., Canada, June 23, 1990, Dave Vedder

GREENLING, ROCK (*Hexagrammos lagocephalus*), 1 lb. 13 oz., Adak, Alaska, USA, Aug. 15, 1988, George D. Cornish

GROUPER, NASSAU (*Epinephelus sriatus*), 38 lb. 8 oz., Bimini, Bahamas, Feb. 14, 1994, Lewis Goodman

GROUPER, BLACK (*Mycteroperca bonaci*), 113 lb. 6 oz., Dry Tortugas, Florida, USA, Jan. 27, 1990, Donald W. Bone

GROUPER, BROOMTAIL (*Mycteroperca xenarcha*), 83 lb., Isla Santa Clara, Salinas, Ecuador, June 28, 1992, Ab. Enrique Weisson P.

GROUPER, GAG (*Mycteroperca microlepis*), 80 lb. 6 oz., Gulf of Mexico, Destin, Florida, USA, Oct. 14, 1993, Bill Smith

GROUPER, GIANT (*Epinephelus lanceolatus*), 263 lb. 7 oz., Anguruki Ck., Groote Eylandt, N.T., Australia, Sept. 9, 1988, Peter C. Norris

GROUPER, GULF (*Mycteroperca jordani*), 106 lb. 3 oz., Baja California, Mexico, Dec. 14, 1989, Kaoru Masubuchi

GROUPER, MALABAR (*Epanephelus malabaricus*), 22 lb., Emerald River, N.T., Australia, March 8, 1987, Andrew Brelsford

GROUPER, RED (*Epinephelus morio*), 39 lb. 8 oz., Port Canaveral, Florida, USA, June 11, 1991, David Lee Fox

GROUPER, SNOWY (*Etinephinelus niveatus*), 23 lb., Miami, Florida, USA, Oct. 10, 1993, Julio A. Mila

GROUPER, TIGER (*Mycteroperca Tigris*), 14 lb. 8 oz., Bimini, Bahamas, May 30, 1993, Michael John Meeker

GROUPER, WARSAW (*Epinephelus nigritus*), 436 lb. 12 oz., Gulf of Mexico, Destin, Florida, USA, Dec. 22, 1985, Steve Haeusler

GROUPER, WHITE (*Epinephelus aeneus*), 15 lb. 1 oz., Dakar, Senegal, Jan. 24, 1984, Michel Calendini

GROUPER, YELLOW-BELLY (*Epinephelus marginatus*), 46 lb. 13 oz., Porto Cervo, Sardinia, Italy, Nov. 15, 1990, Luca Bonfanti

GROUPER, YELLOWEDGE (*Epinephelus flavolinbatus*), 13 lb., Miami, Florida, USA, Dec. 23, 1993, Julio Mila

GROUPER, YELLOWFIN
(*Mycteroperca venenosa*), 34 lb. 6
oz., Largo, Florida, USA, Dec. 7,
1988, Roy Hogrebe

GROUPER, YELLOWMOUTH
(*Mycteroperca interstitialis*), 8 lb.
2 oz., Gulf of Mexico, Tampa,
Florida, USA, May 4, 1991, Skip
Busto

GRUNT, PACIFIC RONCADOR
(*Pomadasys bayanus*), 3 lb. 8 oz.,
Rio Grande de Terraba, Costa
Rica, Jan. 28, 1990, Dr. Craig
Whitehead

GRUNT, WHITE (*Haemulon
plumieri*), 6 lb. 8 oz., North
Brunswick, Georgia, USA, May 6,
1989, J.D. Barnes, Jr.

GRUNTER, SADDLE
(*Pomadasys maculatum*), 7 lb., St.
Lucia, Republic of South Africa,
Dec. 11, 1991, J.J. van Rensburg

GUAPOTE (*Cichlasoma dovii*), 11
lb. 8 oz., San Miguel de
Sarapiqui, Costa Rica, Aug. 16,
1986, Ray Baum

GUITARFISH, BLACKCHIN
(*Rhinobatos cemiculus*), 87 lb. 1
oz., Nouadhibou, Mauritania,
Nov. 30, 1986, Rene Trigoulet

GUITARFISH, GIANT
(*Rhynchobatus djeddensis*), 110 lb.
3 oz., Mackay River, N.S.W.,
Australia, Feb. 8, 1988, Kim F.
Payne

GUITARFISH, SHOVELNOSE
(*Rhinobatos productus*), 19 lb. 3
oz., Oxnard, California, USA, July
15, 1989, Paul David Bodtke

GURNARD, FLYING
(*Dactylopterus volitans*), 4 lb.,
Gulf of Mexico, Panama City,
Florida, USA, June 7, 1986,
Vernon Carl Allen

HADDOCK (*Melanogrammus
aeglefinus*), 11 lb. 11 oz., Perkins
Cove, Ogunquit, Maine, USA,
Sept. 12, 1991, Jim Mailea

HAKE, RED (*Urophycis chuss*), 7
lb. 15 oz., Mud Hole, New Jersey,
USA, March 23, 1994, Steven
Schauermann

HAKE, SILVER (*Merluccius
bilinearis*), 2 lb. 4 oz., Atlantic
Ocean, Hicksville, New York,
USA, March 13, 1991, John
Boesenberg

HAKE, WHITE (*Urophycis
tenuis*), 46 lb. 4 oz., Perkins Cove,
Ogunquit, Maine, USA, Oct. 26,
1986, John Audet

HALIBUT, ATLANTIC
(*Hippoglossus hippoglossus*), 255
lb. 4 oz., Gloucester,
Massachusetts, USA, July 28,
1989, Sonny Manley

HALIBUT, CALIFORNIA
(*Paralichthys californicus*), 53 lb.
4 oz., Santa Rosa Island,
California, USA, July 7, 1988,
Russell J. Harmon

HALIBUT, PACIFIC
(*Hippoglossus stenolepis*), 368 lb.,
Gustavus, Alaska, USA, July 5,
1991, Celia H. Dueitt

HAWKFISH, GIANT (*Cirrhitus
rivulatus*), 9 lb. 3 oz., Salinas,
Ecuador, Aug. 21, 1993, Hugo
Tobar

HERRING, SKIPJACK (*Alosa
chrysochloris*), 3 lb. 12 oz., Watts
Bar Lake, Kingston, Tennessee,
USA, Feb. 14, 1982, Paul D.
Goddard

HIND, RED (*Epinephelus gutta-
tus*), 6 lb. 1 oz., Dry Tortugas,
Florida, USA, Jan. 23, 1993,
Capt. Mark Johnson

HIND, ROCK (*Epinephelus
adscensionis*), 6 lb. 8 oz.,
Ascension Island, United
Kingdom, Nov. 22, 1991,
DeWayne M. Kunkel

HIND, SPECKLED (*Epinephelus
drummondhayi*), 42 lb. 6 oz.,
Destin, Florida, USA, Oct. 18,
1987, Charles D. Houghton

HOGFISH (*Lachnolaimus
maximus*), 19 lb. 8 oz., Daytona
Beach, Florida, USA, April 28,
1962, Robert E. Batson

HOTTENTOT (*Pachymetopon
blochii*), 3 lb. 12 oz., Cape Point,
Republic of South Africa, May 28,
1989, Byron Ashington

HOUNDFISH (*Tylosurus crocodilus fodiator*), 21 lb. 12 oz., Cabo San Lucas, Baja California Sur, Mexico, Aug. 10, 1993, John J. Kovacevich

HUCHEN (*Hucho hucho hucho*), 76 lb. 11 oz., Gemeinde Spittal/Drau, Austria, Feb. 19, 1985, Hans Offermanns

IDE (*Leuciscus idus*), 5 lb. 8 oz., Revsudden, Kalmar, Sweden, Nov. 16, 1987, Luis Rasmussen

INCONNU (*Stenodus leucichthys*), 53 lb., Pah River, Alaska, USA, Aug. 20, 1986, Lawrence E. Hudnall

JACK, PACIFIC CREVALLE (*Caranx caninus*), 29 lb. 8 oz., Playa Zancudo, Costa Rica, Jan. 1, 1994, Ronald C. Snody

JACK, ALMACO [Atlantic] (*Seriola rivoliana*), 78 lb., Argus Bank, Bermuda, July 11, 1990, Joey Dawson

JACK, ALMACO [Pacific] (*Seriola rivoliana*), 132 lb., La Paz, Baja California, Mexico, July 21, 1964, Howard H. Hahn

JACK, BLACK (*Caranx lugubris*), 28 lb. 8 oz., Isla Clarion, Revillagigedo Islands, Mexico, Feb. 24, 1988, David Goldsmith

JACK, COTTONMOUTH (*Uraspis secunda*), 4 lb. 8 oz., Cat Island, Bahamas, May 17, 1991, Linda R. Cook

JACK, CREVALLE (*Caranx hippos*), 57 lb. 5 oz., Barra do Kwanza, Angola, Oct. 10, 1992, Cam Nicolson

JACK, HORSE-EYE (*Caranx latus*), 24 lb. 8 oz., Miami, Florida, USA, Dec. 20, 1982, Tito Schnau

JACK, ISLAND (*Caranx carangoides orthogrammus*), 10 lb. 10 oz., Ewa Beach, Hawaii, USA, March 4, 1992, Jeffrey A. Kagihara, D.D.S.

JACK, MANGROVE (*Lutjanus argentimaculatus*), 19 lb. 2 oz., Fish Rock, N.S.W., Australia, April 22, 1994, Ken Lyons

JACK, YELLOW (*Caranx bartholomaei*), 19 lb. 7 oz., Alligator Light, Islamorada, Florida, USA, Sept. 14, 1985, Peter Lee Ernst

JAWFISH, FINESPOTTED (*Opistognathus punctatus*), 2 lb. 8 oz., Turner Island, Sonora, Mexico, June 11, 1988, Lorna R. Garrod

JEWFISH (*Epinephelus itajara*), 680 lb., Fernandina Beach, Florida, USA, May 20, 1961, Lynn Joyner

JOBFISH, GREEN (*Aprion viriscens*), 24 lb., Cape Vidol, Natal, Republic of South Africa, Nov. 23, 1991, Danie G. de Villiers

KAHAWAI [Australian salmon] (*Arripis trutta*), 19 lb. 4 oz., Currarong, Australia, April 9, 1994, Stephen Muller

KAWAKAWA (*Euthynnus affinis*), 29 lb., Isla Clarion, Revillagigedo Islands, Mexico, Dec. 17, 1986, Ronald Nakamura

KOB (*Argyrosomus hololepidotus*), 119 lb. 14 oz., Knysna, Republic of South Africa, Jan. 25, 1988, Colin Stewart Vowles

KOKANEE (*Oncorhynchus nerka*), 9 lb. 6 oz., Okanagan Lake, Vernon, B.C., Canada, June 18, 1988, Norm Kuhn

LADYFISH (*Elops saurus*), 5 lb., Port St. John, Florida, USA, Sept. 19, 1993, Ron Rebeck

LADYFISH [Senegalese] (*Elops senegalensis*), 7 lb. 14 oz., Nouadhibou, Mauritania, Sept. 20, 1988, Pierre L.J. Cluck

LADYFISH, SPRINGER (*Elops marahnata*), 23 lb. 12 oz., Ilha do Bazaruio, Mozambique, Oct. 28, 1993, Zaqueu Paulo

LAU-LAU [piraiba] (*Brachyplatystoma filamentosum*), 256 lb. 9 oz., Solimoes River, Amazon, Brazil, April 3, 1981, Gilberto Fernandes

LEATHERJACK, BIGMOUTHED (*Oligoplites mundus*), 3 lb. 8 oz., Rio Coto, Puntarenas, Costa Rica, Feb. 6, 1990, Dr. Craig Whitehead

LEERFISH [Garrick] (*Lichia amia*), 52 lb. 3 oz., Catania, Italy, Oct. 17, 1991, Massimo Brogna

LENOK (*Brachymystax lenok*), 5 lb. 6 oz., Maya River, Siberia, CIS, Sept. 13, 1992, Hakan Brugard

LING, EUROPEAN (*Molva molva*), 82 lb., Langesund, Norway, May 4, 1993, Peter Arvidsson

LING, BLUE (*Molva dypterygia*), 35 lb. 6 oz., Trondheimsfjorden, Norway, Nov. 23, 1993, Oyvind Braa

LINGCOD (*Ophiodon elongatus*), 69 lb, Langara Island, B.C., Canada, June 16, 1992, Murray M. Romer

LIZARDFISH, INSHORE (*Synodus foetens*), 2 lb., Bellair Shores, Florida, USA, Nov. 17, 1990, Todd Staley

LOOKDOWN (*Selene vomer*), 4 lb. 10 oz., Angra dos Reis, Rio de Janeiro, Brazil, Nov. 11, 1993, Adolpho A. Mayer Neto

LORD, RED IRISH (*Hemilepidotus hemilepidotus*), 2 lb. 7 oz., Depoe Bay, Oregon, USA, April 26, 1992, Ronald L. Chatham

MACHACA (*Brycon guatemalensis*), 9 lb. 8 oz., Barra del Colorado, Costa Rica, Nov. 24, 1991, Barbara Ann Fields

MACKEREL, ATLANTIC (*Scomber scombrus*), 2 lb. 10 oz., Kraakvaag Fjord, Norway, June 29, 1992, Joerg Marquard

MACKEREL, PACIFIC SIERRA (*Scomberomorus sierra*), 18 lb., Isla de la Plata, Ecuador, March 24, 1990, Jorge Begue W.
and (co-record):
18 lb., Salinas, Ecuador, Sept. 15, 1990, Luis Alberto Flores A.

MACKEREL, SPANISH (*Scomberomorus maculatus*), 13 lb., Ocracoke Inlet, North Carolina, USA, Nov. 4, 1987, Robert Cranton

MACKEREL, BROADBARRED (*Scomberomorus semifasciatus*), 17 lb. 10 oz., Kendrew Island, Dampier, W.A., Australia, Aug. 6, 1992, Glen Edward Walker

MACKEREL, CERO (*Scomberomorus regalis*), 17 lb. 2 oz., Islamorada, Florida, USA, April 5, 1986, G. Michael Mills

MACKEREL, CHUB (*Scomber japonicus*), 4 lb. 12 oz., Guadalupe Island, Mexico, June 5, 1986, Roy R. Ludt

MACKEREL, FRIGATE (*Auxis thazard*), 2 lb. 15 oz., Fish Rock, N.S.W., Australia, March 12, 1994, Wayne Colling

MACKEREL, KING (*Scomberomorus cavalla*), 90 lb., Key West, Florida, USA, Feb. 16, 1976, Norton I. Thomton

MACKEREL, NARROWBARRED (*Scomberomorus commerson*), 99 lb., Scottburgh, Natal, Republic of South Africa, March 14, 1982, Michael John Wilkinson

MACKEREL, SHARK (*Grammatorcynus bicarinatus*), 27 lb. 1 oz., Bribie Island, Brisbane, Queensland, Australia, March 24, 1989, Kathy Maguire

MAHSEER (*Tor tor*), 95 lb., Cauvery River, India, March 26, 1984, Robert Howitt

MANDUBA (*Ageneiosus brevifilis*), 4 lb. 2 oz., Cuiaba River, Mato Grosso, Brazil, June 30, 1992, Luiz Carlos Nolasco

MARGATE, WHITE (*Haemulon album*), 14 lb. 8 oz., South Shore, Bermuda, Nov. 24, 1986, J. Henry Gill

MARLIN, BLACK (*Makaira indica*), 1,560 lb., Cabo Blanco, Peru, Aug. 4, 1953, Alfred C. Glassell, Jr.

MARLIN, BLUE [Atlantic] (*Makaira nigricans*), 1,402 lb. 2 oz., Vitoria, Brazil, Feb. 29, 1992, Paulo Roberto A. Amorim

MARLIN, BLUE [Pacific] (*Makaira nigricans*), 1,376 lb., Kaaiwi Pt., Kona, Hawaii, USA, May 31, 1982, Jay Wm. deBeaubien

MARLIN, STRIPED (*Tetrapturus audax*), 494 lb., Tutukaka, New Zealand, Jan. 16, 1986, Bill Boniface

MARLIN, WHITE (*Tetrapturus albidus*), 181 lb. 14 oz., Vitoria, Brazil, Dec. 8, 1979, Evandro Luiz Coser

MATRINCHA (*Brycon hilarii*), 3 lb. 5 oz., Cristalino River, Mato Grosso, Brazil, June 23, 1993, Sergio Roberto Rothier

MEAGRE (*Argyrosomus regius*), 105 lb. 13 oz., Nouadhibou, Mauritania, March 30, 1986, Laurent Morat

MILKFISH (*Chanos chanos*), 24 lb. 8 oz., Hilo Bay, Hilo, Hawaii, USA, Aug. 25, 1991, Rory Tokeshi

MOJARRA, STRIPED (*Diapterus plumieri*), 2 lb. 4 oz., West Palm Beach, Florida, USA, Aug. 21, 1987, James B. Black, Jr.

MONKFISH, EUROPEAN (*Squatina squatina*), 52 lb. 14 oz., Llwyngwril Beach, North Wales, UK, June 16, 1984, George Steven Bishop

MORAY, SLENDER GIANT (*Thyrsoidea macrura*), 11 lb. 12 oz., St. Lucia, Republic of South Africa, Aug. 29, 1987, Graham Vollmer

MULLET, STRIPED (*Liza tricuspidens*), 6 lb. 13 oz., Hermanus, Republic of South Africa, Oct. 7, 1987, Julius Jerling

MULLET, THICKLIP (*Chelon labrosus*), 7 lb. 11 oz., Barseback, Sweden, March 16, 1991, Bengt Olsson

MULLET, THIN LIPPED (*Liza ramada*), 5 lb. 4 oz., River Taw, Barnstaple, England, June 14, 1984, Raymond John White

MUSKELLUNGE (*Esox masquinongy*), 65 lb., Blackstone Harbor, Ontario, Canada, Oct. 16, 1988, Kenneth J. O'Brien

MUSKELLUNGE, TIGER (*Esox masquinongy and Esox lucius*), 51 lb. 3 oz., Lac Vieux-Desert, Wisconsin/Michigan, USA, July 16, 1919, John A. Knobla

MUSSELCRACKER, BLACK (*Cymatoceps nasutus*), 23 lb. 12 oz., Cape Recife, Port Elizabeth, Republic of South Africa, Feb. 21, 1993, Santie Beukes

NEEDLEFISH, ATLANTIC (*Strongylura marina*), 3 lb. 4 oz., Brigantine, New Jersey, USA, July 18, 1990, Charlie Trost

NEEDLEFISH, FLAT (*Ablennes hians*), 4 lb. 4 oz., St. Lucie, Stuart, Florida, USA, July 30, 1986, Paul T. Gilligan

OILFISH (*Ruvettus pretiosus*), 139 lb. 15 oz., White Island, New Zealand, April 12, 1986, Tim Wallace

OPAH (*Lampris guttatus*), 122 lb. 9 oz., Baja, Mexico, July 31, 1993, Walter Dittman

OSCAR (*Astronotus ocellatus*), 3 lb. 3 oz., Snake Creek Channel, Florida, USA, Nov. 1, 1993, Carlos Rodriguez

OTOLITHE (*Pseudotolithus brachygnethus*), 13 lb. 7 oz., Nouadhibou, Mauritania, March 8, 1986, Francois Sturm

PACU (*Colossoma spp.*), 21 lb. 2 oz., Parana River, Paso de la Patria, Argentina, Jan. 3, 1993, Ken Bohling

PACU, BLACK (*Colossoma brachypomum*), 16 lb., Cutler Ridge, Florida, USA, Feb. 15, 1993, Ronald C. Cotton

PALOMETA (*Trachinotus goodei*), 13 lb., Bimini, Bahamas, Feb. 3, 1991, Capt. Dan Kipnis

PAYARA (*Hydrolicus scomberoides*), 34 lb. 12 oz., La Paragua River Lodge, Paragua, Venezuela, April 11, 1994, Lee Thill

PERCH, NILE (*Lates niloticus*), 191 lb. 8 oz., Rusinga Island, Lake Victoria, Kenya, Sept. 5, 1991, Andy Davison

PERCH, SACRAMENTO (*Archoplites interruptus*), 2 lb. 12 oz., Sonoma County, California, USA, March 21, 1991, Darrell Arnold

PERCH, WHITE (*Morone americana*), 4 lb. 12 oz., Messalonskee Lake, Maine, USA, June 4, 1949, Mrs. Earl Small

PERCH, YELLOW (*Perca flavescens*), 4 lb. 3 oz., Bordentown, New Jersey, USA, May 1865, Dr. C.C. Abbot

PERMIT (*Trachinotus falcatus*), 53 lb. 4 oz., Lake Worth, Florida, USA, March 25, 1994, Roy Brooker

PIAU (*Leproinus piau*), 1 lb. 6 oz., Sao Francisco River, Minas Gerais, Brazil, Aug. 18, 1993, Tobias Rothier

PICKEREL, CHAIN (*Esox niger*), 9 lb. 6 oz., Homerville, Georgia, USA, Feb. 17, 1961, Baxley McQuaig, Jr.

PICKEREL, GRASS (*Esox americanus vermiculatus*), 1 lb., Dewart Lake, Indiana, USA, June 9, 1990, Mike Berg

PICKEREL, REDFIN (*Esox americanus americanus*), 1 lb. 15 oz., Red Hook, New York, USA, Oct. 16, 1988, William G. Stagias

PIKE, NORTHERN (*Esox lucius*), 55 lb. 1 oz., Lake of Grefeern, West Germany, Oct. 16, 1986, Lothar Louis

PIKE-CONGER, COMMON (*Muraenesooc bagio*), 15 lb. 10 oz., Markham River, LAE, Huon Gulf, Papua New Guinea, March 7, 1993, Barry Mallett

PINFISH (*Lagodon rhomboides*), 3 lb. 5 oz., Horn Island, Mississippi, USA, Sept. 4, 1992, William Davis Fountain

PIRANHA, BLACK (*Pygocentrus piraya*), 3 lb., Uatuma River, Brazil, Nov. 23, 1991, Doug Olander

PIRANHA, BLACK SPOT (*Pygocentrus cariba*), 14 lb., Hato Cedral, Apure, Venezuela, Jan. 18, 1991, William T. Miller

PIRANHA, RED (*Serrasalmus nattereri*), 2 lb. 3 oz., Cuiaba River, Mato Grosso, Brazil, July 2, 1992, Fernando A. Martins Salles

PIRAPUTANGA (*Brycon orbinyanus*), 1 lb., Cuibara River, Mato Grosso, Brazil, June 10, 1993, Sergio Roberto Rothier

PIRARUCU (*Arapaima gigas*), 148 lb., Rupununi River, Karanambu, Guyana, April 1, 1953, Ed Migdalski

POLLACK, EUROPEAN (*Pollachius pollachius*), 27 lb. 6 oz., Salcombe, Devon, England, Jan. 16, 1986, Robert Samuel Milkins

POLLOCK (*Pollachius virens*), 46 lb. 10 oz., Perkins Cove, Ogunquit, Maine, USA, Oct. 24, 1990, Linda M. Paul

POMPANO, AFRICAN (*Alectis ciliaris*), 50 lb. 8 oz., Daytona Beach, Florida, USA, April 21, 1990, Tom Sargent

POMPANO, FLORIDA (*Trachinotus carolinus*), 8 lb. 1 oz., Flagler Beach, Florida, USA, March 19, 1984, Chester E. Dietrick

PORGY, BLACK (*Acanthopagrus schlegeli*), 7 lb., West Port, Niigata, Niigata, Japan, March 30, 1992, Yoichi Suzuki

PORGY, JOLTHEAD (*Calumus bajonado*), 23 lb. 4 oz., Madeira Beach, Florida, USA, March 14, 1990, Harm M. Wilder

PORGY, RED (*Pagrus pagrus*), 2 lb. 7 oz., Gibraltar Bay, Dec. 30, 1993, Joseph Anthony Triay

POWAN (*Coregonus lavaretus*), 11 lb. 2 oz., Skrabean, Nymoua, Sweden, Dec. 9, 1984, Jorgen Larsson

PUFFER, OCEANIC (*Lagocephalus lagocephalus*), 7 lb., Sandy Hook, New Jersey, USA, Aug. 28, 1991, Jane Lee Jagen

PUFFER, STRIPEBELLY (*Arothron hispidus*), 4 lb. 7 oz., Iroquois Point, Hawaii, USA, Oct. 31, 1992, George D. Cornish

PUMPKINSEED (*Lepomis gibbosus*), 1 lb. 6 oz., Mexico, New York, USA, April 27, 1985, Heather Ann Finch

QUEENFISH, DOUBLESPOTTED (*Scomberoides lysan*), 2 lb. 8 oz., Lifuka Island, Ha-apai, Kingdom of Tonga, Nov. 27, 1991, Norbert H. Watanabe

QUEENFISH, TALANG (*Scomberoides commersonianus*), 31 lb. 15 oz., Bazaruto Island, Mozambique, Jan. 18, 1991, Hilton Nichols

QUILLBACK (*Carpiodes cyprinus*), 6 lb. 8 oz., Lake Michigan, Indiana, USA, Jan. 15, 1993, Mike Berg

RATTAIL, roundhead (*Coryphaenoides rupestris*), 3 lb. 11 oz., Trondheimsfjorden, Norway, Nov. 26, 1993, Knut Nilson

RAY, BACKWATER BUTTERFLY (*Gymnura natalensis*), 182 lb. 1 oz., Knysna Lagoon, Republic of South Africa, July 11, 1992, Hilton Gervais

RAY, BLACK (*Dasyatis thetidis*), 82 lb. 10 oz., Weston Point Bay, Newhaven, Australia, Jan. 20, 1993, Peter Ronald Blondell

RAY, BLONDE (*Raja brachyura*), 31 lb. 8 oz., Jersey Channel Islands, United Kingdom, April 3, 1989, John Thompson

RAY, BULL (*Pteromylaeus bovinus*), 80 lb. 7 oz., Nouadhibou, Mauritania, Sept. 16, 1986, Pierre Cluck

RAY, BULL [Australian] (*Myliobatis australis*), 124 lb. 8 oz., Neptune Island, Port Lincoln, S.A., Australia, April 13, 1991, Rolf Czabayski

RAY, PAINTED (*Raja microocellata*), 9 lb. 15 oz., Jersey, Channel Islands, England, Aug. 2, 1988, Andrew R.J. Mitchell

RAY, PALE (*Raja lintea*), 19 lb. 15 oz., Langesund, Norway, July 14, 1987, Lars-Goran Westerlund

RAY, SOUTHERN FIDDLER (*Trygonorrhina fasciata*), 14 lb. 12 oz., Marion Bay, Australia, Aug. 11, 1990, Marcel Vandergoot

RAY, SPINY BUTTERFLY (*Gymnura altavela*), 132 lb. 4 oz., Nouadhibou, Mauritania, May 5, 1984, Robin Michel

RAY, THORNBACK (*Raja clavata*), 16 lb. 12 oz., Jersey, Channel Islands, United Kingdom, July 11, 1988, John Thompson

REDFISH [ocean perch] (*Sebastes marinus*), 10 lb. 5 oz., Sorvfer, Finnmark, Norway, July 16, 1990, Ole-Einar Jakobsen

REDHORSE, BLACK (*Moxostoma duquesni*), 1 lb. 14 oz., French Creek, Urica, Pennsylvania, USA, April 30, 1994, Richard E. Faler, Jr.

REDHORSE, GOLDEN (*Moxostoma erythrurum*), 2 lb. 11 oz., French Creek, Franklin, Pennsylvania, USA, April 26, 1992, Kristen E. Faler

REDHORSE, GREATER (*Moxostoma valenciennesi*), 9 lb. 3 oz., Salmon River, Pulaski, New York, USA, May 11, 1985, Jason A. Wilson

REDHORSE, RIVER
(*Moxostoma carinatum*), 5 lb. 9
oz., Limestone Creek,
Mooresville, Alabama, USA,
March 27, 1985, Don Hale

REDHORSE, SHORTHEAD
(*Moxostoma macrolepidotum*), 4
lb. 12 oz., Island Park, Elkhart,
Indiana, USA, May 18, 1984,
William A. Merrick

REDHORSE, SILVER
(*Moxostoma anisurum*), 11 lb. 7
oz., Plum Creek, Wisconsin, USA,
May 29, 1985, Neal D.G. Long

ROACH (*Rutilus rutilus*), 4 lb. 1
oz., Colwick, Nottingham,
England, June 16, 1975, R.G.
Jones

ROCKFISH, CHINA (*Sebastes
nebulosus*), 3 lb. 11 oz., Tatoosh
Island, Neah Bay, Washington,
USA, Aug. 24, 1992, Edward
Schultz

ROCKFISH, BLACK (*Sebastes
melanops*), 10 lb., Puget Sound,
Washington, USA, July 20, 1986,
William J. Harris, DDS

ROCKFISH, BLUE (*Sabastes
mystinus*), 3 lb. 8 oz., Tatoosh
Island, Neah Bay, Washington,
USA, August 11, 1993, Ronald D.
Shelton

ROCKFISH, CANARY (*Sebastes
pinniger*), 10 lb., Westport,
Washington, USA, May 17, 1986,
Terry Rudnick

ROCKFISH, COPPER (*Sebastes
caurinus*), 5 lb. 11 oz., Discovery
Island, Victoria, B.C., Canada,
Aug. 4, 1989, Norman R. Clark

ROCKFISH, QUILLBACK
(*Sebastes maliger*), 7 lb. 4 oz.,
Depoe Bay, Oregon, USA, March
18, 1990, Kelly H. Canaday

ROCKFISH, TIGER (*Sebastes
nigrocinctus*), 4 lb. 14 oz., Depoe
Bay, Oregon, USA, Sept. 4, 1993,
Ronald L. Chatham

ROCKFISH, VERMILLION
(*Sebastes miniatus*), 12 lb., Depoe
Bay, Oregon, USA, June 2, 1990,
Joseph William Lowe

ROCKFISH, YELLOWEYE
(*Sebastes ruberrimus*), 26 lb. 4
oz., Dickson Island, Wells
Passage, B.C., Canada, Nov. 8,
1993, Alan Mace

ROCKFISH, YELLOWTAIL
(*Sebastes flavidus*), 5 lb. 8 oz.,
Cape Flattery, Washington, USA,
Aug. 28, 1988, Steven D. Garnett

ROOSTERFISH (*Nematistius
pectoralis*), 114 lb., La Paz, Baja
California, Mexico, June 1, 1960,
Abe Sackheim

RUDD (*Scardinius erytrophthalmus*), 3 lb. 7 oz., Ljungan River,
Sweden, July 31, 1988, Luis
Kilian Rasmussen

RUNNER, BLUE (*Caranx
crysos*), 8 lb. 4 oz., Bimini,
Bahamas, Sept. 9, 1990, Brent C.
Rowland

RUNNER, RAINBOW (*Elagatis
bipinnulata*), 37 lb. 9 oz., Isla
Clarion, Revillagigedo Islands,
Mexico, Nov. 21, 1991, Tom
Pfleger

SABALO (*Brycon melanopterus*),
9 lb. 9 oz., Rio Tambopata, Peru,
Oct. 10, 1992, James B. Wise,
M.D.

SAILFISH, ATLANTIC
(*Istiophorus platypterus*), 135 lb.
5 oz., Lagos, Nigeria, Nov. 10,
1991, Ron King

SAILFISH, PACIFIC
(*Istiophorus platypterus*), 221 lb.,
Santa Cruz Island, Ecuador, Feb.
12, 1947, C.W. Stewart

SALMON, ATLANTIC (*Salmo
salar*), 79 lb. 2 oz., Tana River,
Norway, 1928, Henrik Henriksen

SALMON, CHINOOK
(*Oncorhynchus tshawytscha*), 97
lb. 4 oz., Kenai River, Alaska,
USA, May 17, 1985, Les
Anderson

SALMON, CHUM (*Oncorhynchus
keta*), 32 lb., Behm Canal, Alaska,
USA, June 7, 1985, Fredrick E.
Thynes

SALMON, COHO (*Oncorhynchus kisutch*), 33 lb. 4 oz., Salmon River, Pulaski, New York, USA, Sept. 27, 1989, Jerry Lifton

SALMON, HYBRID and CHINOOK (*Oncorhynchus gorbuscha*), 14 lb., Lake Huron, Michigan, USA, Aug. 23, 1993, Buddy L. Jacob

SALMON, LAKE (*Lates microlepis*), 18 lb. 4 oz., Lake Tanganyika, Zambia, Dec. 1, 1987, Steve Robinson

SALMON, PINK (*Oncorhynchus gorbuscha*), 13 lb. 1 oz., St. Mary's River, Ontario, Canada, Sept. 23, 1992, Ray Higaki

SALMON, SOCKEYE (*Oncorhynchus nerka*), 15 lb. 3 oz., Kenai River, Alaska, USA, Aug. 9, 1987, Stan Roach

SAMSONFISH (*Seriola hippos*), 80 lb. 7 oz., Cape Naturaliste, W.A., Australia, Jan. 31, 1993, Terry Coote

SAUGER (*Stizostedion canadense*), 8 lb. 12 oz., Lake Sakakawea, North Dakota, USA, Oct. 6, 1971, Mike Fischer

SAUGEYE (*Stizostedion vitrcum and canadense*), 12 lb. 6 oz., Lake Logan, Ohio, USA, March 29, 1993, Daniel Louis D'Amore

SAWFISH (*Pristis spp.*), 890 lb. 8 oz., Fort Amador, Canal Zone, Panama, May 26, 1960, Jack D. Wagner

SCAMP (*Mycteroperca phenax*), 28 lb., Port Canaveral, Florida, USA, Dec. 30, 1991, Charles V. West

SCUP (*Stenotomus chrysops*), 4 lb. 9 oz., Nantucket Sound, Massachusetts, USA, June 3, 1992, Sonny Richards

SEA BASS, NEW ZEALAND (*Polyprion moeone*), 156 lb. 8 oz., White Island, Whakatane, New Zealand, Nov. 2, 1990, Ian Grindle

SEA-PERCH, SPOTTED-SCALE (*Lutjanus johni*), 23 lb. 2 oz., Cairns, Queensland, Australia, March 2, 1986, Mac Mankowski

SEABASS, EUROPEAN (*Dicentrarchus labrax*), 20 lb. 11 oz., Stes Maries de la Mer 13, France, May 6, 1986, Jean Baptiste Bayle

SEABASS, JAPANESE [SUZUKI] (*Lateolabrax japonicus*), 19 lb. 2 oz., Kano River, Numazu-shi, Shizuoka, Japan, Nov. 26, 1988, Yasuaki Ohshio

SEABASS, BLACKFIN, (*Lateolabrax latus*), 18 lb. 4 oz., Naminoura, Wakayama, Japan, Feb. 25, 1990, Takashi Tsujimoto

SEABASS, LEATHER (*Dermatolepis dermatolepis*), 4 lb. 8 oz., Playa Zancudo, Costa Rica, Jan. 23, 1993, Craig Whitehead, M.D.

SEABASS, WHITE (*Atractoscion nobilis*), 83 lb. 12 oz., San Felipe, Mexico, March 31, 1953, L.C. Baumgardner

SEABREAM, DAGGERHEAD (*Chrysoblephus cristiceps*), 16 lb. 1 oz., Algora Bay, Port Elizabeth, South Africa, Oct. 10, 1993, Eddie de Reuck

SEABREAM, REDBANDED (*Pagrus auriga*), 6 lb. 9 oz., Nouadhibou, Mauritania, March 9, 1986, Serge Bensa

SEABREAM, SOUTHERN COMMON (*Pagrus africanus*), 12 lb. 3 oz., Nouadhibou, Mauritania, March 13, 1986, Bernard Defago

SEAROBIN, STRIPED (*Prionotus evolans*), 3 lb. 6 oz., Mt. Sinai, Long Island, New York, USA, June 22, 1988, Michael B. Greene, Jr.

SEATROUT, SAND (*Cynoscion arenarius*), 1 lb. 1 oz., Dog Island, Garrabelle, Florida, USA, Oct. 2, 1993, Kate Nelson

SEATROUT, SPOTTED (*Cynoscion nebulosus*), 16 lb., Mason's Beach, Virginia, USA, May 28, 1977, William Katko

SEERFISH, AUSTRALIAN
(*Scomberomorus munroi*), 20 lb. 6
oz., South West Rocks, N.S.W.,
Australia, July 5, 1987, Greg
Laarkamp

SEERFISH, CHINESE
(*Scomberomorus sinensis*), 89 lb. 4
oz., Nine Pin Islands, Hong Kong,
Oct. 6, 1988, Ken R. Jones

SEERFISH, KANADI
(*Scomberomorus plurilineatus*), 21
lb. 9 oz., Richards Bay, Republic
of South Africa, July 5, 1988, Lisa
Jane Harvey

SENNET, SOUTHERN
(*Sphyraena picudilla*), 2 lb. 1 oz.,
Lake Worth, Florida, USA, Jan.
30, 1988, William J. White, Sr.

SEVENTY-FOUR (*Polysteganus
undulosus*), 35 lb. 4 oz., Mapuzi,
Transkei, Republic of South
Africa, Aug. 17, 1985, Nolan
Sparg

SHAD, AMERICAN (*Alosa
sapidissima*), 11 lb. 4 oz.,
Connecticut River, South Hadley,
Massachusetts, USA, May 19,
1986, Bob Thibodo

SHAD, GIZZARD (*Dorosoma
cepedianum*), 4 lb., Lake
Michigan, Indiana, USA, Jan. 15,
1993, Mike Berg

**SHARK, ATLANTIC SHARP-
NOSE** (*Rhizopcionodon terraeno-
vae*), 14 lb. 10 oz., Sebastian Inlet,
Florida, USA, Feb. 5, 1994,
Stephen Wise

SHARK, BIGEYE THRESHER
(*Alopias superciliosus*), 802 lb.,
Tutukaka, New Zealand, Feb. 8,
1981, Dianne North

SHARK, BIGNOSE
(*Carcharhinus alimus*), 369 lb. 14
oz., Markham River, LAE, Papua
New Guinea, Oct. 23, 1993,
Lester J. Rohrlach

SHARK, BLACKMOUTH CAT
(*Galeus melastomus*), 1 lb. 11 oz.,
Kraakvaag Fjord, Norway, June
17, 1992, Joerg Marquard

SHARK, BLACKNOSE
(*Carcharhinus acronotus*), 41 lb. 9
oz., Little River, South Carolina,
USA, July 30, 1992, Jon-Paul
Hoffman

SHARK, BLACKTAIL
(*Carcharhinus wheeleri*), 74 lb. 4
oz., Kosi Bay, Zululand, Republic
of South Africa, May 25, 1987,
Trevor Ashington

SHARK, BLACKTIP
(*Carcharhinus limbatus*), 270 lb.
9 oz., Malindi Bay, Kenya, Sept.
21, 1984, Jurgen Oeder

SHARK, BLUE (*Prionace
glauca*), 437 lb., Catherine Bay,
N.S.W., Australia, Oct. 2, 1976,
Peter Hyde

SHARK, BONNETHEAD
(*Sphyrna tiburo*), 22 lb. 13 oz.,
Gulf of Mexico, Port O'Connor,
Texas, USA, July 13, 1991, Bill
M. Kirschner

SHARK, BULL (*Carcharhinus
leucas*), 490 lb., Dauphin Island,
Alabama, USA, Aug. 30, 1986,
Phillip Wilson

SHARK, DUSKY (*Carcharhinus
obscurus*), 764 lb., Longboat Key,
Florida, USA, May 28, 1982,
Warren Girle

**SHARK, GREAT HAMMER-
HEAD** (*Sphyrna mokarran*), 991
lb., Sarasota, Florida, USA, May
30, 1982, Allen Ogle

SHARK, GREENLAND
(*Somniosus microcephalus*), 1,708
lb. 9 oz., Trondheimsfjord,
Norway, Oct. 18, 1987, Terje
Nordtvedt

SHARK, GUMMY (*Mustelus
anarcticus*), 67 lb. 14 oz.,
Mcloughins Beach, Victoria,
Australia, Nov. 15, 1992, Neale
Blunden

SHARK, LEMON (*Negaprion
brevirostris*), 405 lb., Buxton,
North Carolina, USA, Nov. 23,
1988, Colleen D. Harlow

SHARK, LEOPARD (*Triakis
semifasciata*), 40 lb. 10 oz.,
Oceanside, California, USA, May
13, 1994, Fred Oakley

SHARK, NARROWTOOTH
(*Carcharhinus brachyurus*), 533
lb. 8 oz., Cape Karikari, New
Zealand, Jan. 9, 1993, Gaye
Harrison-Armstrong

SHARK, OCEANIC WHITETIP
(*Carcharhinus longimanus*), 146
lb. 8 oz., Kona, Hawaii, USA, Nov.
11, 1992, Pamela S. Basco

SHARK, PORBEAGLE (*Lamna
nasus*), 507 lb., Pentland Firth,
Caithness, Scotland, March 9,
1993, Christopher Bennet

SHARK, SAND TIGER
(*Adontaspis taurus*), 350 lb. 2 oz.,
Charleston Jetty, Charleston,
South Carolina, USA, April 29,
1993, Mark Thawley

SHARK, SANDBAR
(*Carcharhinus plumbeus*), 260 lb.,
Gambia Coast, Gambia, Jan. 2,
1989, Paul Delsignore

**SHARK, SCALLOPED
HAMMERHEAD** (*Sphyrna
lewini*), 234 lb., Cape Point,
North Carolina, USA, March 24,
1990, Timothy P. Harlow

SHARK, SHORTFIN MAKO
(*Isurus oxyrinchus*), 1,115 lb.,
Black River, Mauritius, Nov. 16,
1988, Patrick Guillanton

SHARK, SILVERTIP
(*Carcharhinus albimarginatus*),
330 lb. 11 oz., Watamu, Kenya,
Oct. 22, 1991, Christopher Wood

SHARK, SIX-GILLED (*Hexanchus
griseus*), 1,069 lb. 3 oz., Faial,
Azores, Oct. 18, 1990, Capt. Jack
Reece

SHARK, SMALLFIN GULPER
(*Centrophorus moluccensis*), 5 lb.
4 oz., LAE, Huon Gulf, Papua
New Guinea, Feb. 13, 1993, Justin
Mallett

**SHARK, SMOOTH HAMMER-
HEAD** (*Sphyrna zygaena*), 249 lb.
1 oz., Azores Bank, Faial Azores,
Aug. 17, 1993, Nigel T. Gibbs

SHARK, SPINNER
(*Carcharhinus brevipinna*), 190
lb., Flagler Beach, Florida, USA,
April 3, 1986, Mrs. Gladys Prior

SHARK, TIGER (*Galeocerdo
cuvier*), 1,780 lb., Cherry Grove,
South Carolina, USA, June 14,
1964, Walter Maxwell

SHARK, WHITE (*Carcharodon
carcharias*), 2,664 lb., Ceduna,
South Australia, April 21, 1959,
Alfred Dean

SHARK, WHITETIP REEF
(*Triaenodon obesus*), 40 lb. 4 oz.,
Isla Coiba, Panama, Aug. 8, 1979,
Jack Kamerman

SHARKSUCKER (*Echeneis
naucrates*), 4 lb. 7 oz., Boca
Raton, Florida, USA, Aug. 4,
1990, Richard F. Bertok

SHEEPSHEAD (*Archosargus
probatocephalus*), 21 lb. 4 oz.,
Bayou St. John, New Orleans,
Louisiana, USA, April 16, 1982,
Wayne Desselle

SHEEPSHEAD, CALIFORNIA
(*Semicossyphus pulcher*), 21 lb. 8
oz., Huntington Beach,
California, USA, Dec. 2, 1992,
Jack Dalla Corte

SIERRA, ATLANTIC
(*Scomberomorus brasiliensis*), 13
lb. 7 oz., Maracaibo, Venezuela,
May 12, 1985, Edgar C. Jimenez

SKATE (*Raja batis*), 144 lb.,
Tobermory, Isle of Mull, Scotland,
Nov. 16, 1984, Brian J. Swinbanks

SKATE, BIG (*Raja binoculata*),
91 lb., Humbolt Bay, Eureka,
California, USA, March 6, 1993,
Scotty A. Krick

SKATE, STARRY (*Raja radiata*),
9 lb. 5 oz., Hvasser, Norway, Oct.
10, 1982, Knut Hedlund

SKIPJACK, BLACK (*Euthynnus
lineatus*), 26 lb., Thetis Bank,
Baja California, Mexico, Oct. 23,
1991, Clifford K. Hamaishi

SMOOTHHOUND, FLORIDA
(*Mustelus norrisi*), 30 lb. 6 oz.,
Gulf of Mexico, Destin, Florida,
USA, April 1, 1992, Stephen L.
Wilson

**SMOOTHHOUND, STAR-
SPOTTED** (*Mustelus manazo*), 12
lb. 9 oz., Lae, Huon Gulf, Papua
New Guinea, Feb. 13, 1993, Justin
Mallett

SMOOTHHOUND, STARRY
(*Mustelus asterias*), 10 lb. 8 oz.,
Nab Rocks, Isle of Wight,
England, July 18, 1984, Sylvia M.
Steed

SNAKEHEAD (*Channa argus*),
13 lb. 7 oz., Yazawanuma,
Yamagata, Japan, May 13, 1990,
Kazuhiro Takeda

SNAPPER [squirefish] (*Pagrus
auratus*), 37 lb. 14 oz., Mottiti
Island, New Zealand, Nov. 2,
1992, Mark Hemingway

SNAPPER, GUINEAN [African
cubera] (*Lutjanus agennes*), 89 lb.
15 oz., Blieron, Cavally River,
Ivory Coast, March 3, 1987,
Daniel Pichard

SNAPPER, MALABAR (*Lutjanus
malabaricos*), 17 lb. 7 oz., Cairns,
Queensland, Australia, Aug. 3,
1989, Gregory Ronald Albert

SNAPPER, PACIFIC CUBERA
(*Lutjanus novemfasciatus*), 78 lb.
12 oz., Bahia Pez Vela, Costa Rica,
March 23, 1988, Steven C. Paull

SNAPPER, AMARILLO
(*Lutjanus argentiventris*), 11 lb.,
Playa Zancudo, Costa Rica,
March 12, 1993, Roy Ventura
Roig

SNAPPER, BLACK (*Apsilus
dentatus*), 7 lb., Little San
Salvador, Bahamas, April 24,
1992, Donald E. May

SNAPPER, BLACKFIN
(*Lutjanus buccanella*), 7 lb. 3 oz.,
Bahamas, Aug. 25, 1993, Ron
Mallet

SNAPPER, COLORADO
(*Lutjanus colorado*), 20 lb. 8 oz.,
Playa Zancudo, Costa Rica,
March 19, 1993, Craig
Whitehead, M.D.

SNAPPER, CUBERA (*Lutjanus
cyanopterus*), 121 lb. 8 oz.,
Cameron, Louisiana, USA, July 5,
1982, Mike Hebert

SNAPPER, DOG [Atlantic]
(*Lutjanus jocu*), 20 lb., San
Salvador, Bahamas, June 5, 1992,
Tom Prater, Sr.

SNAPPER, GRAY [mangrove]
(*Lutjanus griseus*), 17 lb., Port
Canaveral, Florida, USA, June 14,
1992, Steve Maddox

SNAPPER, GREENBAR
(*Hoplopagrus guntheri*), 17 lb. 3
oz., Bahia de la Paz, Bahia, Jan.
24, 1994, Jerry D. Lairson, Sr.

SNAPPER, LANE (*Lutjanus
synagris*), 7 lb., Gulf of Mexico,
Perdido Pass, Alabama, USA,
June 23, 1991, Suzanne Ridgon

SNAPPER, MULLET (*Lutjanus
aratus*), 7 lb., Playa Zancudo,
Costa Rica, March 15, 1994,
Ronald C. Snody

SNAPPER, MUTTON (*Lutjanus
analis*), 28 lb. 5 oz., Gulf of
Mexico, Florida, USA, Sept. 4,
1993, Bennie D. Kilgore

SNAPPER, PAPUAN BLACK
(*Lutjanus goldiei*), 42 lb. 5 oz., Fly
River, Papua New Guinea, Sept.
22, 1992, Len Bradica

SNAPPER, RED (*Lutjanus
campechanus*), 46 lb. 8 oz.,
Destin, Florida, USA, Oct. 1,
1985, E. Lane Nichols III

SNAPPER, SILK (*Lutjanus
vivanus*), 18 lb. 5 oz., Gulf of
Mexico, Venice, Florida, USA,
July 12, 1986, James M. Taylor

SNAPPER, TWOSPOT RED
(*Lutjanus bohar*), 27 lb. 8 oz.,
Ogasawara Islands, Hahajima,
Tokyo, Japan, Aug. 9, 1990,
Fujiko Shimazaki

SNAPPER, VERMILLION
(*Rhomboplites aurorubens*), 7 lb. 3
oz., Gulf of Mexico, Mobile,
Alabama, USA, May 31, 1987,
John W. Doss

SNAPPER, YELLOWTAIL
(*Ocyurus chrysurus*), 8 lb. 8 oz.,
Gulf of Mexico, Ft. Myers,
Florida, USA, July 24, 1992,
Suzanne Axel

SNOOK, PACIFIC BLACK
(*Centropomus nigrescens*), 57 lb.
12 oz., Rio Naranjo, Quepos,
Costa Rica, Aug. 23, 1991,
George Beck

SNOOK, PACIFIC BLACKFIN
(*Centropomus medius*), 3 lb., Playa
Zancudo, Puntarenas, Costa Rica,
June 10, 1990, Dr. Craig
Whitehead

SNOOK, PACIFIC WHITE
(*Centropomus viridis*), 23 lb.,
Playa Zancudo, Puntarenas, Costa
Rica, June 29, 1990, Dr. Craig
Whitehead

SNOOK, COMMON
(*Centropomus undecimalis*), 53 lb.
10 oz., Parismina Ranch, Costa
Rica, Oct. 18, 1978, Gilbert Ponzi

SNOOK, FAT (*Centropomus
parallelus*), 7 lb. 4 oz., Miami,
Florida, USA, Oct. 9, 1992,
William John Parry, Jr.

SORUBIM, SPOTTED
(*Pseudoplatystoma coruscans*), 44
lb., Miranda River, Mato Grosso,
Brazil, Aug. 30, 1993, Sandy
Blum

SORUBIM, TIGER
(*Pseudoplatystoma tigrinum*), 36
lb. 8 oz., Rupinuni River,
Karanambo, Guyana, Dec. 4,
1981, William T. Miller

SPADEFISH, ATLANTIC
(*Chaetodipterus faber*), 14 lb.,
Chesapeake Bay, Virginia, USA,
May 23, 1986, George F. Brace

**SPEARFISH,
MEDITERRANEAN** (*Tetrapturus
belone*), 90 lb. 13 oz., Madeira
Island, Portugal, June 2, 1980,
Joseph Larkin

SPLAKE (*Salvelinus namaycush
and Salvelinus fontinalis*), 20 lb.
11 oz., Georgian Bay, Ontario,
Canada, May 17, 1987, Paul S.
Thompson

STARGAZER, NORTHERN
(*Astroscopus guttatus*), 10 lb. 4
oz., Shark River Inlet, New Jersey,
USA, Aug. 10, 1988, Leslie E.
Katona, Sr.

STEED, BARBEL [igoi]
(*Hemibarbus barbus*), 1 lb. 10 oz.,
Ono, Hyogo, Japan, March 20,
1992, Masahiro Oomori

STEENBRAS, BLACK
(*Cymatoceps nasutus*), 69 lb. 12
oz., Umngazana, Transkei,
Republic of South Africa, July 6,
1990, Neville R. Sparg

STEENBRAS, RED (*Petrus
rupestras*), 124 lb. 12 oz., Aston
Bay, Eastern Cape Coast, South
Africa, May 8, 1994, Terry Colin
Goldstone

STINGRAY, ATLANTIC
(*Dasyatis sabina*), 7 lb. 6 oz.,
West Bay, Galveston, Texas, USA,
July 4, 1993, Richard M. Olszak,
Jr.

STINGRAY, DIAMOND
(*Dasyatis brevis*), 102 lb., Mission
Bay, San Diego, California, USA,
Aug. 7, 1993, Roger Ehlers

STINGRAY, ROUGHTAIL
(*Dasyatis centrovra*), 294 lb.,
River Gambia, The Gambia, Nov.
4, 1988, Iain Foulger

STINGRAY, ROUND (*Urolophus
halleri*), 3 lb., Santa Clara River,
Ventura, California, USA, Sept. 3,
1989, Paul David Bodtke

STINGRAY, SOUTHERN
(*Dasyatis americana*), 229 lb.,
Galveston Bay, Texas, USA, June
2, 1991, David Lee Anderson

STUMPNOSE, RED
(*Chrysoblephus*), 12 lb. 12 oz., St.
Croix Island, Port Elizabeth,
South Africa, Dec. 20, 1993,
Craig Saunders

STURGEON, BELUGA (*Huso
huso*), 224 lb. 13 oz., Guryev,
Kasakhstan, May 3, 1993, Merete
Lehne

STURGEON, LAKE (*Acipenser
fulvescens*), 92 lb. 4 oz., Kettle
River, Minnesota, USA, Sept. 11,
1986, James Michael DeOtis

STURGEON, SHORTNOSE
(*Acipenser brevirostrum*), 11 lb. 2
oz., Kennebacis River, N.B.,
Canada, July 31, 1988, Lawrence
Guimond

STURGEON, SHOVELNOSE
(*Scaphirhynchus platorynchus*),
10 lb. 12 oz., Missouri River,
Loma, Montana, USA, June 14,
1985, Arthur James Seal

STURGEON, WHITE (*Acipenser
transmontanus*), 468 lb., Benicia,
California, USA, July 9, 1983,
Joey Pallotta III

SUCKER, FLANNELMOUTH (*Catostomus latipinnis*), 2 lb. 6 oz., Colorado River, Colorado, USA, July 7, 1990, Karen A. DeVine

SUCKER, LONGNOSE (*Catostomus catostomus*), 6 lb. 9 oz., St. Joseph River, Michigan, USA, Dec. 2, 1989, Ben Knoll

SUCKER, SPOTTED (*Minytrema melanops*), 2 lb. 11 oz., Hall's Lake, Rome, Georgia, USA, March 6, 1985, J. Paul Diprima, Jr.

SUCKER, WHITE (*Catostomus commersoni*), 6 lb. 8 oz., Rainy River, Loman, Minnesota, USA, April 20, 1984, Joel M. Anderson

SUNFISH, GREEN (*Lepomis cyanellus*), 2 lb. 2 oz., Stockton Lake, Missouri, USA, June 18, 1971, Paul M. Dilley

SUNFISH, GREEN [hybrid] (*Lepomis cyanellus and Lepomis macrochirus*), 1 lb. 3 oz., Walker Farm Lake, Olive Branch, Mississippi, USA, April 6, 1986, Troy M. Wright

SUNFISH, LONGEAR (*Lepomis megalotis*), 1 lb. 12 oz., Elephant Butte Lake, New Mexico, USA, May 9, 1985, Patricia Stout

SUNFISH, REDBREAST (*Lepomis auritus*), 1 lb. 12 oz., Suwannee River, Florida, USA, May 29, 1984, Alvin Buchanan

SUNFISH, REDEAR (*Lepomis microlophus*), 4 lb. 13 oz., Merritt's Mill Pond, Marianna, Florida, USA, March 13, 1986, Joey M. Floyd

SURFPERCH, BARRED (*Amphistichus argenteus*), 3 lb. 12 oz., Morro Bay, California, USA, March 14, 1992, Marvin L. Green

SWEETLIPS, PAINTED (*Plectorhynchus pictus*), 15 lb. 3 oz., Moreton Island, Queensland, Australia, July 24, 1993, Kathy Maguire

SWORDFISH (*Xiphias gladius*), 1,182 lb., Iquique, Chile, May 7, 1953, L. Marron

TAIMEN (*Hucho taimen*), 92 lb. 8 oz., Keta River, Russia, Aug. 11, 1993, Yuri Orlov

TARPON (*Megalops atlanticus*), 283 lb., Lake Maracaibo, Venezuela, March 19, 1956, M. Salazar

TARPON (*Megalops atlanticus*), 283 lb. 4 oz., Sherbro Island, Sierra Leone, April 16, 1991, Yvon Victor Sebag

TAUTOG (*Tautoga onitis*), 24 lb., Wachapreague, Virginia, USA, Aug. 25, 1987, Gregory Robert Bell

TENCH (*Tinca tinca*), 10 lb. 3 oz., Ljungbyan, Sweden, July 2, 1985, Dan Dellerfjord

THREADFIN, AFRICAN (*Alectis alexandrina*), 5 lb. 15 oz., Nouadhibou, Mauritania, Nov. 8, 1986, Gerrard Nadal

THREADFIN, KING (*Polynemus sheridani*), 23 lb. 5 oz., Port Hurd, Bathurst Island, N.T., Australia, Nov. 15, 1991, Brett Smith

THREADFIN, KING (*Polynemus sheridani*), 23 lb. 5 oz., Bathurst Island, N.T., Australia, May 4, 1991, Peter A. Taylor

THREADFIN, MOI (*Polydactylus sexfilis*), 7 lb., Hanalei, Hawaii, USA, Sept. 3, 1988, Harry H. Paik

TIGERFISH (*Hydrocynus vittatus*), 21 lb. 13 oz., Zambesi River, Zimbabwe, July 31, 1986, Brent Reg Gavin Hudson

TIGERFISH, GIANT (*Hydrocynus goliath*), 97 lb., Zaire River, Kinshasa, Zaire, July 9, 1988, Raymond Houtmans

TILAPIA (*Tilapia spp.*), 6 lb., Lake Okeechobee, Clewiston, Florida, USA, June 24, 1989, Joseph Michael Tucker

TILEFISH, BLUELINE (*Caulolatilus microps*), 2 lb. 6 oz., Pompano Beach, Florida, USA, May 24, 1992, Gabriel David Olander

TILEFISH, GOLDEN-EYED
(*Caulotilus affinus*), 1 lb. 8 oz.,
Palya Zancudo, Costa Rica,
March 10, 1993, Craig
Whitehead, M.D.

TILEFISH, SAND (*Malacanthus
plumieri*), 2 lb. 4 oz., Key Largo,
Florida, USA, June 23, 1991,
Rachel S. Olander

TOADFISH, OYSTER (*Opsanus
tau*), 3 lb. 10 oz., Ocracoke, North
Carolina, USA, May 19, 1990,
Stuart C. Lee

TOLSTOLOB
(*Hypophthalmichthys spp.*), 35 lb.
4 oz., Danube River, Austria, Nov.
10, 1983, Josef Windholz

TOPE (*Galeorhinus galeus*), 72
lb. 12 oz., Parengarenga Harbor,
New Zealand, Dec. 19, 1986,
Melanie B. Feldman

TRAHIRA (*Hoplias malabari-
cus*), 2 lb. 2 oz., Hato el Cedral,
Apure, Venezuela, July 18, 1991,
William T. Miller

TREVALLY, BIGEYE (*Caranx
(Caranx) sexfasciatus*), 15 lb. 8
oz., Waianae, Hawaii, USA, March
6, 1992, Darryl R. Bailey

TREVALLY, BLUE (*Caranx
(Carangoides) ferdau*), 2 lb. 5 oz.,
Iroquois Point, Hawaii, USA, Oct.
4, 1992, George D. Cornish

TREVALLY, BLUEFIN, (*Caranx
(Caranx) melampygus*), 96 lb.,
Christmas Island, Republic of
Kiribati, Dec. 19, 1987, Harvey K.
Minatoya, M.D.

TREVALLY, BRASSY (*Caranx
(Caranx) papuensis*), 9 lb. 11 oz.,
Isigaki Island, Okinawa, Japan,
April 12, 1991, Fumio Suzuki

TREVALLY, GIANT (*Caranx
(Caranx) ignobilis*), 145 lb. 8 oz.,
Makena, Maui, Hawaii, USA,
March 28, 1991, Russell Mori

TREVALLY, GOLDEN (*Caranx
(Gnathanodon) speciosus*), 22 lb.
14 oz., Exmouth, W.A., Australia,
Aug. 17, 1990, Keith C. Deimel

TREVALLY, WHITE (*Caranx
(Pseudocaranx) dentex*), 23 lb. 5
oz., Lord Howe Island, N.S.W.,
Australia, March 5, 1987, David
John Mack

**TREVALLY, YELLOWSPOT-
TED** (*Carangoides fulvaguttatus*),
22 lb. 6 oz., Amani-Ohshima,
Japan, March 5, 1994, Hiromi
Shimoebisu

TRIGGERFISH, GRAY (*Balistes
capriscus*), 13 lb. 9 oz., Murrells
Inlet, South Carolina, USA, May
3, 1989, Jim Hilton

TRIGGERFISH, OCEAN
(*Canthidermis sulffamen*), 12 lb.,
Key West, Florida, USA, Feb. 27,
1994, Nicholas Gikas

TRIGGERFISH, QUEEN
(*Balistes vetula*), 12 lb., Ponce
Inlet, Florida, USA, Aug. 11,
1985, Cindy Pitts

TRIPLETAIL (*Lobotes surina-
mensis*), 42 lb. 5 oz., Zululand,
Republic of South Africa, June 7,
1989, Steve Hand

TROUT, APACHE
(*Oncorhynchus apache*), 5 lb. 3
oz., White Mountain Apache
Reservation, Arizona, USA, May
29, 1991, John (TRES) Baldwin

TROUT, BROOK (*Salvelinus
fontinalis*), 14 lb. 8 oz., Nipigon
River, Ontario, Canada, July
1916, Dr. W.J. Cook

TROUT, BROWN (*Salmo trutta*),
40 lb. 4 oz., Little Red River,
Heber Springs, Arkansas, USA,
May 9, 1992, Howard L. (Rip)
Collins

TROUT, BULL (*Salvelinus
confluentus*), 32 lb., Lake Pond
Orielle, Idaho, USA, Oct. 27,
1949, N.L. Higgins

TROUT, CUTBOW
(*Oncorhynchus mykiss and clarki*),
5 lb. 7 oz., Spinney Mt. Reservoir,
Hartzel, Colorado, USA, Oct. 3,
1993, Karen A. DeVine

**TROUT, CUTTHROAT
LAHONTAN** (*Oncorhynchus
clarki*), 41 lb., Pyramid Lake,
Nevada, USA, Dec. 1925, John
Skimmerhorn

TROUT, GOLDEN
(*Oncorhynchus aguabonita*), 11
lb., Cooks Lake, Wyoming, USA,
Aug. 5, 1948, Charles S. Reed

TROUT, LAKE (*Salvelinus
namaycush*), 66 lb. 8 oz., Great
Bear Lake, N.W.T., Canada, July
19, 1991, Rodney Harback

TROUT, MASU (*Oncorhynchus
masou*), 8 lb. 13 oz., Kuzuryu
River, Fukui, Japan, May 27,
1993, Masanori Kakehi

TROUT, OHRID (*Salmo letnica*),
14 lb. 4 oz., Platte River,
Wyoming, USA, Jan. 26, 1986,
Kim Darwin Durfee

TROUT, OHRID (*Salmo letnica*),
14 lb. 4 oz., Watauga Lake,
Tennessee, USA, March 28, 1986,
Richard L. Carter

TROUT, RAINBOW
(*Oncorhynchus mykiss*), 42 lb. 2
oz., Bell Island, Alaska, USA, June
22, 1970, David Robert White

TROUT, RED-SPOTTED MASU
(*Oncorhynchus masou macrosto-
mus*), 2 lb. 11 oz., Monobe River,
Kochi, Japan, March 19, 1994,
Yuji Shimasaki

TROUT, TIGER (*Salmo trutta
and Salvelinus fontinalis*), 20 lb.
13 oz., Lake Michigan,
Wisconsin, USA, Aug. 12, 1978,
Pete M. Friedland

TRUNKFISH (*Lactophrys
trigonus*), 5 lb. 14 oz., Tavernier
Creek, Key Largo, Florida, USA,
Nov. 24, 1985, Edward Shaw

TUNA, BIGEYE [Atlantic]
(*Thunnus obesus*), 375 lb. 8 oz.,
Ocean City, Maryland, USA, Aug.
26, 1977, Cecil Browne

TUNA, BIGEYE [Pacific]
(*Thunnus obesus*), 435 lb., Cabo
Blanco, Peru, April 17, 1957, Dr.
Russel V.A. Lee

TUNA, BLACKFIN (*Thunnus
atlanticus*), 42 lb., Challenger
Bank, Bermuda, July 18, 1989,
Gilbert C. Pearman
    and (co-record):
42 lb., June 2, 1978, Alan J. Card

TUNA, BLUEFIN (*Thunnus
thynnus*), 1,496 lb., Aulds Cove,
Nova Scotia, Canada, Oct. 26,
1979, Ken Fraser

TUNA, DOGTOOTH
(*Gymnosarda unicolor*), 288 lb.
12 oz., Kwan-Tall Island, N.
Cheju-Do, Korea, Oct. 6, 1982,
Boo-Il Oh

TUNA, LONGTAIL (*Thunnus
tonggol*), 79 lb. 2 oz., Montague
Island, N.S.W., Australia, April
12, 1982, Tim Simpson

TUNA, SKIPJACK (*Katsuwonus
pelamis*), 41 lb. 14 oz., Pearl
Beach, Mauritius, Nov. 12, 1985,
Edmund K. R. Heinzen

TUNA, SLENDER (*Allothunnus
fallai*), 21 lb. 10 oz., Dunedin,
New Zealand, April 19, 1993,
Carl Angus

TUNA, SOUTHERN BLUEFIN
(*Thunnus maccoyi*), 348 lb. 5 oz.,
Whakatane, New Zealand, Jan.
16, 1981, Rex Wood

TUNA, YELLOWFIN (*Thunnus
albacares*), 388 lb. 12 oz., Isla San
Benedicto, Revillagigedo Islands,
Mexico, April 1, 1977, Curt
Wiesenhutter

TUNNY, LITTLE (*Euthynnus
alletteratus*), 35 lb. 2 oz., Cap de
Garde, Algeria, Dec. 14. 1988,
Jean Yves Chatard

TUSK-FISH, BLACK-SPOT
(*Choerodon schoenleinii*), 20 lb. 15
oz., Bribie Island, Queensland,
Australia, June 19, 1988, Olga
Mack

VIMBA [Zahrte] (*Vimba vimba*),
2 lb. 8 oz., Olandsan, Sweden,
May 1, 1990, Sonny Pettersson

VIMBA [Zahrte] (*Vimba vimba*),
2 lb. 7 oz., Hossmoan, Kalmar,
Sweden, June 9, 1987, Luis Kilian
Rasmussen

WAHOO (*Acanthocybium
solandri*), 155 lb. 8 oz., San
Salvador, Bahamas, April 3, 1990,
William Bourne

WALLEYE (*Stizostedion vitreum*), 25 lb., Old Hickory Lake, Tennessee, USA, April 1, 1960, Mabry Harper

WARMOUTH (*Lepomis gulosus*), 2 lb. 7 oz., Guess Lake, Yellow River, Holt, Florida, USA, Oct. 19, 1985, Tony David Dempsey

WEAKFISH (*Cynoscion regalis*), 19 lb. 2 oz., Jones Beach Inlet, Long Island, New York, USA, Oct. 11, 1984, Dennis Roger Rooney
and (co-record):
19 lb. 2 oz., Delaware Bay, Delaware, USA, May 20, 1989, William E. Thomas

WEEVER, GREATER (*Trachinus draco*), 3 lb. 11 oz., Gran Canaria, Canary Islands, Spain, March 31, 1984, Arild J. Danielsen

WELS (*Silurus glanis*), 72 lb. 12 oz., Volga Delta, Astrakhan, CIS, Oct. 31, 1990, Jorg Marquard

WHITEFISH, BROAD (*Coregonus nasus*), 9 lb., Tozitna River, Alaska, USA, July 17, 1989, Al Mathews

WHITEFISH, LAKE (*Coregonus clupeaformis*), 14 lb. 6 oz., Meaford, Ontario, Canada, May 21, 1984, Dennis M. Laycock

WHITEFISH, MOUNTAIN (*Prosopium williamsoni*), 5 lb. 6 oz., Rioh River, Saskatchewan, Canada, June 15, 1988, John R. Bell

WHITEFISH, ROUND (*Prosopium cylindraceum*), 6 lb., Putahow River, Manitoba, Canada, June 14, 1984, Allan J. Ristori

WHITING, EUROPEAN (*Merlangius merlangius*), 2 lb. 8 oz., Kraakvaag Fjord, Norway, June 24, 1992, Joerg Marquard

WOLFFISH, ATLANTIC (*Anarhichas lupus*), 52 lb., Georges Bank, Massachusetts, USA, June 11, 1986, Frederick Gardiner

WOLFFISH, NORTHERN (*Anarhichas denticulatus*), 37 lb. 7 oz., Holsteinsborg, Greenland, Aug. 19, 1982, Jens Ploug Hansen

WOLFFISH, SPOTTED (*Anarhichas minor*), 51 lb. 7 oz., Holsteinsborg, Greenland, Aug. 20, 1982, Jens Ploug Hansen

WRASSE, BALLAN (*Labrus bergylta*), 9 lb. 9 oz., Clogher Head, County Kerry, Ireland, Aug. 20, 1983, Bertrand Kron

WRASSE, HUMP-HEADED MAORI (*Cheilinus undulatus*), 20 lb. 15 oz., Aitutaki, Cook Islands, New Zealand, Sept. 18, 1990, Toby DeJong

WRASSE, PURPLE [hou] (*Thalassoma purpureum*), 2 lb. 9 oz., Kalapana, Hawaii, USA, Feb. 8, 1992, Chris Hara

WRECKFISH (*Polyprion americanus*), 106 lb. 14 oz., Sao Miguel, Azores, Portugal, Aug. 2, 1985, Friedrich Schopf

YELLOWTAIL, ASIAN (*Seriola lalandi aureovittata*), 40 lb. 5 oz., Miyake Island, Tokyo, Japan, Oct. 23, 1982, Masahiko Kuwata

YELLOWTAIL, CALIFORNIA (*Seriola lalandi dorsalis*), 79 lb. 4 oz., Alijos Rocks, Baja California, Mexico, July 2, 1991, Robert I. Welker

YELLOWTAIL, SOUTHERN (*Seriola lalandi lalandi*) 114 lb. 10 oz., Tauranga, New Zealand, Feb. 5, 1984, Mike Godfrey

ZANDER (*Stizostedion lucioperca*), 25 lb. 2 oz., Trosa, Sweden, June 12, 1986, Harry Lee Tennison

3

RODS

The first rods were tree limbs long enough to extend a line into a body of water and strong enough not to snap while the angler was playing a fish. By the 1850s, fishermen had attached three or four strips of flexible cane bamboo tips onto tapered poles made from such durable woods as hickory. As technology improved, so the amount of bamboo increased, culminating in the "classic" eight-strip laminated style.

Major innovations in man-made material happened after World War II. Fiberglass rods appeared, made by two techniques: one consisted of glass fibers impregnated in cloth that was wrapped around steel templates for size and taper; the other involved glass fibers wrapped around a light wood core and wrapped with a cellophane film before being heated. Although other rod materials are now more popular, some fishermen still prefer fiberglass' relatively greater "give," which produces a more sensitive feel for setting hooks. Fiberglass also survives in heavy-duty saltwater rods.

High-modulus graphite ("modulus" means "stiffness") is now the overwhelming material of choice for almost all kinds of rods. Invented in Britain for aerospace use and introduced into the fishing world by Fenwick in 1973, graphite offers two-thirds the weight and up to 10 times the stiffness of fiberglass.

Graphite is carbon fiber that comes from the residue of crude oil, post-refining sludge that is extruded into polyacrylic nitrate fibers. Through a series of baking operations, the fibers are carbonized and oxidized so the molecules become stiff graphite fibers. The fibers are placed onto a supporting "scrim" layer (usually fiberglass), after which they go into a matrix of epoxy resin shaped for the desired length and taper. The graphite is then wrapped around a mandrel, or form; how the fibers are wrapped determines the rod's taper and other characteristics. Finally, the graphite is subjected to at high-pressure compression to achieve its strength.

Very few graphite rods are made of pure graphite. A rod that is, for example, "95% graphite" contains 5% of another material, most often fiberglass. This is a common practice, since many rodmakers feel that pure graphite is too brittle.

The stiffness of graphite rods is described by their **MODULUS** expressed per square inch, or p.s.i. A high modulus number, in the area of 44 million p.s.i., indicates that the blank was rolled under a substantial amount of pressure and the graphite was well bonded. Over the past several years, boron has been making a strong move to become an alternative to graphite. Although fans of graphite have serious reservations, other fishermen feel that boron equals and even surpasses graphite's sensitivity and durability.

Before the advent of man-made materials, rods made of bamboo were standard. Bamboo fly rods are now considered handsome vestiges of a bygone era, able to cast tight loops but very fragile in all but the most experienced of hands. Only a handful of anglers routinely use them, although they are displayed as collectibles by many more people. Craftsmen still turn out handmade cane rods, especially the fly-fishing variety. Even if you come across a bamboo rod in workable condition in somebody's attic, consider the species strictly of historical interest (translation: stick to the man-made, more affordable variety).

General Considerations

The flexibility of a rod's shaft (or "blank"), the manner in which it bends and how rapidly it straightens, determines its "action." In rods with "fast" action, only the top one-third flexes, while the entire shaft of a "slow" action rod does the bending. A rod described as having "progressive" action has a tip that bends more than the middle section, which in turn bends more than the butt end. In other words, a parabola instead of a circle.

As a general rule, stiff rods have faster action, which allows casts of greater distances and makes maneuvering a lure easier. A stiff fly rod tends to produce tighter line loops between the back- and the forecast. More flexible rods with slower action are preferable for more delicate presentations.

Rods used for plastic worm and jig-fishing tend to have firm tips for greater sensitivity and ease in setting the hook. Live bait, however, calls for a rod with relatively slow action, since too strong a "snap" will rip worms and other fleshly creatures off the hook. Bottom-fishing requires a relatively strong rod because bait is more likely to become caught on objects on the bottom.

The **REEL SEAT** is the part of the rod by which a reel is attached. Two sliding rings allow some degree of adjusting the reel's position along the grip. Another choice is a **FIXED BUTT CAP** with one sliding ring. Somewhat more popular are

the **UPLOCK** (where the reel seat fits into a slot at the grip's top end) and the **DOWNLOCK** (the seat fits into a slot at the rod's butt end); in both instances, a sliding ring or screw holds the other end of the reel seat in place.

An example of a downlock seat.

(Many surf-casting fishermen who don't want to take the chance of rough use and big fish tearing the reel off a rod simply tape their reels to their rods; they use the most durable packing tape they can find to secure the reel to a cork base, then leave the rig in place throughout the entire season.)

Whatever the style, seats made out of machined metal are more precisely and durably made than ones that are stamped. Nickel silver is prized for its self-lubricating quality, with aluminum a very acceptable alternative.

GUIDES, through which line passes along the length of a rod, come in two main styles. The single-foot variety is wrapped onto the blank by its sole projection. The two-foot's twin projections may make it twice as secure, but since the number of wraps by which guides are held in place are thought to affect a rod's action, many fishermen prefer single-foot guides, which require half as many wraps.

Silicon carbide is the most durable material for guides. It's also the most expensive, so aluminum oxide is more prevalent.

Although cork is the traditional material for handles (and remains so for pistol-grip rods), most baitcasting fishermen prefer an EVA foam composition. Foam is more durable and it offers greater "gripability," especially when wet.

Multipiece rods are joined together by ferrules. The open cylindrical end, called the "female," fits over the solid end, or "spigot" or "male."

"Pack" rods are designed for easy carrying while traveling. They consist of three (or four) to seven component pieces. Thanks to the strength of man-made materials, they are just as durable as one- or two-piece rods, and with little to no objectionable action.[*]

Also designed for ease of transportation, telescopic rods slide into themselves, like the shafts of folding umbrellas. Commonly used for saltwater fishing, they are found more infrequently as freshwater angling tools.

Baitcasting Rods

The "right" length and weight of a baitcasting rod depends in large part on the weight of the particular lure that you plan to use. Manufacturers have grouped rods according in the following table:

	ROD LENGTH (IN FT.)	LURE WEIGHT (IN OZ.)
Extra-Light:	6 to 6½	⅛ to ¼
Light:	5½ to 6½	¼ to ½
Medium:	4½ to 6	⅝ to ¾
Heavy:	4½ to 7½	¾ to 1¼

Rods that fall into the "medium" group are considered the best for all-around, general-purpose fishing. Bass fishermen favor them, while anglers after muskies and pike choose heavy rods. Light rods are best for panfishing.

You'll note that there's a fair amount of overlapping in rod lengths among the categories. That's because proper length is also a function of the kind

[*]Another example of a "pack" rod of sorts, as well as of tackle telemarketing, is the Pocket Fisherman. This rod-and-reel combo that folds into a small carrying case has been promoted by super-salesman Ron Popeil (of Veg-O-Matic chopper fame) in infomercials to the tune of 1.25 million sold.

of conditions you must cope with and the kind of presentation you're aiming for. A short rod delivers a lure in a relatively flat trajectory, which is essential if you're fishing in a heavily wooded area. On the other hand, and foliage permitting, longer rods tend to cast bait in a high arc.

Rods used for the technique known as **FLIPPIN'** (the "g" is almost never written, much less pronounced), or an underhand or "slingshot" cast, tend to be slightly longer than those intended for **PITCHIN'**, which is an overhand or sidearm presentation. Both have a flexible tip. The rest of the blank, or its lower 80%, is stiff, in order to toss heavy bait a good distance (pitchin') and to penetrate heavy weed cover (flippin'). There is now a tendency to use the same rod for both techniques, with a compromise length 7½ feet.

Flippin' rods can easily double as pitchin' rods.

Relatively short "pistol-grip" handles have a hook projection for the caster's index finger. The one-handed style is popular for baitcasting and is usually found on short (5 feet–6 feet) rods where, according to its fans, pistol-grips permit snappier and more accurate casts.

Pistol Grip.

The "triggerstick" handle is similar, in that it also offers index-finger support, but the handle itself is longer, usually long enough to accommodate a two-handed casting grip. Triggerstick handles are most often found on flippin' and pitchin' rods.

Length would be a handicap in rods used in ice-fishing. The typical rod used for that purpose is

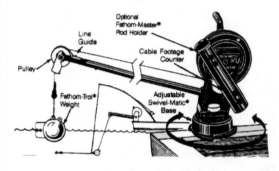

Triggerstick.

no more than 3 feet in length; many ice-fishermen make their own rods from remnants of longer rods that have snapped.

Saltwater Rods

Subtlety of presentation is not much of a factor when surf-casting 50 yards to a bluefish or trolling for tarpon, so rods made of fiberglass and composite are found as frequently as those made of graphite.

Rods are designated according to their strength; specifically, the amount of force needed to bend a rod 90°. The International Game Fish Association established the following classifications for trolling rods in conjunction with the organization's world record-keeping:

Ultra-Light: 6-, 12-, and 20-lb.
Light: 30-lb.
Medium: 50-lb.
Heavy: 80-lb.
Ultra-Heavy: 130-lb.
Without Limit: 130-lb. to 180-lb.

To be recognized by the IGFA, these "classified" rods must be composed of two sections, either separable or one-piece. The rod blank itself (called the "tip") must measure a minimum of 40 inches with five guides plus the tip-top. The butt, or handle, cannot be longer than 27 inches. The tip may be made of fiberglass or graphite, while the butt may be made of metal or fiber and have a grip of cork, rubber, or other material.

Rods used for fishing from anchored boats (known as "bottom-fishing") usually measure 10 feet or less. The IGFA classifies these rods into 6-,

12-, 20-, and 30-pound-weight categories.

Surf-casting rods are built for ultra-long casting, up to 200 feet or more. Medium-length rods are from 6 feet to 10 feet, while long rods measure between 10 feet and 15 feet. Most are made of graphite, fiberglass, or a composite.

Boat rods, those monster pieces of tackle used for blue-water fishing, are designated according to their line class, or the **TEST STRENGTH** of the line that is designed to be used on them. A rod with a line class of 20-pounds, for example, is meant to carry 20-pound line. Big-game rods, such as those used for tuna, range in length from 5 feet 6 inches to 6 feet and take line between 50 and 130 pounds.

Rods attached to downrigger trolling tackle measure about 8 feet and take 8- to 20-pound line.[*]

When a fish strikes, the line is released from the weight, and the downrigger's motor rewinds the cable, returning the weight to the boom tip and out of interference range.

A downrigger. [courtesy Penn Rells]

Playing a big-game saltwater fish generates a great deal of line friction against a rod's guides, so

[*]A **DOWNRIGGER** is an electric battery-operated device that maintains bait at a predetermined depth. The fishing rod's line is snapped to a weight at the end of the downrigger's stainless-steel cable. The cable is lowered from the tip of the downrigger's 2-foot or 4-foot boom until the desired depth is reached. A footage counter on the downrigger indicates the depth of the weight. Using that data, the fisherman or boat captain can release or rewind cable to compensate for any changes in depth due to the boat's speed and the ocean's current.

rods used for that purpose have roller (also called pulley) guides. Fishermen routinely inspect these guides, because a jammed pulley is worse than useless.

Spinning Rods

One of the advantages to spinning tackle is its ability to present lighter bait that baitcasting gear can. Accordingly, line thickness becomes relevant, as is lure weight. The following table tells that tale:

	LINE DIAMETER (IN MM)	LURE WEIGHT (IN OZ.)
Ultra-Light:	.005 to .008	⅟₁₆ to ⁵⁄₁₆
Light:	.008 to .010	¼ to ⅜
Medium:	.010 to .012	⅜ to ⅝
Heavy:	.012 to .013	½ to 1
Extra-Heavy:	.015 to .024	1 to 4

With regard to length, most freshwater spinning rods range from 5½ feet to 7 feet. The upper end of that spectrum is most effective for longer casts. There are also two-handed spinning rods for salmon and steelhead fishing that are 7 feet to 8 feet in length.

Saltwater fishing from boats calls for spinning rods between 6 feet and 10 feet that can cast lures weighing between ¾ ounce to 2 ounces.

Surf-casting spinning rods are divided into four categories:

	ROD LENGTH (IN FT.)	BAIT WEIGHT (IN OZ.)
Super-Light:	8 to 10	¾ to 1
Light:	11 to 12½	1 to 2¾
Medium or Semi-Heavy:	13 to 15	2¼ to 3½
Heavy:	16+	3½+

HARDWARE

Unlike line coming out straight from a baitcasting reel, line cast from a spinning reel emerges in spirals. The guide on a spinning rod closest to the reel must therefore be large enough to accommodate the spiral, but it must also be small enough to keep the spiraling line from slapping against the rod. The other guides (more often single-foot than snake in style) progressively reduce the size of the spiral. That's why the guides on spinning rods diminish in size down to the smallest one at the tip-top. Ceramic-lined guides are best at dissipating heat caused by friction.

Spinning rods use three types of mechanisms to hold the reel. Sliding rings slip onto the reel handle to hold the reel in place by tension against the handle. A fixed-reel seat screws the reel in place; there is greater security, but the metal corners can chafe your fingers. A sliding-reel seat combines the first two devices and has the advantage of great comfort and security.

Not all spinning rods are designed for light tackle fishing. Many boat rods and surf-casting rods are big brawny members of that family.

Fly Rods

In baitcasting and spinning, the weight of the bait provides the force that carries the line during a cast. That's why such rods are described in terms of optimum bait weight.

In fly casting, however, the line moves because of its own weight is carried by the energy generated by the propelling force of the rod during the cast. Accordingly, rods are described in terms of the weight of the line that they are intended to hold (see page 67 for a discussion of fly line weight).

The following broad classifications give an indication of which weights are designed for particular kinds of fly-fishing:

1-weight through 3-weight: for small trout and panfish sought with delicate presentations of tiny light flies on small, slow-moving streams.

4-weight through 6-weight: for general, all-purpose trout fishing.

7-weight and 8-weight: for relatively larger streams and lakes and for bass fishing (where more line weight is needed to "punch" heavier bass flies).

9-weight through 11-weight: for salmon and steelhead fishing, where casts between 40 feet and 70 feet are routinely needed on fast rivers. These weights are also appropriate for bonefish, permit, and small tarpon, especially on saltwater flats where ocean winds are an ever-present factor.

12-weight through 15-weight: for playing and landing such substantial deep-sea quarry as sailfish, tarpon, and tuna.

Somewhat muddying the waters is the ability of modern rods to accommodate slightly lighter or heavier line weight. Some anglers who want a bit more distance routinely use a line one weight heavier than the rod calls for: 6-weight line on a 5-weight rod, for example. By the same token, line that is one weight lighter produces slightly greater sensitivity (thinner line also cuts through wind better than line with a thicker diameter does).

As for action, the stiffer a fly rod, the further it will cast a fly. That makes sense, because a stiff rod can generates a faster action (think of it in terms of more "snap"). Faster action in turn generates higher line speeds, which produce greater distances.

Conversely, a more supple, or "slow," rod will toss a fly in more of a lazy lob, a characteristic that's desirable for more delicate presentations.

The action you'll want depends on the kind of fishing you'll do. Bear in mind that the vast majority of casts made for trout (bass and panfish too) are 25 feet and under, well within the parameters of a medium-action rod. The ability to throw a fly 70 feet or further is an enviable skill, but not something that a novice trout angler needs.

However, casts of from 40 feet to 70 feet are routine when coping with wind and longer distances across saltwater flats or salmon and steelhead rivers.

With regard to length, if you remember that a fly rod is, in John Merwin's phrase, a "flexible lever," you'll understand the physics of why longer rods are able to develop and deliver greater power. Unless they're confining their fishing to small streams with heavy overgrowth, novice fly-casters in pursuit of trout would do well to select a rod in the 8-foot to 9-foot range. A 9-foot length is appropriate for salmon and steelhead fishing.

A rod's weight is also a factor. The difference of an ounce or two may not seem like much when you're looking over a selection in a tackle shop or catalog, but even that small amount of weight will add up over a day on the water. All else being equal, most people select a lighter rod.

HARDWARE

The rule of thumb is one guide for each foot of rod plus the tip-top. That translates into a total of 8 guides for a 7-foot rod.

In his book *Advanced Fly Fishing* (Delacourt, 1992), Lefty Kreh points out that line that passes through the butt guide (the guide closest to the handle) during a cast does not go straight through, but at an angle from below. A small butt guide restricts the amount of line that passes through in that fashion; Kreh prefers a butt guide that's slightly larger than a fly rod's other guides (16mm for 1-weight to 6-weights, 20mm or 24mm for heavier rods). As for the type of guide, Kreh argues that snake guides create less friction that the one-foot variety, and they weigh less too. The additional wrapping that a two-foot guide requires, he adds, has a negligible effect on a rod's action.

Fly rod handles, which are traditionally made of cork, come in a variety of shapes. The cigar is the most popular, although its tapered shape offers relative little support to the fisherman's thumb. The bulge at the top of the half-wells style of handle and the twin bulges of the full-wells offer far greater support, making them preferable for heavier tackle and bigger fish.

(See Figures at right)

Heavier rods often have a fighting butt, a knob at the handle end that can be pressed against the angler's stomach and thus offer better leverage for fighting salmon, steelheads, and saltwater species. Such butts are de rigueur on two-handed "Spey" rods traditionally used for salmon and sea trout along British lochs and rivers.

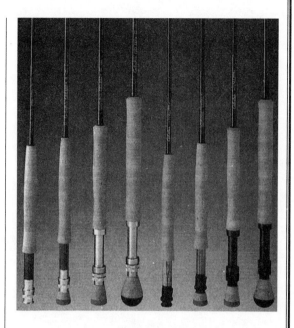

A variety of fly rod butts. The rods fourth and eighth from the left have fighting butts.

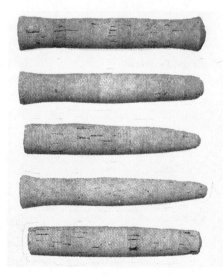

Fly rod grip styles. From top: Full-Wells, Reversed Half-Wells, Super Fine, Western, Cigar.

Before You Buy

Even within such categories as baitcasting, fly-fishing, and blue-water, quarry (that is, the species of fish you're after) and conditions will largely determine your choice of rod. As with other tackle, you can learn a great deal about what is appropriate through (1) magazine articles; (2) advertisements; and (3) word-of-mouth, whether from users or tackle shop recommendations. The latter should never be underestimated, since the best-selling "Ugly Stick" baitcasting rod owes its success to word-of-mouth as much as to Shakespeare's innovating advertising campaign.

When examining a rod:

1. Sight along its length, checking for straightness as you rotate the rod.

2. Are the guides lined up straight and are the wrappings secure? Whatever the style of rod, its wraps need an even coat of varnish to prevent the wrapping thread from coming apart and fraying.

3. If the handle is made of cork, is it solid and snug? Avoid cork that's dried and cracked, with lots of pits and gouges.

4. Is the reel seat snug and secure? The only way to tell for sure is to try it, either with a borrowed reel or one of your own that you brought with you.

5. How does the rod feel? You can cast a half-dozen rods of the same length, weight, and material but made by different manufacturers, and you might have six different reactions. The only infallible method of determining how well you like a rod is to conduct a hands-on trial. Rig a candidate with reel and line if you can, then take it outside and cast until you get a good feeling for the rod's particular properties and idiosyncrasies. If the seller won't let you rig the rod, insist on trying a number of "false" casts.

Then comes the matter of cost. How much should a good rod cost (or, put another way, why are some rods more expensive than others)?

Better materials and more careful craftsmanship cost more than cheaper materials and run-of-the-mill workmanship. A rod made of premium graphite, solid hand-machined fittings, and a defect-free cork handle will handle better, last longer, and look better than one that rolls off a mass-production assembly line. Sure, you can get away with a cheap rod, but if you're planning to make fishing a lifetime sport, not to spend a little extra (okay, sometimes a lot extra) for a rod that you can grow to know and use for many years is false economy.

Packaged "starter" sets that include a rod and reel cost less, but that's because the tackle tends to be the manufacturer's "bottom of the line." It's false economy. Similar to a would-be musician's starting out on a "learner" instrument, the kind of results that would encourage you to continue are difficult to come by; cheaply-made (i.e., inexpensive) rods lack the action and sensitivity that leads to immediate enjoyment and quick progress. If you're uncertain whether fishing will be a long-term sport for you, consider borrowing a good rod until you've decided whether you want one of your own.

Care and Maintenance

The greatest enemy of a fishing rod is human negligence. Car doors and windows, one fisherman ruefully pointed out, are the serial killers of the rod-destroying felons. Far better to invest in a carrier, either one that can be mounted like a ski rack on a car roof or, if the size of your vehicle permits, one that can carry rods on the inside.

A rod left on the ground can be stepped on. One left leaning against the sides of cars is likely to be caught by a gust of wind and blown underfoot or transported into the path of an oncoming vehicle. Similarly, a rod that juts out of a boat can be snapped by a passing log, boulder, pier, or another boat. A rod needn't be snapped in two to be harmed; a bent blank, reel seat, or one or more guides and ferrules will affect the rod's action and function.

Fly-fishermen learn to carry their rods butt end first, so in case they drop the rods, the tips and guides are protected. There's also less risk in snagging an overhead branch, a good reason for carrying any kind of rod in that fashion through wooded areas.

Toting more than one rod can be a handful, a problem to which multi-rod carriers are a solution. Carrying even one rod, especially when you break it down into its component pieces, is likely to produce a tangled line. The Rod Buddy™, composed of two rubber clamps, holds the rod pieces together, and it secures the line in the process (Marine Innovations, P.O. Box 21040, St. Catharines, Ontario L2M 7X2 Canada).

Cleaning a rod prolongs its condition and life. After removing the reel and breaking the rod down into its components, use a damp cloth to wipe away dirt, sand, vegetation, or any other debris. Saltwater rods deserve a more thorough cleaning. Fleece mitts (the kind used to wash car bodies) make good tackle cleaners. Dip one into soapy water and swab the rod, then rinse the rod in freshwater to remove all traces of corrosive salt. You may need to use a soft brush to remove dried fish scales, dried algae, and anything else that's stuck to the rod.

Then dry the rod with a clean, soft cloth, paying particular attention to the ferrules, guides, and reel seat. While you're at it, check to see whether guides and ferrules might have become loose or bent. If so, take the rod to a qualified person to make the necessary repairs.

Keeping a rod in a cloth sleeve keeps dust and other dirt off the rod. Storing and transporting a rod in a hard protective case greatly reduces the chance of its being stepped on, snapped, or otherwise trashed. If your rod didn't come with its case, you can buy one at most tackle shops or mail-order outlets. Or, you can make your own from a length of PVC pipe and two rubber stoppers.

A rod case. [courtesy Plano]

Further Reading

There are excellent entries on all the varieties of rods in *McClane's New Standard Fishing Encyclopedia and International Angling Guide* by A.J. McClane (Henry Holt, 1974).

The *Dorling Kindersley Encyclopedia of Fishing* (Dorling Kindersley, 1994) is a British import. Its full-color illustrations and brief descriptions of rods often need translation for this side of the pond, but the chapters on tackle provide a panoramic view of fresh- and saltwater gear.

The New American Trout Fishing by John Merwin (Macmillan, 1994) includes a thoughtful discussion of fly rod manufacture, properties, and uses.

New rods based on improved technology are forever being offered. Fishing magazines include annual "new tackle roundup" articles that describe any such innovations in design and composition, usually based on hands-on research. You'll also get the low-down—with the expected sales pitch—from the tackle manufacturers' catalogs.

Rod-Making
Made Easy

"What's the best way to start?" we asked a half-dozen people who have some experience making their own rods. "Find a teacher," was the unanimous answer. That's not to say that making a rod is particularly difficult, but like most do-it-yourself projects, the guidance of a more experienced person saves time and eliminates wasted effort and its accompanying stress. And since rod-building involves using a number of specialized tools, whoever provides the instruction may own such equipment and let you use it, a good idea while you decide whether you want to make such a capital investment.

Finding a teacher should be no more difficult than inquiring at your local tackle shop; if the proprietor or sales clerk can't oblige, he or she often knows of someone else who can. Or you can find someone through your local fishing club or chapter of Trout Unlimited, Izaak Walton League, B.A.S.S., or similar organization.

However you approach rod-building, you'll begin by selecting a blank, the heart of the rod. You'll base your choice on several factors: length, action, weight, and line or bait size. If you have a favorite rod, chances are good that you can get a blank made by the same manufacturer.

Other ingredients consist of a reel seat, a handle, ferrules, a set of guides, thread to wrap the guides, cement, varnish or another finish, and brushes with which to apply the finish.

The machinery that you'll need to buy or borrow are a rod-wrapper lathe and a slow-rotating drying motor that helps achieve a smooth glassy finish on your custom-made, handmade rod.

Most tackle shops and catalogs carry the items you'll need. In addition to the ones listed on pages 290–309, the following firms specialize in tools, blanks, and other components.

Barry Kustin Rods & Components
8589 Nevada Ave.
West Hills, CA 91304
(818) 992-5747

Bellinger Reel Seats
3482 El Dorado Loop S.
Salem, OR 97302
(503) 364-8219

Blue Ridge Rod Company
P.O. Box 6268
Annapolis, MD 21401
(410) 224-4072
fax: (410) 573-0993

Clemens Custom Tackle
444 Schantz Spring Rd.
Allentown, PA 18104
(215) 395-5119

Elkhorn Rod Company
P.O. Box 2525
Loveland, CO 80539
(303) 227-4707
fax: (303) 667-9435
Offers a beginner's rod-building kit (9-foot, ⅝-weight, 4-piece).

Midland Tackle
66 Route 17
Sloatsburg, NY 10974
(914) 753-5440

Powell
P.O. Box 3966
Chino, CA 95927
(916) 345-3393

Research Engineers Company
RR 1, Box 1605
Morrisville, VT 05661-9704
(802) 888-7200
fax: (802) 888-7021

Shoff Tackle
P.O. Box 1227
Kent, WA 98035-1227
(206) 852-4760

Winston Rod
P.O. Drawer T
Twin Bridges, MT 59754
(406) 684-5674

Books

One catalog calls *The New Advanced Custom Rod Building* by Dale Clemens (1987) the "Bible for the all-around rod builder," and many other sources hold it in equally high esteem.

Anyone interested in graphite rods will want to know about *The Custom Graphite Fly Rod: Design and Construction* by Skip Morris (1989) and *Handcrafting a Graphite Rod* by Luis Garcia (1994).

Bamboo rods are the ultimate angling artifact. If and when you deem yourself ready to tackle such a project, *Handicrafting Bamboo Fly Rods* by Wayne Cattanach (1992) draws on the author's three decades of experience; there's even a computer disk to help in rod design.

More technical, yet (according to those who know about such matters) the definitive work on the subject is *A Master's Guide to Building a Fly Rod*, 3rd edition, by Everett Garrison and Hoagy B. Carmichael (1995).

Secret Fresh and Salt Water Fishing Tricks by George Leonard and Jacques P. Herter (1965) includes a hefty section on building these rods for fly-, spin-, and baitcasting-fishing.

Manufacturers and/or Dealers of Rods

Abu Garcia
21 Law Drive
Fairfield, NJ 07004-3296
(201) 227-7666

All Star Graphite Rods Inc.
9750 Whithorn
Houston, TX 77095
(713) 855-9603
fax: (713) 855-4530

American Fly Fishing Co.
3523 Fair Oaks Blvd.
Sacramento, CA 95864
(800) 410-1222

L.L. Bean, Inc.
Freeport, ME 04033
(800) 221-4221

Berkley
One Berkley Drive
Spirit Lake, IA 51360-1041
(800) BERKLEY
fax: (712) 336-5183

Biscayne Rods
425 E. 9th St.
Hialeah, FL 33010
(205) 884-0808
fax: (205) 884-3017

Browning Fishing/Zebco Corp.
P.O. Box 840
Tulsa, OK 74101-0840
(918) 836-3542
fax: (918) 836-0514

Castaway Graphite Rods, Inc.
118 Cap Conroe Dr.
Montgomery, TX 77356
(409) 582-1677

Castle Arms
P.O. Box 30070
Springfield, MA 01103
(413) 567-8268

Cortland Line Company
Kellog Road
P.O. Box 5588
Cortland, NY 13045-5588
(800) 847-6787

Daiwa
7421 Chapman Avenue
Garden Grove, CA 92641
(714) 898-6645
fax: (714) 898-1476

Diamondback Co.
P.O. Box 308
Stowe, VT 05672
(802) 253-4358

Eagle Claw Fishing Tackle/Wright & McGill Co.
4254 E. 46 Ave.
Denver, CO 80216
(303) 321-1481
fax: (303) 321-4750

East Branch Rods
206a Route 9W
Haverstraw, NY 10927
(800) 337-EROD
fax: (914) 942-5485

Falcon Graphite Rods
821 West Elgin
Broken Arrow, OK 74012
(918) 251-0020
fax: (918) 251-0021

Fenwick
14799 5242 Argosy Ave.
Huntington Beach, CA 92649
(714) 879-1066
fax: (714) 891-9610

Fishing Specialties
315 Short St.
Auburn, MI 48611
(517) 622-6347
fax: (517) 622-6347

Green River Rodmakers
Box 817, RR 4
Green River, VT 05301
(802) 257-4553

Hardy (USA) Inc.
10 Goodwin Plaza
Midland Oark, NJ 07432
(201) 481-7557
fax: (201) 670-7190

Hexagraph Fishing Rods
2703 Rocky Woods
Kingwood, TX 77339
(800) 870 4211
fax: (713) 224-7574

HT Enterprises
P.O. Box 909
Campbellsport, WI 53010
(414) 533-5080

Johnson Fishing (Mitchell)
1531 East Madison Ave
Mankato, MT 56002
(507) 345-4623

Kiwi Outfitters
P.O. Box 80654
Baskersfield, CA 93380-0654
(805) 399-0485

Lake Country Products
P.O. Box 367
Isle, MN 56342
(612) 676-3440

Lamiglas
P.O. Box U
Woodland, WA 98674
(206) 225-9436

G. Loomis Inc.
1359 Downriver Drive
Woodland, WA 98674
(800) 622-8818
fax: (206) 225-7169

Martin
P.O. Box 270
Tulsa, OK 74101
(918) 836-5581
fax: (918) 836-0514

Normark Corp.
10395 Yellow Circle Dr.
Minnetonka, MN 55343
(612) 933-7060
fax: (612) 933-0046

Orvis
Historic Route 7A
Manchester, VT 05254
(800) 815-5900

Penn Fishing Tackle
    Manufacturing Company
3028 West Hunting Park Ave.
Philadelphia, PA 19132
(215) 229-9415
fax: (215) 223-3017

Powell Rod Co.
P.O. Box 4000
Chino, CA 95927
(800) 228-0615

Quantum
P.O. Box 270
Tulsa, OK 74101
(918) 836-5581
fax: (918) 836-0514

Redington Rod Co.
2324 E. Indian St.
Stuart, FL 34997
(407) 223-1342

Sage
8500 Northeast Day Rd.
Bainbridge Island, WA 98110
(800) 533-3004
fax: (206) 842-6830

St. Croix of Park Falls Ltd.
P.O. Box 279
Hwy. 13 N
Park Falls, WI 54552
(715) 762-3226
fax: (715) 762-3293

Scott Fly Rods
P.O. Box 889
Telluride, CO 81435
(800) 728-7208
fax: (303) 728-5031

Shakespeare
3801 Westmore Drive
Columbia, SC 29223
(800) 334-9105
fax: (803) 754-7342

Shimano
P.O. Box 19615
Irvine, CA 92713-9615
(714) 951-5003
fax: (714) 951-5071

Silstar
P.O. Box 6505
West Columbia, SC 29171
(803) 794-8521
fax: (803) 794- 8544

South Bend Sporting Goods
1950 Stanley Street
Northbrook, IL 60065
(800) 622-9662
fax: (708) 564-3042

Thomas & Thomas
P.O. Box 32
Turners Falls, MA 01376
(413) 863-9727

Thorne Brothers Custom Rod &
    Tackle
7500 University Ave. NE
Minneapolis, MN 55432
(612) 572-3782

Tycoon Fin-Nor Corp. (Fin-Nor)
2021 SW 31 St.
Hallendale, FL 33009
(305) 966-5507
fax: (305) 966-5509

U.S. Line Co.
P.O. Box 531
Westfield, MA 01086
(800) 456-4665

R.L. Winston Rod Co.
109 East Third Street
Twin Bridges, MT 59754
(406) 684-5674
fax: (406) 684-5533

Zebco
P.O. Box 270
Tulsa, OK 74101
(918) 836-5581
fax: (918) 836-0514

4

REELS

eels used to be dismissed as being nothing more than a gizmo for storing line. Not any more, though. The array of reels found in all types of fishing demonstrates an effort on the part of the tackle industry to create high precision, durable instruments that perform an active and essential role in the process of playing and landing fish.

Two preliminary items: Whether a reel is designed for baitcasting (known in saltwater circles as a "conventional" reel), spinning, spin-casting, or fly-fishing, the concept of "drag" is central to any discussion of reels. **DRAG** is simply resistance, which translates into the amount of tension that a line (including a leader, if any) can take before it breaks. To prevent such breakage, reels contain drag mechanisms that automatically disengage the reel spool and thus release line when a certain pressure is reached.

The **GEAR RATIO** of a reel indicates the number of revolutions it takes to rewind a certain length of line. As a general rule, each revolution picks up approximately 5 inches of line, so that a reel with a gear ratio of 3:1 retrieves some 15 inches (4:1=20", 5:1=25", etc.).

Baitcasting Reels

The earliest recorded reference to a line-holding device mounted on the end of a rod is said to have appeared the literature of third-century China, although a reel very definitely is pictured in a thirteenth-century print from that country. In 1651, Thomas Barker refers in his *The Art of the Angler* to a "wind, to turn with a barrel to gather up line."

Before the nineteenth century, revolving-spool reels were made either of wood or bronze in the English single-action style. The first modern American baitcasting reels were crafted by a succession of Kentucky-based watchmakers (why the Bluegrass State accounted for so much reel-making activity remains unexplained). An early and important innovation of that era was a gear mechanism that allowed several revolutions of the spool for each turn of the crank handle; when another watchmaker devised a 4:1 gear ratio, the first quadruple multiplier reel was born. Other advancements later in that century included click-and-drag springs and level-wind mechanisms.

A baitcasting reel, circa 1950.

What distinguishes baitcasting reels from those used in other types of fishing is the revolving spool from which the weight of the bait pulls the line. This ability to release the line at high speeds also gives rise to a major potential problem, that of **BACKLASH,** the bird's nest tangle of line that happens when a spool spins faster than the line is released. To eliminate that hazard, many reels contain magnetic "brake" mechanisms that limit the speed at which the spool revolves during a cast; the brake can be adjusted to reflect the weight of the plug or whatever other bait the reel is being asked to cast.

Another potential problem with baitcasting reels involves uneven line distribution during the rewind; too much line on one side or in the middle of the spool creates lumps that can interfere with the reel's action. The solution, developed during the last century, is a **LEVEL-WINDER DEVICE,** an elongated loop that slides back and forth across the spool to ensure that the line lays even and flat.

A baitcasting reel with a level-winder. [courtesy Abu Garcia]

Getting the bait out to where fish are is just one job of a baitcasting reel. Landing a fish is another task, and these reels, particularly for salt-water fishing, employ either of two kinds of braking systems against the drag produced by a hard-fighting fish. The **STAR DRAG** consists of a series of discs that increase or decrease pressure against the spool's drum. It's a durable system that is operated by one or two star-shaped wheels mounted between the reel casing and the winder.

A baitcasting reel with a star drag system. [courtesy Daiwa]

As its name suggests, the **LEVER DRAG SYSTEM** contains a single lever that exerts pressure against the reel drum. Many fishermen consider reels with this system more sensitive than those with star drags. Adjustable drags automatically downshift to a lower gear that is more efficient in fighting big fish (much as low gears on bicycles afford more power). Some surf-casting reels have two-speed retrieval systems for even more precise control.

In either case, both star and lever drags often need to be readjusted according to bait weight and conditions throughout the course of the day and often while a fish is being played and landed.

As for how initially to set the drag of a baitcasting reel, the standard practice is to hold the rod at a 45° angle and then press the bar on the reel that releases the line. Adjust the drag control so the plug (or whatever other bait you're using) descends slowly until it touches the ground. The plug shouldn't drop like a rock, just "slide," with no additional line coming off the reel once the plug touches down.

Ball bearings have become standard components of both saltwater and freshwater reels. They reduce friction for smoother rewinding under tension and at greater speeds.

Reels used for big-game (or "blue-water") ocean fishing might be described as "freshwater reels on steroids." Made of anodized aluminum or graphite for maximum resistance to corrosion, they are substantial pieces of equipment both in size (some weigh 10 pounds or more) and cost.

Some saltwater reels have attached electric motors, handy for rewinding line from depths of up (or down) to 300 feet, but are heavy to handle. That's why many ocean-going fishing vessels have shelves mounted along their railings to support these cumbersome attachments.

Tackle manufacturers continue to fine-tune baitcasting reel technology. For example, some now have levers that disengage the clutch lot to let out more line without requiring the angler to turn the reel handle, while gyroscope-style rotors reduce wobble while the line is rewound. Even handle knobs have been designed to be more ergonomically sound—their contours accommodate fingertips better than the round knobs did.

A spinning reel's components. [courtesy Penn Reels]

Spinning Reels

First developed in nineteenth-century Britain, **SPINNING REELS** were improved in Britain and France and introduced into the U.S. before World War II. The technique quickly grew in popularity when people discovered that the absence of a rotary spool meant the virtual elimination of backlashes. Moreover, with no rotating spool that needed a relatively heavy bait to activate it, spinning permitted the use of lightweight bait, ¼ ounce or even less; this greater range of bait was another major plus. Finally, fewer moving parts meant that spinning reels were easier, and therefore less expensive, to manufacture, and consumers certainly did not object to the lower price.

One would think that a spool with a very large diameter would be most efficient, since the larger the diameter, the less potential interference with the line during a cast. However, a diameter that is too large forces the escaping coils of line to become equally too large. The coils will then slap against the rod, robbing the cast of distance and accuracy.

The most popular type of line retrieval mechanism is the **BAIL**, a metal hoop across a spinning reel spool's face. One end is on the pick-up bracket, the other on the rotating cup. The bail is opened manually by a flick of the angler's finger, then closes when the winding handle is cranked; the line moves along the bail until it reaches the roller and then onto the spool.

A system found on older reels is the **AUTO-MATIC PICK-UP ARM**. It consists of a single curved arm that swings out of the way during the cast. As soon as the winder handle is turned, the arm strikes a cam and swings back to pick up the line.

A **MANUAL PICK-UP** is simply a roller on the revolving cup. The angler's forefinger slips the line over the roller. Because it has the fewest working parts, the manual pick-up is the least likely to fail.

Drag is adjusted by tightening or loosening the nut found either at the front of the spool or at the rear of the reel. A reel that has it drag adjustment knob on the front of the spool cannot accommodate the snap-off spools that make changing lines literally a snap. However, reels that have the knob on the rear can.

A spinning reel with a rear drag system. [courtesy Abu Garcia]

The **ANTI-REVERSE LOCK** is a ratchet that prevents a reel from letting line unwind, except for the drag mechanism. Most spin-fishermen keep it on all the time in conjunction with a properly-set drag (you can always flip the bail if you want to unwind line to a deeper depth). It's particularly useful feature for such "single-handed" operations as netting a fish.

Whichever features you select, the choice of spinning reel should be based on line weight and line capacity. The following categories describe the range:

Ultra-Light: up to 8 lb.-test
Light: 8 to 15 lb.-test
Medium: 15 to 30 lb.-test
Heavy: above 30 lb.-test

Spin-Casting Reels

A **SPIN-CASTING REEL** is a spinning reel with a closed face. The enclosure is usually a rounded hood with a small hole on its face through which the line passes. The fisherman's thumb on a release button or knob on the back end of the reel controls the line during a cast: the moment pressure on the button relaxes, no further line is released.

With regard to line retrieval, a pin winds around inside the hood to settle the line onto a cup. Some reels have more than one pin, which makes for a faster rewind.

Friction and line capacity are the two main considerations of spin-casting reels. With regard to friction, monofilament is the line of choice; braided line creates too much resistance, while mono glides off the spool and through the hole. The hood makes line capacity somewhat restrictive, although not impossibly so.

Most "kiddie" fishing sets include a spin-casting reel. That's because spin-casting tackle is easier to use than a spinning rod and reel. Although you don't have the same accuracy of line control, since the release button is an all-or-nothing mechanism, a little bit of practice is all it takes for anyone can learn to gauge the amount of time the button should be held down to achieve a respectable cast.

That's not to say, however, that all spin-casting reels should be considered "kid stuff." More sophisticated features now include a 4:1 ratio retrieval, star drag systems, and "power" handles for better grip.

Two spin-casting reels with thumb-release knobs. [courtesy Daiwa]

Fly Reels

The first reels used in fly-fishing were wooden affairs inspired by bobbins. Technology took a giant step forward when in 1874 Charles F. Orvis was awarded a patent for a ventilated (that is, having holes in its sides), narrow-spool reel. Another more recent innovation was the exposed rim that permits braking by the palm of the angler's hand.

A fly reel. [courtesy Orvis]

Fly reels are categorized primarily according to the range of line weights that they are intended to hold (for a discussion of fly line weights and the rods for which they are designed, see pages 67 and 46). Reels designed for the lightest weights, 1 through 5, are necessarily smaller than those meant for salmon, steelhead, and especially deep-sea fishing.

The weight of a fly reel becomes crucial to establish optimum balance. A reel that is too heavy means that the rod itself will feel too light, and that will interfere with line control while you cast. A reel that is too light, however, makes a rod feel too heavy, especially at its tip. This too creates casting problems. In the best of all worlds, a rod and reel will have their center of balance just in front of the grip.

Many fly reels adjust for drag by means of a single triangular pawl held by a spring against a geared wheel. Since pawls can slip and spring coils can lose their tension, a more precise mechanism is a padded disc that applies pressure against the spool, much as disc brakes retard an automobile's forward movement. The least adjustable resistance control comes from the click ratchet, activated by an all-or-nothing on–off switch.

Resistance can be applied manually by letting your the flat of your hand rub against a reel's rim. This is possible, however, only on a reel designed for "rim palming"; that is, one with an exposed rim.

Even the sound a reel makes can be a matter of choice. Some fishermen enjoy the loud clicks that a ratchet arrangement make, especially the coffee-grinder "rat-tat-tat" heard when a big fish strips line off such a reel. Others prefer a more understated and harmonious sound. The only functional difference, some big-game anglers feel, is that clicking ratchet systems can deprive line tension of consistent pressure.

One sound that a big-game fly-fisherman doesn't enjoy hearing is that of a reel handle knob cracking against his knuckle. A big fish can yank line so hard and fast that the reel's spool will rotate in excess of 5,000 rpms.
ANTI-REVERSE REELS eliminate this danger; the spool rotates as the line goes out, but the knob does not.

A system of internal springs and gears characterize the
"AUTOMATIC" FLY REEL. A flip of the lever (usually with your little finger), and the mechanism springs into action, pulling the slack in the line back onto the reel spool. Many anglers, especially who release lots of line fishing for salmon and steelheads, swear by automatics. Others who prefer greater human control sneer at them, citing poor drag control and relative little line capacity with no backing.

More widely accepted examples of mechanical advantage are **MULTIPLIER REELS**. Their gear systems (typically, a 3:1 retrieve ratio) offer faster line retrieval, very much of an asset when trying to land any of the larger and hard-fighting freshwater or saltwater species.

Before You Buy

Whichever kind of reel you consider, you'll become aware that reels are precision instruments. Some, however, are more precise than others, usually with regard to the materials from which they are made and the care and accuracy of the assembling process.

The finest quality reel are made from bar stock metal that is honed to exact specifications. Another method is to cast metal parts out of molds, a somewhat less expensive process. According to a March 1993 article in *Fly Rod & Reel*, the difference between the two techniques is "negligible" (or, put another way, a matter of personal bias). Other reels are molded from plastic or graphite, or mass-produced from stamped metal. One benefit of the lower end of this craftsmanship spectrum is that mass-produced reels tend to accept abrasion, bangs, and other traumas better than their handmade ultra-precision brethren. . . they just keep on clicking.

Some reels come only in right- or left-handed models. Others can be adjusted to be worked by either hand. But as Gary Soucie points out, switching hands on the rod after casting is hardly a big deal. You cast with your stronger hand and arm, so playing a big fish with that side of your body makes more sense.

With regard to material, brass or steel are extremely durable. So are such man-made material as graphite. Plastic, however "space-age" it may be hyped, remains at the fragile end of the spectrum.

Reels with thick coats of finish are more scratch-resistant than those with thin anodized or baked finishes. Reel feet that are screwed on are stronger than one that are riveted. Plastic pawls tend to crack or wear out faster than pawls made of metal.

When inspecting a reel:

1. Look and feel for any imperfections.
2. Check for loose, wobbling parts as you wind the reel, especially the spool and the spool release (and any spare spools that you're also considering buying).
3. Test the drag system. Listen for clicks as you rotate the spool.
4. Make sure the spool is large enough to accommodate enough line for the type of fishing you plan to do. That's a particularly important consideration in "blue-water" ocean fishing, where a reel must be able to hold 400 feet or more of line (and if a fly reel, line plus backing).
5. Finally, confirm that any defects that occur during a warranty period will be corrected or the reel can be exchanged.

Care and Maintenance of Reels

Reels are precision instruments, so dropping or otherwise subjecting them to abuse won't do them or you any good. If you do drop a reel, immediately remove any dirt, sand, or other debris that may be clogging the mechanism. Make sure, too, that no screws have come loose or that, if it's a spinning reel, the pick-up bail is not bent.

A saltwater reel should be lightly rinsed in freshwater after each use to remove any traces of salt. If possible, remove the spool to remove any water trapped there. Dry the reel with a clean absorbent cloth, then apply a slight amount of reel oil on internal moving parts. After reassembling the reel, put just a drop of household oil on any external moving parts (reel oil is too thick).

Any drag mechanism that includes cork or rubber should be kept fully released when not in use. Otherwise the soft material will become indented and/or stiff.

Freshwater reels should be cleaned with a clean cloth or a silicon rag, with external moving parts periodically receiving a drop of household oil.

The need to store and transport reels in cases is as important as it is for rods. Leather or cloth reel bags are designed for that purpose (plastic "zip-up" sandwich bags make a handy substitute). Padded reel cases are even sturdier. So are tackle boxes, in which many anglers keep their baitcasting and spinning reels safe and secure amid plugs, bobbers, hooks, and other gear.

Further Reading

As with the companion subject of rods, reels are well treated in *McClane's New Standard Fishing Encyclopedia and International Angling Guide* by A.J. McClane (Henry Holt, 1974).

Full-color illustrations and brief descriptions appear in the *Dorling Kindersley Encyclopedia of Fishing* (Dorling Kindersley, 1994).

The New American Trout Fishing by John Merwin (Macmillan, 1994) includes a thoughtful discussion of fly reels.

Manufacturers of Reels

Abel Automatics, Inc
165 Aviador St.
Camarillo, CA 93010
(805) 484-8789
fax: (805) 482-0701

Ascent Reels
2516 Fulton St.
Berkeley, CA 94704
(510) 848-9582
fax: (510) 548-6664

Abu Garcia
21 Law Dr.
Fairfield, NJ 07004-3296
(201) 227-7666

L.L. Bean, Inc.
Freeport, ME 04033
(800) 221-4221

Berkley
One Berkley Dr.
Spirit Lake, IA 51360-1041
(800) BERKLEY
fax: (712) 336-5183

Billy Pate Reels
900 Northeast 40th Court
Oakland Park, FL 33334

Browning Fishing/Zebco Corp.
P.O. Box 840
Tulsa, OK 74101-0840

(918) 836-3542
fax: (918) 836-0514

Charlton Outdoor Technologies
1179-A Water Tank Rd.
Burlington, WA 98233
(206) 757-2609
fax: (206) 757-2610

Cortland Line Company
Kellog Rd.
P.O. Box 5588
Cortland, NY 13045-5588
(800) 847-6787

Daiwa
7421 Chapman Ave.
Garden Grove, CA 92641
(714) 895-6645
fax: (714) 898-1476

Eagle Claw Fishing Tackle/Wright & McGill Co.
4254 E. 46 Ave.
Denver, CO 80216
(303) 321-1481
fax: (303) 321-4750

Fenwick
5242 Argosy Avenue
Huntington Beach, CA 92649
(800) 642-7637
fax: (714) 891-9610

Hardy (USA) Inc.
10 Goodwin Plaza
Midland Park, NJ 07432
(201) 481-7557
fax: (201) 670-7190

HT Enterprises
P.O. Box 909
Campbellsport, WI 53010
(414) 533-5080
fax: (414) 533-5147

JS Foster Corp. (Islander Reels)
517 Kelvin Rd.
Victoria, B.C. V82 1C4 Canada
(604) 384-3242
fax: (604) 386-3177

Johnson Fishing (Mitchell)
1531 East Madison Ave.
Mankato, MT 56002
(507) 345-4623

Lamson & Goodnow Mfg. Co.
    (Lamson)
45 Conway St.
P.O. Box 128
Shelburne Falls, MA 01270
(800) 872-6564
fax: (413) 625-9816

Martin/Zebco
P.O. Box 270
Tulsa, OK 74101
(918) 836-5581
fax: (918) 836-0514

Orvis
Historic Route 7A
Manchester, VT 05254
(800) 815-5900

Peerless Reel Co.
427-3 Amherst St.
Nashua, NH 03063
(603) 595-2459

Penn Fishing Tackle
    Manufacturing Company
3028 West Hunting Park Ave.
Philadelphia, PA 19132
(215) 229-9415
fax: (215) 223-3017

Quantum
P.O. Box 270
Tulsa, OK 74101
(918) 836-5581
fax: (918) 836-0514

Ross Reel USA
1 Ponderosa Ct.
Montrose, CO 81401
(303) 249-1212
fax: (303) 249-1834

Sage
8500 Northeast Day Rd.
Bainbridge Island, WA 98110
(206) 842-6608
fax: (206) 842-6830

St. Croix of Park Falls Ltd.
P.O. Box 279
Hwy. 13 N
Park Falls, WI 54552
(715) 762-3226
fax: (715) 762-3293

Scientific Anglers
3M Center 225-3N
St. Paul, MN 55144
(800) 525-6291
fax: (612) 736-7479

Shakespeare
3801 Westmore Drive
Columbia, SC 29223
(800) 334-9105
fax: (803) 754-7342

Shimano
P.O. Box 19615
Irvine, CA 92713-9615
(714) 951-5003
fax: (714) 951-5071

Silstar
P.O. Box 6505
West Columbia, SC 29171
(803) 794-8521
fax: (803) 794-8544

South Bend Sporting Goods
1950 Stanley Street
Northbrook, IL 60065
(800) 622-9662
fax: (708) 564-3042

STH Reels USA Inc.
1000 15th St.
P.O. Box 816
Marathon, FL 33050
(800) 232-1359
(305) 743-3519

Valentine Fly Reels
P.O. Box 95
Chartley, MA 02712
(508) 226-0040

Zebco
P.O. Box 270
Tulsa, OK 74101
(918) 836-5581
fax: (918) 836-0514

5

LINES

The earliest fishing lines were strips of animal sinew, later replaced by pieces of twine or thin rope that were also knotted together into workable lengths. By the Middle Ages, braided or twisted horse-tail hair had become the material of choice. Silk was added until it finally replaced horsehair entirely. In order to make the line float, fishermen dressed it with oil or grease, and whether floating or not, line needed to be thoroughly dried after each use to retard rotting. Deep-sea fishermen favored another fabric, linen, which was braided or twisted into line.

The 1940s and 1950s saw several major technological advances. Sporting goods manufacturers realized that the extruded polymeric amide known as nylon, first used for parachutes and women's stockings, produced a thin tough line that was perfect for fishing (single-strand nylon is now known generically as "monofilament"). Other petrochemical materials, such as Dacron®, followed. Scientific Anglers was the first, in 1949, to coat synthetic line with a substance that caused fly line to float better and more durably than any silk.

Innovations of this decade include Du Pont's Kevlar™ and other so-called "super" lines. Amazingly strong and thin, they have changed almost all forms of fishing.

Baitcasting and Spinning Lines

Line used for these methods are either monofilament (a single strand) or braided from more than one strand of whatever material is used. These materials include:

NYLON: Monofilament, or single-strand nylon, offers all-around versatility. Its ability to stretch up to 35% is excellent for absorbing the recoil of a heavy plug or a fish's strike. It's also inexpensive and easy to knot, although knots in soft, waterlogged mono line have a tendency to loosen. There are disadvantages, though. The same ability to stretch means reduced sensitivity when a fish plays with or strikes bait. Mono's "memory," or its tendency to remain in coils (it "remembers" being coiled on a reel's spool), can adversely affect casting distance and accuracy. Moreover, any nick or knot dramatically reduces mono's strength, so the line must be constantly inspected and frequently replaced.

CO-FILAMENT: The core of co-filament is made of monofilament that is stiffer and stronger than standard mono, which is co-filament's outer layer. The result is a line with less "give" and memory and more abrasion resistance. Saltwater anglers favor co-filament for bottom-fishing.

DACRON®: Du Pont's trademark for its polyester fiber, Dacron® stretches to a maximum of 10%, far less than monofilament. It absorbs less water and is less resistant to sunlight deterioration than nylon is. Many anglers favor Dacron® lines for trolling because of its high visibility and sensitivity to strikes. On the other hand, tying knots in Dacron® requires considerable care.

TERYLENE™: This polyester line approximates the characteristics of older silk lines, having a buoyancy between nylon and Dacron®.

WIRE: Wire lines are primarily used for medium to deep trolling. Wire is sensitive (you'll feel every movement of your bait—and fish), strong, and abrasion-resistant. Although it has a tendency to twist, that can be overcome by using one or more swivels.

A single-strand line sinks faster than one that is multi-strand, a benefit when you're trying to get depth in a hurry, yet it is no less durable. Another variety of wire line, lead core, is made of Dacron® or nylon braided around lead wire; Gary Soucie points out that Dacron® stretches less than nylon and helps hold the line's shape when tension stretches the lead core (as it invariably does).

Of the materials of which wire line is made, stainless steel is the most popular for its strength and durability. A nickel–copper alloy marketed under the brand name Monel™ is a close second. Copper, which tends to corrode in salt water, is a better freshwater choice.

"SUPER-STRENGTH" FIBERS: A spun-gel polyethylene, Kevlar™ (a Du Pont trademark) is five times stronger than steel by weight. An example of its strength: Kevlar™ is used in bulletproof vests and as maritime cables to moor ships (a ¼-inch Kevlar™ rope has a strength of 6 tons). Thanks to the strength of Kevlar™ and such other similar fibers and brands as Spectra™ and IronThread™, the chance of losing a lure or a lunker due to line breakage has become virtually nonexistent. In fact, you're more likely to snap your graphite rod or straighten a hook that is snagged on

a log than snap a braided super-strength line.

Among other properties of super-strength line is its smaller diameter, approximately one-third the size of nylon monofilament or Dacron®. Thinner lines create less drag, a particular useful feature when bottom-fishing where a line's "belly," or bow, detracts from the fisherman's ability to feel a strike. Despite their small size, these lines come in tests in the 30- to 130-pound range, although IronThread™ has come out with a 6-pound-test that is as thin as sewing thread.

Another plus is that super-strength lines have virtually no stretch. That allows a faster hook-set that takes less effort. Gone is the need for Herculean "jaw-breaker" hook-ups, thanks to the line's strength and less stretch (3%–5%, compared to monofilament's 20%–30% and often more). Super-strength line requires less line on your reel, since you'll be able to hook and hold a fish without its running all over the lake before you can bring it to your boat.

Super-line also has no "memory" as nylon and Dacron® do, so the line gives bait better action. The line also lies limp in the water, without curling.

Why then, you might well wonder, would anyone choose such antediluvian line as nylon or Dacron® monofilament instead of this space-age braided marvel? First of all, there are times when monofilament's stretch is preferable. This stretchability allows a fish to take the bait deeper into its mouth even while you're setting the hook.

Then too, people have complained that super-lines don't hold knots very well. In response, manufacturers have promoted special knots for this material, as well as a super-glue that is as strong as the line itself (you'll also need a super-sharp knife to cut the line; many standard clippers won't make a dent). Another objection is that it's relatively expensive compared to monofilament. On the other hand, it lasts longer than mono, so you won't need to replace it very frequently. Then too, you'll need less since any fish taken on super-strength line won't run all over the lake before you can haul it into your boat (some anglers use monofilament as spool-filling backing for their super-strength line).

Once you've decided on the material, you will need to decide between monofilament or braided line. Mono absorbs less water than braided line, and it produces less friction for longer casts. Because spinning lines need some stiffness so the line will "spring" off the spool, mono works better than braided line for that purpose.

However, braided line, which is limper than mono, is easier to cast off a baitcasting reel, and surf-casters tend to favor it for their revolving-spool reels. Some prefer nylon because it holds knots better than Dacron®, which, others argue, has less stretch and sinks faster and better for bottom-fishing.

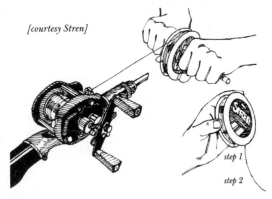

[courtesy Stren]

step 1
step 2

HOW TO FILL YOUR REEL

Improper loading of your reel can cause line twist which can greatly reduce casting accuracy and distance. Worse yet, it can cause you to lose fish.

You can avoid problems by having your reel filled on a linewinding machine at your favorite sporting goods store. However, it pays to learn how to do it yourself because most line problems occur at lakeside, miles from the nearest winder.

Filling a Revolving-Spool Reel

Insert a pencil into the supply spool to allow the fishing line to feed smoothly off the spool. Have someone hold each end of the pencil while you turn the reel handle. Keep proper tension on the line by having the person holding the pencil exert a slight inward pressure on the supply spool.

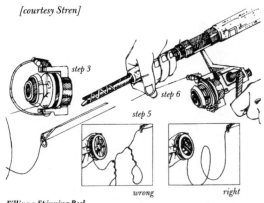

[courtesy Stren]

step 3
step 6
step 5
wrong
right

Filling a Spinning Reel

You fill a spinning/open-face reel differently than a baitcast reel because you must allow for the rotation of the pick-up bail which may cause the line to twist.

Follow these steps:

1. Have someone hold the supply spool or place it on the floor or ground.
2. Pull the line so that it spirals (balloons) off the end of the spool.
3. Thread the line through the rod guides and tie the line to the reel with the bail in the open position.
4. Hold the rod tip three to four feet away from the supply spool. Make fifteen to twenty turns on the reel handle, then stop.
5. Check for line twist by moving the rod tip to about one foot from the supply spool. If the slack line twists, turn the supply spool completely around. This will eliminate most of the twist as you wind the rest of the line onto the reel.
6. Always keep a light tension on fishing line when spooling any reel. Do this by holding the line between the thumb and forefinger of your free hand.

[courtesy Stren]

Filling a Spin-Cast/Closed-Face Reel

Use the same procedure (steps 1 to 6) described for filling a spinning reel. Remember to partially remove the reel cover so you will be able to see the spool and the rotation of the pickup pin. This is critical to insure that you do not underfill or overfill the spool.

The thickness of a line affects castability. A heavy line will not cast well with a light bait on its end, nor will a plug or other artificial bait move with its intended action if it is towed on a line that is too heavy. By the same token, heavy bait will not stay attached very long when on light-weight monofilament line. Also, with regard to thickness, thicker lines tend to last longer, because there's more of it to resist abrasion.

Another element is the relationship between line and rod. A stiff rod needs a heavy line to perform, while a light rod needs a much finer line.

But, you may well ask, if modern super-strength "unbreakable" lines hold almost anything tied to them, why not routinely use a heavy test? The answer is that no matter what the material of which the line is made, the thinner the line, the easier it is to cast, the greater its sensitivity and the less visibility it shows to a fish. That's why experts counsel using the lightest line possible for the appropriate conditions.

Moreover, to go after lake or pond fish that weigh under five pounds by using a line that tests at 10 times that weight strikes many people the sporting equivalent of hunting squirrels with an elephant gun.

These are the reasons why, notwithstanding the availability of super-strength lines, many freshwater pond and lake bait- and spin-fisherfolk seldom venture beyond the 10-pound to 12-pound-test range, with 20 pounds the maximum for pickerel and muskie anglers.

A line's test or breaking-point rating becomes an important factor for anyone who plans to go after a world-record catch. The International Game Fish Association rates and monitors manufacturers' test ratings, and the organization will grant record status only to fish caught on lines that measure no more than 5% above or below the maker's declared test rating. Such IGFA approval is marked on the line packaging.

A complete discussion of the relative benefits and disadvantages of monofilament versus braided lines can be found on page 193 of Gary Soucie's *Hook, Line, and Sinker: The Complete Angler's Guide to Terminal Tackle* (Henry Holt, 1994).

Fly Lines

Fly lines are made of lengths of nylon or Dacron® that have been covered with a polyvinyl chloride wrap. Fly lines come in a variety of types, each with its own properties for specific purposes.

Weight-forward line. [courtesy Scientific Anglers]

Double-tapered line. [courtesy Scientific Anglers]

Level line. [courtesy Scientific Anglers]

WEIGHT-FORWARD (abbreviated WF) is the most popular line for general-purpose fly-fishing and is recommended as the easiest for novices to use. The first 30 feet are heavier than the rest of the line, which is known as the running line; the weight up front permits longer casts than those made on double-tapered lines. The thinner mid-section, however, makes roll-casting more difficult.

DOUBLE-TAPERED (DT), of which the first 10 or 12 feet are tapered, has a narrower and lighter front section than the one found on a weight-forward line. That enables a fly to be presented with greater delicacy. Making roll casts is easier too, since the heavier line behind lifts the front section off the water. Mending this type of line is also easier, again because of the heavier mid-section.

Both ends of the line are tapered in this way, so you can simply remove and reverse the line on your reel when the first portion needs to be replaced. That feature was more of a plus in the days before lines were as durable as they are today and when rod guides weren't so friction- and wear-resistant. Nevertheless, double-tapered lines continue to have their fans for reasons of economy as well as technique.

SHOOTING TAPER (ST), OR SHOOTING HEAD: This length of weighted line, usually 30 feet in length, is attached to a lighter running line by a loop. The weight allows maximum casting distance, which is especially useful when fishing in wide, fast rivers for steelheads and salmon. Line is stripped out preparatory to being cast, and to prevent it from drifting into tangles, the line is often kept in a shooting basket strapped to the angler's waist.

LEVEL LINE (see below) is typically used as running line, although monofilament is an acceptable substitute. If you choose mono, which is less expensive and sinks faster than level fly line, you'll want 20-pound test for line weight up to 7 weight, and 30-pound test above 7.

One drawback to shooting tapers is that the line must be retrieved almost back to the head before you can cast again. That's a problem when you need to get your fly to a fish in a hurry.

BUG-TAPERED/BASS LINES (BT): The front portion of these lines is shorter than in the normal weight-forward. That profile permits an additional "punch" that's necessary when casting heavier bass "bug" flies.

SALTWATER TAPER (ST): This line is similar in profile to a bass line, again to provide extra casting "punch." However, the line casing composition is more durable; the toughness is

needed to resist the chemical reaction of salt water and the abrasiveness of sand, rocks, and other aspects of a marine environment.

LEVEL (L): This line has no taper whatsoever and, accordingly, many people find it the most difficult to cast with delicacy and for distance. Still, it's a reasonable choice for using live bait and other situations where a delicate presentation isn't necessary. It is also often used behind a shooting taper.

TRIANGLE TAPER (TT): Invented by legendary angler and innovator Lee Wulff, triangle taper begins with a 40-foot section tapered down toward the tip, behind which the line tapers back another 10 feet (that's what "triangle" refers to; the line's cross-section itself is round). This WF-DT hybrid thus encourages both casting for distance and with delicate presentations.

SPECIALTY LINES:

TARPON TAPER has a short front head and taper for accurate and delicate casts using a minimum of line. Similar to bass taper lines,

BONEFISH TAPER and saltwater taper also have short heads. These heads make delivering distance casts relatively difficult, but the line works better under windy conditions than a longer-casting line would.

Another classification of fly lines is in terms of buoyancy:

FLOATING (F): Floating lines, which have microscopic hollow glass "micro-balloon" beads in their coating, are essential for surface-fishing dry flies. A line that floats is easy to lift off the water surface and, therefore, to cast. In addition, it is the most versatile type of line, since it can be used in shallow water and, with the addition of a sinker or heavy fly, in deep water too.

SINKING (S): Sinking lines have tiny bits of weighted material in their coating. Used for wet flies, nymphs, and streamers, a sinking line is useful for fishing at depths and over long distances. It will keep a fly at a more or less constant depth in ways that a floating line with a sinker or weighted fly will not; the latter tends to pull the fly up with each tug or strip of the line.

FLOATING/SINKING (F/S): Better known as "sink-tip" line, its front portion (usually the first 6 feet), sinks while the rest of the line floats. Within this category of line is a range of speeds with which the tip sinks:

SLOW-SINKING: $1\frac{1}{4}$ to $1\frac{3}{4}$ inches per second (this and the following other rates will vary according to water conditions). Used when you want your fly to ride just below the water's surface.

FAST-SINKING: $2\frac{1}{2}$ to 3 inches per second. For depths between 5 feet and 15 feet.

EXTRA-FAST: $3\frac{1}{2}$ to 4 inches per second. For depths from 15 feet to 20 feet.

Beyond these are the so-called "Super-Sinker" and "Super-Fast" types used in deep holes and in the sort of fast rivers in which salmon and steelhead are found.

INTERMEDIATE (I): This is in a sense a sinking line, but one that sinks so slowly that it tends to stay just below the surface. Many people find it useful on lakes or ponds when wind creates a choppy surface.

WEIGHT

The **WEIGHT** of a fly line is based on a standard computed in grains (not ounces) based on the weight of a line's first 30 feet:

Fly rods are constructed to accommodate specific line weights, so your choice of rod will make selecting the proper line weight automatic. (For more on rod weights, see the section on fly rods, page 46.) Be aware, however, that most rods can handle a line weight one above or below the rod's designation; 6-weight line on a 5-weight rod will produce a bit more "punch."

You can now translate the arcane mysteries of fly line designation. A line marked "WF-5-F" translates into weight-forward, 5-weight, and floating.

COLOR

Whether fish respond to colors the way that other creatures do remains a subject of conjecture. Many fishermen feel that as long as a floating line rests on top of the water, color is irrelevant; fish seem to react more to shadows than to hues. Moreover, eye-catching colors from light pastels to bright neons are more visible to anglers, especially at dusk or during foggy conditions. However, as for sinking lines, the choice is for dark colors that act as underwater camouflage.

BACKING

Unlike baitcasting and spinning line, fly line is not attached directly to the reel. A length of line called **BACKING** is used, and for two reasons. Backing fills up space on the reel's arbor to give the fly line a thicker base; the larger reel diameter means less rewinding is necessary to retrieve line. Backing also offers additional line, something of a safety margin in case a fish runs through all of the fly line.

Until recently, almost all backing was made of thin braided Dacron® or similar material. It ranged

LINE WEIGHT #:	1	2	3	4	5	6	7	8	9	10	11	12
WEIGHT: (in grains)	60	80	100	120	140	160	185	210	240	280	330	380

in test strengths from 12 pounds to 30 pounds, with 18 pounds or 20 pounds as the typical choice for most freshwater fishing. A heavier test is appropriate for saltwater game fish.

Writing in the February 1995 issue of *Fly Fishing* magazine, Lefty Kreh suggested that 150 yards of backing is more than sufficient for any species of shallow-water fish. However, twice that amount and up to 400 yards is appropriate for billfish, tuna, wahoo, and large mackerel.

A new breed of backing appeared two or three years ago. Made of super-strength material, it offers a thinner diameter that translates into more backing on a reel. Another benefit is greater strength than conventional backing. But, as Kreh was quick to point out in the same article, thin line (under 30-pound test) has the potential to dig into the layer of backing underneath it. The result is breakage when the line fails to unwind properly. To prepare level layers, thin super-strong backing must be wound on a reel with firm, even pressure and in smooth layers that extend from one end of the spool to the other.

Backing is attached to the reel spool by an overhand knot and to the fly line by a nail knot. The "classic" way to measure the correct amount is a multi-stage process: (1) Wind the fly line, front end first, onto the reel; (2) join the back end of the fly line to the backing; (3) wind the backing onto the reel over the fly line until the spool is filled; (4) unwind everything (without tangling any of the line or backing); (5) tie the backing to the spool and rewind fly line-side-out.

Line Care

Nicks and chips in its outer core will not only weaken any fly line, but will diminish a floating line's buoyancy. Therefore, to practice your casting

on a blacktop driveway or a rocky field isn't the wisest of ideas. Neither is to cast a line that has no leader, since abrasion to the front of the line will weaken that section.

Floating line can be cleaned in warm water to which a small amount of mild liquid detergent as been added. Wipe the line with a sponge, rinse in clear water, and wipe again with a clean sponge.

Liquid or liquid-soaked cloth cleaners wipe away dirt and restore a line's waterproof property. Silicon-based liquids and pastes designed to clean and polish automobile finishes work well for this purpose. Some cleaners contain Teflon™, which reduces friction against a rod's ferrules to produce longer casts.

Sound environmental practice includes disposing of used line properly. Whether an entire spoolful or just lengths, line can easily become a snare that birds and animals can't escape. Keep unwanted line with you and either incinerate it in your campfire or take it home.

An equally sound dental practice is not to bite off pieces of line after you've tied a knot. Line, and especially the new unbreakable variety, is strong enough to chip teeth. Use a clipper or a knife instead.

Leaders

A **LEADER** is a piece of line or wire that connects the line to the bait. Many bait and spinning fisherfolk simply dispense with leaders, preferring to tie their hooks or lures directly to the line.

That's good news for muskies, pickerel, and other species of fish whose razor-sharp teeth that can weaken or cut through even the strongest of super-strength lines. To reduce this likelihood, savvy freshwater anglers who pursue these species use leaders made of extra-heavy monofilament or wire. Which material to choose depends on the species you'll encounter and the conditions under which you'll fish. Monofilament leaders are strong, stretchy, flexible, and inexpensive. Wire, however, is essential if you're going after sharks and other heavy and tough deep-sea denizens. It is also more resistant than monofilament to sharp rocks and coral, and unlike mono, sunlight won't cause it to deteriorate. Among wire's drawbacks are the relative difficulty in handling it and the possible interference with the "natural" movement of the lure or live bait to which it is attached.

If you're going to use a wire leader, stainless steel is stronger than, and therefore preferable to, tin or brass, and a single solid strand is less obtrusive than braided (also called stranded) wire. For a more detailed analysis of types of wire leaders, see *Hook, Line, and Sinker* by Gary Soucie, page 223.

The weight and energy of a big game fish can easily snap a line, which is why deep-sea fishermen use a **SHOCK LEADER**. That's a short (perhaps 2 feet long) length of monofilament that absorbs the concussive impact of a big fish's initial strike and ongoing fight.

There's a similar need in trolling to absorb the additional force produced by a fish striking against tackle on a moving boat. A **MONO TROLLING LEADER** may be up to 100 feet long to keep the bait or lure down deep.

RELEASE LEADERS developed in saltwater catch-and-release tournaments. They are short pieces of wire with a snap attached; the boated fish is released either by unsnapping the leader or cutting it. The procedure is based on the theory that a fish released with a hook and short length of wire in its mouth stands a far better chance of survival than one whose mouth has been mangled in an attempt to remove the hook.

In the realm of "package deal" leaders and hooks, **SNELLED HOOKS** have lengths of permanently-attached monofilament leaders. The theory is that the force used to set the hook when a fish strikes is absorbed along the hook shank instead of directly to where the line is tied to the hook's eye.

Other pre-tied rigs are more complicated affairs that mix hooks, leaders, spinners, snaps, and swivels in a variety of combinations. Some contain leaders that hold more than one hook, while others have metal arms that keep two or more leaders apart.

FLY LEADERS

Unlike lures and live bait, flies cannot be attached directly to a fly line. Fly lines are too thick and heavy to allow a delicate casting presentation. Trout, in particular, are spooked by the splash of a line striking water, and all species react suspiciously when a fly is tied to line that to them must seem as thick as a ship's cable. The fly needs to be "distanced" from the line, and that's where leaders come into play.

The original fly leaders were lengths of braided horsehair, after which anglers used lengths of animal gut. Twentieth-century technology produced nylon, and monofilament leaders remain the material of choice.

Anatomically, a fly line leader is composed of three parts: the **BUTT**, or thick end, approximately 60% of the total leader length; a thinner mid-section of about 20%; and an even thinner **TIPPET**, to which the fly is tied, also about 20%.

Leaders come in two styles.

KNOTTED LEADERS are composed of three to eight sections of plain or braided monofilament of successively thinner diameter (the braided butt variety afford a bit of shock-absorbing "give" when a fish strikes). An advantage is that broken or nicked sections can be accurately replaced. However, the knots that hold these sections together can become weakened with use. The knots also have a tendency to pick up weeds and other debris, still another reason why not everyone uses this style.

The **KNOTLESS**, or plain, style of leader is a single strand of tapered monofilament. This material can stretch up to 10% or slightly more, so that too has a shock-absorbing property.

Leader thickness is expressed according to the diameter of their tippets. The calculation is based on the **"RULE OF 11"**: the tippet size (expressed in a number followed by the letter "X") plus the tippet diameter equals .011. For example, a 6X leader's tippet measures .005 (6+.005=.011... "6" really means ".006").

The follow table indicates the dimensions and strengths of trout leaders sold under the Stren label:

Leader size:	0X	1X	2X	3X	4X	5X	6X	7X
Lb. test:	15	12	10	7	5	4	2.8	1.9
Tip diameter:	.011	.010	.009	.008	.007	.006	.005	.004
Butt diameter:	.023	.023	.023	.023	.023	.023	.023	.023

Just as rod weight largely dictates line weight, the size of a fly (or nymph or streamer or bass bug) will determine the proper thickness of a leader. A fly should not only appear lifelike, but a leader must be able to "**TURN OVER**" properly, a phrase that means a leader's ability to go through all the phases of a cast and then settle on the water with neither too much nor too little force (a salmon-size streamer tied to a light leader will plop down, if it hasn't already snapped off during the back cast's crack-the-whip stage).

A rule of thumb helps us determine the correct leader thickness size. Known as the **RULE OF THREE**, it involves dividing the fly size by the number 3, with the result rounded off to the nearest leader size. For example, a size 16 dry fly would be suited to a 5X leader. However, some people still prefer to use the **RULE OF FOUR**, which provides a heavier leader that was preferable in the days before leaders were made of the more durable synthetic material of today.

Such rules are now made even more complicated by the advent of super-strong "fluorocarbon" leaders and tippets (purists put the word in quotes because the material is really polyvinylidene fluoride). The advantages are several, beginning with fluorocarbon's near-invisibility, which spooks fewer fish. Fluorocarbon is also very resistant to abrasion and breakdown from exposure to sunlight (on the other hand, nylon and similar synthetics deteriorate from both ultraviolet light and age). And unlike nylon, which can lose up to 40% of its strength after two hours of use, fluorocarbon won't absorb water.

On the other hand, cost-conscious fishermen point out that fluorocarbon leaders are two to three times more expensive than those made of nylon.

Leaders come in lengths that range from 4 feet up to 15 feet for freshwater fishing, and even longer for saltwater (tarpon fishermen routinely use leaders that end in 100-pound-test shock tippets). For most streamside trout angling, 7½ feet and 9 feet are typical. Conditions and quarry are factors in determining the appropriate length. Fishing with a dry fly for wily trout on a large clear pond or slow-moving stream calls for a relatively long leader, to keep as great a "reality" distance as possible between line and fly. Windy conditions may call for a shorter leader, better for "punchy" casting. Shorter leaders will work well for bass and other less spooky species. They also let wet flies and nymphs go deeper. Thicker leaders can accommodate relatively heavy flies, such as bass bugs.

Leaders are attached to fly lines by knot or loop. The most frequently used knot is the nail knot. A "Chinese-handcuff" loop (often in a bright eye-catching color that doubles as a strike indicator) is wormed onto the end of the line, then fastened by super-glue. A "square-knot" over-and-under knot connects that look with one on the end of the leader (some leaders are pre-looped, while others need one tied at the butt end).

These loop devices inspired an innovative interchangeable leader system, such as the one packaged by Orvis. "Mini Lead Head" attachments allow a floating line to be instantly converted into a sinking-tip line.

Changing or replacing a fly requires clipping off a piece of tippet, a process that reduces not only the leader's length but its taper. At some point the taper becomes inappropriately thick for the size fly you've been using. Replacing an entire leader is an expensive and time-consuming proposition, but there's an alternative: simply tie on a length of tippet material. That involves carrying a supply of spools in a variety of sizes. Many fly-fishing vests have a series of small pockets designed to accommodate tippet spools, or you can invest in a dispensers that has room for up to a half-dozen spools.

LEADER AND TIPPET CARE

Tippet dispensers, as well as leader wallets, prevent unwanted kinks, nicks, and tangles that weaken the monofilament material. No matter how you store or carry leaders and tippet material, monofilament should be kept out of the light, which causes the material to deteriorate, and extreme heat, which hastens that reaction even more.

Some anglers replace all their leaders and tippet material annually, although others claim they've had no untoward experiences with older material.

Knots

The adage about a chain being only as strong as its weakest link might have been inspired by lines and knots. There are knots for every purpose under and above water: to attach line to a reel spool, leaders to line, hooks and other terminal tackle to line, and line to line.

Which knot to use depends on such factors as type and size of line and terminal tackle, whether (if you're tying two lines together) the lines are of equal or unequal diameter, and the knot strength you require. That last element is more relevant than it would seem to be, since almost all knots diminish line strength to some degree.

Among his other talents, Lefty Kreh is widely (and highly) regarded as a knot expert; his magazine articles make reference to a knot-testing machine, a mechanical arbiter of such matters. Kreh and Mark Sosin, the well-regarded saltwater angler and commentator, collaborated on *Practical Knots II* (Lyons & Burford, 1991), an update of their earlier best-selling manual.

Orvis publishes two references that are designed for on-site use: *Waterproof Knot Booklet* and *Saltwater Knot Booklet* are both printed on durable waterproof paper.

Other good sources of information about knots comes from manufacturers of lines and other tackle, as the following illustrations demonstrate.

A literary footnote: E. Annie Proulx credits the redoubtable reference tome, *The Ashley Book of*

KNOTS TO HOLD TERMINAL TACKLE

Improved Clinch Knot

This is a good knot for making terminal-tackle connections and is best used for lines up to 20-pound test. It is a preferred knot by professional fishermen and angling authorities.

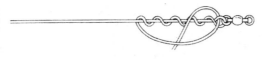

1. Pass line through eye of hook, swivel or lure. Double back and make five turns around the standing line. Hold coils in place; thread end of line around first loop above the eye, then through big loop as shown.

2. Hold tag end and standing line while coils are pulled up. Take care that coils are in spiral, not lapping over each other. Slide tight against eye. Clip tag end.

[courtesy Stren]

Blood Knot

The blood knot is used to connect lines of unequal diameter, such as tying a tipit to a tapered leader for fly fishing.

[courtesy Berkley]

Perfection Loop

Use the Perfection Knot to tie a loop at the end of your leader.

1. To start the loop, double the end of the leader back on itself, then take a single turn around the standing leader as is shown in Step 1.

2. The end of the leader should pass between the front and back loops formed in Step 1. Next, pull the back loop through the front loop, as the arrow in Step 2 shows.

3. Finally, pull the knot tight and trim off the tag end, as in Step 3.

[courtesy Cortland]

Fast Nail Knot

Perfect for connecting fly line to tapered leader... and easy to do!

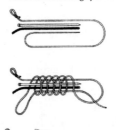

1. Lay components into position as shown: nail, fly line, leader butt, and leader tip.

2. Grasp extension of leader butt, wrap back towards fingers five turns.

3. Pinch wraps between thumb and forefinger of left hand. Pull tip end of leader through.

4. Tighten hard to imbed wraps into fly line finish. Clip ends closely.

[courtesy Cortland]

Palomar Knot

This knot is equally as good as the improved Clinch for terminal tackle connections and is easier to tie, except when using large plugs. It, too, is used by most of the pros.

1. Double about 4 inches of line and pass loop through eye.

2. Let hook hang loose and tie overhand knot in doubled line. Avoid twisting the lines and don't tighten.

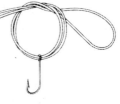

3. Pull loop of line far enough to pass it over hook, swivel or lure. Make sure loop passes completely over this attachment.

4. Pull both tag end and standing line to tighten. Clip tag end.

[courtesy Stren]

THE UNI-KNOT

Here is a system that uses one basic knot for a variety of applications. Developed by Vic Dunaway, author of numerous books on fishing and editor of *Florida Sportsman* magazine, the Uni-Knot can be varied to meet virtually every knot tying need in either fresh or salt water fishing.

The Basic Knot

1. Run line through eye of hook, swivel or lure at least 6 inches and fold to make two parallel lines. Bring end of line back in a circle toward hook or lure.

2. Make six turns with tag end around the double line and through the circle. Hold double line at the point where it passes through eye and pull tag end to snug up turns.

3. Now pull standing line to slide knot up against eye.

4. Continue pulling until knot is tight. Trim tag end flush with closest coil of knot. Uni-Knot will not slip.

[courtesy Stren]

Knots by Clifford W. Ashley (Doubleday), as the inspiration for her Pulitzer Prize-winning novel *The Shipping News*. Moreover, quotations and illustrations from Mr. Ashley's work serve as headnotes and headpieces for the novel's chapters.

Line and Leader Accessories

CLIPPERS

Got a tag end of line after you tied on your lure or hook? Lots of people cut it off by biting through. Using your teeth is risky business, dentists say,

Spider Hitch

This is a fast, easy knot for creating a double-line leader. Under steady pressure it is equally strong but does not have the resilience of the Bimini Twist under sharp impact. It is not practical, however, with lines above 30-pound test.

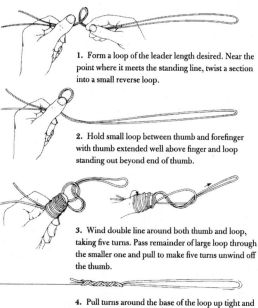

1. Form a loop of the leader length desired. Near the point where it meets the standing line, twist a section into a small reverse loop.

2. Hold small loop between thumb and forefinger with thumb extended well above finger and loop standing out beyond end of thumb.

3. Wind double line around both thumb and loop, taking five turns. Pass remainder of large loop through the smaller one and pull to make five turns unwind off the thumb.

4. Pull turns around the base of the loop up tight and snip off tag end.

[courtesy Stren]

especially when you try to chomp through any of the super-strength lines.

Far better to use a clipper, either a fingernail-trimming variety, or one that's specially designed for fishing line (many of these come equipped with tiny needles for cleaning hook eyes). You can carry it on a lanyard around your neck or attach it via a retractable "zinger" to your vest.

LEADER/TIPPET GAUGE

To be certain that a leader needs a new tippet or that their ends are of compatible thicknesses, you might invest in a leader/tippet gauge that measures such diameters. It's small enough to be carried in a vest pocket or attached to the vest by a retractable "zinger."

KNOT-TYING TOOLS

The nail knot is a sturdy way to attach leader to line. Trouble is, it's an intricate knot to tie, so anyone who has trouble with it may want to invest in a needle-like device that makes tying it a snap.

LEADER STRAIGHTENER

Because monofilament has a "memory," a leader, which is packaged coiled, will remain that way unless and until it is straightened. A device composed of two pieces of leather, rubber, or a synthetic fabric through which the leader is rubbed will de-coil the monofilament. Most fly-fishers carry such a leader straightener in their vests.

LEADER DRESSING

The sheen of fly-leader monofilament right out of a package is, some anglers feel, visible to fish. Rubbing the leader with a liquid "gink," a kind of synthetic mud, eliminates the glare.

Manufacturers of Line

Allied Signa
P.O. Box 31
Petersburg, VA 23804
(804) 520-3242

American Fishing Wire
205 Carter Dr.
West Chester, PA 19380
(800) 824-9473

Ande Inc.
1310 West 53 Street
West Palm Beach, FL 33407
(407) 842-2474

Angler Sport Group/Airflo
6619 Oak Orchard Rd.
Elba, NY 14058
(716) 757-9958

Berkley
One Berkley Drive
Spirit Lake, IA 51360-1041
(800) BERKLEY

Cortland Line Company
Kellog Road
P.O. Box 5588
Cortland, NY 13045-5588
(607) 756-2851

Fenwick (IronThread™)
5242 Argosy Avenue
Huntington Beach, CA 92649
(714) 897-1066

FTN Industries
P.O. Box 157
Menominee, MI 49858
(906) 863-5531

Gudbrod
P.O. Box 357
Pottstown, PA 19464
(215) 327-4050

HT Enterprises
P.O. Box 909
Campbellsport, WI 53010
(414) 533-5080

Izorline International
813 Gardena Blvd.
Gardena, CA 90247
(310) 324-1159

Mason Tackle Co.
P.O. Box 56
Otisville, MI 48463
(313) 631-4571

Maxima Fishing Lines
5 Chrysler Street
Irvine, CA 92718
(213) 515-2543

New Tech Sports
7208 McNeil Dr.
Suite 207
Austin, TX 78729
(512) 250-0485

Oldham Lures (Terry Oldham's Spectra™)
Rt. 1, Box 94
Wimberley, TX 78676
(512) 874-2842

Orvis
Historic Route 7A
Manchester, VT 05254
(800) 815-5900

Phantom Tackle
11130 Petal St.
Suite 500
Dallas, TX 75238
(214) 349-8228

PRADCO
P.O. Box 1587
Fort Smith, AR 72902
(800) 422-FISH

R.J. Tackle, Inc.
5719 Corporation Circle
Fort Myers, FL 33905
(813) 693-7070

Royal Wulff Products
Lew Beach, NY 12753
(914) 439-4060

Safariland Ltd. (Spectra™)
3120 E. Mission Blvd.
Ontario, CA 91761
(800) 347-1200
fax: (800) 336-1669

Scientific Anglers
3M Center 225-3N
St. Paul, MN 55144
(612) 733-6066

Stren
Remington Arms Co.
1011 Centre Rd.
Wilmington, DE 19805
(800) 537-2278

T & C Tackle (T.U.F.-Line)
P.O. Box 198
Schertz, TX 78154
(210) 659-5268

Tackle Marketing Inc.
3801 W. Superior St.
Duluth, MN 55807
(218) 628-0206

Triple Fish Fishing Line
321 Enterprise St.
Ocoee, FL 34761
(407) 656-7834

U.S. Line Co.
P.O. Box 531
Westfield, MA 01086
(800) 456-4665

Versitex
3545 Schuylkill Rd.
Spring City, PA 19475
(215) 948-4442

Western Filament
630 Hollingworth Dr.
Grand Junction, CO 81505
(303) 241-8780

6

FLOATS, SINKERS, SPINNERS, SWIVELS, SNAPS, AND TACKLE BOXES

Floats

Floats (or bobbers, or bobs, or drifters, or strike indicators—call them what you will) are a mainstay of still fishing. The bait (usually live bait) remains suspended in the water waiting for a fish to come along. The fish strikes, the float jiggles, then disappears below the surface, and everybody knows there's a fish on the line. What could be simpler?

But fishing with a float isn't limited to the bare-foot-boys-with-cheeks-of-tan among us. Veteran anglers know that using a float is a good way to keep bait at whatever lake or pond depth at which fish are taking. Plus, having a visual cue that a fish is interested in your bait certainly helps knowing when to set the hook.

Evidence of the widespread use of floats and other strike indicators is the number of types and shapes of such devices. In addition to the most common red-and-white sphere secured to the line by a spring-operated hook is a bewildering array of shapes, sizes, and weights.

The appropriate size and shape of a float depends on the weight of the bait, water current speed, and wind conditions. For example, a fat round plastic bobber works in still ponds and lakes, but the drag that its creates may present far too much resistance for a fast-moving stream or river. That's where a long thin dart-like float made of ultra-light balsa wood would provide greater sensitivity.

As a general rule, tall and thin floats are more sensitive and offer less wind resistance. However, there is a point of diminishing returns; too sensitive a float when used with live bait will signal underwater activity whenever the minnow on your hook moves. Also, too light a float cannot accommodate a relatively heavy sinker, hook, and bait.

Sometimes, however, you will want to retard the speed of a float in a particularly fast-moving current. In that case, you would want to use a float that is weighted with lead shot.

HEAVY FLOATS also provide needed weight when you're trying to cast light bait a considerable distance, especially if you're using spinning or spin-fishing tackle.

TALL FLOATS, such as quills and barrels, are appropriate for choppy current conditions, riding high enough on the rough surface to be visible.

LONG STEMS also sink below surface drift and stay out of the wind.

Among other types of floats are **DRIFT BOBBERS**, submerged floats, that keep bait off the bottom.

SPINNING BUBBLES are made of clear plastic into which water can be poured to adjust the buoyancy; these are designed for casting. So are **POPPING CORKS**, cigar-shaped wooden or plastic floats that make a splash or plop when cast and thus attract the more curious species of fish.

Floats are attached to lines by three methods. The above-mentioned spring hook is simple to operate, but the spring doesn't always stay always tight enough to keep the line from sliding through. Other floats have an eye through which the line is threaded or a clip through which the line is slid and then slip-knotted.

SLIP FLOATS, with releasable stopper-like fasteners, make life easier in that regard: the fastener is released, the line length readjusted, and then the fastener reapplied.

Some floats attach to a line at both their top and bottom, but the more sensitive styles are fastened only at the bottom.

Floats range from several inches long and many ounces in weight to something as light and sensitive as a porcupine quill (yes, actual porcupine quills are used as floats). There's no hard-and-fast rule about appropriate size and weight for every situation; that's why carrying a selection in your tackle box is essential.

With regard to colors, floats traditionally have highly visible red tops, with brown as a good neutral color for bottom halves. Some floats add a yellow band between the red and brown. Its purpose is to indicate when a fish is biting at the bait from below; the bobber will rise, at which point you should set the hook.

High-tech has hit the float world in the form of battery-operated lighted floats that are especially useful for night fishing. One variety flashes a red light to indicate a strike; another blinks yellow until the float sinks, at which point the light becomes red.

STRIKE INDICATORS

Fly anglers have their own variety of strike indicators that they use for nymph fishing. One type is a small wooden float that threads onto the leader and is kept in place by a toothpick. Another is a small patch of synthetic fabric that sticks onto the line by means of adhesive backing. Becoming increasingly popular is a fluorescent-colored putty-like substance, a pinch of which is applied to the leader.

Or you can always tie a small length of colored yarn to your line, the way folks did in the old days.

Sinkers

Sinkers, or weights, are a staple item in all varieties of fishing where you want to get your bait down to the fish's level. Measured by weight in ounces (or fractions thereof), sinkers come in a variety of shapes. According to tackle authority Gary Soucie, the **BANK SINKER** should be considered the general all-around choice. The hexagonal teardrop shape produces the least amount of air resistance during a cast. It's also the steadiest in the air; other shapes wobble, which throws off attempts at accuracy. That shape also sinks faster and therefore is most able to come close to the spot where the fisherman intends it to go.

Among other popular shapes, the **CLINCHER** has wings at either end; the line passes through a groove along the body of the sinker and the sinker is secured in place when the wings are pinched around the line. Some of this style have rubber grips for better security. The **TORPEDO** is another of the fitted- or fixed-shape sinkers. **SLIP WEIGHTS**, which are bullet-shaped, are an essential part of fishing with Texas- and Carolina-rigged plastic worms. The line is threaded through the hole that runs through the weight, and the worm's head fits snugly against the weight's concave base. Some slip weights have built-in rattles to attract bass and other curious species. **EGG SINKERS** also have holes that run through them.

CASTING SINKERS have swivel ends, while bank sinkers have eyes at one end of their teardrop shape. All these types are designed to slide along the bottom without being caught in weeds or other underwater snagging growth.

As the name implies, **PYRAMID SINKERS** are triangular in shape. They are intended to dig into the lake or ocean bottom and stay in one place.

BB-sized **SPLIT SHOT WEIGHTS** that pinch onto a line are used by both bait and fly-fishing. Fly anglers also use wraparound strips of metal, which are especially useful for getting and keeping a nymph along the bottom of a stream.

The choice of sinker shape is often determined by the bottom of the body of water. Mud, silt, sand, gravel, and other slick bottoms call for sinkers that can grip into the surface; the grapnel shape, for example, is effective under such conditions. On the other hand, uneven bottoms, such as rock piles, need a flat sinker that won't become wedged.

Trolling requires a weighted line to keep the bait or lure down deep and, equally important, to keep it stable. Such specialized trolling weights such as **RUDDERS**, **FOLDING KEELS**, and **CRESCENTS** reduce erratic movement in all planes.

Once upon a time, lead was the universal favorite material for sinkers. It's heavy and it's also cheap, so losing a sinker was no big deal. However, lead has fallen out of favor in some circles. Environmentalists cite numerous cases of wildfowl fatalities caused by ingesting lead shotgun pellets and lead sinkers. A movement to ban the use of

lead sinkers entirely has received the support of many fishing and conservation groups, and some amount of federal legislation is expected over the next few years. Far better, conservationists say, is tin, bronze, and other nontoxic metals and alloys.

An excellent discussion of the relative merits of various kinds of sinkers is found in Gary Soucie's *Hook, Line, and Sinker*.

Spinners

We've encountered spinners as an integral part of spinnerbait lures, but they can also be used on their own. Many fishermen attach a spinner to a simple hook rig as an attractor, either for bottom-fishing or trolling. If you do, remember as you select the blade shape that long thin blades tend to spin faster than short wide ones. Larger blades, which offer more resistance, sink more slowly than small blades, and they also turn more slowly.

Most spinners have built-in swivels. If not, you'll have to attach one yourself.

A single-blade spinner attached to a deer-hair plug.

A double-bladed spinner attached to a wet fly.

Swivels

Swivels, which prevent lines from becoming twisted, are widely used by live-bait fishermen. They are less frequently used with freshwater plugs, however, since a swivel can affect—and even negate—the action of some crankbait. On the other hand, surf-casters regularly use swivels and snaps with their plugs, since swivels are essential for shock leaders.

Swivels are also routinely used in trolling and drift-fishing, since line that is constantly being pulled through the water has a tendency to spiral. **THREE-WAY** and **CROSSLINE SWIVELS** have been designed for such use.

Swivels that include ball bearings, which reduce friction, are more efficient than those that have a sliding friction mechanism. **BEAD CHAIN SWIVELS** have the advantage of several rotating elements, so if one bead link jams, there are others that will still work.

There are two basic ways to attach a swivel. The one that has rings on both ends requires tying the line and/or leader twice (that is, once on each end). The other style of swivel has a ring on the top but a snap on the bottom; the snap facilitates changing leaders or hooks, a useful feature when you're in a rush to get your line back in the water.

Whichever you choose, buy the sturdiest you can find. Brass is the material of choice because of its strength, but just because a swivel is made of brass don't necessarily mean it's well machined. Cheaply made snaps tend to bend or snap when under pressure, and many an angler has regretted being penny-foolish after losing a good-size fish to a cheap swivel.

For the last word on swivels, including a discussion of how torque affects terminal tackle, see page 130 of *Hook, Line, and Sinker* by Gary Soucie.

Snaps

Snaps are a convenient was to change hooks and lures. They come in a variety of styles and sizes. The **LOCK SNAP** is most popular, primarily because its hole in the clasp case secures the ends of the snaps. Another favored style is the strong and lightweight **ONE-PIECE**, or **DUO-LOCK**. A favorite of saltwater anglers is the **COASTLINE**; its loop grows tighter under stress, but doesn't open. Other styles are the **AMPERSAND**, the **BUTTERFLY**, and the **CONNECTING-LINKS**.

Proper size will depend on thickness of line and/or leader and the size and weight of hook or lure. As a rule, use as small a snap as your tackle can accommodate; snaps that are too large tend to distract fish from the bait.

And as for strength and durability, steel is preferable to brass.

Tackle Boxes

The first tackle boxes were metal rectangular containers of the "toolbox" variety with one removable compartment tray. Most were secured by two or more hinged snaps on the front and by a built-in lock opened with a tiny key.

Boxes now comes in many styles, most of which bear slight resemblance to the original:

TRUNK: several tiers of unfolding, stackable trays.

FLAT BOX: side compartments with transparent lids.

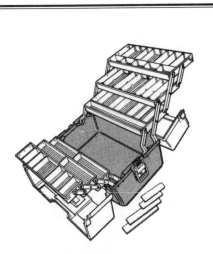

Trunk style. [courtesy Plano]

Drawer-box style. [courtesy Flambeau]

Flat-box style. [courtesy Plano]

Hip-roof style. [courtesy Woodstream]

DRAWER BOX: up to four sliding compartments below a top compartment under the lid. One or more drawers may be designed to accommodate spinnerbaits.

HIP-ROOF: two facing tiers of up to three drawers that unfold away from each other when the box is opened. Additional items can be stored on the box's bottom compartment.

HANGING RACKS: deep boxes in which plugs and spoons hang on removable racks to prevent tangling and permit rapid drying. Most of these boxes have compartments for spare spinnerbait and buzzbait blades and skirts.

TACKLE TOTES: sturdy fabric tote bags with outside compartments and internal pockets and pouches. These spaces accommodate lures,

Hanging-rack style. [courtesy Plano]

scent bottles, reels, rain gear, and other essentials. Some totes have built-in vinyl pockets for storing plastic worms and other soft bait. Otherwise, separate vinyl binders and bags are available.

Metal tackle boxes are now almost impossible to find; rugged, lightweight, and rustproof plastic has become the material of choice. Adjustable dividers make "customizing" shelves and drawers to accommodate individual items an easy matter. Boxes with flip-open tops allow reaching for frequently used items without the need to wade through other gear.

BEFORE YOU BUY

How commodious a tackle box do you need? It depends on the amount of tackle you plan to carry. There are two approaches regarding tackle box sizes. One goes on the theory that "you never need it till you need it"; a box that can hold everything you might possibly need is worth the expense and the effort, since items left at home aren't very useful. The other approach is a variant of Parkinson's Law and states that "stuff expands to fill available space." Professional tournament fishermen carry large tackle boxes because their bait requirements are based on their knowledge of how to cope with very specific conditions. The rest of us don't have that kind of

expertise, so it's far more sensible to carry only those lures, bobbers, etc., that you think you'll need.

The above debate becomes somewhat academic if you always fish from a boat that has lots of storage compartment space. However, if you're sharing a small boat with another angler or more, common courtesy dictates that you don't hog the storage space. The solution may be to own more than one tackle box of different sizes and use them according to particular situations and conditions.

Soft plastic worms, grubs, and similar bait are made of materials that can eat through certain plastics. If a tackle box isn't designated as "plastic worm-proof," you'll have to store such items in smaller boxes or bags inside the tackle box.

Smaller bags and boxes are also of great help in organizing a tackle box's contents. Hooks, jig heads, sinkers, small bobbers. . . all can live in plastic containers. Some boxes have adjustable compartments.

Sturdy handles and latches are tackle box essentials. Imagine the feeling of seeing your box fly open and its contents spill all over the ground or, worse yet, into the water. Some fishermen take the additional precaution of snapping an elastic cord or cable around the box's girth just to make sure such accidents won't happen.

Manufacturers

Flambeau Products Corporation
15981 Valplast Rd.
P.O. Box 97
Middlefield, OH 44062
(800) 457-5252
fax: (216) 632-1581

Plano Molding Co.
431 S. South St.
Plano, IL 60545-1601

(708) 552-3111
fax: (708) 552-9737

Rubbermaid Inc.,
   Specialty Products
1147 Akron Rd.
Wooster, OH 44691
(216) 264-6464
fax: (216) 287-2052

Soft Pak USA
N. Hwy. 65
P.O. Box 98
Branson, MO 65616
(800) 366-4751
fax: (417) 334-5220

Woodstream Corp.
Elko Group Inc.
P.O. Box 327
Lititz, PA 17543
(800) 800-1819
(717) 626-1912

7

HOOKS

Found among the artifacts of northern European cultures, the oldest fish hooks were fashioned from acutely-angled twigs or, for greater durability, harder wood, the bones of animals, and the beaks and claws of birds. Whatever material these early hook-makers selected, they honed the end into a sharp point, often with a barb to prevent the fish from disgorging the hook (although some hooks were designed to ride perpendicular to the line and thus catch in a fish's throat). Some hooks had holes through which a line could be threaded and tied, while other required knotting the line around the hook's shank, similar to the way hooks are now snelled. As civilization's "ages of metal" developed, hooks were made of bronze and then iron.

The modern era of hook-making started in seventeenth-century England, where manufacturers of sewing needles diversified into producing steel hooks. The Great Fire that leveled much of London in 1664 dispersed many of that city's industries; needle-making was one, and its practitioners relocated to the Worcestershire town of Redditch. Until the beginning of the nineteenth century, virtually all hooks came from that town, of which the venerable firm of Partridge of Redditch remains a notable inhabitant (as they have been since the firm's beginning, all Partridge hooks are handmade).

As sport-fishing grew in popularity, other companies in other countries met the demand.

O. Mustad, of Oslo, Norway, now the world's largest manufacturer, opened its doors in 1832, and the French firm of Veillard Migeon et Cie (abbreviated to VMC) started in 1910. Some 20 years later, the Denver-based Wright & McGill turned out its first Eagle Claw hooks. Among other well-known manufacturers are Umpqua and the Japanese firms Daiichi and Tiemco (the latter abbreviated to TMC).

Manufacture

Almost all fish hooks are composed of 80% or more carbon steel. The machine-made manufacturing process begins with malleable steel wire cut into pieces that are twice as long as the length of metal needed to make the hook. Both ends of the piece are sharpened by either mechanical or chemical means into points. The piece is cut in half, which results in two hooks. A barb is formed on the sharpened end and an eye on the other end, and then the wire is twisted into the desired hook shape.

The steel is cold-forged tempered for strength and durability. After this hardening process, the hooks are scoured to remove the oxide scale coating. One process, called chemical deburring or bright dipping, removes the outer layer of steel and so eliminates burrs and other rough spots for a smoother, sharper hook. A layer of lacquer or another finish comes next; bronze or a blue-black color known as "japanned" are common. The process ends with a visual inspection and packaging.

Hook Sizes

A hook's size is based on its **GAP**, or the distance from the point to the shank measured perpendicular to the shank. However, anyone expecting to find a universal sizing system that corresponds to such absolute measurements as inches or millimeters will be sadly disappointed. The widely-used Redditch System and others are only relative within themselves, and even within a particular system, hooks designated as the same size will vary according to their different shape. As with most other things, familiarity with the products of particular manufacturers, as well as with hooks in general, will lead to a better understanding of this seemingly complicated subject.

As the size-number of a hook increases, its actual size grows smaller, so that a 20 hook is smaller than a 10 hook. Not precisely half as small, but simply smaller, just as it is larger than, for example, a 24. Fly hooks are measured by even numbers (28 is the smallest), whereas hooks used for other types of fishing are numbered consecutively.

There are hooks larger than 1s, and they are designated by a number followed by a slash and a "0" (pronounced "aught"). These hooks grow in size as do their numbers, so a 4/0 is larger than a 3/0. . . here you will note that numbers above 1/0 run consecutively.

Hook Weight

Wire diameter or weight is expressed by a scale based on the letter "X" and the words "Fine" and "Stout," the latter describing the hook wire's relative thickness. The scale ranges from 1X to 3X. Fine wire, such as that used for dry flies, is easier to set in a fish's mouth, as well as better for keeping live bait alive. Stout hooks tend to be sturdier.

Eye Shape and Position

EYE SHAPE

The most common shape is the **BALL EYE**, a simple round circle. A **TAPERED EYE**, which grows narrow at its end, somewhat reduces the weight of a hook. Both the ball eye and the tapered eye often have gaps between the end of the eye and the shank, which some anglers feel increases the chance of fraying the line or leader.

To prevent this possibility, a **LOOPED EYE** is formed by the hook's wire bent into an eye and then doubling back along the shank; hooks for salmon and steelhead flies customarily are made this way.

A **NEEDLE EYE**, an elongated hole like the ones on sewing needles, makes it easy to push bait to cover the entire hook or beyond.

A **FLATTENED EYE** may have a small hole or even none at all. If there is no hole, the line or a leader will be attached by means of a snell knot, which many people feel is less likely to fray and eventually break. Some hooks come with pre-attached leaders; a line of Wright & McGill "Eagle Claw" hooks is a classic example.

Finally, a **BRAZED EYE** is one that is coated with brass for additional strength.

A snelled hook. [courtesy Eagle Claw]

Because the size of an eye is proportional to the size of the hook, threading line or leaders onto smaller hooks becomes a difficult chore for people with poor eyesight. However, Orvis has come to the rescue with its line of "Big Eye" hooks for sizes 16 and smaller.

POSITION

There are three positions of an eye relative to the shank: RINGED, or parallel to the shank; TURNED-UP, and TURNED-DOWN.

The turned-up eye, which is used for traditional British trout, as well as salmon and steelhead flies, permits a relatively quick, rake-like penetration when a fish strikes.

On the other hand, a turned-down eye puts the hook closer to the line of penetration and is, accordingly, more widely used, although some anglers feel that the turned-down eye of hooks size 22 or smaller interfere with the tiny gaps.

Shank Types and Length

The STRAIGHT SHANK runs in a direct line from the eye to beginning of bend.

The HUMPED SHANK has one or more humps that prevent a lure body from rotating.

Similarly, a BARBED SHANK has serrated projections that hold baits such as plastic worms more securely on the hook.

A STEP SHANK, or KEEL HOOK, is weighted so the hook rides upright to help avoid snagging on weeds.

Like the turned-down eye, a CURVED-DOWN SHANK is designed to bring the line of pull closer to the penetration point, while a

CURVED-UP SHANK allows a faster, though shallower, penetration. Within these two categories are curves of a variety of angles, as the illustrations show.

If there is no other specific designation, a shank is considered standard length. Otherwise, there will be an "X" preceded by a number and followed by the words "Long" or "Short" (some types have names, such as the Carlisle, a long-shanked variety). That translates as follows: a "1X Long" has the shank length of the next larger hook size (a 12 would have the shank length of a 10), but would still have the gap width of a 12. By the same token, a 12 in "2X Long" would have the length of an 8, while a 12 in "2X Short" is as long as a 16.

The Carlisle. [courtesy Mustad]

8X Long is the longest size commonly available, and 5X Short the smallest.

The Bend

The ROUND BEND, considered the "classic" shape, is a simple semi-circle that extends from the end of the shank to the point.

The SPROAT has a more elongated but uniformly rounded curve, while the LIMERICK and the O'SHAUGHNESSY have the sharpest angles of the bend directly behind their points.

The ABERDEEN has a round bend and a wide gap.

The Aberdeen. [courtesy Mustad]

The O'Shaughnessy. [courtesy Mustad]

The Sproat. [courtesy Mustad]

Points Types and Positions

Although the **SPEAR POINT**, the most common, varies in precise shape from manufacturer to manufacturer, its point and barb resemble the flat edge of a spear head.

The **NEEDLE POINT** is ground on all sides for maximum "bite."

Despite its name, the **HOLLOW POINT** is solid, but is tapered into slightly concave sides for rapid penetration.

The **KNIFE-EDGE POINT** has a flat and wide surface, especially useful for big-game fishing.

The **BARBLESS POINT** has become particularly popular among catch-and-release anglers, who claim that the lack of a barb enhances penetration, despite the chance that a fish may be able to shake the hook more easily if it has no barb.

There are four point positions relative to the rest of the hook. The **STRAIGHT POINT** runs parallel to the shank. The **ROLL POINT** has only the point bent up toward the shank. In the **BENT-IN POINT**, a greater portion of the end of the hook loops out and then bends in, making disgorging the hook more difficult. Conversely, the **KIRBY** (named after a noted hook-maker and contemporary of Izaak Walton) or **BENT-OUT POINT**

exposes the tip of the hook for faster penetration.

Although offset hooks may make deeper strikes in most species, they are more difficult to set in hard-mouthed fish and are more likely to bend when a big fish puts up a big fight. They also rotate while being trolled. Similarly, sharp angles in a hook's bend tend to weaken the hook, while perfectly round bends tend to open under stress.

An offset worm hook. [courtesy Heddon/PRADCO]

Others

WEEDLESS HOOKS contain thin strands of metal or rugged filament that run from or just behind the eye to above the point; when they work, and that don't always, the strand keeps the hook from becoming entangled.

BAIT-HOLDING HOOKS are designed to hold live or artificial bait such as plastic worms. Some models have small projections that extend below the eye and provide an extra "finger" to grip the bait. Others have barbed shanks that do the same job, or spiral wiring along the shank that works well with dough balls and other soft bait.

DOUBLE or **TREBLE HOOKS** are clusters most often found on baitcasting lures and spoons. Although some people feel that multiple hooks just as easily snag a fish as hook one (and are therefore somehow less sporting), as Gary Soucie points out, they're widely used on plugs because they catch fish. That's also why they're routinely used by saltwater and ice-fishermen. You should be aware, however, that doubles and trebles more easily catch weeds and other underwater obstructions, and they're harder to remove from a fish if your goal is catch-and-release.

Salmon. [courtesy Mustad]

Diametrically opposed to treble hooks is the **PARTRIDGE TAG** (for "Touch And Go") hook. Instead of a point it has a second eye, so that no fish is ever hooked. Just having a fish attracted to the bait—usually a fly—is satisfaction enough for the hook's users.

Giant tuna. [courtesy Mustad]

Shark hook. [courtesy Mustad]

To Barb or Not to Barb

Some fishermen routinely remove the barbs from the hooks they use, while others buy only barbless hooks in the first place. Their reasoning: in addition to feeling that barbless hooks penetrate more easily, they contend that barbs tear larger holes in a fish's mouth than necessary. Fishermen who practice catch-and-release want to do as little as possible to jeopardize a fish's chance of returning safe and sound to the water. Losing an occasional fish that spits out or slips off a barbless hook,

such people would argue, matters less than the fish's ultimate welfare.

On the other hand, there are those anglers who say a barbless hook is likely to slip out of the mouth of a fighting fish, only to be engaged again before the fish can completely eject the hook. A prolonged struggle can therefore result in several punctures, a recurrence that can be avoided by using a barbed hook that catches and holds only once. Moreover, expert anglers know how to remove a barb without causing damage by tearing away flesh.

The answer: If you plan to release a fish and don't think you're sufficiently skillful in removing barbed hooks, better fish barbless. Otherwise, the choice is yours.

Hook Care

How sharp should a hook be? A good indication of a sharp hook is one that will dig into the flesh of your finger or hand as you lightly drag it across. Another less hazardous test is to run its point across your thumbnail. Use as little pressure as possible, and if the point makes a scratch in your nail, the hook is sharp enough. If not, and even new hooks sometimes lose their razor-sharp edge during packaging and shipping, use a file to touch up the point. Carborundum files specifically designed for the purpose are available at tackle shops and through catalogs. Alternatives include carborundum or steel fingernail files, automobile ignition-point files, and even, for tiny hooks, the abrasive striking surface of a new matchbook cover.

Hooks used in saltwater fishing, particularly for species that have tough gristly mouths, need to be especially well honed. Fisherfolk after these species routinely sharpen their hooks, usually into a single triangle or a double-triangle "diamond" point.

Electric hook sharpeners facilitate this process, and the devices are growing popular among freshwater bait anglers. Those people who use one need to be aware that heat from an overheated motor can weaken a hook's tempered strength.

Storing hooks can be as uncomplicated as keeping them in their original packaging, especially if they came in plastic boxes. Otherwise, they can be jabbed into in a piece of cork or kept in special holders, although some people prefer airtight containers that retard rusting. Spring-tension racks for snelled hooks keep the leaders from becoming tangled, while form-fitting plastic covers prevent double and treble hooks on plugs and spoons from snagging other pieces of tackle.

Wherever you keep your hooks, don't forget before putting them away to rinse those that have been in salt water with freshwater, then dry thoroughly.

Hook Safety

No matter how careful you think you are, at some point in your fishing career you're going to be hooked. One day you may reach into your tackle box and yank out your hand, the victim of a bare hook ambush. Or you'll lose your grip as you're attaching a fly to your line, and its hook will become embedded in a finger. A fishing buddy may catch you in his back cast, or a sudden breeze can toss your cast back into your face.

Moral: fish hooks can be dangerous, so always treat them accordingly. That's also a reason why fishermen wear caps and sunglasses, which do more than keep off rays and glare. They protect against hooks, so please dress accordingly.

And should worst come to worst, this book's chapter on medical care includes instructions on hook removal and follow-up first aid treatment (see pages 240–241).

Manufacturers and Distributors of Hooks

Daiichi/Angler Sport Group
6619 Oak Orchard Road
Elba, New York 14058
(716) 757-9958
fax: (716) 757-9066

Excaliber
Heddon/PRADCO
P.O. Box 1587
Fort Smith, AR 72902
(800) 422-FISH

Gamakatsu U.S.A. Inc.
P.O. Box 1794
Tacoma, WA 98424
(206) 922-8373

fax: (206) 922-8447

O. Mustad & Son [USA] Inc.
P.O. Box 838
Auburn, New York 13021
(315) 253-2793

Owner American Corporation
17965 Von Karman, Suite 111
Irvine, CA 92714
(714) 261-7922
fax: (714) 261-9399

Partridge of Redditch Ltd.
Redditch, Worcestershire B97 4JE
England

011-44-527-543555 or 550575
fax: 011-44-527-546956

Tiemco
Umpqua Feather Merchants
P.O. Box 700
Glide, OR 97443
(800) 322-3218

Tru-Turn
P.O. Box 767
Wetumpka, AL 36092
(800) 421-5768
fax: (205) 567-9788

Wright & McGill Co. (Eagle Claw)
P.O. Box 16011
Denver, CO 80216
(303) 321-1481

8

BAIT

Perhaps the easiest way to understand the elements of what makes a bait effective is in terms of the applicable sense or senses of a fish. That is, what exactly stimulates the creature to go for a particular lure, fly, or live bait?

SIGHT

Motion attracts fish, or at least attracts their attention to the object that is in motion. Plastic worm tails wiggle, jig skirts do a "hula"-like shake, animal or synthetic hair undulate, and jointed plugs sway from side to side. In all cases, it's their movement that draws a fish's notice.

Whether fish see color as humans do is a matter of some conjecture, but it's beyond argument that color is another visual cue. Some species more susceptible to particular colors than other species are. For example, largemouth bass seem to prefer such dark colors as black, gray, and purple. One color that seems to attract most species is red, and the best guess is simply because it's the color of blood.

SOUND

Fish "hear" in the sense that they pick up vibrations through their lateral line sensory system. Some aggressive species, like bass, are attracted by sound, which is thought to stimulate their belligerent nature. The erratic sound pattern of a lure that's retrieved in a stop-and-go action replicates the noise made by a wounded or otherwise distressed baitfish, and that's music to the ears of many species.

However, some species (trout, for one) react negatively to sound, equating unfamiliar noises with the presence of predators. That's why anglers who do not approach trout waters in a stealthy manner or whose casts smack against the water soon discover that they have frightened fish away.

SMELL

Certain odors attract fish, and an angler who uses live or scented baits is taking advantage of that appeal. Science has made some bait scents particularly sophisticated, such as the ones that duplicate the hormonal secretions triggered by fear (thus giving the bait the aroma of a fish under attack) or that duplicate sex attractors.

On the other hand, many scents repel fish. Motor oil, some sunscreens, and even unadorned human odor fit into that category. That's why cleaning your hands with special preparations that neutralize eliminate or neutralize the scents is a good idea.

TOUCH/FEEL

Fish are sensitive to vibrations, and they will pick up the "shock waves" that emanate from a vibrating bait (the "wounded prey" syndrome again). Also appealing to the sense of feel, plastic worms feel lifelike to an inquisitive fish.

TASTE

Those species of fish that have barbels, such as the catfish, are able to "taste" a prospective meal with their feelers, so they needn't ingest the food to tell whether it's acceptable. Otherwise, a fish will spit out anything that fails to appeal to its sense of taste.

Most baits appeal to more than one of a fish's senses, especially when fished in a particular way. For example, a colored plastic worm bumped along a lake bottom in a stop-and-go manner appeals to sight and sound.

A thoughtful and useful analysis of the elements of a lure's effectiveness can be found in *Hook, Line, and Sinker* by Gary Soucie (Henry Holt); the serious fisherman would do well to study Mr. Soucie's conclusions in some detail. In order of importance, the author lists seven factors: (1) running depth, or ability to stay at the level at which fish are; (2) speed, or the velocity at which the lure is intended to be moved; (3) action, or a lure's behavior; (4) appropriate size, since fish tend to seek the largest food it can eat with the least effort; (5) visual contrast; (6) color; and (7) pattern and finish detail, such as bead eyes or patches of red paint behind the lure's "head" to replicate gills.

Even the briefest glance through a tack shop catalog reveals a staggering number of plugs, spoons, jigs, and other kinds of lures. Why so many? one might ask.

A former tackle company executive had an answer. In a sense, lures are like pet food and baby food: the ultimate consumers (whether fish, dogs and cats, or babies) don't make the decision about what to buy. We fishermen do, and lure companies, who are after all in the business of selling lures, invest lots of time, effort, and money in creating choices for us, all in the name of what we're led to believe a fish will want. The more new lures and variations on older ones adorn tackle shop shelves, the more likely that we as fishermen will buy.

But what makes us buy a specific lure? Word-of-mouth is one way. Someone wins a club tournament or just catches a big fish on something—say, a lightweight floating jerkbait that he just happened to buy—and the next thing the local tackle shop owner knows, he's sold out of that lure. Someone else catches a big fish on that lure, and everyone becomes convinced that it's the only lure you'll ever need. . . until it doesn't work, and you try something else.

A step above local word-of-mouth is the well-established marketing technique of celebrity endorsement. Nothing succeeds like success, and a professional need only mention that he caught the lunker that tipped the scales to win a big tournament on a particular plug. Then watch how sales of that lure take off like a turbo-powered bass boat, especially if the professional "shares his secret" via a magazine advertisement or TV commercial.

There are fashions in fishing tackle as in most other lines of products, which such endorsements often create through a kind of ripple effect. If, for example, lightweight topwater stickbait plugs figure in one or two tournament victories, not only the makers of those particular plugs but many other plug manufacturers will beat the drum for the "hottest lure on the lake." Or at least until the next "hot" plug comes along.

But there's more to selling lures than advertising "smoke and sizzle." There's what a *Wall Street Journal* article (October 5, 1994) termed "technically sophisticated consumer-preference surveys—on fish." As part of the age-old quest to discover the reasons why a fish choose one bait over another, a biologist and a chemist at Berkley (the tackle manufacturer, not the California university) have been conducting what is essentially consumer research. A monorail that circles a 6-foot-deep indoor pool stocked with sport fish tows a variety of lures, with an underwater video camera to record the fish's reaction. Data is analyzed and conclusions drawn, and the results appear on the market as Berkley products.

When asked about the elements of an "all-purpose" bait, a number of veteran fishermen were quick to point out that perhaps the single most important thing to remember is that bait that suggests a wounded or otherwise helpless prey stimulates a fish's predator instinct.* Just as the weakest land animals are the easiest to catch and, therefore, are the first choice of carnivorous predators, fish baits that replicate the movements of a wounded baitfish are especially appealing to predator fish. And when that action is combined with the color red, which seems to awaken a fish's blood-lust, we can begin to understand why the red-and-white striped metal spoon (which originated as the Dardevle™) is widely considered the most universally effective artificial lure ever made.

That's not to say, however, that a red-and-white striped metal spoon works all the time. If it did, there would be no need for the thousands of plugs, spoons, jigs, flies, and other types of bait that the mind of man has concocted over the years. The best bait is that which catches fish at any given time, and what works can change from minute to minute (if indeed anything at all happens to work at any given time). As one angler ruminated, "What's best?—you'd have to ask a fish, and fish tend to be close-mouthed on the subject."

*This doesn't apply to dry flies or nymphs, which are intended to resemble insects, not baitfish. Some species of fish, most notably trout, are attracted to specific insects through a complex triggering reaction that makes fish choose a specific "hatch," to the exclusion of all other food choices.

Joe Hughes is publicist for PRADCO (Plastics Research and Development Corporation), the world's largest manufacturers of artificial lures. He's also the writer/narrator of The Nine Characteristics of Crankbaits, *an audiotape that's available from PRADCO. Few commentators are better qualified to discuss the practical application of lure research and design on fishing techniques (and vice versa).*

The Artificial Lure Manufacturing Process: From Conception to Final Product

BY JOE HUGHES

Walking down the aisles of one of the many "Outdoor Expos," held annually in cities throughout the U.S., one can be overcome by the literally hundreds of artificial lures yearning for attention by the fishing public. At fishing seminars, usually conducted by fishing professionals or experts in the field, some of the most-asked questions are, "How do I make sense out of what's available? How can I make good decisions about what to purchase?"

For the weekend or novice angler, there are a couple of avenues that may yield the right answers.

First, there's always trial and error, but that can be expensive and sometimes disappointing. One could also take the advice of the local experts and limit choices to the proven artificial lures that have a reputation for being productive on a specific, favorite body of water.

However, anglers, by nature, are always looking for an edge—that old or new lure which, for whatever reason, seems to be the key for a specific type of angling. It is this attitude that is one of the driving forces of a remarkably diverse and extremely competitive segment of the fishing industry. . . lure design and manufacturing.

And, for the angler who would like to make the best choices of the lure products available, knowing how manufacturers approach the design of individual lures will aid in the selection process.

ASKING THE QUESTION: SOLVING THE PROBLEM

In 1896, while sitting on the banks of the "Old Mill Pond" in Michigan, James Heddon quietly passed the time whittling away at a stick he'd found on the ground. After shaving all the bark and tapering both ends of the 6-inch stick, Heddon simply tossed his creation into the nearby water. What happened next changed the face of fishing for all time.

That whittled stick, bobbing lightly on the surface, suddenly disappeared within a vicious swirl. Moments later, the stick returned to the surface, only to be smashed again by a fish mistaking the stick for an easy meal.

Heddon, an avid angler, recognized immediately that something special had occurred. A predator, in this case a largemouth bass, had mistaken his whittled stick for a baitfish.

In Heddon's case, the answer came before the question. Yes, sport fish would hit an artificial lure. And from that brief and unexpected encounter on the Old Mill Pond, James Heddon created one of the most prestigious and successful artificial lure manufacturers of all time.

Granted, the first manufactured lures from the Heddon plant were not sophisticated in design, especially by today's standards. However, based upon the large quantities of various sport fish available during that period, any baitfish imitation with a balanced action and decent coloration seemed to produce.

As more and more individuals fell prey to the lure of catching sport fish with artificials, additional lure manufacturers appeared. This new and growing competition created a spiraling sophistication in the design of artificial lures that has evolved into a high-tech industry of specialization.

This space-age competition is dramatically illustrated by an abundance of specific lures that have been designed to solve specific fishing problems. There are suspending minnow lures that have their largest following during the cool and cold waters of spring. Crankbaits or diving plugs have been created that will dive to depths of 15 feet and more on a normal cast-and-retrieve. Weedless lures have been designed for specific types of moss, specifically hydrilla. Surface lures have been designed and modified to create a specific sound when retrieved. Lure patterns and colors have been created for waters of a particular color: muddy, stained, or clear. And, artificial lure sizes now range from the creatively small "critter" ultra-lights to huge minnow plugs that approach a foot in length. . . each size category specifically targeted to various species of game fish.

In each case, a fishing problem was first defined and then, through the creativity of a relatively small group of designers, the problem was solved. The resulting lure, created with all the sophistication that the current manufacturing processes allow, tried to make a certain type of fishing more effective, more enjoyable. The consumer would be the ultimate judge of the success of the designer/manufacturer to solve the problem.

THE NINE CHARACTERISTICS OF LURE PROBLEM SOLVING

When it comes to solving a fishing problem with an artificial lure, there are six primary and three secondary characteristics that must be addressed. By understanding these characteristics and how each specific lure exhibits different levels of performance within each characteristic' category, one may quickly become an expert with that lure.

The following characteristics are the building blocks of every surface lure, diving crankbait or minnow plug: (1) depth, (2) speed, (3) action, (4) sound, (5) size, (6) buoyancy, (7) color, (8) shape, and (9) scent.

Crankbaits.

DEPTH: THE ULTIMATE CHARACTERISTIC

Regardless of the species of fish being sought, depth of lure presentation is the ultimate key to success. It is therefore understandable that from a design standpoint, depth of operation is the first consideration when creating a new crankbait or minnow plug. (For this discussion we will consider only those lures that float at rest and dive when they are retrieved.)

Generally speaking, the size of the lure's diving lip determines the depth at which it will run. Small-lipped minnow lures generally work from 1 foot to 3 feet. Larger crankbaits with large diving lips may attain depths of 15 feet or more. And, the larger the diving plane that is required for additional depth, the larger the lure's body must be to allow for overall balance of the product.

The key for anglers is to learn the depth range that was designed into the lure and then explore the ways to adjust this depth range to fit the situation at hand. Most manufacturers print a suggested depth range on the back of the lure package. These ranges offer a good place to begin your depth expectations.

To personalize the printed depth range, consider the following presentation modifications. (Unless otherwise stated, all depth suggestions are based upon a retrieve that has the rod tip pointed down at its steepest angle and without the tip penetrating the surface.)

A longer cast allows the lure more distance with which to attain the maximum depth. Therefore longer rods, which allow longer casts, will deliver additional depth. Lighter lines and the new smaller-diameter lines, such as Super Silver Thread, create two positive depth scenarios.

First, lures cast for greater distance on lighter lines, and this extra distance yields greater depth.

Second, lighter/smaller lines create less resistance in the water during the retrieve. This reduced resistance, especially with lures that have the line tie on the diving lip of the lure (as opposed to the nose of the lure) adds depth to the retrieve.

Conversely, heavier lines with larger diameters retard lure depth to varying degrees.

By raising one's rod tip to a 12 o'clock position during the retrieve, one may severely retard the depth a lure may attain.

SPEED: A COMPONENT OF DEPTH AND STABILITY

The speed at which a lure will exhibit its designed action and still maintain a true-running stability in the water is a critical design characteristic.

During the late 1970s, when buzzbaits became a popular bass lure, reel manufacturers rushed to develop and market high-speed gears within their product lines. If one compares the average retrieve (turn of the handle) of a 4.3:1 gear ratio to a 5.3:1 gear ratio, one will find that the faster gears retrieve a lure almost twice as fast as the slower gears.

Without knowing it, the reel-makers created a serious problem for all crankbait manufacturers. When reels with faster gear ratios moved lures much more rapidly through the water, design flaws were exposed and problems in running stability were created where no problems existed before.

To solve this problem, a serious evolution in lure design and assembly evolved. First, sonic welding began to replace gluing as the method by which plastic lure halves were joined together. The chemical bonding of the halves tended to create a slight imbalance in the lure, and that imbalance was exploited by the greater retrieve speeds in the new reels.

Screw-in-type line ties, the point at which the lure is attached to one's line, became obsolete. In their place, force-driven line ties were created. This new system allowed more perfect alignment of each and every lure's line tie.

One of the more recent evolutions in the lure manufacturing process has been the adaptation by certain companies (Rebel, Heddon, Bomber, Cordell, and Riverside) to the CAD–CAM system. This "Computer Assisted Design–Computer Assisted Machining" system is state-of-the-art equipment that allows for accelerated speed and rigid accuracy in both the design and manufacture of hard- and soft-plastic artificial lures.

All of these new design innovations were, in part, the result of the effects of speed on crankbaits. The process to minimize the negative effects of speed on lures is continuing. However, it may be said that the lures of the nineties are dramatically more stable, over a wider range of speeds, than lures of previous decades.

From an angling standpoint, there are a couple of critical aspects that must be considered in reference to lure speed. Both are related to the depth a lure may attain.

First, just as heavier lines create a resistance in water that retards lure depth, so does the speed of retrieve. Faster retrieves tend to limit the ability of a lure to dive. The added resistance on the line, caused by speed, can remove up to 2 feet from the designed maximum depth of the lure. In a game of inches, 2 feet may keep one well above the structure that needs to be ticked or bumped to create the maximum number of strikes.

Additionally, from a visual perspective, one may determine the best speed to work a diving plug for maximum depth. Simply retrieve the lure on a short cast and notice the point at which the lure begins to exhibit a good, strong, and steady action. When you see and feel the lure begin to wobble, this is the speed, with the rod tip down, that will allow the lure to attain its maximum designed depth.

Remember, the reel has a marked effect on lure depth. Know the gear ratio of your equipment and resist the comfortable turning of the handle. Rather, adjust the turn of your reel handle to the speed necessary to accomplish the depth you deem necessary.

ACTION: MORE THAN A WOBBLE

As a lure designer begins his thought on a new problem-solving lure, the action that will be built into the lure is of critical concern. Should the lure exhibit a thin minnow-style wiggle or a larger, harder, pulsating wobble?

More and more, these action characteristics are tailored to the specific fishing conditions the lure will face. For shad or baitfish imitations that are designed for cool and cold clear-water use, the thin tight-wiggle action is most accepted. For warmer water presentations—especially in stained and muddy water—larger, wider wobbles that displace much more water are more desirable.

The desired action is strictly a function of lure design. Body style, diving-lip design, and placement, along with hook arrangement and internal weighting, affect the lure's ultimate action. It is a critical process that illustrates the value of a seasoned and creative lure designer.

From a fishing standpoint, after one has selected the proper "built-in" action for the waters to be fished, one may also expand on the action characteristics of each lure. Jerking or twitching minnow-style plugs creates an erratic action that stimulates strikes. Hitting structure with a crankbait creates what is called the ricochet effect. Upon contact the lure moves erratically, right or left off the structure. After the ricochet, a simple "stop" in action can be a major key to drawing strikes.

By not only utilizing the built-in action of the lure, but also creating erratic actions on your own, you can almost be guaranteed of additional success.

Sound: What the Fish "Hears"

Make no mistake, all crankbaits, minnow plugs, and surface lures create what we perceive as sound. Even crankbaits without rattles, thought to be silent, develop a rhythmic rattling through the action of their hooks. A 4-inch balsa minnow will create almost as much noise as does a 2-inch, rattle-equipped fat plug.

We should then understand that sound is a product of action. A lure sitting dead still in the water will create no sound as we know it. As action is applied, water is displaced, creating percussion waves within the water. These pressure waves may be read or felt by the lateral lines of fish. Internal rattles and hook noise, as a product of action, compliment the displacement frequencies created by the lure's body.

Sub-surface sound, for the purpose of a simple explanation, may be classified as a product of frequency and amplitude. All lures create a frequency of sound that may be "heard" by fish. Amplitude is the level or volume of that frequency.

It was in the sixties that Rebel Lures completed a rather significant bit of research into "frequency" as it related to the products they were manufacturing. Basically, their research pointed out that the top-selling casting plugs of the past had one major similarity: Most exhibited a "frequency," under water, that fell within a relatively narrow range. If we assume that these lures, none of which were Rebels, sold extremely well because they caught fish, then we must seriously consider the "right" sound as a major design component of all lures.

Remember, to our ears some lures may sound dramatically louder than others. However, the frequencies of these different-sounding lures may be closely related. When one hits the "A" key on a piano, it is still an "A" whether one hits the key lightly or bangs on it.

From the angler's point of view, the softer amplitudes within the desired frequency ranges tend to be more productive in clearer waters, while the louder amplitudes are more acceptable in stained or muddy water.

It may be suggested that the matching of the right "action" of a lure with the right "amplitude" of sound (frequency) in relation to the type of water one is fishing may dramatically affect the fish-catching results.

Size: The Eliminator

Size, as a function of lure design, is directly related to the types of fish the designer wants to target. However, from the point of view of an angler's choice, size has a wide range of application.

Most of us have heard the old adage, "Use a

big bait to catch a big fish." One can't really challenge that statement because large lures tend to eliminate all but the large sport fish. At the same time, smaller lures, especially the ultra-light "critter" lures, don't eliminate anything. From the smallest perch and bream to legal muskies, these small, ⅛-ounce to ¹⁄₁₂-ounce lures catch everything that swims. Their only drawbacks, in reference to larger sport fish, is that line in the 2- to 6-pound-test range is necessary for casting. Also, these lighter lures have a restricted depth range that usually prevents them from attaining depths that are necessary to consistently entice larger game fish in major rivers, lakes, and reservoirs. Within the confines of a small stream, pond, or lake, these ultra-light lures offer the ultimate in fishing success.

The key is to select a lure size and appropriate equipment to target the activity you desire. If you want to fish for everything within a body of water, scale down. If, however, larger species are your target, choose a lure size that approximates the size of the most abundant forage in the waters you are fishing.

It is interesting to note that as a function of size, most major lure manufacturers offer a wide range of body sizes and depth possibilities within each lure family. The Rebel Crawfish family is a good example. Currently, Rebel offers the crawfish in both shallow- and deep-running models that range in size from 1½ inches to 3 inches long. Bomber's Model "A" family exhibits five shallow and deep runners that range in size from 2 inches to 5 inches long. The largest of these, the 9A, is a deep-diving lure that may be cast and cranked to depths in excess of 12 feet.

Within each family of lures the action and sound characteristics are relatively uniform. This allows the angler to move up or down in size and change the depth of presentation without compromising the other characteristics that are important within the type of water being fished.

BUOYANCY: A CHARACTERISTIC COMING-OF-AGE

Of all the primary lure characteristics designed into a fishing lure, buoyancy has, until recently, been relatively ignored by the angler. However, as professional bass anglers began to modify certain minnow plugs—specifically the 5½-inch Smithwick Rogue—so that the lure would "suspend" when a retrieve was stopped, a new and extremely productive fishing technique evolved.

This suspending quality allowed professional anglers to make long casts and work a minnow-shaped plug very slowly around submerged brush and vegetation. This technique is especially productive in the cool and cold waters of early spring and summer. By making a retrieve last for minutes, anglers offered sport fish (in this case, largemouth and smallmouth bass) an opportunity to capture these slow-moving, sometimes stationary lures.

There are two possible reasons for the productivity of this technique. First, fish are cold-blooded, and during cooler water periods they don't tend to chase fast-moving lures. Second, by suspending a lure and then twitching it much like a topwater offering, the angler creates the impression of a severely injured baitfish that is unable to escape. This sends a message of an easy meal that opportunistic predators sometimes can't resist.

As the professionals' modifications began to win major tournaments, manufacturers responded with factory-created suspending lures of their own. Among the most prominent are the Suspending Smithwick Rogue and the Suspending Bomber Long "A." It should be noted that although these suspending models exhibit a wiggling action, their actions seem retarded when they are compared to their more buoyant cousins. This is a function of the internal weights necessary to suspend the lure.

By illustrating this point, additional light is focused on the critical balance necessary within each lure to attain the right depth at the right speed with the right action and sound.

Be aware, also, that other buoyancy characteristics, such as the ability to sink or rise rapidly, are functions of lure design; the knowledge of what your lure's buoyancy characteristics are is important to presenting the lure properly. The more you know your lure, the more productive you will make it be.

COLOR, SHAPE, AND SCENT: VERY IMPORTANT
SECONDARY CHARACTERISTICS

Color as a function of lure design is, more often than not, dictated by the desires of the consumer. In turn, consumer desire is dictated by the productivity of certain patterns in the water being fished. As a standard rule, one may expect lures to be offered in varying patterns that represent baitfish or crawfish, which are the two most-utilized forage available.

Remember, each sport fish makes the final decision of whether to accept or reject a target based upon what it sees. Visibility, then, is a key to understanding why the brighter, fluorescent patterns seem to produce better in stained and muddy waters, while chrome and gold with background colors of black, blue, or purple tend to produce better in clear-water environments.

The eyes of a sport fish have evolved over millions of years, and tests have determined most fish see color in some way that allow them to tell the difference and make a choice. Products, specifically the Color-C-Lector, created by Dr. Loren Hill, correlated the ability of largemouth bass to see certain colors more easily under varying conditions of light intensity and water clarity. In the selection

of the right color for the conditions faced, any edge may be a huge advantage.

Shape, as a function of lure design, is a relatively easy decision. Thin minnow-shaped plugs and flat-sided crankbaits tend to represent forage and have the ability to influence the action characteristics of the lure. Fatter, rounder crankbaits may represent both forage and crawfish imitations, and are usually associated with wider wobbles and exaggerated actions.

The form or look of a lure is the creative license of the designer. If all the primary characteristics of the lure are to one's liking—if it looks good—it gets fished with more intensity.

Scents are present on everything and must be considered with regard to fishing lures. Negative scents, such as human odor, may have an effect on lure productivity. On the other hand, natural scents, such as Riverside's Real Crawfish, Real Baitfish, or Real Worm, offer the angler the opportunity to match a real scent with the type of artificial being fished. Not only do these scents mask potentially negative odors that fish react to, but they also offer a natural scent that can influence whether a fish will accept or reject a target.

Slower-moving, bottom-hugging lures such as jigs and soft plastic worms should always be coated with an appropriate scent. In fact, some of the newer soft plastics, like Riverside's Floating Air Series, offer air pockets into which scent may be placed.

MOTIVATION FOR NEW-PRODUCT DEVELOPMENT

One of the most-used, yet misleading, comments about artificial lure design and manufacture is, "Lures are designed to catch fishermen, not fish." Make no mistake, the lure industry is a business and, although driven in part by fashion, the ultimate success or failure of a product is measured by the product's ability to catch fish.

Where does the motivation to develop new products come from? Basically, it is market-driven. Anglers all over the world are constantly searching for a new lure that will perform better under the circumstances that a fisherman faces. And manufacturers constantly attempt to tap into this aggressive, interested market segment. How different manufacturers participate in this quest for new-product business may vary. However, the underlying foundation for all new-product development is good ideas.

PRADCO, the parent company for the brand names Rebel, Bomber, Haddon, Cordell, Smithwick, Lazy Ike, Riverside, and Creek Chub, considers every possible avenue of new-product ideas. PRADCO's professional fishing team continually offers suggestions about how a particular fishing problem can be solved. A good example of such professional input was the introduction in 1994 of the Pro Autograph series. This family of new lure colors and modifications of existing lures was totally driven by the ideas of the participating professionals. Included in this series are serious modifications to two popular surface lures. Denny Brauer's Baby Torpedo has a much larger rear prop and internal rattles, both resulting in a louder lure that creates much more surface commotion. Zell Rowland's three-hooked Zara Spook permits smaller hooks that offer dramatically better hook penetration when strikes occur on long casts. In each case, the resulting "new" lure better solves the perceived problem as defined by the designer-pro.

The changing conditions of our fisheries also provide opportunities for new-product development. One example of environmental changes that affect lure design comes from the spread of various grasses; in particular, hydrilla and coon-tail moss.

During the past decade, the introduction of grasses to new bodies of water has not only increased the number of fish that the body of water can support, but it has also created problems in how to catch the fish that live in and around this green structure.

Weedless single-hook soft-plastic lures like the Soft-Classic Pop-R and Zara Spook were designed specifically for this type of structure. Larger and much heavier jigs have also been designed to penetrate the structure, while the addition of rattles makes these jigs much more productive in heavy cover.

Perhaps the best example of how a changing fishing environment affects lure choice, and ultimately design, is the story of Lake Erie.

Traditionally Lake Erie's western basin has been a murky, even muddy, fishery that allowed basic shallow-water techniques to be the dominant method. However, with the accidental introduction of the zebra mussel, one of nature's most proficient water cleaners, the western basin's shallow-water fishery almost disappears after the spring spawns of walleyes and smallmouth bass. The much-clearer waters have altered the habits of baitfish, sending them to deeper waters of the central and eastern basins as the water temperature increases. Game fish, especially the walleye, follow.

This relocation of summertime baitfish has dictated a change from the traditional casting of weight-forward spinners around and above shallow reefs to the more technical trolling techniques widely associated with the clear, open water of Lake Ontario or Lake Michigan. In turn, the clearer waters resulted in new walleye trolling lures; special colors and exceptional depth abilities lead the list of innovations.

With all the input from professional anglers and changing fisheries environments, as well as suggestions made by consumers, manufacturers usually rely on one or two individuals who are responsible for lure design. In the case of PRADCO, Jim Gowing of Altus, Arkansas, and Charlie Medley of Gainsville, Texas, carry that responsibility. The main lures in the PRADCO catalog reflect the abilities of these men to be both creative and responsive to the fishing public's needs and wishes. Their creativity is a special skill that allows them to transform a concept into a fishing lure that earns the respect of discriminating anglers.

Conclusion

When the lure designer begins to solve a fishing problem, many considerations must be made. The closer the finished product comes to the designer's desires, the better the problem will be solved. By learning the characteristics that are present in each lure, an angler can begin to make more sophisticated judgments as to which lure to use when to solve the problem at hand. Make the nine correct choices and you'll know as much about the lure as the original designer.

And if you know that much about the lures you use, you will be a much better angler.

Live Bait

Worms

"Worms have played a more important part in the history of the world than most persons would at first suppose."

Charles Darwin (1896)

Picture the most elemental kind of fishing in America: a barefoot-boy-with-cheek-of-tan sauntering down to the old fishin' hole. He's holding his pole in one hand. And in his other. . . a can of worms.

That's not just a slice of Norman Rockwell nostalgia. There may be millions of fishermen whose tackle boxes overflow with the latest high-tech, space-age plastic bait, but there are also a substantial number who prefer to fish with real live bait. And that begins with worms.

The species most often used for fishing is the earthworm, or more specifically, the nightcrawler. You can pick up a day's supply at most tackle shops and at many rural gas stations and general stores.

One general store in a small Kentucky town features a coin-operated vending machine on its front porch: when a handful of quarters is inserted, out pops a cardboard carton containing a dozen night-crawlers. The machine isn't refrigerated, however, and unfortunately for the worms and for my fishing prospects, the worms that popped out one summer evening showed the effects of the machine's exposure to direct sunlight earlier in the day.

As their name would suggest, people used to find nightcrawlers by digging after sunset. A damp patch of soil or lawn, especially following a rain, is a likely spot. If randomly turning over the soil doesn't prove fruitful, the worms will be encouraged to come up, and at any time of day, after a charge of electricity is sent into the ground. An automobile battery or a small generator can be the power source, but be careful not to give yourself a shock. One good jolt and worms will appear on the surface.

Under rocks and logs is another popular worm hangout (newts too, which also make good bait).

To have a fresh and healthy quantity of worms always on hand, try raising your own. You can buy a supply from local gardening stores and nurseries, or by mail from commercial vermiculturists. For the latter, check the classified sections of such magazines as *Field & Stream* (among the regular adver-

FAVORITE BAIT

A pop music magazine features a column in which readers are invited to submit a list of their "Desert Island Discs," favorite recordings that they would take along to keep them company if they were stranded on a desert isle.

In the same spirit, a number of anglers were asked to choose their three favorite flies, lures, and/or bait. However, fishermen being an ornery sort, not everyone abided by the three-limit rule.

ANGUS CAMERON, WESTON, CONNECTICUT, AUTHOR AND EDITOR:

"If I had to rate wet flies in order of my preference, it would be: (1) Green Machine; (2) Green Butt (sometimes called the Conrad); (3) Casseboom; (4) Black Buck Bug; (5) Undertaker; (6) Silver Rat; (7) Shady Lady (Rusty Rat). Among dry flies: (1) Bomber; (2) White Wulff."

ARNOLD FALK, KEENE, NEW HAMPSHIRE, RECREATIONAL FLY-FISHERMAN:

"For dry flies, I would choose an Adams Parachute, a good all-around fly for many conditions; an Irresistible, which is a good floater and easy to see in low light; and a Renegade, which works when 'standards' aren't working and can be fished wet or dry.

"For wets/nymphs, I would select a Wooly Worm/Wooly Bugger: easy to tie and easily weighted, they can be used for both trout and bass; and a Hare's Ear nymph, which seems to work best for my local trout. Among streamers, I pick the Muddler Minnow, my absolutely all-around favorite that can do everything; the Clouser's Minnow: great for bass, and sinks like a brick; and the Mickey Finn: when other stream-ers aren't working, this one might.

"On those infrequent times I go spin-fishing, I generally use a jointed minnow for trolling and casting. My #1 choice for 'meat' fishing is a Junebug spinner with a single hook with a worm or half a crawler. These spinners come in various sizes and seem to catch everything and anything depending on how they are fished. My wife, Ginny, caught walleye out of the Connecticut River using that rig."

JERRY O'CONNOR, LAGRANGE, KENTUCKY, RECREATIONAL BASS FISHERMAN:

"I like plastic worms, particularly the purple Culprit. When Texas-rigged, a ⅛-ounce weight gives it a lot better action. Among spinnerbaits, I use tandem blades in the spring and willow blades when the water is warm. I choose dark colors when the water is dark; otherwise, chartreuse. Mud Bugs bury in mud, and when they're 'stirred up,' they behave like crawdads. Orange and yellow seem to be the colors that work best for me."

RICH PAGANO, WASHINGTON, DC, FORMER COLORADO FLY-FISHING GUIDE:

"Which three flies I would choose depends on whether I was interested in fishing for fun or for numbers. If I wanted big trout, I would choose three Wooly Buggers, all size 4: one black, one olive, and one white. If I wanted lots of trout, I would choose three nymphs, all size 14: a Gold Ribbed Hare's Ear, a Prince nymph, and an olive Bead Head. But if I were willing to wait for perfect conditions, I would choose three dry flies, all size 22: a black Midge (my own pattern), an olive Comparadun, and a gray Usual. I prefer dry fly fishing."

(continued)

NICK KARAS, ST. JAMES, NEW YORK, AUTHOR
AND OUTDOOR COLUMNIST:

*"As far as my three favorite lures are
concerned. . . yes, I do have three which I can talk
about. They are the Dardevle™ spoon, the
Muddler Minnow, and the bucktailed jig. What is
unique about these three is that they can all be
used effectively in either fresh- or salt water.*

*"The only-one-lure on a desert island is the
bucktailed jig. It can be fished on the bottom and
in the mid-section of the water column by varying size and speed or retrieve. Size of jig to use is
determined by the size of the prey you're after.
Color selection starts with one's basic white, then
chartreuse. Green is the last color to turn blue in
the depths. I prefer a swinging hook jig; that is, a
head with an eyelet on the back, under the hairs,
and the hook attached to the eye. This enhances
the swinging action of the pork rind.*

*"The Muddler Minnow is an all-around lure,
and because it was designed to resemble a baitfish,
it can also be used effectively in salt as well as freshwater. It is unique among artificial fly lures
because it can be fished as a dry, a wet, and a
streamer. If it isn't treated with silicone floatants,
it will sink readily with the aid of saliva. It can
also be fished on a spinning rod with a split-shot a
dozen inches ahead of the lure.*

*"The spoon, or Dardevle (brand name), can
be used in salt water (e.g., the bunker spoon) and
it does catch marine species, but it is best used in
freshwater and will take any predaceous, piscivorous fish, and that includes almost all freshwater
fishes from trout to pike, and many in-between.
It too can fish a range of levels in the water
column, and this is dependent upon the weight
and size of the spoon and the speed of the retrieve.
With this lure, color is less important than the
wobbly action it imparts when drawn through
the water. It swims like a wounded baitfish.
While color does come into play, and while the
most effective historically has been the red-and-
white Dardevle, it is the chrome underside that
does most of the work."*

tisers is Hugh Carter of Plains, Georgia, a relative
of the former President).

Earthworms should live in a commercially
available habitat or any well-ventilated (fine mesh
screening works well) wooden or plastic carton.
They will thrive in a compost mixture made from
fallen leaves and manure or freshly shredded leaves.
The mixture should be kept moist, not wet, and at a
temperature between 40° F and 60° F.

Feed your brood every few days: apples,
banana peels, cabbage, tomatoes, and tea leaves are
all excellent. Coffee grounds, however, are too
acidic. A handful of ground eggshells supplies
much-needed calcium. Some people routinely add
ice cubes to worm boxes during warm weather.

Not all your worms will survive. You'll need to
remove the dead ones promptly, or else their
decomposing bodies will raise the temperature of
the worm-house.

Ready-made alternatives are sold as worm farms
or ranches. They are ventilated polystyrene containers that come with a supply of bedding and food.

Before you set off fishing, exposing worms to
cold temperature, either by refrigeration or immersion in ice water, will cause them to "plump up" and
thus be more tempting to fish. That's why adding ice
cubes to their traveling accommodations makes
sense during summer months. Plumping-up can also

be done by injecting air into nightcrawlers with a hypodermic syringe or a similar commercial device.

Strange but true, the vibrations from being driven over bumpy unpaved roads or over off-road terrain can injure worms (minnows too), so cushioning your live bait supply is a good idea.

Bloodworms and other species are also popular bait, and they can be obtained and maintained as earthworms are. So can sandworms, which are especially effective when trolled for striped bass.

A Euphemistic Aside: Some fly-fisherman who otherwise turn up their noses at live bait have been known on occasion to fish with worms. Perhaps to appear less compromised, the anglers refer to them as "garden hackle."

MINNOWS

Any number of species constitute members of what go under the general heading of "minnows." They include the alewife, dace, shiner, and chub.

You can catch these baitfish using a seine net (if legal in your locale). You can also make a trap from a re-lidded empty can into which a number of small holes have been punched. Use small chunks of meat or fish heads as bait, and leave the trap in a lake or pond overnight. In the morning, you're likely to find lots of minnows, as well as crayfish and leeches.

Or, you can always buy minnows by the dozen at bait shops.

However you get them, the fish will stay healthiest if they're kept in special buckets that have tiny holes that let fresh water flow through. Aeration can be accomplished either by immersing the bucket in a lake or stream, or by using a portable electric aerator (more sophisticated—and expensive—buckets have built-in aerators).

OTHER FISH

Among popular saltwater live baits are bunkers, snappers, tinker mackerel, mullet, and herring, all small enough to become the dinner of striped bass, bluefish, fluke, and other surf offshore species. Live eels are a favorite along the East Coast for catching stripers at night.

The phrase "live bait" may be sometimes be somewhat misleading with regard to these baitfish. The fish that they're intended to attract don't seem to object to dead bait, so bunker and mullet, for example, are often chopped into bite-sized pieces.

LEECHES

Leeches, a class of segmented worms, are best known for their ability to bite and then suck the blood from other creatures. Nevertheless, leeches are a favorite food of many freshwater species and, as such, make good bait. Those anglers who have no squeamish feelings about handling leeches (those who do can use plastic replicas) will find them available at many bait stores.

The best method of keeping leeches alive is to store them in a pail of unchlorinated refrigerated water, with the refrigerator's temperature maintained at just above freezing. When the water in the pail begins to turn cloudy, transfer the leeches to another pail of water at the same temperature.

The aftermath of a leech's bite is more itchy than painful, the result of an anticoagulant that the leech transmits. If a leech latches onto you, pry it off and then apply a dusting of antiseptic powder to the wound.

CRICKETS AND GRASSHOPPERS

These terrestrials often hop or fly into ponds and streams, making them a familiar menu item for bass, trout, and most other fish. Sweeping a butterfly net through a meadow's tall grass will usually produce enough crickets and 'hoppers for a day's fishing. So will examining the under-leaves of meadow and field shrubbery.

Crickets and grasshoppers will remain alive if they are kept in a cool environment. A cardboard box filled with damp grass works well. So do cricket holders/dispensers that are sold at tackle shops and through mail-order houses. The insects stay in the jug-shaped basket or plastic container, to be released one at a time into the narrow end and held there in a clip-like device while you slide your fishhook through the insect's back. At no time do you touch the critter, which has benefits for more than the squeamish: you won't run the risk of accidentally squashing the insect or letting it fly away.

CRAWFISH

Whether you pronounce it "crawfish" or "crayfish," these little lobster look-alikes make tempting bait for bass, pike, pickerel, and other relatively large species. Look for them under underwater rocks or in weed-beds, and keep them alive in a cool, moist environment. Plastic or paper cartons will work if you keep them out of direct sunlight.

FROGS

Small green frogs, pickerel frogs, and bullfrogs are the most common varieties of amphibians used for bait. Using a net (or your bare hands if you have the reflexes of "Kung Fu"'s Caine), capture them in the shallow areas of ponds, streams, and lakes. If you hunt at night, shining a high-beam flashlight in their eyes will transfix them.

Keep the frogs in a container with damp leaves, moss, or grass.

"PRESERVED" LIVE BAIT

To define "live" as "organic" or "once-living" may be stretching the point, but if we do, the following types of bait qualify under this category.

The best-known "preserved" bait is pork rind, an essential element of the "jig'n'pig" technique. The most popular shape is split-tail, the ends of which flutter as they move through the water. Other patterns are skirts, frogs, and eels/worms. Pork rind comes in a variety of colors, some embedded with sparkles and other varieties of glitter. A number of manufacturers enhance the pork's scent and flavor (including additional salt).

A variation of pork rind shaped from single pieces of pork are those made from compressed pork that have been molded into jig tails, skirts, and other patterns. These too can be tarted up with glitter and enhanced with regard to odor.

Salmon eggs are packed in jars, in brine or another preservative. Their color is usually embellished, so the eggs glow with a fluorescence instead of their normal pale hue.

Grass shrimp, leeches, maggots, and mealworms are among the species of preserved bait marketed under the Uncle Josh label. Resembling tiny mummies, they are nontoxic and easy to handle.

Traditional catfish bait comes under the "preserved" heading. Balls and cubes of bread dough, pork pellets scented with fish or blood, nightcrawler links, and nightcrawler-and-cheese links are all proven catfish attractors. They are chiefly used on trot lines, which are strings of up to 25 hooks, each on a foot-long line, that stretch across or along a river or stream.

Anyone who thinks that fish aren't vegetarians should try a kernel of fresh or canned corn at the end of a hook. Panfish seem to like nothing better, as do trout, perhaps mistaking the kernel for roe.

Blueberries work too, especially on hatchery-raised fish. Hatcheries feed their fingerlings pellet food, which make a splash when they hit the water. Toss a handful of berries into a stream or pond and watch the chumming start a feeding frenzy. Then put a blueberry on your hook, cast it with a noisy plop, and get ready to set your hook.

Scents

Among a fish's most active senses is its sense of smell, to which the angling industry has responded with a virtual pharmacopoeia of attractor scents to increase the appeal of your lures. They range from concentrated extract of actual crawfish and baitfish to garlic-based liquids to laboratory-concocted synthetics. Some contain such visual attractors as "scales" that adhere to your plug. At least one oozes a trail of "blood," while for a true multimedia experience, SparklScales Plus™ features an additive that causes bubbles.

Scents that comes in pump-nozzle bottles or (less environmentally-sound) aerosol cans can be sprayed directly on to the lure. Otherwise, applicator devices do the job, including one with a lid operated by a pedal so your hands never touch the impregnated bait.

That raises the question of how to get rid of unwanted scent on your hands. Uncle Buck's® Scent Remover takes care of that chore, and it also eliminates other unwanted odors.

Within that category is the odor of us humans. According to some scientists, many species of fish find an element of human odor particularly repugnant, made more so after we come in contact with such other turnoffs as motor fuel. Using fishing scents is a way to mask these and other unwanted odors, not to mention the positive benefit of attracting fish.

Then why doesn't everyone use scents? you may be wondering.

Some people tried, drew a blank, and were thus soured on the idea. Other fishermen believe that fish that are biting will take anything, but when they're not, nothing on earth (or land or water) will induce them to bite.

Then too, the benefits of scents are admittedly limited. Scents seem to work best only when a fish has spotted a lure and is interested enough to investigate, yet just because you've impregnated your crankbait with eau de shad doesn't necessarily mean the fish will strike. Scents are not magnets, so don't expect that a dose applied to your lure will draw every fish in the lake. All the scent does is increase the possibility of such success. And to fisherman who like to play the odds, that's good enough for them.

An article in *The Wall Street Journal* (October 5, 1994) describes the efforts of a biologist involved in bait research for Berkley. Like humans, fish detect only a few flavor elements even though foods are composed of thousands of different elements, and it's the scientist's task to isolate and identify those which fish find the most palatable. In addition to flavors that appeal to most varieties of fish, the kinds that are used in Berkley's Power Bait line, research is also focusing on "species-specific" odors and tastes. Some progress is reported, the proof coming from the tankful of fish that live in Berkley's laboratories.

Call them "focus-groupers," if you wish.

9

L U R E S

I n a sense, "lure" would describe any bait, since the purpose of all is to attract fish. However, fishermen distinguish among live bait, artificial flies (at the heart of fly-fishing), and a wide range of what are essentially plastic, wood, or metal decoys designed to look like baitfish.

Plugs

Like many other artificial baits, **PLUGS** are designed to resemble baitfish, either specific species or "generic" fish. In many cases, the names of plug categories reflect the technique by which the lure is fished.

CRANKBAIT

CRANKBAITS are plugs with plastic or metal "lips" that cause the plug to move through the water with an undulating plane-and-dive "porpoising" action. The length and the angle of the lip determines the lure's motion and the depth to which it will sink, seldom more than 10 feet to 15 feet without extra weight, lead-core-line or the use of a downrigger.

Crankbaits come in a variety of shapes and sizes. Some are long and slender, while others have potbellies. Some are one-piece, while others are jointed to move laterally as well as up-and-down.

Those that contain rattle compartments attract fish audibly as well as visually. Almost all crankbait (almost all plugs, for that matter) have double or treble hooks, one customarily mounted on the front part of the belly and a second under the tail.

Flash Dancer, a medium diver— ⅜ *oz. [courtesy Hank Roberts/Fred Arbogast Co.]*

*Jitterbug—*⅝ *oz. [courtesy Hank Roberts/Fred Arbogast Co.]*

Big Bud.® [courtesy Heddon]

Another universal feature are the eyes that are painted or mounted on these fish replicas. Highly reflective eyes made by a holographic process are popular because of their realistic appearance.

Crankbaits that are characterized as **DARTERS** have notched lips instead of a plate. **CHUGGERS** (of which the Jitterbug™ is a classic example) have wide plates in either side of the lure's "head."

Some crankbaits, however, have no lips or notches at all (you'll discover that exceptions and variations run rampant throughout the subject of lures, if not all baits). Shaped like shad, these plugs sink when there is no pressure from the line, then rise when they are retrieved; the line eye mounted above what would be the shad's head keeps the lipless/plateless/notchless crankbait on a vertical plane.

STICKBAIT

These elongated plugs are worked on the water surface. Some **STICKBAITS** have metal cups on their faces to create the action of a wounded baitfish. Most stickbaits have none, however; their action comes solely from how the fisherman manipulates his rod tip.

Jumping Minnow, a stickbait. [courtesy PRADCO]

POPPERS

Also in the crankbait category are **POPPERS.** Their concave or flat heads create a "popping" sound as they are retrieved. Surface-feeding fish, especially bass, find the sound particularly appealing.

Hula Popper—⅝ oz. [courtesy Fred Arbogast]

Bayou Boogie. [courtesy Heddon]

SPINNERBAIT

The "classic" **SPINNERBAIT** is a V-shaped rig with a hook on one arm and a spinner blade on the other. The blade's rotation produces vibrations that attract fish to the hook, which is covered by a plastic skirt or a plastic worm, a strip of pork or another "edible" item, or a streamer or bucktail (the popular Mepps series fits into this category), or a minnow or other live bait.

Bomber Bushwacker™, a spinnerbait. [courtesy PRADCO]

Blades comes in three shapes. The largest is the **COLORADO BLADE.**

Its oval blades rotate the slowest of the three types and take the biggest "bite" through the water. The **WILLOWLEAF,** slender and pointed at both ends, is the fastest spinning, emitting a relatively low amount of vibration. The **INDIANA BLADE** looks and functions somewhere between the first two patterns.

BLADE SIZE CHART

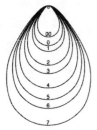

Colorado Blade

Indiana Blade

Willow Leaf Blade

[courtesy Bass Pro Shops]

Asymmetrical blades create an erratic and irregular pulsating motion that resembles a fish in serious distress. Similarly, the depth of a blade's "cup," or concave bend, affects the amount of vibration the blade produces.

Most spinnerbaits have a small U-shaped piece of metal called a **CLEVIS**. The clevis, by which the blade is attached to the axis around which it spins, also allows the blade to revolve with minimal fraction. In addition to a clevis, a spinnerbait will usually have a small bead that acts as a ball bearing and prevents the clevis from rubbing against the shaft.

An alternative style is the **THROUGH-BLADE**, in which the axis passes through a hole in the blade.

Spinnerbaits composed of more than one blade produce a variety of actions. Multi-blade types often use one Colorado and one willowleaf mounted either on a single axis or on separate arms on either side of the hook. The two blades may rotate in the same direction or they may counter-rotate. Most fishermen feel that tandem rigs ride higher in the water than those that have a single blade.

Silver or nickel seems to be the perennially popular blade color. Gold and brass are close seconds, especially in darker water. Brightly painted blades have their fans too. The choice of blade color often determines the color of the skirt that covers the hook (e.g., silver blade and white skirt), although there is some latitude for contrasting colors too.

Spinnerbaits come in sizes that range from ⅛ ounce to 1 ounce, with blade sizes from No. 2 to No. 7. Hooks, which can be single, double, or treble, are sized in proportion to the rest of the bait.

Some lipless crankbait plugs qualify as spinnerbait when they have one or more propeller-shaped blades at their front or rear.

Dying Flutter.™ *[courtesy Heddon]*

BUZZBAIT

BUZZBAITS are first cousins to spinnerbaits. However, instead of a simple lightweight blade, a buzzbait has one or two heavier square- or diamond-shaped counter-rotating blades mounted on a wire at right angles to the wire that holds the hook. A topwater lure, the buzzbait is rapidly retrieved, its "eggbeater" noise and torpedo-like wake produced by counter-rotating blades attracting fish to the plastic skirt on the hook. Some buzzbait also have rattles and other noisemakers that add to the racket, especially useful under poor or naturally dim lighting conditions.

The wire projection on an "in line" buzzbait is angled back so the buzzer is on the same plane as the hook.

SPOON

The simplest yet often the most effective form of plug, the **SPOON** is nothing more than a piece of oval metal with an attached single or multiple hook. Although it may be all silver, bronze, or another metallic color, one side is often painted with alternating bands of color, of which red and white (as in the well-regarded Dardevle™) is a particularly devastating combination.

A spoon that is concave or spiral in shape produces a wobbling movement. Whatever their particular shape, however, spoons revolve when being retrieved or trolled. The line will become twisted, which can—and should—be overcome by the use of a swivel.

Rebel Arrowhead™ weedless spoon. [courtesy Rebel]

JIG

Viewed in its simplest form, a **JIG** is a sinker-and-hook combination. The sinker portion provides the weight to drop the jig down to what-ever depth the angler wishes. The hook holds the choice of wide variety of skirts, tubes, and other attractors that are attached to or mounted on the jig head.

The name "jig" comes from the hopping movement of the folk dance. That's how jigs are typically fished, in an up-and-down jerky move-ment. Not always, however; jigs are often cast from

boats or from shore, in which case they are retrieved much like any other lure.

The shape of a jig's head helps to determine the rate of sinking: pointed or round heads meet less water resistance than flat or broad heads, which are designed to sink more slowly. Jig heads made of plastic or other buoyant material also fall more slowly than metal heads.

The head shape also determines how well a jig can contend with underwater foliage cover. Bullet sinker-shaped heads penetrate weeds most easily when being retrieved, although they also have a tendency to become wedged in underwater rocks and wood cover.

Heavy stand-up heads of more than $\frac{3}{8}$ ounce are often the choice of fishermen working a flat, clear lake or pond bottom. Their angled heads present a high profile, and the noise made by the jig head striking the bottom also attracts fish.

Many jig heads are equipped with weed guards that reduce, if not altogether eliminate, the problem of snagging underwater vegetation. Some heads have one or more wire or projections that extend from the head almost to the hook's point.

More common are weed guards in the form of bunches of fiber bristles. These have varying degrees of flexibility: stiff bristles are useful to penetrate tough weeds, although some particularly tough bristles are strong enough to immobilize a jig. To adapt them to specific conditions, fishermen often trim and/or spread the bristles apart.

Tube jig with external weight. [courtesy BASSMASTER®]

Most jig-head hooks are the cutting point vari-ety, not the straight needle shape. Those made of relatively thin wire most easily penetrate a fish's mouth, although at the expense of strength. Either straight or turned hook eyes are usually set perpendicular to the shank and angled at 60° or 90° for easier and faster hook-setting.

The short compact shanks of "flippin' " jig hooks permit the rig to be dropped into narrow spaces. These hooks also have wide gaps, upturned eyes, and larger barbs that help set the hook quickly. In contrast, jigs used for casting have longer shanks and smaller gaps.

Jigs also make use of sound as an attractor. Heads with built-in rattles can be either a hollow head filled with BB shot or a shot-filled chamber mounted behind the head like a collar. With regard to the effectiveness of these noisemakers, an article in the March 1994 issue of *The In-Fisherman* suggests that "soft jigging motions don't activate the sound chambers. It takes a sharp wrist snap that raises the bait about six inches to produce a sound." The article goes on to say, however, that rattle chambers also produce fish-attracting bubbles.

Jig hooks need not be covered only by plastic skirts. Enjoying great vogue through their success are combinations of "jig plus. . . " led by the "JIG'N'PIG," in which a piece of processed pork rind is threaded on the hook. This rig is equally popular with saltwater fishermen, who may call their jigs "tins," but who also attach pork strips.

Plastic Worms

Among the most popular bass, walleye, and panfish lures are plastic worms. They come in a rainbow of colors, some plain and some spangled, and in a variety of lengths. Some are impregnated with scent (although Gary Soucie suggests that these scents are more effective at masking human odor than at attracting fish).

Plastic worms are most often rigged **TEXAS-STYLE**: a bullet-shaped sinker above the hook, with the hook point buried in the worm. The weight keeps the bait close to the bottom, with a minimal amount of restriction of movement, while the embedded hook makes the rig virtually weed-proof.

Plastic worm rigged Texas-style. [courtesy BASSMASTER®]

An alternative set-up is the **CAROLINA-RIG**. A swivel sits between the sinker and the hook, so that the worm will ride off the bottom. A way to maintain the sinker's position is by jamming its hole with a small piece of toothpick.

Carolina-Rig Worm. [courtesy BASSMASTER®]

The material of which plastic worms are made can dissolve some hard plastics. That's the reason for "worm-proof" tackle boxes. If your tackle box isn't invulnerable this way, you can store your supply of plastic worms in expendable plastic containers inside the box.

Plastic Slugs

First cousins to plastic worms are **PLASTIC SLUGS**, distinguished by their elongated and forked or skirted tails that are meant to resemble leeches or crayfish.

Tube Lures

Pieces of latex tubing, cut from 4 inches to 5 inches in length, make effective worm-like lures. Saltwater anglers make tube eels from 16+ inches pieces of latex mounted on two or more hooks. Similarly, tube lures are soft plastic cylindrical bodies, 3 inches to 4 inches in length, that end in tentacle-like strands.

(Sales)Pitching Lures

Telemarketing hit the fishing world in a big way when two lures came on the TV screen scene.

First was the Flying Lure™, basically a jig head with most of its weight toward the rear; the lure sinks backwards when tension on the line is relaxed during the retrieval ("it swims away from you"). That's especially useful for probing hard-to-reach underwater nooks and crannies, as viewers learned from a lengthy TV infomercial in which professional anglers demonstrated its action. The program ended with details about the package of jig heads, soft-body baits, tackle box, and instructional brochure.

The rest was merchandising history. Enough viewers mailed in their money or called the toll-free number to turn the Flying Lure™ into the country's best-selling lure for several consecutive years. Now also sold in stores and through catalogs, the item comes in standard, weedless, and saltwater jig heads and a plethora of soft-body baits shapes and colors.

Then came Roland Martin's Helicopter Lures™, soft-plastic baits with three rotor blades. Spokesman Martin, a successful bass tournament professional and host of his own TNN TV show, makes much of the lure system's ability to get to and then through otherwise inaccessible cover and

holes. The package includes the lures, hooks, a box, and how-to booklet and video.

Infomercials tend to be aired at odd hours, so catching them is pretty much a hit-or-miss affair (insomniacs seem to have the best chance). But, say those who have tried Helicopter Lures™ and Flying Lures™, both systems are worth knowing about and getting to know.

Videos

The following videos describe baitcasting and spinning baits and how to use them. They are available from Bass Pro Shop:

Deep-Diving Crankbaits, with Shaw Grigsby (45 min.)

Take 'em Topside, with Chet Douthit (45 min.)—buzzbaits, propbaits, and stickbaits.

Worm Fishin', with Woo Daves (45 min.)—flippin', pitchin', and casting worms.

Fishing the Incredible "Slug-o"™, with Stacy King (60 min.)—rigging and fishing techniques for Slug-o™ and floating plastic worms and lizards.

The Carolina Rig, with Stacy King (45 min.)

Manufacturers of Lures and Bait

To list the many hundreds of lure manufacturers and their product lines would be an impossibility in a book of this scope. Accordingly, the following representative roster includes information on where to write or phone for information about their products.

Note: Although every effort was made to indicate trademark and service mark protection, the absence of such symbols should not be assumed to indicate the lack of such protection.

Accardo Tackle
3708 Conrad
Baton Rouge, LA 70805
(504) 355-0863
Popping Minnow and Parker Minnow bass poppers.

Action Plastics
3927 Valley E. Industrial Dr.
Birmingham, AL 35217
(800) 874-4829
Flutter Bug plastic worms; Super Goober.

Aggravator Lure Co.
22 Cinderwood Cove
Maumelle, AR 72113
(800) 655-5873
Aggravator spoons.

American Lure Company
98 Gordon Commercial Drive
LaGrange, GA 30240
(706) 882-9099
Sugar Worm; Gator Grub.

Fred Arbogast Co.
313 W. North St.
Akron, OH 44303
(800) 486-4068
Jitterbug crankbaits; Hula Popper; A.C. Plug.

Bait Rigs Tackle Company
P.O. Box 44153
Madison, WI 53744
Slo-Poke Jig'n Combo.

Bagley Bait Co.
P.O. Box 810
Winter Haven, FL 33882
(813) 294-4271
Kill'r B's, Balsa B's, and Hustle Bug crankbaits.

Bass Assassin Lures
Rte. 3, Box 248
Mayo, FL 32066
(904) 294-1049
Assassin; Lizard Assassin; Shad Assassin; Twitch Assassin.

Berkley
One Berkley Drive
Spirit Lake, IA
(712) 336-1520
"Power" plastic worm, shad, grub, etc., series.

Blakemore Sales Corp.
P.O. Box 1149
Branson, MO 65616
(417) 334-5340
Road Runner jighead/spinner; Branson Bug.

Blue Fox Tackle Co.
645 North Emerson
Cambridge, MN 55008
(612) 689-3402
Spinnerbaits, buzzbaits, Super Vibrax spinners, jigs, and skirts.

Charlie Brewer's Slider Co.
P.O. Box 130
Lawrenceburg, TN 38464
(815) 762-4700
Slider lures system.

Browning/Zebco Corp.
P.O. Box 840
Tulsa, OK 74101
(918) 836-5581
Poe's Classic Super Cedar crankbaits.

Bull Dog Lures
3609-A S. College
Bryan, TX 88801
(409) 846-5473

"–Dog" line of buzzbaits and spinner-baits; Tripple Rattle Back jigs.

Bumper Stumper Lures
402 East Highway 121
Lewisville, TX 75061
(214) 420-0365
Buzzbaits and spinnerbaits.

Creme Lure Co.
P.O. Box 6162
Tyler, TX 75711
(903) 561-0522
Plastic worms.

Classic Manufacturing
P.O. Box 1249
Clermont, FL 34712
(407) 656-6133
Culprit lures and soft plastics.

Coastal Lures
P.O. Box 485
Orange Park, FL 32067
(904) 272-0562
Bass Flash crankbaits.

Daiwa
7421 Chapman Ave.
Garden Grove, CA 92641
(714) 895-6645
Team Daiwa TD Lures crankbait series.

Eppinger Manufacturing Co.
6340 Schaefer Highway
Dearborn, MI 48126
(313) 582-3205
Dardevle™ spoons; Spinning Wiggler.

Fenwick
5242 Argosy Drive
Huntington Beach, CA 92649

(714) 897-1066

Methods series of crankbaits; Shallow Crank crankbait.

Flow-Rite of Tennessee
107 Allen St.
Bruceton, TN 38317
(901) 586-2271

Original Formula Fish Scented Baits series.

Hart Tackle Co.
P.O. Box 898
Stratford, OK 74872
(800) 543-0774

"Throb" buzzbaits and spinnerbaits; jigs and soft plastics.

Hilderbrandt
P.O. Box 50
Logansport, IN 46947
(219) 722-4455

Tin Roller spinnerbait; Headbanger buzzbait.

Horizon Lure Co.
P.O. Box 330
Huntington, TX 75949
(409) 876-3943

Ghost Minnow spinnerbait.

Johnson Worldwide Associates
222 Main St.
Racine, WI 53403
(800) 227-6432

Silver Minnow spoon.

Kalin Company
Box 1234
Brawley, CA 92227
(800) 782-2393

Hologram series.

Bill Lewis Lures
P.O. Box 7959

Alexandria, LA 71304
(318) 487-0352

Rat-L-Trap series of jerkbaits.

Luck "E" Strike USA
P.O. Box 587
Cassville, MO 65625
(417) 847-3158

Lunker City
P.O. Box 1807
Meriden, CT 06450
(203) 276-1111

Slug-o™ soft jerkbait.

Lunker Lure
115 E. Illinois Ave.
Carterville, IL 62918
(618) 985-4214

Lunker Lure buzzbait; Rattle Back jig.

Luhr-Jensen & Sons, Inc.
P.O. Box 297
Hood River, OR 97031
(800) 366-3811

Wooden J-Plug crankbaits; "Live Image" Dodgers crankbait; Power Dive Minnow crankbait.

Magna Strike Inc.
224 Buffalo Ave.
P.O. Box 69
Freeport, NY 10520
(516) 378-1913

Grandma™ crankbait; Equalizer™ crankbait.

Mann's Bait Company
604 State Docks Road
Eufaula, AL 36027
(205) 687-5716

Stretch and Loudmouth series of crankbaits and spinnerbaits; Mann-O-Lure™ jig-style lures.

Mepps
626 Center Street
Antigo, WI 54409
(715) 639-2382

Aglia®, Black Fury®, and Comet® spinners; spoons.

MirrOlure
1415 E. Bay Dr.
Largo, FL 34641
(813) 584-7691

Surface Popper series; twitchbaits, crankbaits; trolling lures.

Mister Twister, Inc.
P.O. Drawer 996
Minden, LA 71058
(318) 377-8818

Buzzbaits and soft plastics.

Norman Lures
P.O. Box 580
Greenwood, AR 72936
(501) 996-2125

Rip-N-Ric jerkbait; Professional Edge series of crankbait.

Normark Corp.
10395 Yellow Circle Dr.
Minneapolis, MN 55343
(612) 933-7060

Rapala: Shad Rap™ series of crankbaits; Rattlin' Rapala jerkbait; spoons.

Panther Martin
Harrison-Hoge Industries, Inc.
200 Wilson Street
Port Jefferson Station, NY 11776
(800) 852-0925

Panther Martin series of spinners; Fire Tiger spinnerbait.

PRADCO
P.O. Box 1587
Fort Smith, AR 72902
(800) 422-FISH

Pro Autograph series of PRADCO lures; Bomber Model "A" (including Flat "A," Fat "A," and Long "A") crankbaits; Rebel® Pop-R series of crankbait and Rebel Minnows; Cotton Cordell Big-O and Wally Diver crankbaits; Heddon Zara Spook® surface plug, Torpedo propeller spinnerbait, and Crazy Crawler topbait; Smithwick Rattlin' Rogue.

SAS Marketing
220 White Plains Road
Tarrytown, NY 10591
(800) 342-3838

Roland Martin's Helicopter Lure™.

Snag Proof Manufacturing Co.
11387 Deerfield Road
Cincinnati, OH 54242
(513) 489-6483

Weedless lures.

Southern Lure Company
P.O. Box 2244
Columbus, MS 39704
(601) 327-4557

Jerk jerkbait.

Stanley Jigs
P.O. Box 722
Huntington, TX 75949
(409) 876-5713

Jigs and spinnerbaits.

Storm Manufacturing Co.
P.O. Box 720265
Norman, OK 73070
(405) 329-5894

ThunderSticks™ stickbaits; Wart series of crankbaits.

Strike King Lure Company
174 Highway 72 West
Collierville, TN 38017
(901) 853-1455

Mirage Pro series of spinnerbaits; skirts; buzzbaits.

Uncle Josh Bait Company
P.O. Box 130
Fort Atkinson, WI 53538
(414) 563-2491

Pork rind; scents.

United Brands International
1489 Market Circle
Port Charlotte, FL 33953-3804
(813) 255-0061

Flying Lure™.

Varonon Bait Co.
805 Oak Ridge Drive
Birmingham, AL 35214
(205) 791-1985

Soft plastics.

Yakima Bait Company
P.O. Box 310
Granger, WA 98932
(800) 527-2711

Worden's Lures series; Rooster Tail® spinner with hackle tail; Poe's Ace-In-The-Hole; Super Toad crankbait.

Zetabait, Inc.
9559 Foley Lane
Foley, AL 36535
(205) 943-1902

Soft plastics; jerkbaits.

OTHER MANUFACTURERS

Acme Tackle Co.
P.O. Box 2771
Providence, RI 02907
(401) 331-6437

Apex Tackle Corp.
P.O. Box 988
South Sioux City, NE 68776
(402) 494-3009

Bad Dog Lures
Snyder Co.
P.O. Box 636
Dodge Center, MN 55927
(507) 374-2955

Bass 'N Bait Co.
8780 Ft. Amanda Rd.
Spenserville, OH 45887
(419) 647-4501

Comet Tackle
72098 Old 21 Rd.
Kimbolton, OH 43749
(614) 432-5550

Custom Jigs & Spins
P.O. Box 27
Glenview, IL 60025
(708) 729-9050

Double D Lures
2500 Chinook Trail
Maitland, FL 32751
(407) 628-9648

Fish-Tek Manufacturing Co.
4235 NE 27 St.
Des Moines, IA 50317
(515) 262-7419

Freshwater Tackle Co.
P.O. Box 518
Deerwood, MN 56444
(218) 534-3837

Hopkins Fishing Lures
1130 Boissevain Ave.
Norfolk, VA 23507
(804) 622-0977

HT Enterprises
P.O. Box 909
Campbellsport, WI 53010
(414) 533-5080

Islander Manufacturing
9287 Horseshoe Island
Clay, NY 13041
(315) 695-2754

Jawtec Worms
P.O. Box 1181
Forney, TX 75127
(800) 544-4842

JB Lures
RR2, Box 16C
Winthrop, MN 55396
(507) 647-5696

Jig-A-Whopper Inc.
P.O. Box 3546
Mankato, MN 56001
(507) 386-1878

Lake Country Products (Lakco)
P.O. Box 367
Isle, MN 56342
(612) 676-3440

Lindy-Little Joe
P.O. Box C
Brainerd, MN 56401
(218) 829-1714

Marble Hall, Inc.
1426 N. 27th Lane
Phoenix, AZ 85009
(602) 269-0708

Northland Fishing Tackle
3209 Mill St. NE
Bemidji, MN 56601
(218) 751-6723

R.J. Tackle, Inc.
5719 Corporation Circle
Fort Myers, FL 33905
(813) 693-7070

Reef Runner Tackle Co.
P.O. Box 939
Port Clinton, OH 43452
(419) 798-9125

Shearwater Tackle
P.O. Box 32103
Fridley, MN 55432
(612) 323-9829

Tackle Marketing, Inc.
3801 W. Superior St.
Duleth, MN 55807
(218) 628-0206

Turner Jones' Micro Jigs
3514 Carriage Dr.
Springfield, MO 65809
(417) 883-6723

Water Life, Inc. (Rebaki)
P.O. Box 10300
Alexandria, VA 22310
(703) 960-5820

10

FLIES

One reference book of trout, salmon, bass, and saltwater fishing flies contains more than 1,200 patterns. If we add to that number only their widely accepted variations and then consider how many new patterns have been created since the book was published almost 10 years ago, the cast of characters would increase by at least 500 more.

Why so many patterns? One answer is that artificial flies are have been designed and constructed to replicate the almost limitless variety of insects and other forms of life.[*]

Over the years, people have identified thousands of insect and fish species that are part of the diet of all sorts of fish. Because species of insects vary from region to region even within the same part of the world (for example, entomologists have found some 25,000 species of beetles in the U.S. alone), anglers have come up with many designs to duplicate (called "imitators") or just suggest ("attractors") these items on a fish's menu.

"Matching the hatch," or using an artificial fly that represents the insect species that is "coming off the water" at that particular moment, is often the only way to interest the fish in what you have to offer. But if no hatch is taking place or it's one of those times when fish aren't playing by "the rules,"

[*]Although the word "fly" is most closely associated with insects, it also applies to patterns that represent such non-buggy creatures as baitfish, frogs, and even landlubbers like field mice (which often end up falling into lands and ponds and becoming snacks for passing bass).

the sensible angler needs to be well prepared with a well-stocked arsenal of artificials.

Human imagination and our sense of aesthetics provide still one more reason for so many different patterns. Even above and beyond a pattern's ability to attract fish, many people feel that a design and its variations are worth perpetuating—and sharing—simply for the sake of beauty.

An Overview of Fly Types

DRY FLIES

The "classic" image of fly fishing calls to mind a fly floating on the surface of a stream, one that has been cast to a rising trout or to one that has just risen. Fishing to an identifiable and specific quarry, as opposed to randomly seeking fish, has great visual and visceral appeal, and that's why many anglers consider fishing "drys" the ultimate experience.

MAYFLIES

If fishing a dry is considered the "classic" technique, then **MAYFLIES** are the "classic" dry pattern. Designed to replicate the adult *Ephemerpotera* (the mayfly's scientific name), patterns in this category are distinguished by upright wings and relatively long tails.

Whether a dry or another type, all its elements should be in certain proportions to each other and to the size of the hook. The mayfly's **HACKLE** (the equivalent of an insect's legs) should be three-quarters the length of the wings or half as long as the hook's gap. The tail should be as long as the wings, while the body should be two-thirds the length of the hook's shank.

In addition to a hackle traditionally tied perpendicular to the hook shank, the **"PARA-CHUTE"** style has the hackle parallel to the shank. Parachute flies ride lower on the water, and as the name suggests, the position of the hackle allows the fly to land softly and right-side-up.

Parachute Olive Hare's Ear.

Of all mayfly patterns, as well as quite possibly all other varieties of dry flies, the Adams is the most widely popular. Someone has called it the "Big Mac" of flies—over 8 billion served, and few flyboxes lack this pattern.

ADAMS
hook size range: 10–20
wings: grizzly hackle tips
hackle: mixed brown and grizzly
body: gray dubbing*
tail: mixed brown and grizzly

Other popular mayfly patterns include:

ROYAL COACHMAN *(supposedly designed by a coach driver)*
hook size range: 8–14
wings: white duck quill
hackle: brown

---

*"**Dubbing**" is fine strands of fur or synthetic material that makes the body of a fly. Unless otherwise indicated, the "recipes" for the flies described in this chapter refer to dubbed bodies in the indicated colors.

body: peacock herl separated by a band of red floss
tail: black-tipped brown golden pheasant

LIGHT CAHILL
hook size range: 12–16
wings: speckled wood duck
hackle: white or cream
body: cream
tail: white or cream

BLUE WING OLIVE
hook size range: 14–22
wings: dark dun hackle tips
hackle: dark dun
body: brown/olive
tail: dark dun

BIVISIBLE *(so-called because it's meant to be visible to the fisherman as well as to the fish)*
hook size range: 10–16
body: two or three brown, black, or ginger hackles
hackle: one white hackle feather
tail: same color as the body

QUILL GORDON
hook size range: 10–16
wings: lemon wood duck
hackle: medium dun
body: stripped peacock quill with gold wire ribbing
tail: medium dun

The noted angler/writer/inventor Lee Wulff substituted deer hair for feathers as the wings and tails of certain patterns. The Royal Wulff would thus differ from the traditional Royal Coachman as follows:

ROYAL WULFF

hook size range: 8–14
wings: white deer hair
hackle: brown
body: peacock herl separated by a band of red floss
tail: white deer hair

CADDIS

CADDIS FLIES replicate the order *Trichoptera*, a group of insects that are most easily identified by their swept-back wings. Correct caddis proportions call for the wing to be one and one-third times the length of the hook shank, while the height of the hackle is three-quarters the length of the shank.

Popular patterns begin with the Hair-Wing Caddis:

HAIR-WING CADDIS

hook size range: 10–18
wings: black, olive, brown, or gray deer hair
hackle: dark dunn
body: olive and brown

Another widely used caddis is the Henryville Special.

HENRYVILLE SPECIAL

hook size range: 12–20
wings: lemon wood duck with mallard overwing
hackle: ginger
body: olive floss with palmered ("palmered" = wrapped around the hook shank) grizzly hackle

STONEFLIES

Adult **STONEFLIES,** of the order *Plecoptera,* have double wings that are folded over their bodies. Popular patterns of these flies, which are used primarily in Western waters, include:

STIMULATOR

hook size range: 4–10
wings: natural elk or deer hair

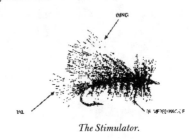

The Stimulator.

body: yellow, orange, or olive with palmered brown hackle
tail: natural elk or deer hair
head: amber, with wound grizzly hackle

GOLDEN STONE

hook size range: 4–10
wings: light elk hair
hackle: golden ginger
body: yellow with palmered ginger hackle
tail: light elk hair

MIDGES

Humans know some tiny two-winged insects of the order *Chironomid* as gnats and mosquitoes. Characterized by their minuscule size, these flies are tied on equivalently small hooks.

ADAMS MIDGE

hook size range: 20–24
hackle: mixed brown and grizzly
body: gray
tail: mixed brown and grizzly

TERRESTRIALS

Ants, beetles, grasshoppers, and other land-dwelling insects often fall off overhanging trees and bushes into streams and ponds. Sometimes they're blown there by gusts of wind. No matter how they get there, terrestrials are favorite fare of fish, and so are their equivalent flies.

BLACK ANT

hook size range: 10–20
wings: dun hackle tips
hackle: black
body: black, tied into two segments

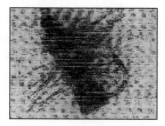

The Black Ant.

LETORT HOPPER

hook size range: 8–14
wings: speckled turkey, with brown deer hair as over-wing
body: yellow
head: spun deer hair

BLACK BEETLE

hook size range: 8–14
body: peacock herl with palmered black hackle
wing: gray goose wing stretched across top of fly

Deer hair, which has a good buoyancy quality, is used to make the Adams Irresistible and the Rat-Faced McDougal. The hair is spun around the hook's shank until it flares. Then it is trimmed to make the fly's *body:*

ADAMS IRRESISTIBLE

hook size range: 8–14
wings: grizzly hackle tips
hackle: mixed grizzly and brown
body: spun and clipped gray deer hair
tail: brown hackle fibers

RAT-FACED MCDOUGAL

hook size range: 8–14
wings: dark ginger
hackle: dark ginger
body: spun and clipped light deer hair
tail: dark ginger

WET FLIES

Although any fly that is fished below the water surface is considered "wet," a category that might be called "true wet" resemble larger and streamlined drys that, according to some commentators, fish may consider to be as much baitfish as insects. Many dry patterns, such as the Light and Dark Cahill and the Royal Coachman, have their equivalents in this form, but there are also exclusively "wet" patterns.

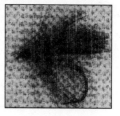

A wet fly.

The Hornberg is one:

HORNBERG

hook size range: 8–12
wings: mallard over yellow
hackle: mixed grizzly and brown
body: silver tinsel
cheek: jungle cock

Two other classic "wets" are:

LEADWING COACHMAN

hook size range: 10–14

wings: mallard duck quills

hackle: brown

body: peacock herl

PARMCHENE BELLE

hook size range: 8–12

wings: red and white duck quill

hackle: red and white

body: yellow floss with gold ribbing

tail: red and white hackle fibers

Dry flies replicate the adult stage of insects. However, before insects emerge as adults, they pass through several sub-surface stages. The intermediate stage between egg and adult for mayflies and stoneflies is as a nymph. Caddis flies metamorphose from eggs into larva (a wingless feeding stage) and then pupa (a non-feeding and immobile phase) before they becoming adults.

All these immature phases have their counterparts as fishing flies. Together with several other types of flies, they are grouped under the broad category "wet." The oldest type of fly, wets remain the most productive. Although some anglers resort to them only if dry fly-fishing is unproductive, everyone should bear in mind that the vast majority of a fish's diet comes from sub-surface food, especially the immature stage of whatever insects inhabit a particular stream, river, or pond.

NYMPHS

Easily the most popular nymph pattern is the Gold-Ribbed Hare's Ear:

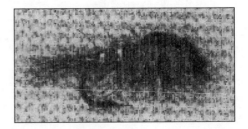

GOLD-RIBBED HARE'S EAR

hook size range: 6–18

wingcase: wood duck

body: black, brown, gray, or olive with gold tinsel ribbing

tail: wood duck

Other popular patterns are:

ZUG BUG

hook size range: 10–14

wingcase: mallard

hackle: brown

body: peacock herl with silver tinsel ribbing

tail: peacock

COMPRA NYMPH

hook size range: 4–18

wingcase: brown

hackle: ginger

body: yellow brown

MONTANA

hook size range: 8–14

wingcase: black chenille

hackle: black, palmered as legs

body: black chenille abdomen over yellow chenille thorax

tail: black

CADDIS LARVA AND PUPA

Patterns based on the immature stages of caddis flies include the following "generic" types:

CADDIS LARVA

hook size range: 12–16
body: olive, light yellow or brown with fine gold tinsel ribbing
hackle: brown, tied as legs
head: same color dubbing as body

CADDIS PUPA

hook size range: 16–20
body: gray, cream, olive, or brown with monofilament ribbing
wing: mallard quill
legs: wood duck
head: same dubbing as body

Many caddis larva and pupa flies have heads made of bronze bead. The tiny metal is meant to give the impression of air trapped in an insect's head sac. Then too, the weight of the bead serves as a sinker to get the fly down to bottom-feeding fish.

STREAMERS

There's no question that streamers are meant to resemble baitfish. Many streamers are made of long clumps of deer hair that move through the water with the sinuous motion of a fish's body.

One of the world's most popular streamer patterns is the Mickey Finn:

MICKEY FINN

hook size range: 4–14
wings: layered yellow, red, and yellow bucktail
body: silver tinsel

Other well-regarded patterns include:

MUDDLER MINNOW

hook size range: 4–14
head: flared deer hair
wings: brown deer hair and mottled turkey
body: gold tinsel
tail: turkey quill

MATUKA

hook size range: 4–10
wings: four grizzly, olive, or furnace hackle feathers tied vertically
hackle: grizzly, olive, or furnace
body: gray, olive, or yellow yarn with silver tinsel ribbon

GRAY GHOST

hook size range: 2–12
wings: four gray hackle feathers over golden pheasant
body: orange floss with silver tinsel ribbing
throat: peacock herl, white bucktail, and golden pheasant
shoulders: silver pheasant

BLACK LEECH

Lead Eye Leech.

hook size range: 4–10
wings: black marabou tied at top of hook shank

body: formed by the tied marabou
tail: black marabou

A saltwater streamer.

WOOLY WORM/BUGGER

Is it perceived as a nymph, a leech, or perhaps some sort of baitfish? That's a question that only a fish can answer, but if you ask any angler which fly wins the all-around "can't live without" prize, the answer will almost certainly be the Wooly Worm or the Wooly Bugger.

The Wooly Worm.

Which is which? Technically, one made with palmered hackle feathers is a Worm, while palmered marabou (the soft plumage of a stork) makes it a Bugger. Either way, the Wooly is frequently weighted with lead wire wrapped around the hook shank.

Like many effective items, the Wooly is simplicity itself. That's why it's the first pattern that most fly-tyers learn to create:

WOOLY WORM/BUGGER
hook size range: 6–16
body: black, brown, olive, gray, or white chenille palmered with grizzly, black, or white hackle feather or marabou

tail: red yarn for Wooly Worm; marabou for Wooly Bugger

Fashion Notes from Unlikely Sources: The Wooly Bugger holds the distinction of being the only fly to be featured in the "Style" section of *The New York Times.* Published in the wake of the success of the movie *A River Runs Through It,* the article suggested that a pair of Wooly Buggers tied on barbless hooks would make stunning earrings.

BASS FLIES

Although freshwater bass willingly take streamers and other large flies, certain patterns have been earmarked for largemouth, smallmouth, and other species. Some have cork or plastic bodies; others are all feather:

A plastic head bass fly.

HAIR BUG
hook size range: 1/0–4
legs: thin rubber stripswings
body: bands of black, yellow, and white spun and clipped deer hair
tail: yellow marabou and white saddle hackle

A mini hair bug popper.

MOUSE

hook size range: 1/0–2

body: brown spun deer hair clipped to the outline of a field mouse, with leather ears and bead eyes glued in place

tail: leather strip

SALMON FLIES

Salmon flies are as strikingly ornate in design as their names are exotic:

COSSEBOOM

hook size range: 2–10

tail: olive floss

body: olive floss with silver tinsel ribbing

wing: gray squirrel

throat: yellow hackle

SILVER DOCTOR

hook size range: 2–10

tail: golden pheasant

body: silver tinsel

wing: layered brown, blue, red, and yellow calf tail

throat: blue hackle

beard: guinea hackle

JOCK SCOTT

hook size range: 2–10

tail: golden pheasant wings

body: yellow floss and black goat with silver tinsel ribbing

wing: red, yellow, and blue calf tail with peacock and brown calf tail

throat: black hackle

UNDERTAKER

hook size range: 2–10

wings: black bear

body: green and red butt behind peacock herl with gold tinsel ribbing

throat: black hackle

SALTWATER FLIES

The growth in popularity of fly-fishing for tarpon, bonefish, and other species spawned innumerable patterns. The following three have become standards (both the Lefty's Deceiver and the Blonde series are tied in a variety of colors).

LEFTY'S DECEIVER

hook size range: 3/0–2

body: silver Mylar™

tail: 4 saddle hackles

hackle: matching bucktail or calf tail

cheek: Mylar™ strips

HONEY BLONDE

hook size range: 2–6

wings: yellow bucktail

body: gold tinsel

tail: yellow bucktail

PINK SHRIMP

hook size range: 2–6

body: silver Mylar™ with palmered pink hackle

tail: pink hackle fibers

back: pink bucktail stretched over hook shank

Tackle shops and mail-order firms that include ready-tied flies among their wares offer both basic and more specialized patterns in a range of hook sizes. Many of these commercially-tied flies, especially those in basic patterns, are made in Thailand, Sri Lanka, and other third-world countries where tyers frequently spend their entire working lives cranking out only one pattern.

You'll hear a difference of opinion over these mass-produced imports. Some people feel that the assembly-line approach creates acceptable, if not high, standards of quality. Others believe the imports tend to be sloppily made. The alternative?—some stores buy their flies from professional North American tyers, often from self-styled "trout bums" who keep body and soul together by selling flies that are tied by expert anglers.

Both imported and domestic flies have a nasty habit of becoming irretrievably caught in upper tree branches and on inaccessible underwater rocks and logs. That's why you'll need to carry several of each of the patterns recommended for the type of fishing you'll do, and in different sizes too. Anglers heading to unfamiliar waters often wait until they reach their destination, then purchase appropriate

patterns in the right sizes at local tackle shops. Or they phone ahead to a shop, lodge, or guide and inquire what to bring.

Tying Your Own Flies

Although hooking into a fish on a store-bought fly is exciting, an even greater buzz comes from success with a fly that you tied. That's why at some point in their careers, just about all fly-fishermen try their hand at turning out their own fur-and-feather concoctions.

Basic "hardware" consists of a vise to hold the hook, a bobbin to hold a spool of thread, scissors, waterproof cement, a pair of hackle pliers, and a whip finisher tool to tie off the thread. You'll also need hooks in different sizes, shapes, and weights, several spools of pre-waxed colored thread, a quantity of yarn (especially chenille, since your first attempt at tying is likely to be a Wooly Worm/Bugger). Other items include a variety of dubbing material and dubbing wax (used to make dubbing adhere to the thread), feathers for hackles, wings, and tails, and bucktail and other deer hair.*

Although these items and materials are available separately, entry-level fly-tying kits offer everything you'll need to get started. Then, if and when you decide you're hooked, you can invest in better equipment; starter-kit vises, for example, lack many features found in more sophisticated—and, accordingly, costly—vises.

Above and beyond what's included in kits, the books at the end of this chapter include reference works for tyers at all levels of experience. They will,

---

*And that's just the beginning. There's no end to the supplies with which experienced tyers surround themselves: wire, floss, foam and rubber (for insect bodies and legs), tinsel and other shiny metallic and synthetic threads, and epoxy for making the heads and bodies of saltwater flies. Even within these categories are a bewildering and panoramic range of products, each of which has its own use (and partisans among the fly-tying community).

in turn, refer you to more specialized volumes based on the kind of fish and fishing you plan to do.

VIDEOS

Instructional videos are a good way to learn fly-tying basics and more advanced techniques. Some that come highly recommended are:

Classic Dry Flies **with Dick Tailleur, Vols. I and II (90 min. each)**

Tying Trout Flies **with Gary Borger (60 min.)**

Jack Dennis' Fly Tying Basics **(60 min.)**

Poul Jorgensen on Fly Tying: My Favorite Fishing Flies, **Vols. I and II (100 min. each)**

Practical Trout Flies, **with Bob Lay and Al Beatty (120 min.)**

How to Tie and Fish the Caddis Fly, **with Gary LaFontaine, Mike Lawson, and Jack Dennis (120 min.)**

Tying Bass Flies, **with Dave Whitlock, Vols. 1 and 2 (65 min. each)**

Tying Saltwater Flies, **with Jimmy Nix, Vols. 1 and 2 (90 min. each)**

Tying Hatch Simulator Flies, **with Doug Swisher (60 min.)**

Tying Attractor Flies, **with Doug Swisher (60 min.)**

People who prefer "live" instruction will be pleased to discover that many tackle shops offer individual and group classes. In addition to the benefits of one-on-one instruction, many classes provide all the necessary tools and materials, so you needn't make a capital investment before deciding whether fly-tying is your bag. A growing number of colleges and universities offer classes as part of adult education programs. Then too, local chapters

of such organizations as Trout Unlimited and Federation of Fly Fishers can often put you in touch with a member who'll be happy to take you under his or her wing.

Fly Care

Whether store-bought or homegrown, flies will last longer and remain literally in better shape if stored in containers that have been specially designed for that job.

Fly boxes and wallets have two purposes: One is to keep flies from being crushed. The other is to allow fishermen to select a particular fly easily and safely, the latter referring to the ever-present possibility of dumping the box's contents or letting the wind blow them away.

The top-of-the-line models of boxes for dry flies are made of anodized aluminum and feature individual compartments, each of which has a spring-loaded transparent lid. When one compartment is open, only its contents run the risk of being spilled or blown away. Other aluminum models hold flies by their hooks in durable ripple foam.

Most foam-lined boxes come in plastic, in most cases equally serviceable as metal and certainly less costly. Ripple foam or other terraced or layered designs give the hackles of dry flies plenty of elbow room, far better than flat surfaces that tend to crush delicate feathers.

Unlined "see-through" plastic boxes comes in many sizes and with varying numbers of compartments. This type of container is not for the clumsy, though, since people who use them run the risk of dumping the entire contents at one time or watching everything blow away in an unexpected gust of wind. Still, plain compartmentalized boxes are inexpensive and convenient if handled correctly.

An innovative version of this type features adjustable dividers, so that you can customize the container according to your needs on any given day. The better boxes have watertight gasket-like rubber fittings around the top in case they're dropped into a stream or pond.

Wet flies, nymphs, and streamers aren't quite so delicate as drys. They can live quite comfortably in folding leather- or fabric-covered wallets that fit easily into vest pockets. The flies themselves stay in place by being hooked into the foam or sheepskin lining.

A popular type of box for wets has rows of clips or coils to hold the flies. Some models have clips on one inside cover and foam on the other so that both wets and dries can be carried in the same box.

Conclusion: There's no reason why you must limit yourself to only one style of container. Most fishermen use a variety, storing their flies at home in plain plastic boxes and then transferring the ones they plan to use into smaller and more secure cases.

Foam rubber or synthetic sheepskin fleece patches that clip or pin onto the front of a vest are a convenient way to carry a handful of flies or to dry off a fly after it's been used. Many vests come with permanently-attached fleece patches, but anglers who fish with barbed hooks may prefer foam rubber. Although sheepskin tends to hold hooks more securely than foam does (and it lasts longer), freeing a barb from its fleecy grasp often takes more effort than some people care to make.

Without proper care, feathers become moldy and hooks rust. Make sure your flies are thoroughly dry before putting them away. If, however, a fly's feathers have dried out or are stuck together, it's usually not beyond salvation. Holding the fly in a stream of steam coming out from a tea-kettle spout usually does the trick.

Books on Flies and Fly-Tying

Dyeing and Bleaching Natural Fly Tying Materials, **by A.S. Best (Lyons & Burford, 1993).**

Production Fly Tying, **by A.S. Best (Pruett, 1989).**
According to the author, "production" means tying more than one fly at a time. Be that as it may, he shares hints, prejudices, and other techniques on all aspects of creating what comes as close to perfection as an artificial fly can ever be.

Designing Trout Flies, **by Gary Borger (Tomorrow River Press, 1991).**
For more experienced and adventurous tyers.

The Simon & Schuster Guide to Trout and Salmon Flies, **by John Buckland (Simon & Schuster, 1986).**
A pocket-sized compendium of flies from all over the world.

The Art of the Trout Fly, **by Judith Dunham (Chronicle Books, 1988).**

The Atlantic Salmon Fly: The Tyers and Their Art, **by Judith Dunham (Chronicle Books, 1991).**
Two handsomely photographed collections that spotlight the handiwork of many of the world's best tyers.

The Orvis Fly Patterns Index, **by John Harder (Viking Penguin, 1990).**
Photos and "recipes" for essential patterns in all categories.

Salmon Flies: Their Character, Style and Dressings, **by Poul Jorgensen (Stackpole Books, 1978).**

Tying Dry Flies, **by Randall Kaufmann (West Fisherman, 1990).**
A well-regarded manual by a prolific and widely respected writer.

Caddisflies, **by Gary LaFontaine (Lyons & Burford, 1987).**
A definitive work on the subject.

The Complete Book of Fly Tying, by Eric Leiser (Knopf, 1977).

Orvis Guide to Beginning Fly Tying, by Eric Leiser (The Countryman Press, 1993).

The Complete Book is often cited as the best introduction to the subject, while the *Orvis Guide* is equally worth a place above your workbench.

The Book of Fly Patterns, by Eric Leiser (Knopf, 1993).

A comprehensive reference for somewhat more experienced tyers that novices will soon "grow into."

Micropatterns: Tying and Fishing the Small Fly, by Darrel Martin (Lyons & Burford, 1994)

Field & Stream calls this book "required reading for every angler who fishes over the 'tired' trout of today."

The Art of Tying the Nymph, by Skip Morris (Frank Amato Publications, 1993).

Fly Tying Made Clear and Simple, by Skip Morris (Frank Amato Publications, 1992).

Bug Making, by C. Boyd Pfeiffer (Lyons & Burford, 1993).

What the Trout Said, by Datus Proper (Lyons & Burford, 1989).

A thorough and thoughtful analysis of fly design based on the behavior of trout and of the insects themselves.

A Flyfisher's Guide to Saltwater Naturals and Their Imitation, by George V. Roberts, Jr. (Ragged Mountain Press/McGraw-Hill, 1994).

Fly Rod & Reel magazine suggests that this manual to the saltwater equivalent of matching the hatch "should be the standard for a long time to come."

Fly Tying Tips (revised), by Dick Stewart (Mountain Pond Pub., 1993).

Valuable shortcuts and remedial advice for tyers at all levels.

The Fly Tyer's Primer, by Richard W. Tailleur (Lyons & Burford, 1986).

Mastering the Art of Fly Tying, by Richard W. Tailleur (Stackpole Books, 1979).

Both books demonstrate why the author's reputation as a top teacher and tyer is so well deserved.

Fly Tying Tools and Materials, by Jacqueline Wakeford (Lyons & Burford, 1992).

The first and last word on fly-tying "hardware."

Salt Water Fly Tying, by Frank Wentink (Lyons & Burford, 1991).

What you'll need to know about this fast-growing aspect of saltwater fishing.

Note: Almost all the works listed in the "Books on Fly-Fishing" section of Chapter 13 (see pages 147–150) cover fly selection and how to use them.

11

ICE-FISHING

Ice-fishing is often treated like something of a breed apart from other angling disciplines. It usually gets its own section in books, the implication being that ice-fishing such a specialized calling that readers are either devotees (and as such, will devour the material) or else they couldn't care less and could be counted on to blithely skip to the next chapter.

Ice-fishing has its own section here because it's an activity that uses equipment which, except for the bait, tends to be unlike gear found in other kinds of fishing.

Discussions of ice-fishing almost invariably begin with the matter of keeping warm. If you've ever spent a winter in the upper Midwest or Canada, especially around the Great Lakes (the hotbed, so to speak, of ice-fishing), you're well aware that hypothermia is a significant and ever-present consideration. Thermal underwear and layers of turtlenecks, flannel shirts, and sweaters, all worn below a cocoon of a quilted and hooded jumpsuit, are standard apparel when the wind-chill factor reaches the brutal stage. Waterproof and insulated footwear is equally essential; some fishermen routinely attach cleats to the soles of their boots. A woolen watch cap is traditional; it's practical too, since it can fit snugly under a jumpsuit hood. Among types of gloves, some ice-fishermen prefer the fingertip-less variety that allow greater

digital dexterity, although neoprene Glacier Gloves® are far more water-resistant and warm. Sunglasses are necessary protection against glare coming off frozen lakes that are usually covered with a layer of snow.

Another way to reduce the brunt of winter is to fish from an ice-fishing shack. Towed into position as soon as a frozen lake is capable of supporting it, a shack may be anchored in one spot for weeks on end, or moved around more frequently (if the latter, its foundation may include skis or a sled). Shacks are customarily made of wood and heated by a wood-burning or butane gas stove or by a gas or electric heater. Shelves and/or cabinets provide storage space for tackle and extra clothing. Furnishings may include hot plates or more sophisticated cooking facilities and even a portable TV set (for those fishermen who couldn't bear to miss watching a Packers or Vikings game).

Less permanent, but wholly functional, are windscreens rigged of canvas stretched between durable metal frames. Somewhere between these and wooden shacks are the polyester tents and shelters sold by many tackle shops and catalogs. Features include Velcro® window flaps, sturdy plastic floors (some with precut holes), cushioned seats, and equipment lockers.

Or, if the ice is thick enough to support vehicles, you'll see people eying their tip-ups from the comfort of trucks or 4 × 4s.

Ice-fishing is a relatively passive form of fishing, and whether you're in a shelter or out in the open, you'll want to sit on something comfortable while you wait for a strike. Folding stools are easier on the body than boxes or upturned buckets; some come with storage compartments.

Safety is a second important factor. "STANDARD" ice is considered clear, blue, hard ice above the still water of a pond or lake. Such ice over the running water of a river is approximately 20% weaker, while slush ice is approximately 50% weaker. The American Pulpwood Association's "Ice Thickness Table" suggests the following permissible loads based on standard ice's thickness in inches:

2":	one person on foot
3":	group in single file
7½":	one car (2 tons)
8":	light truck (2½ tons)
10":	truck (3½ tons)
12":	heavy truck (7–8 tons)

However, some people will not fish on any ice less than 5 inches thick or drive a light truck on ice less than 15 inches thick.

There are two primary techniques used in ice-fishing. JIGGING calls for a short rod, from 2 feet to 3 feet in length. Although available commercially, many jigging rods are homemade: the tip section of a broken spinning or fly rod mounted onto a cork or foam handle. Once upon a time, any reel used on it was a rudimentary affair, basically a spool with little or no drag adjustment, but now small spinning reels are widely seen. Some jigging rods have no reel; line is looped around two hooks mounted above the handle and unwrapped as needed.

The other technique is to use a TIP-UP, an apparatus that signals, usually by tripping a flag, that fish is on the line. A reel is mounted on one end of the tip-up or else it is suspended underwater. The advantage to the former style is that you don't have to lift the entire tip-up out of the water

before setting the hook and retrieving a fish. On the other hand, wet line on an underwater reel doesn't freeze to the spool as it's apt to do if exposed to cold wind and air.

Instead of holding your jigging rod all the time or propping it on a can or box, you might consider a rod holder with a fluorescent orange handle. There are even rods with built-in holder handles designed to keep the rods at a proper angle over the hole (and also keep the reel above ground snow and ice).

The most elementary tip-ups are made of two crossed sticks, but more sophisticated systems have flashing lights and wind-powered mechanisms that jig the bait below.

That's not to say that ice-fishermen can't use both techniques. Most state laws permit one angler to use two lines, so one can be a stationary tip-up and the other a portable jigging rod that the fisherman carries to as many holes in the ice that he cares to make.

Dacron® line covered with vinyl or Teflon™ is a popular choice for either system, the test depending on the target species of fish. Braided line has its supporters, although some fishermen claim that maneuverability is lost when water gets between the strands of braiding and then freezes. SpiderWire™ makes a super-strength polyethylene line that its manufacturers claim becomes stronger as it gets colder. Nor will it become brittle, even at temperatures of −60° F.

Both jigging and tip-ups use live and artificial bait. Popular live baits are minnows, smelts, ciscos, grubs, and worms. Another traditional choice is a single fish eye, appropriated from earlier catches of the day. Live bait is customarily carried in a bucket; water tends to freeze more slowly in those made of Styrofoam.

Jigs and teardrop-shaped spoons, some with

hair or feather attached, lead the list of favorite lures. Light jigs of 1/16 ounce work best for perch and other small fish, while jigs weighing 1/4 ounce or more are appropriate for lake trout, pickerel, and other larger species. Because ice-fishing is a vertical activity, flat jigs and spoons work well; fish are attracted by the fluttering motion that the lures make during their descent.

Although bobbers are unnecessary on tip-ups, they are standard terminal tackle on jigging rig. Sinkers are useful for both techniques, not only to get the bait down to where the fish are, but to act as a depth-finder (if you're not using an electronic bottom-finder). One method is to lower a sinker line, then mark the line at the point where slack indicates that the sinker reached the bottom. Another is to attach hooks at various points along the line; where bites occur is where the fish are.

But the first step is to chop a hole in the ice. The most popular hardware for this purpose is an auger drill powered by hand or a gas motor. An alternative is a spud, a long-handled chisel for chipping ice away.

A slotted spoon is essential to remove layers of ice that will inevitably re-form over open holes. Or you can use a plastic cover, some models of which have a built-in tip-up. Another choice is something known as an Anti-Freeze Device, a cover with a thin plastic straw-like tube through which line can slide even if the hole freezes up.

A hole approximately 3-feet wide doesn't give much room to net a fish once it's brought to the surface. That's why a gaff is the customary way to prevent fish from escaping.

State and local laws vary with regard to the maximum number of lines that one angler is permitted to use, as well as the maximum number of hooks. In New York State, for example, five tip-ups and two hand-lines are the maximum (at this writing); each tip-up must be identified with the name and address of the fisherman, who must be present when the lines are in the water.

Other regulations may be different from what you're used to obeying during non-winter seasons, so make sure you know what's legal and what isn't. You'll also want to learn any local customs, particularly with regard to picking a spot or spots that are too close to someone else's hole or holes.

That becomes even more of a factor when fishing on popular lakes where the number of shacks gives the scene the appearance of a small village.

Ice-fishing isn't for everyone. Like aquavit with a beer chaser, it's an acquired taste, enjoyable only after you take the time and make the effort to become accustomed to it. But its fans claim that the thrill of an unseen fish below your feet taking your bait is just as exciting, if not more so, than thrills found in other kinds of fishing. They also point with pleasure to the sociability factor: the companionship of other anglers who, like themselves, don't let the minor inconvenience of subfreezing temperatures keep them from fishing.

Books and Videos on Ice-Fishing

Perhaps because of its Minnesota base of operations, *The In-Fisherman* seems to cover the world of ice-fishing more thoroughly than other general-interest magazines. Regional magazines published in Wisconsin, Minnesota, Michigan, and other northern states also do a good job.

The In-Fisherman produced a pair of videos: *Ice Fishing Secrets I* (52 min.) and *Ice Fishing Secrets II* (60 min.). The former features an introduction to jigging and tip-ups, while the sequel focuses on more advanced techniques, including the use of depth-finders and other electronic devices.

A good book on the subject is *Ice Fishing: Methods and Magic* by Steven Griffin (Stackpole Books, 1985), which gives an appetite-whetting taste of the sport's general appeal and lifestyle.

Another how-to book that many devotees of the sport recommended is *Ice Fishing: A Complete Guide. . . Basic to Advanced* by Jim Capossela (The Countryman Press, 1992).

Freshwater Fishing: 1000 Tips from the Pros by Henry Waszczuk and Italo Labignan (Key Porter Books, 1993) contains a chapter full of meaty how-to hints. So does *The Sports Afield Fishing Almanac*, edited by Frank S. Golad (Lyons & Burford, 1989).

Ice-fishing in Minnesota.
[photo courtesy Minnesota Office of Tourism]

12

CLOTHING

Footwear

Many anglers, especially those who fish from a boat, favor athletic shoes of the jogging/sneaker type. Comfortable and relatively lightweight, they provide traction even when the boat's deck or its bottom is wet.

Shoes and boots of the style that's become generically known as "Bean boots" (after its innovator, the eponymous L.L. Bean) have waterproof rubber bottoms and leather uppers. They're especially good for walking along shorelines or over rugged terrain. A steel shank makes them durable, while molded heels and soft rubber or gum soles increase their comfort.

The Red Ball Guide Boot is 11 inches high and has rubber bottoms. Its uppers are made of 1000 denier nylon. Its Thinsulate® bootie can be removed when insulation is not required, and its liner wicks away moisture from the feet. Similar boots from other manufacturers may contain moisture-wicking liners made of Gore-Tex®.

SOCKS

Since few things are more uncomfortable than spending a day with cold and/or clammy or completely wet feet, the choice of socks is important. Polypropylene and silk both wick moisture away from the skin, which makes either fabric an excellent choice for a liner to be worn under cotton, wool, acrylic, or wool/acrylic socks, depending on the degree of warmth you seek.

Waders

Not all fishing requires working your way into position to meet the fish halfway. There are even anglers who wade but don't need special clothing, such as the bonefishermen who wear short pants or swimsuits while they work warm-water flats. But for those who challenge chilly streams and colder rivers and coastal surf, waders are essential for warmth and safety.

Waders come in two types. The one you'll need depends entirely on the type of water that you fish. Hip waders (also called "hippers") are designed for water that comes up no higher than pelvis-deep. Chest waders are appropriate for deeper water. Although chest-highs can be rolled down to hip height when the weather and water level permit, many anglers don't like the excess material, and so owning both hippers and chest-highs makes some sense.

Within these types are two categories. The boot-foot wader contains an attached rubber boot. Its advantage is convenience, since you won't spend time lacing and unlacing wading shoes. But the boots tend to be heavy and bulky, qualities that give much-needed warmth and stability while surf-casting in the ocean. They also offer less ankle and heel support than separate wading shoes and boots do. That's less of a problem on smooth, relatively level surfaces (such as, again, when surf-fishing on sandy-bottom stretches of coastline) than when coping with the uncertain footing of a rocky-bottomed mountain trout stream or a rushing salmon river or a rocky surf.

That's a compelling argument for wading shoes, the kind worn with stocking-foot waders. They are made of synthetic leather uppers and felt soles. Some soles come with attached metal studs for easier and safer walking on muddy bottoms, although many angler prefer plain felt soles for rocky stream bottoms.

The best wading shoes have a padded collar at the back, a sturdy tongue, solid eyelets, and a thick and sturdy polyester "felt" sole. Although lacing shoes takes somewhat longer than slipping into their boot-foot cousins, that chore becomes somewhat easier for shoes with "speed lace" eyelets or bindings made of Velcro® strips.

The first waders were made of rubber. Some still are, and these are the type that some surf-fishermen continue to use. Lighter-weight nylon and other synthetics came next, and they remain the most durable (in the sense of tear-resistant) material. Multi-layered designs using waterproof and abrasion- and crack-resistant fabrics keep the wearer warm as well as dry; waders that retain body heat are a big plus on cold days and/or in frigid waters. Accordingly, and depending on the climate in which they fish, many anglers choose multi-ply material that come in up to four layers. Among the strongest and most comfortable are a four-layer system composed (starting with the layer closest to the body) of a nylon liner, a closed-cell polyurethane foam, an insulator felt, and an insulating aluminum film covered by a waterproof polyurethane coating.

Stretch fabrics like neoprene revolutionized waders. Neoprene hugs the wearer's body and thus reduces the chance of water entering and collecting. Moreover, this form-fitting style traps and retains the wearer's body heat. And when tempera-tures rise to the point that insulation isn't welcome (and where water level permits), neoprene chest waders can be rolled down and worn waist-high.

Gore-Tex® is a fabric that is highly regarded for its "breathability"; it is composed of layers of billions of holes that are too small for drops of water to pass through, but large enough for human perspiration to escape. Despite the tiny holes, the fabric gets high marks for durability.

Why then choose a wader made of anything other than a stretch fabric? Cost is one factor; nylon and rubber are less expensive. Weight is another reason: single layers of nylon are far lighter and cooler for summer use, and they're equally durable in situations where there's little chance of snagging or otherwise puncturing the material.

The sizing of boot-foot chest waders is based on a combination of shoe size and inseam length, with the inseam measured from crotch to floor. (Some manufacturers also provide chest size and height and weight ranges for additional reference.) Inseams usually have a 4-inch range; for example, 30 inches to 34 inches for a size 8 foot. Stocking-foot sizes offer a slightly larger range of inseam; in one instance, a wader that accommodates sizes 9 to 11 shoes has an inseam range of 30 inches to 36 inches.

However, since people come in all sizes and shapes and combinations of sizes and shapes, not everyone with a size 8 foot can comfortably wear an inseam in the indicated range, even when stretchy fabrics are involved. A comfortable fit is essential for ease of casting and lack of chafing. However, don't despair if you don't find your perfect fit on your first try. Different manufacturers make their waders in different shapes, so keep shopping around. Trying on waders before you buy a pair is always a good idea, but if that's not possible, dealing with a mail-order firm that has a good exchange policy is the next best course.

Many serious anglers have their waders custom-made. You send in your measurements, and the manufacturer tailors the garment accordingly. Custom-made waders are not inexpensive, but one devotee suggested that prorating the additional cost over four or five years of wear makes the expense less painful.

As for "extras," built-in knee-pads add comfort and durability, while hand-warmer front pockets are useful in cold weather. And far more than something in the "extra" department, women anglers have been pleased to learn that a number of manufacturers now offer waders specifically designed to fit the female form.

Certain accessories make wading easier and safer. Socks made of neoprene or another synthetic are worn over the foot of a stocking-foot wader; the sock's top folds gaiter-like over the boot-top to keep gravel and other debris out of the shoe.

Any chest wader that isn't form-fitting requires a wading belt. The belt straps tightly around the wearer's chest to keep out water in case of a dunking, a serious matter because drownings have resulted from water-filled waders. A quick-release buckle is also of inestimable value in the unhappy event you need to get out of your waders in a hurry to swim for your life.

Unless your chest waders come with their own suspenders, you'll need a pair. Snaps are somewhat easier to attach but less secure than buckles or buttons-and-buttonholes.

Inflatable suspenders are activated by CO_2 cartridges and sinking. Also in the safety vein, cleats that strap onto wader boots or shoes (think of chains on auto tires) give considerably more traction than studded soles do. The most widely used brand is "Corkers," which has become something of a generic name for the item.

While not exactly part of your wardrobe, a wading staff can save your day (if not your life) in the event you need to cross difficult water. The wood or metal one-piece types are strong but can be unwieldy when not being used. The folding variety has the advantage of being able to be worn on your belt when not in use.

What to wear under waders depends on the climate and how much you want to avoid the clammy clutches of evaporating perspiration. Polypropylene or silk socks and underwear wick moisture away to your next layer of clothing, usually a second pair of wool or cotton socks. Polar fleece wading pants don't ride up under waders, thanks to their elastic foot stirrups. Otherwise, most fishermen find that sweats, long johns, or jeans work perfectly well.

WADER CARE

The best way to prolong the life of waders, no matter what the material, is to keep them high and dry. Waders that are tossed in a corner are prone to suffer scrapes and other abrasions and punctures. Any residue moisture invites mildew and other unwelcome flora and fauna. Boot and wader hangers are specifically designed for storage and drying.

No matter how tight the fit, some amount of water will seep into wading shoes. Most people don't mind putting on wet shoes, since the wader's stocking foot comes between feet and the shoe itself. If, however, dry shoes is an imperative, a circulating-heat boot drier will speed things up considerably.

Despite the best care, holes will happen at some point in a wader's life. Punctures in rubber waders can be patched, and those in nylon waders can be taped with industrial-strength self-adhesive tape. Although neoprene has a tendency to self-seal small punctures, special cements are available, often as part of repair kits that include detailed instructions.

Soles wear out faster than the rest of wading shoes do, and replacement kits give shoe bottoms a new lease on life.

Transporting waders is easier with a wader pack. Its mesh sides or top expedite drying, and the carpet pad that's part of most packs is a blessing to bare feet when changing in and out of shoes in the middle of the great outdoors (that is, a carpet of pine needles isn't such a blessing).

Pants

Many, if not most, fishermen wear plain ol' jeans. That's not to say, however, that there are no pants specifically designed for fishing. One style, unsurprisingly, is manufactured by a jeans company: the Wrangler Angler. Made of cotton, it includes pockets for such gear as pliers and knives. Rear pockets are secured by Velcro® flaps, a useful feature to keep possessions out of Davy Jones' locker.

Short pants are appropriate for fishing the flats along the Florida Keys and other warm places. Quick-drying and cotton-soft Supplex® has become the material of choice for shorts and for long- and short-sleeved shirts. However, since Supplex® tends to trap perspiration, some garments are treated in a process known as Intera, which draws moisture along the cloth's surface to increase the rate of evaporation.

For those days that you can't decide between long pants and shorts, you might try "zip-off" pants: zippers that run around the trouser legs at mid-thigh instantly convert the garment into shorts.

Shirts

The most essential consideration for any fishing shirt is that it not restrict movement. That's why they are cut to be generously roomy, especially around the armholes.

Shirts should also have collars that can turned up to protect against the wind and the sun's rays. Some anglers favor button-down collars, which won't flap in the breeze but can always be unbuttoned and turned up.

Sun rays that are reflected off water produce particularly nasty burns. Long-sleeved shirts, which offer protection for your entire arm, are traditional. Button-tabs on some models secure the sleeves when you want to roll them up.

All types of fishing require lots of items that you'll want easy access to. That's why fishing shirts are made with a plethora of pockets (even if you wear a vest, you'll never complain about having too many pockets). Among those items designed with the fisherman in mind, Cabela's Guide Shirt is a short-sleeved 5-pocket number with a D-ring for attaching additional items.

Vests

Before there were fishing vests, anglers carried their gear in their pockets or in small bags worn over their shoulders. Then the legendary Lee Wulff had a better idea, and the fishing vest was born.

The fishing vest—and because Wulff was best known as a fly-fishing guru, we'll begin with the fly-fishing vest—is marked by pockets. Big pockets, little pockets, pockets on the outside and inside, and even on the back. That's to accommodate the myriad items to which a fly-fisher needs ready access. And that's "ready" as in "immediate," not "wait a minute until I wade to shore, fumble through my bag, and then wade back."

The number of pockets varies from vest to vest, ranging from 8 up to 30 or more. Some pockets are closed by rustproof metal or plastic zippers, others by flaps secured by Velcro®, while still others have no flaps or fastenings at all.

How many pockets you require on your vest depends primarily on how much gear you plan to carry. Most novices (and many experts) need no more than 10 or 12 pockets to accommodate all their gear; one or two large expandable ones for fly boxes; a couple of others for floatants and desiccants; others for leaders and tippet material (some vests have small inner pockets for individual tippet spools); and the rest for strike indicators, leader sink-gink, sunglasses, and fishing license. That doesn't include items that are carried on the vest itself by means of retractable wire "zingers" (usually, line nipper and hook-removing hemostat pliers, to name just two), as well as a landing net hanging down the back.

Other features can include one or more D-rings for attaching such items as a wading staff; a fleece patch for drying flies; Velcro® rod-holding tabs; buckle straps for carrying traveling rods in their tubes; and hand-warmer pockets on the front of the vest.

Vests come in varying lengths. Those that extend below the wearer's waist have room for the most pockets, but if you're going to wade in deep water, you may want to sacrifice space for one of the so-called "shortie" models.

The best-designed vests have deep armholes that permit unrestricted casting. Because a fully-laden vest will carry several pounds of gear, a bias-cut, non-binding collar will distribute pressure evenly against the wearer's neck. Some vests have padded collars for just that purpose.

A "shortie" vest. [courtesy Orvis]

As for material, cotton or a cotton blend is most common, with such synthetics as Supplex® providing even greater durability. Many anglers favor mesh for greater coolness and less weight, but you should be advised that objects tend to become snagged in mesh faster than in solid cloth.

Since a bright-colored vest will alert fish to the wearer's presence, solid and somber hues like tan, olive green, gray, or camouflage are most popular and the most readily available. Even within that spectrum, green or tan is appropriate for anglers who fish where there's lots of background foliage. By the same token, gray or slate blue will reduce the visual effect of standing out against open sky.

If there's any question about size, opt in favor of roominess. Fishing in cold weather means that you'll wear your vest over a sweater or a jacket (or both), while roomy vests allow air to circulate on warm days whatever the season. Another argument for roominess in cotton vests is that cotton is likely to shrink after a number of dunkings-and-dryings.

Since just about everyone welcomes pockets, other anglers besides the fly-fishing variety wear vests. Those designed for baitcasting and spinning fans who spend a fair amount of time in boats often include flotation safety features, either built-in "life-preserver" foam or an apparatus for inflation. The latter can either be the automatic inflating variety by which CO_2 cartridges are automatically activated, or the manually inflating type where the wearer blows into a valve (some automatics have this backup capability). Whistles attached to vests come in handy when there's a need to signal for help.

Fishermen who don't like the idea of vests, but do like their safety features, might consider separate flotation suspenders.

Alternatives to Vests

Harking back to the pre-Wulff era, gear bags are making a comeback (actually, they never left), especially those that can be worn around the waist.

Other choices include the chest fly box, and the fishing belt with its large main compartment and five smaller ones.

Jackets

Among the styles of nylon and nylon-acrylic wind- and water-resistant jackets are those with built-in sweatshirt linings and hoods. At the top of the line is a bomber-style jacket made of Airex™ flotation foam.

Fly-fishermen tend to favor fleece pullovers made of nonabsorbent, quick-drying, and breathable Polartec™.

Rain Gear

Since precipitation is capable of insinuating itself almost anywhere, the most effective foul-weather gear makes every effort to keep the wearer hermetically sealed against moisture. That includes such features as covered seams, elasticized or Velcro® cuffs, collar-flap tabs, and covered pockets.

With regard to fabric, synthetics have pretty much taken over where oilskin and rubber once reigned. Hypalon™ laminate is one popular fabric. So is a nylon/Supplex® combination with a Zepel™ anti-moisture repellent surface.

Gore-Tex® is as "breathable" for rainwear as it is for waders; the fabric repels rain but allows perspiration to escape.

Our British cousins, who are no strangers to rising damp, discovered that cotton impregnated with paraffin wax repels moisture in a major way. Wax jackets, originated by Barbours but now manufactured by several other companies, is particularly popular among the sporting set. Waxed cotton is not quite so waterproof as synthetics are, but the process does the job (and has a certain British field sports cachet for those who care about such matters). The paraffin wears off, so the garments must be periodically re-waxed, an odorous chore best done in a well-ventilated area.

Wading jackets for fly-fishing are waterproof (not just water-resistant), with large chest pockets and often a hood and a drawstring waist to keep out the elements. Many are light enough to be folded and carried in a vest's pouch pocket.

Headgear

Hats are essential, no matter what the climate or time of year. Hats retains valuable body heat during cold weather, and they help prevent sunburn when the sun shines. Equally important, headgear protects against wayward flying fishhooks whatever the weather.

The choice of fishing headgear is as varied as the imagination of those who wear them. To those of you to whom image is everything, you can top off your individual "look" in any number of ways: floppy hats with cords that tie under the chin or caps with long bills in front and back (to keep the sun off your neck as well as your face) for the explorer/adventurer look; ten-gallon Western hats for the Rocky Mountain fly-fisher look; "Sherlock Holmes" deerstalker caps and tweed cloth caps for the English chalk-stream or Scottish or Irish salmon-river look; baseball-style "gimme" caps with or without logos or funny sayings for whatever look they're meant to convey. . . the choice is yours. But please remember to wear a hat.

One hat that's growing in popularity among anglers is "The Tilley Hat," a canvas number that features a cord that runs over the crown and ties securely under the wearer's chin. A layer of closed-cell polyethylene in its crown enables the hat to float under most conditions should it part company from the wearer's head.

Gloves

Ray Scott, founder of the Bass Anglers Sportsman Society (familiarly known as B.A.S.S.), devised a glove he calls "The Udder Hand." Its latex rubber fingers and thumb give a good grip on slippery fish. The glove also provides protection against hooks and fish teeth. When not in use, it adheres to your belt by a Velcro® holder (available through Bass Pro Shop).

For ice-fishing or any other cold-weather angling, the neoprene Glacier Glove® has a curved-finger design that the manufacturer says provides comfort and flexibility. When the thermometer dips even lower, polypropylene liners can be worn underneath.

Fly-fishermen prefer finger-less wool or acrylic gloves. This style doesn't restrict dexterity or sensitivity (e.g., when stripping line) while keeping the rest of your hand warm.

Sunglasses

You may not consider sunglasses as clothing, but covering your eyes is just as essential to your comfort and safety as covering the rest of your body.

Water reflects ultraviolet radiation (UVR), particularly the more damaging portion of the light-wave spectrum designated as "UV-B." Exposure can cause an inflammatory reaction of the cornea and of the conjunctiva, the tissue that covers the inner eyelid and eyeball. The effect feels as though there's a foreign body in your eye, and occasionally great pain and spasm of the eyelid. Some ophthalmologists believe that prolonged exposure to UV-B results in cataract formation in the lens. That's why the regular use of sunglasses is recommended.

The American National Standards Institute devised a labeling system that sunglasses manufacturers voluntarily follow. There are three categories: "Cosmetic" glasses filter 70% of UV-B; "general purpose" filter 95%; and "special purpose" block 97%. Anglers can further reduce the amount of any type of UVR by wearing frames with side shields, brow bars, and nose shields.

With regard to color, brown lenses reduce glare on bright days, while amber improves vision on cloudy days or under dim light. Gray enhances true colors.

Polarized lenses do not change the amount of UVR filtered from direct sunlight, but they do filter light that is reflected off water. The resulting elimination of glare lets us spot fish more easily, particularly on bright days.

Better-made lenses increases vision and decrease eye fatigue. Most glasses are now made from unbreakable polycarbonate; the coating process that makes them scratch-resistant adds to the cost, but to most wearers the increased cost is well worth it. Photochromatic lenses, which grow darker or lighter according to available light, are also more costly than lenses that remain only one shade.

Among sunglasses specifically made for fishing are bifocals with magnifiers for close-up threading work on the lower half. Spring-hinge glasses let magnifying lenses pop up and out of the way when you don't need them.

Few things are more frustrating yet more avoidable than losing your glasses overboard. Cords that extend from earpiece to earpiece let glasses dangle around your neck when you're not using them. Elastic straps hold glasses in place. Take your choice, but use one of them.

Support Belts

Hours of standing and casting along a shore or from a boat tends to take its toll. One result is fatigue and pain in the lower lumbar region of the back, sometimes temporary but sometime chronic. That's why several manufacturers took a cue from items worn by construction workers and others involved in heavy labor.

Elastic support belts designed for fishermen do in fact relieve lower back stress. Many users prefer the kind with built-in suspenders that keep the belt in place while the wearer is casting or playing a fish. Other models feature an adjustable belt

that threads through trouser loops for the same purpose.

Support belts are even inching toward the "vest" category: Valeo, for example, makes one that includes a built-in tool pouch, D-ring, and accessory clip.

Fishing-Inspired Clothing

How about neckwear with fishy motifs: tie on a Royal Wulff pattern (on a navy background), Grey Ghost (maroon), or Blue Rat (blue-and-red or cream-and-red stripes). A Royal Wulff bowtie is available too. Barnard-Maine Ltd., P.O. Box 275, Castine, ME 04421, phone: (800) 962-1526.

Alynn Neckwear has several handsome cravat patterns, including assorted flies on "Gone Fishing" and the self-explanatory "Reels and Creels." The ties are available at gift shops around the country; to find out where, phone (800) 252-5966.

Kits to make belts and pillows featuring fanciful fish and flies, deep-sea scenes, and other fishing patterns are available from The Joy of Needlepoint, 207 Countryside Dr., Franklin, TN 37064, phone: (800) 545-8028. The firm, which will mount your handiwork once you've finished, will custom-design patterns too.

Most tackle and outdoor clothing shops carry T-shirts with fishing motifs. Like bumper stickers, they range from the mildly ribald ("The Way to a Fisherman's Heart Is Through His Fly" and "Lure Collectors Love Old Hookers") to the sublime ("I Fish, Therefore I Am" and "Nullum Gratuitum Prandium—There Is No Free Lunch").

Some others that caught our eye (manufacturers or distributors in parentheses):

"Walk Softly and Carry a Big Fish"; and "Twist
& Trout" (Quality Classics);
"I Fish, Therefore I Lie" and Alaska fishing
themes (Apone's T-Shirt Cache);
"Wader, There's a Fly in My Soup!" (M.
Hammond);
The muskie, pike, catfish, crappie, bluegill, wall-
eye, and largemouth bass patterns (Tee-
Shirts of Florida);
"Coast & Keys" International Game Fish
Association World collages of "Atlantic
Coast Offshore Game Fish"; "Pacific Coast
Offshore Game Fish"; and "Florida Keys
Offshore Game Fish" (see address for
International Game Fish Association in
Chapter 23, page 257);
"Catch & Release" (Eddie Bauer);

Fly Rod & Reel magazine's cover design;
"The One Who Dies with the Most Toys Wins"
(design includes lots of fishing gadgets);
"No Clear Line Between Religion and
Fishing" (from *A River Runs Through It*);
and the Madison, Beaverkill, Battenkill, and
Bighorn patterns (Orvis);
Placket-front polo shirts with salmon fly or Royal
Coachman "logo" (L.L. Bean);
"I'd Rather Be Fishing with Dad" and
"Something Fishy" (a cat swimming among
three trout)(available from Westbank
Anglers. . . see "Mail-Order Houses and
Tackle Shops" section in Chapter 27 for
address)

Clothing Manufacturers and Sales Outlets

Action Optics
Box 2999
Ketchum, ID 83340
(800) 654-6428

All-American Sportswear
836 Cooper Landing Rd.
Cherry Hill, NJ 08002
(609) 779-965

Apone's T-Shirt Cache
436 W. 4th Ave.
Anchorage, AK 99501-2364
(800) 770-1007
fax: (907) 272-1019

Bausch & Lomb Optics
42 East Ave.
Rochester, NY 14604
(716) 338-6000

Eddie Bauer (outdoor clothing)
P.O. Box 3700
Seattle, WA 98124-3700
(800) 426-8020

L.L. Bean (outdoor clothing)
Freeport, ME 04033
(800) 221-4221

Columbia Sportswear
Box 3239
Portland, OR 97203
(800) 547-8066
(503) 289-6602

Ex Officio (outdoor clothing)
1419-A Elliott Ave.
Seattle, WA 98119
(206) 283-1471
fax: (206) 286-9012

Fenwick (outdoor clothing)
5242 Argosy Avenue
Huntington Beach, CA 92649
(714) 897-1066

Glacier Glove
4890 Aircenter Circle #210
Reno, NV 89502
(800) 728-8235

Goldeneye Vests
P.O. Box 6387
Bozeman, MT 59771
(406) 586-2228

Graylite Outdoors Standard
   Safety Equipment Co.
   (waders)
431 N. Quintin Rd.
Palatine, IL 60067
(708) 359-1400
fax: (708) 359-2885

M. Hammond
214 Dimmick Ave.
Venice, CA 90291
(310) 452-5107

Hobie Sunglasses
1030 Calle Sombre
San Clemente, CA 92673
(800) 554-4335

Hodgman, Inc. (waders)
1750 Orchard Rd.
Montgomery, IL 60538
(800) 323-5965
fax: (708) 897-7558

Korkers Inc. (wading cleats)
P.O. Box 166
Grand Pass, OR 97526
(503) 476-6823
fax: (503) 479-1281

G. Loomis Inc. (outdoor clothing)
1359 Downriver Drive
Woodland, WA 98674
(800) 622-8818
fax: (206) 225-7169

Travel Wader/O.S. Systems
P.O. Box 864
Scappoose, OR 97056
(503) 543-3126
fax: (503) 543-3129

Orvis (outdoor clothing)
Historic Route 7A
Manchester, VT 05254
(800) 815-5900

Patagonia Inc. (outdoor clothing)
P.O. Box 150
Ventura, CA 93002
(805) 643-8616
fax: (805) 653-6355

Quality Classic Sportswear
3000 Lind Ave. SW
Renton, WA 98055
(800) 735-7185
fax: (206) 251-0883

Red Ball/Servus (waders)
9300 Shelbyville Rd.
Louisville, KY 40222
(800) 451-1806
fax: (502) 327-6001

Simms Fishing Products (vests
   and waders)
P.O. Box 3645
Bozeman, MT 59715
(406) 585-3557
fax: (406) 585-3562

Specialized Eyewear
27601 Forbes Rd.
Laguna Niguel, CA 92677
(714) 582-2347

Stream Designs (vests)
350 5th Avenue, Suite 5310
New York, NY 10118
(800) 876-3366

Stream Line (outdoor clothing)
7865 Day Rd. W.
Bainbridge Island, WA 98110
(206) 842-8501

Tarponwear (outdoor clothing)
P.O. Box 2272
Jackson, WY 83001
(307) 739-9755
fax: (307) 739-9817

T Shirts of Florida
4201 NE 12th Terrace
Fort Lauderdale, FL 33334
(800) 327-3665
fax: (305) 565-3340

Tilley Endurables (hats)
300 Langner Road
Buffalo, NY 14224
(800) 338-2797

Valeo Outdoors (support belt)
W 229 N 1680 Westwood Drive
Waukesha, WI 53186
(414) 547-9474

1 3

BOOKS AND MAGAZINES

It's been said about sporting literature that "books can't make you a good player, but they can make you a better player."

That holds true for fishing. Nothing—and that includes the most descriptive prose, the most stunning photography, or the most accurate graphics—takes the place of actually wetting a line. (The same point applies to videos and CD-ROMs: no matter how technologically dazzling, virtual reality comes out second-best against actual reality.)

But, as the saying suggests, books on fishing can make us better fishermen, and in several ways. Thanks to instructional texts (and we can include videos here too) by a variety of experts, we don't have to "reinvent the wheel" whenever we're ready to try something new. Reading the texts becomes the equivalent of taking master classes from which we can benefits in many areas: tackle selection, "reading" water and understanding structure, and techniques involved in casting, hooking, playing, and landing fish. And unlike "live" lessons, books let us go back to review particular points again and again; we can read and reread with the time to

think about the hows and whys and wherefores, and at our own pace too.

Books expand our horizons in other ways. We can learn the history of a particular kind of fishing, often from the pens and perspectives of people who made the history. We learn about places, from the strange and exotic to familiar locales that we see described in a new light. Raconteurs and essayists show us aspects of fishing—and often of ourselves—that increase our enjoyment of the sport in ways that we never dreamed of.

Convinced? Probably—after all, you're reading a book even as we speak.

The Ultimate Fishing Guide is a sourcebook, and almost every one of its section contains references to further reading; the chapters on species, tackle, and vacations in particular contain extensive bibliographies. However, certain books merit special mention for having proved particularly valuable in the preparation of *The Ultimate Fishing Guide*. Certain others may not otherwise fit into a convenient niche in other chapters or section of this book, yet should not be ignored.

Any and all would make useful additions to anyone's basic library (they're listed in no particular order).

McClane's New Standard Fishing Encyclopedia and International Angling Guide by A.J. McClane (Henry Holt, 1974).

Species, tackle, techniques. . . *the* reference book for any and all fishermen.

Hook, Line, and Sinker: The Complete Angler's Guide to Terminal Tackle, by Gary Soucie (Henry Holt, 1994).

The first (and last) word, including technical analyses, on what goes on the "business end" of a fishing line.

The Complete Angler's Catalog, by Scott Roederer (Johnson Books, 1985).

"Complete" is right—the author described and assessed everything in the fly-fishing universe, from tackle and clothing to schools and catalogs to books and art. It's a shame the book is out of print, but don't let that stop you fly-fishing enthusiasts from searching for and snagging a copy.

Fishing Fundamentals, by Wade Bourne (The In-Fisherman, 1988).

A useful introduction to tackle and techniques.

Fishing with Ray Bergman, edited by Edward C. Janes (Simon & Schuster/Fireside, 1989).

This collection of Bergman's *Outdoor Life* columns makes a useful guide to the range of freshwater equipment and techniques.

Freshwater Fishing: 1000 Tips from the Pros, by Henry Waszczuk and Italo Labignan (Key Porter Books, 1993).

Straightforward help hints for a variety of styles of fishing.

Fishing Basics, by Gene Kugach (Stackpole Books, 1993).

Another good introduction.

The Striped Bass, by Nick Karas (Lyons & Burford, 1994).

A comprehensive guide to this popular saltwater species (and to saltwater fishing in general).

New American Trout Fishing, by John Merwin (Macmillan, 1994).

Among the book's other assets, an analysis of fly-fishing tackle in theory and practice.

The Complete Guide to North American Freshwater Game Fish, by Henry Waszczuk and Italo Labignan (Key Porter Books, 1992).

How to locate, recognize, and catch them.

Simon & Schuster's Guide to Saltwater Fish and Fishing, by Angelo Mojetta (Simon & Schuster/Fireside, 1992).

Although European in design and approach, a handy little guide.

The L.L. Bean Game and Fish Cookbook, by Angus Cameron and Judith Jones (Random House, 1983).

In addition to the recipes, there's a good feeling for what sport-fishing is all about.

Fly Fishing with Children: A Guide for Parents, by Philip Brunquell, M.D. (The Countryman Press, 1993).

Equally valuable for other kinds of fishing.

The Travelling Angler, by Ernest Schweibert (Doubleday, 1991).

Even if we're never going to all the places that the author recommends, we can still dream, can't we?

Advanced Fly Fishing Techniques: Secrets of an Avid Fisherman, by Lefty Kreh (Delacourt, 1992).

A giant step toward advancing your skills is to profit from this book.

The Orvis Guide to Flyfishing, by Tom Rosenbauer (Lyons & Burford, 1984).

The best-selling book on the subject (perhaps on any fishing subject), and deservedly so.

Production Fly Tying, by A.S. Best (Pruett, 1989).

A sensible (if somewhat unorthodox) approach to fly-tying.

The Book of Fly Patterns, by Eric Leiser (Knopf, 1993).

An essential reference work for any fly-fisherman or -tyer.

Practical Saltwater Fly Fishing, by Mark Sosin (Lyons & Burford, 1989).

An expert on the subject shares his skills and enthusiasms.

UltraLight Spin-Fishing: A Practical Guide for Freshwater and Saltwater Anglers, by Peter F. Cammann (The Countryman Press, 1994).

This compact volume contains a surprisingly large amount of information on tackle and techniques.

The Fishing Doctor, by Robert F. Jones (John Boswell Associates/Villard Books, 1992).

Not a book about an angling physician, but a compendium of tackle, techniques, and reference sources, packaged with a zip-around vinyl cover so it can be carried in tackle boxes.

Finally, the "Buyer's Guide Issue" of *Fishing Tackle Retailer* magazine (published by B.A.S.S.) contains the most complete listing of manufacturers' names, addresses, and phone numbers to be found throughout the industry.

Note: Books on fish species and fishing vacation opportunities are included in chapters 1 and 16.

Fishing Book Publishers and Book Dealers

Until a decade or so ago, almost all the major book publishers included fishing titles on their lists. Some, most notably the distinguished A.A. Knopf, Inc. (whose eponymous owner was an avid angler), had ongoing and active outdoor publishing programs.

Now only a handful of "majors" publish any fishing books at all, and those only sporadically. Deserving special mention is Simon & Schuster, whose imprints (especially Fireside Books), regularly serve up John Gierach and other literate luminaries.

Why don't more "majors" publish fishing books? Most are now owned by entertainment conglomerates that devote their attention and resources to finding and marketing best-sellers. Until commercially successful authors like Howard Stern discover that the word "fly" has meanings other than sartorial, these publishers will continue to shy away from what they consider special-interest subjects of limited appeal, like fishing. And even though Howell Raines' *Fly Fishing Through the Midlife Crisis* (William Morrow, 1993; paperback edition by Doubleday/Dolphin, 1995) enjoyed a stay on the best-seller lists, the book's popularity had more to do with the author's literary abilities than his angling efforts.

There's good news, though. Smaller independent "niche" publishers have admirably stepped in to fill the breach. The following four firms are the most active, as you will notice from the preponderance of their titles that appear throughout this book. Their catalogs are easily available for the asking. Every literate or otherwise savvy angler should have—and use—them.

Lyons & Burford
31 West 21 Street
New York, NY 10010
(212) 620-9580
fax: (212) 929-1836

Stackpole Books
P.O. Box 1831
Harrisburg, PA 17105
(800) READ-NOW

Frank Amato Publications
P.O. Box 82112
Portland, OR 97282
(503) 653-8108
fax: (503) 653-2766

The In-Fisherman
Two In-Fisherman Drive
Brainerd, MN 56401-9999
(218) 829-1648
fax: (218) 829-3091

Cy DeCosse Incorporated specializes in direct mail-order sales. Its Hunting and Fishing Library® includes more than a dozen well-written and -photographed hardcover instructional books on fishing that come close to being mini-encyclopedias (visualize any of the Time-Life how-to series, and you won't be far off).

Since there are only a handful of such titles (as distinguished from the swarms of books from the publishers mentioned above), we can list them here:

The Art of Freshwater Fishing
Cleaning and Cooking Fish
Fishing with Live Bait
Largemouth Bass
Panfish
Fishing with Artificial Lures
Walleye
Smallmouth Bass
Guide to Freshwater Gamefish of North America
Trout
Secrets of the Fishing Pros
Fishing Rivers and Streams
Fishing Tips and Tricks
Fishing Natural Lakes
Northern Pike and Muskie
Fishing Man-Made Lakes
Art of Fly Tying

Titles may be ordered separately or as part of a series.

Cy DeCosse Incorporated
5900 Green Oak Dr.
Minnetonka, MN 55343
(800) 328-3895

Another notable series, Doubleday's "Outdoor Bibles" trade paperbacks, covers a range of sports, includes the following:

The Bass Fisherman's Bible, revised by Erwin A. Bauer.

The Fly Fisherman's Bible, by Jim Bashline.

The Freshwater Fisherman's Bible, 3rd edition, by Vlad Evanoff.

The Panfisherman's Bible, by John Weiss.

The Saltwater Fisherman's Bible, revised by Erwin A. Bauer.

The Trout and Salmon Fisherman's Bible, by Jim Bashline.

A number of tackle manufacturers also publish books, often in magazine-format form. Among those that do are Scientific Angler/3M, PRADCO, Penn Reels, Universal Vise Co., and Umpqua Feather Merchants.

Titles are listed in their respective catalogs.

Many dealers who specialize in angling books advertise regularly in fishing magazines, especially the ones devoted to fly-fishing.

AB Bookman's Weekly
P.O. Box AB
Clifton, NJ 07015
(201) 772-0020
fax: (201) 772-9281

Another source of information is *AB Bookman's Weekly*, the "trade journal" of specialist (including antiquarian) booksellers. There's an annual special issue devoted to sporting books.

The Anglers Art
P.O. Box 148N
Plainfield, PA 17081
(808) 848-1020

This firm offers a 160-page catalog of "books for the fly-fisherman." As such, it is essential for angling bibliophiles of any discipline.

Angler's & Shooter's Bookshelf
Box 178
Goshen, CT 06756
(203) 491-2500

Armchair Angler
209D Falles Drive
New Milford, CT 07646

Judith Bowman—Books
Pound Ridge Road
Bedford, NY 10506
(914) 234-7543
Reputedly the largest of the angling book dealers.

Callahan & Co.
Box 505
Peterborough, NH 03458
(603) 924-3726
Gary Esterbrook
P.O. Box 61453
Vancouver, WA 98666
A huge catalog of fly-fishing books.

Sportsmen's Encore
342 West 84 Street
New York, NY 10024
(212) 333-6918—day
(212) 362-7865—evening
A small but select list.

Wilderness Adventures Sporting Books
P.O. Box 1410
Bozeman, MT 59771
(800) 925-3339
Almost exclusively fly-fishing, together with hunting and some other outdoor sports.

Libraries

The following libraries have notable collections of books, manuscripts, photographs, and artifacts of interest to angling bibliophiles:

CALIFORNIA

California State University, Fullerton

The university library's Captain P. Markham Kerridge Angling Collection includes material on fishing, conservation, ichthyology, and travel.

CONNECTICUT

Connecticut College, New London

The library's Wilbur and Dorothy Downs Collection includes early nineteenth-century American and British titles, more contemporary limited editions, albums of trout and salmon flies, and an uncataloged group of books on fishing techniques.

FLORIDA

International Game Fish Association, Pompono Beach

The IGFA's International Library of Fishes is an impressively substantial repository of books, films, photographs, and artifacts on game fish, angling, and related subjects.

MASSACHUSETTS

Harvard University, Cambridge

Harvard's Widener Library holds an extensive array of angling books that includes the Fearing Collection, with over 15,000 books, manuscripts, and photographs.

Sturgis Library, Barnstable

The Henry Crocker Kittredge Maritime History Collection contains many works on the early days of New England's fishing industry.

MISSOURI

Central Missouri State University, Warrensburg

The library contains more than 150 different editions of Izaak Walton's *The Compleat Angler*, as well as other books by and about that author.

NEW HAMPSHIRE

University of New Hampshire, Durham

In the university's library are some 2,000 volumes on fishing, with an emphasis on trout and salmon fly-fishing and fly-tying.

NEW JERSEY

Princeton University, Princeton

The Kenneth H. Rockey Angling Collection, the Otto Von Kienbusch Angling Collection, and other material makes this university's library one of the world's important repositories of books, especially rare ones, on the subject.

NEW YORK

Adirondack Historical Association, Blue Mountain Lake

Books, prints, photographs, and artifacts on all aspects of fishing in the Adirondacks Mountains.

C.W. Post Center of Long Island University, Greenvale

The library's Franklin B. Lord Collection includes many nineteenth-century books on fishing.

Catskill Fly Fishing Center and Museum, Livingston Manor

Although the emphasis in on conservation and ecology programs, the Museum contains tackle and other artifacts associated with the history of fly-fishing in this country.

Columbia University, New York

Columbia's Butler Library holds the Elliott V. Bell Collection of more than 500 fishing books dating back to the seventeenth century.

Gladdings International Sport Fishing Museum, South Otselic

A collection of old and contemporary books on fishing-related subjects.

OHIO

Public Library of Cincinnati and Hamilton County, Cincinnati

The Rare Books Division includes a large fishing collection.

PENNSYLVANIA

Layfayette College, Easton

The library's Robert Tinsman Angling Collection includes 58

editions of *The Compleat Angler*, while the Robert S. Conahay, Jr. Atlantic Salmon Collection features more than 1,000 trout and salmon flies, many of which are mounted and framed.

Free Library of Philadelphia, Philadelphia

The Rare Book Department holds the Evan Randolph Collection of more than 1,200 angling prints.

University of Pittburgh, Pittsburgh

The Hillman Library owns one of the world's largest collections of *The Compleat Angler*, with more than 230 editions.

VERMONT

American Museum of Fly Fishing, Manchester

A large and important collection of books, photographs, and artifacts that cover the history of fly-fishing.

Who (Pale Evening) Dun-Its

BY JOSEPH GUGLIELMELLI

When something is dropped into a river or a lake in a mystery novel, it is usually a body, not a fishing line. Remember the Sicilian message in Mario Puzo's *The Godfather*? However, fishing, as both sport and business, has provided the backdrop for a surprising number of mystery novels.

Acknowledged masters of the genre could not resist the image of the dead body clutching a fishing rod. If you mention Rex Stout and fish in the same sentence, most fans will conjure up a tantalizing gourmet meal on the table of his detective Nero Wolfe at his brownstone on West 35th Street. But in the novella "Immune to Murder" found in *Three for the Chair* (Bantam), Wolfe and his legman Archie Goodman are forced to catch not only their dinner (baked brook trout Montbarry), but also a killer at an upstate New York fishing lodge. In his unmistakable wisecracking style, Archie describes the allure of the sport:

> *Ever since I caught my first shiner at the age of seven in an Ohio creek, at the sight of wild water I have always had twin feelings: that there must be fish in it and that they need to be taught a lesson.*

Although a spinning rod and reel adorn the cover of *The Singing Sands* by Josephine Tey (Collier/Macmillan), the vacationing Scotland Yard inspector Alan Grant uses fly rod and reel when pursuing trout and salmon in northern Scotland. Although angling may be incidental to the plot, it certainly enhances this work by one of Britain's legendary mystery writers.

Dame Ngaio Marsh gave new meaning to the familiar phrase "red herring" in her aptly titled *Scales of Justice* (Berkeley). A huge trout known as the Old 'Un had defied and outsmarted local fishermen for years until the day Colonel Cartarette is found murdered on the riverbank with the legendary fish beside the body.

Current mystery writers are even more enthusiastic about the sport. William G. Tapply, a contributing editor to *Field & Stream*, has written a series of more than a dozen novels featuring Brady Coyne, a Boston-based lawyer who would rather be fishing when he isn't solving mysteries. Tapply knowingly and lovingly conveys the pleasures of nature and fishing through New England in these wonderfully written mysteries. Fishing figures prominently in *Dead Meat* (Ballantine), where Coyne must find a murderer at a Maine fishing camp. In describing Brady fishing for trout, Tapply writes:

> *The little Orvis rod was a wand in my hand. The current surged around my knees. The*

gaudy little fly [a Royal Coachman] bobbed and drifted, and then there was a quick burst of silver. I struck too late and felt a momentary tug before the fly came free. I cursed, but not with enthusiasm. I felt too good to care very much about failing to hook a trout.

Tapply has also written several nonfiction books on the sport.

If bluefishing is among your passions, Philip R. Craig is your man. Jeff Jefferson, Craig's protagonist in five novels to date, is an ex-Boston cop who has retired to Martha's Vineyard for the fishing, but is reluctantly drawn into investigating murder on the island. The opening chapter of Craig's first novel, *A Beautiful Place to Die* (Avon), entertainingly details Jackson's preparations for bluefishing before the sun rises.

Carl Hiassen turns his satiric eye on professional sport-fishing in *Double Whammy* (Warner Books). Private eye R.J. Decker is hired to catch a cheater on the bass fishing tournament circuit, but there is too much money at stake in winning to rule out a murder or two if necessary. For those with a bizarre sense of humor, Hiassen is laugh-out-loud funny. Only Hiassen could imagine a funeral where the deceased is buried in a casket converted from the dead man's bass boat. By the way, the title refers to a bass lure.

Mystery writers have not overlooked commercial fishing. In *Polar Star* (Ballantine), Martin Cruz Smith finds murder on a Russian factory ship where fish are caught, cleaned, and frozen while sailing on the Bering Sea. Arkady Renko, formerly a Moscow policeman, has hidden himself among the ship's menial workers after the events of the best-selling *Gorky Park*. But Renko must once again become an investigator when the ship's fishing nets bring up from the sea bullheads, cod, and a

dead woman. Smith effortlessly weaves detailed research about life aboard one of these vessels into a suspenseful story.

Alaskan waters also provide the setting for *Dead in the Water*, by the Edgar Award-winning Dana Stabenow (Berkeley). Kate Shugak, a fiercely independent private investigator of Aleut descent, goes undercover on a commercial crab boat to solve the disappearance of two crew members. The back-breaking physical labor of these commercial fishermen is vividly described in this novel.

Margaret Maron's *Shooting at Loons* (Mysterious Press) is set in a community of commercial fishermen on the coast of North Carolina. Judge Deborah Knott, introduced in the award-winning *Bootlegger's Daughter*, must solve the murder of a local fisherman while a battle rages between the residents who make their living from the sea and "dingbatters" who want to develop the coastline into a resort for the wealthy. The portrait of North Carolina fishermen in this mystery makes it well worth reading.

First published in 1938, *Death Is No Sportsman* by Cyril Hare (Harper Perennial) takes place along a prototypical English chalk stream. Someone is found murdered along its bank, and the local police inspector makes good use of his familiarity with classic British angling attitudes and traditions to land the perpetrator.

Death on a Cold River by Bartholomew Gill (William Morrow) captures the ambiance and allure of salmon fishing in Ireland. You may unravel the puzzle before the police do, but you won't fault the author's impressively detailed knowledge of fly-fishing and fly-tying.

Any one of these mysteries deserves a place in a fisherman's library alongside the Nick Adams stories of Hemingway or *A River Runs Through It*. One thing is certain—if you start reading one before bedtime, you won't sleep, especially "with the fishes."

Joseph Guglielmelli is the owner of The Black Orchid Bookshop at 303 East 81 Street, between First and Second Avenues, in New York, NY; phone: (212) 734-5980.

Books on Fly-Fishing

Why has fly-fishing spawned more books than any other aspect of angling? The reason may be that because fly-fishing is so contemplative, it generates the most food for thought. Or because, as its practitioners claim, it is the most "technical" of all the form of fishings; if so, its theories about such matters as casting techniques, choice of flies, and "reading" streams prompt analyses and spark counterarguments much akin to jesuitic or Talmudic disputations.

Whatever the reason for the breadth and depth of fly-fishing literature, the following titles are representative of well-regarded "how to" manuals, standard references, classic and contemporary prose (from literary works to cartoon collections), and photography. Particular books have been singled out for comment because of particular personal appreciation or the recommendations of others.

INSTRUCTION

Flies in the Water, Fish in the Air: A Personal Introduction to Fly Fishing, by Jim Arnosky (The Countryman Press, 1992).

An original account of the author's love for fly-fishing, together with angling tips. Young adults will find this a particular appealing guide.

Fly Fishing for Bonefish, by Dick Brown (Lyons & Burford, 1993).

Fly Fishing with Children: A Guide for Parents, by Philip Brunquell, M.D. (The Countryman Press, 1993).

Written by a father of a young fisher-woman, this guide will help other parents introduce their children to the sport. High marks go to the emphasis on user-friendly tackle and techniques, safety tips, and ways to focus a youngster's attention to his or her environmental responsibilities.

Wade a Little Deeper, Dear: A Woman's Guide to Fly Fishing, by Gwen Cooper and Evelyn Haas (Cortland Library/Lyons & Burford, 1989).

A hospitable primer for novices, with such wide-ranging advice (aside from how to fish) as what to take along in the way of creature comforts and what to do when the fish aren't biting (e.g., bird-watching).

The Orvis Guide to Saltwater Fly Fishing, by Nick Curcione (Lyons & Burford, 1993).

Fishing a Highland Stream, by John Inglis Hall (Lyons & Burford, 1992).

Fly Fishing Basics, by Dave Hughes (Stackpole Books, 1993).

Dry Fly Fishing, by Dave Hughes (Frank Amato Publications, 1994).

Advanced Fly Fishing Techniques: Secrets of an Avid Fisherman, by Lefty Kreh (Delacourt, 1992).

Expert advice clearly expressed by one of the sport's greats make this book essential reading even for those at the novice level.

A Modern Dry Fly Code, by Vince Marinaro (Lyons & Burford, 1988).

An important book by an important commentator.

The Practical Fly Fisherman, by A.J. McClane (Lyons & Burford, 1989).

With a new introduction by Paul Schullery, this classic still holds water, and then some.

The Orvis Guide to Flyfishing, by Tom Rosenbauer (Lyons & Burford, 1984).

This manual has sold more copies than any other book on the subject, and for good reason: comprehensive and clear advice.

Prospecting for Trout: Flyfishing Secrets from a Streamside Observer, by Tom Rosenbauer (Delacourt, 1993).

This analysis of "reading" water teaches us how to think like a fisherman, if not like a fish.

Fly Fishing Made Easy, by Michael Rutter and David Card (Globe Pequot Press, 1994).

A good primer, with good chapters on "reading" streams and on float- and boat-fishing.

Practical Saltwater Fly Fishing, by Mark Sosin (Lyons & Burford, 1989).

Required reading from an acknowledged expert on saltwater fishing.

Inshore Fly Fishing, by Lou Tabory (Lyons & Burford, 1992).

Another essential volume for saltwater anglers.

L.L. Bean Fly-Fishing Handbook, by Dave Whitlock (Lyons & Burford, 1984).

One of the best-selling introductions to the subject.

Joan Wulff's Flycasting Techniques, by Joan Wulff (Lyons & Burford, 1987).

For everyone who wants to improve his or her casting for distance, accuracy, and a feeling of accomplishment.

Joan Wulff's Fly Fishing: Expert Advice from a Woman's Perspective, by Joan Wulff (Stackpole Books, 1991).

Everyone, regardless of gender, will profit from reading this primer.

REFERENCE

Trout, by Ray Bergman (Outlet Book Co., 1991).

The Fly Fisherman's Bible, by Jim Bashline (Doubleday, 1993).

The Illustrated Encyclopedia of Fly-Fishing, by Silvio Calabi (Henry Holt, 1993).

The sum of the entries comprises a comprehensive education on tackle, techniques, noted personalities, and historical developments.

PanAngling's World Guide to Fly Fishing, by Jim C. Chaprailis (PanAngling, 1987).

The New American Trout Fishing, by John Merwin (Macmillan, 1994).

Insightful and useful chapters on species, equipment, fishing techniques, history, and more put this marvelous volume in the "if you could have only one book. . . " category.

The Complete Book of Fly Fishing, 2nd edition, by Tom McNally (Ragged Mountain Press/McGraw-Hill, 1994).

Trout Stream Insects: An Orvis Streamside Guide, by Dick Pobst (Lyons & Burford, 1991).

American Fly Fishing: A History, by Paul Schullery (Lyons & Burford, 1992).

Traces the sport and its most influential practitioners from fly-fishing's earliest days in this country.

Lee Wulff on Flies, by Lee Wulff (Stackpole Books, 1985).

ESSAYS/HUMOR/ PHOTOGRAPHY

Silver Swimmer: The Struggle for Survival of the Wild Atlantic Salmon, by Richard Buck (Lyons & Burford, 1993).

Dances with Trout, by John Gierach (Simon & Schuster, 1994).

Even Brook Trout Get the Blues, by John Gierach (Simon & Schuster, 1992).

Sex, Death and Fly-Fishing, by John Gierach (Simon & Schuster, 1990).

Trout Bum, by John Gierach (Simon & Schuster, 1986).

The View from Rat Lake, by John Gierach (Simon & Schuster, 1988).

Where the Trout Are All as Long as Your Arm, by John Gierach (Simon & Schuster, 1991).

Often described as the most readable fly-fishing essayist now writing, this Montaigne of the Mountains turns a good phrase while telling a good tale.

Halcyon Days, by Bryn Hammond (Ragged Mountain Press/McGraw-Hill, 1992).

Fly Fishing, by J.R. Hartley (pseudonym)(HarperCollins, 1991).

An entertaining parody of a British sporting memoir.

Fly Fishing Tales, by Terry Hefferman (Viking Studio Books, 1994).

Photographer Hefferman's work accompanies essays by Zane Grey, Ted Williams, Herbert Hoover, Papa Hemingway, and others; the result is a compact but visually stunning volume.

Portrait of the Tweed, by Ian B. Jones (Sterling, 1993).

Salmon fishing on one of Scotland's premier rivers.

The Habit of Rivers: Reflections on Trout Streams and Fly Fishing, by Ted Leeson (Lyons & Burford, 1993).

A collection of essays that one reviewer predicts is "destined to be a classic."

Fishing and Thinking, by A.A. Luce (Ragged Mountain Press/McGraw-Hill, 1993).

Confessions of a Fly Fishing Addict, by Nick Lyons (Simon & Schuster, 1989).

Spring Creek, by Nick Lyons (Grove-Atlantic, 1992).

The noted writer-publisher spins a mean yarn, writing with erudition, insight, and charm.

A Dictionary of Fly-Fishing, by C.B. McCully (Oxford University Press, 1992).

Etymology (not entomology) this time, and a stunning piece of scholarship: the author traces the origins of the sport's words and phrases, making much use of the *Oxford English Dictionary* along the way.

The Bright Country, by Harry Middleton (Simon & Schuster, 1993).

On the Spine of Time: An Angler's Love of the Smokies, by Harry Middleton (Simon & Schuster, 1992).

Thoreau-like essays that reflect the late writer's passion for fishing and for the places where he fishes.

How to Fool Fish with Feathers, by Paul Margolis and Jeff MacNelly (Simon & Schuster, 1992).

The political columnist and the Pulitzer Prize-winning cartoonist blend their talents in what is a very entertaining introduction to fly-fishing; the question-and-answer-format works well too.

The Way of the Trout: An Essay on Anglers, Wild Fish, and Running Water, by M.R. Montgomery (Knopf, 1991).

Highly recommended for the author's thought-provoking perceptions.

Uncommon Waters, edited by Holly Morris (Seal Press, 1991).

This anthology, the first one of women's writings about fishing, contains essays, poems, and stories that reflect a female—but also a universal—viewpoint.

Fear of Fly Fishing, by Jack Ohman (Simon & Schuster, 1988).

When the humor hits the mark, it's very funny.

Sports Afield Treasury of Fly Fishing, by Tom Paugh (Delacourt, 1992).

An anthology of much of the best writing about the sport.

Pavlov's Trout: The Incomplete Psychology of Everyday Fishing, by Paul Quinnett (Keokee Publishing, 1994).

An inquiry into why we fish and why we fish the way we do.

Fly Fishing Through the Midlife Crisis, by Howell Raines (William Morrow, 1993; paperback edition by Doubleday/Dolphin, 1995).

One man's progress from bait-fishing for bass to fly-fishing for trout, full of ruminations about what he learned on the way. In a sense the literary equivalent of the movie *A River Runs Through It* (insofar as both attracted considerable public attention to fly-fishing), the book made best-seller lists in both its hardcover and paperback editions.

The Complete Angler's Catalog, by Scott Roederer (Johnson Books, 1985).

Although this stunning compendium of virtually everything that's available in the world of fly-fishing is out of print and more than a decade old, ferreting out a copy to own still makes good sense.

Saltwater Fly Fishing Magic, by Neal and Linda Rogers, with Lefty Kreh and Stu Apte (Earth & Great Weather Pub./Lyons & Burford, 1994).

Stunning photographs by some of the world's best anglers/photographers.

Casting Illusions: The World of Fly Fishing, by Tom Rosenbauer (text)(Thommason-Grant, 1994).

Another front-runner in the race for the title of "the world's most beautiful fishing photography." Rosenbauer's introductory text nicely complements the illustrations.

Home Waters: A Fly-Fishing Anthology, edited by Gary Soucie (Simon & Schuster, 1991).

An anthology of essays on favorite fishing spots from such a mixed bag as Vance Bourjaily, Thomas McGuane, Viscount Gray of Fallodon, and former President Jimmy Carter.

Editors in the Steam, edited by Tom Tolmay (Halo Books, 1992).

What could be more literate than a handful of book and magazine editors reflecting on delights they find in fly-fishing? Silvio Calabi, Gary Soucie, John Randolph, Nick Lyons, Peter

Barrett, and a half-dozen others provide a literate and pleasurable paperback package.

Trout Magic, by Robert Traver (Simon & Schuster, 1989).

Trout Madness, by Robert Traver (Simon & Schuster, 1989).

The author of *Anatomy of a Murder* was an inveterate fly-fisherman; he was also a graceful essayist, as these two volumes demonstrate.

The Fly Fisher's Reader, edited by Leonard M. Wright, Jr. (Simon & Schuster, 1990).

Ernest Hemingway, Sparse Gray Hackle, Corey Ford, and Theodore Gordon are just some of the "legends" whose essays comprise this well-assembled anthology.

Salmon on a Fly, by Lee Wulff (John Merwin, ed.)(Simon & Schuster, 1992).

Thirty essays by the master on what salmon fishing meant to him.

BOOKS ON CASSETTES

Audio books have hit the fishing world too. The following titles are available at many fly shops as well as bookshops:

A River Runs Through It, by Norman Maclean. Read by Ivan Doig (3 cassettes; 4 hrs.).

Trout Bum, by John Gierach. Read by the author (2 cassettes; 2½ hrs.).

Tales of the Trout, Vol. 1: Eastern Streams; Vol. 2: Western Rivers. Both read by Ernest Schweibert (90 min. each).

Afield with Lee Wulff. Read by the author (90 min.).

Magazines

Magazines provide an important service, for that's where avid anglers can learn how to improve their fishing techniques (often in articles by noted experts), read about new products, discover tantalizing vacation spots, find out tournament results, and even be entertained by fishing fiction, all under one roof and (usually) every month. General-interest periodicals literally and figuratively cover the waterfront, while special interests are also well served in publications that cater to their own portion of the fishing universe.

A note about general-interest magazines that cover other field sports: fishing tends to take a backseat to hunting in issues published during fall and winter months.

Among the major national magazines are:

American Angler
Abenaki Publishers, Inc.
P.O. Box 4100
Bennington, VT 05201-4100

Published bimonthly. "How-to" and "where-to" articles on fly-fishing, with a strong emphasis on flies and fly-tying. A new sibling publication, *Saltwater Fly Fishing*, is aimed at the growing number of marine fly buffs.

Bassin'
NatCom Inc.
15115 S. 76th E. Avenue
Bixby, OK 74008

Published eight times a year (January, February, March, April, May/June, July/August, September/October, and November/December). Straight-ahead articles on all aspects of bass fishing, from tackle and techniques to vacation spots. There are columns by noted tournament fisherman too.

Bassmaster
B.A.S.S.
5845 Carmichael Rd.
Montgomery, AL 36117

Published monthly (but bimonthly in July/August and September/October). Available only to members of the Bass Anglers Sportsman Society (B.A.S.S.), of which it is the official publication. Excellent how-to articles on bass fishing, as well as analyses of new products and the results of B.A.S.S.-sanctioned competitions.

The Complete Sportsman's Fishing
Harris Publications, Inc.
1115 Broadway
New York, NY 10010

An annual (last year's was entitled *The Complete Sportsman's Fishing '95*) that is published in time for the New Year. Its contents includes "true-life adventure" articles on where and how to catch a variety of species. The blurbs that describe the "Buyer's Guide Section"'s new products sound as if they are copied from manufacturers' press releases.

Field & Stream
Times Mirror Pub Co.
2 Park Avenue
New York, NY 10016

Published monthly. There's something very comforting about receiving *Field & Stream* every month: it's likely to have been the first fishing magazine you ever came across, since it recently celebrated its centennial.

Articles and fiction pieces cover a wide range of fresh- and saltwater fishing topics, with a strong emphasis on conservation.

The Fisherman
L.I.F. Publishing Corp.
14 Ramsay Rd.
Shirley, NY 11967

Published weekly in editions for New England, Long Island, New Jersey Delaware Bay, and Florida. Articles on fishing news, technique, new products, and (since it's a weekly) up-to-date fishing reports for the areas that each edition covers.

Fly Fisherman
Cowles Magazines, Inc.
6405 Flank Drive
Harrisburg, PA 17112-2753

Published six times a year (February, March, May, July, September, and December). Essential for fly-fishing and fly-tying enthusiasts, with authoritative articles on tackle, techniques, and travel. Contributors include many well-known anglers/writers.

Fly Rod & Reel
P.O. Box 370
Camden, ME 04843

Published six times a year (January/February, March, April, May/June, July/October, and November/December). Another well-written and well-edited "how-to/where-to/what-to" publication that anyone interested in fly-fishing would find indispensable. Particularly strong in the book and video reviews and the new products departments.

Flyfishing
Frank Amato Publications
P.O. Box 82112
Portland, OR 97282

Published five times a year: January/February, March/April, May/June, July/October, and November/December). News, instruction, and other facets of fly-fishing. . . frequent articles directed at novice anglers.

Gray's Sporting Journal
Morris Communications Corp.
P.O. Box 2123
Augusta, GA 30903-2123

Published seven times a year (February, March, May, July, September, November, and December). A handsome effort that contains at least one article about fishing per issue, along with hunting and other so-called field sports. The emphasis on "the good life" focuses on such concerns as top-of-the-line tackle, exotic and/or famous fishing and vacation spots, and elegant cuisine. The niche that the magazine fills is admittedly posh, and it fills it nicely.

The In-Fisherman
Two In-Fisherman Drive
Brainerd, MN 56401-0999

Published seven times a year (December/January, February, March, April, May/June, July/August, September, and October/November). Emphasis on freshwater bait- and spin-casting, with how-to articles that take an in-depth and technical approach (e.g., schematic drawings, graphs) approach. As such, *The In-Fisherman* might be considered the *Scientific American* of fishing magazines. (The In-Fisherman organization also publishes *Walleye Insider*.)

Outdoor Life
Times Mirror Pub. Co.
2 Park Avenue
New York, NY 10016
Published monthly. Like its cousin *Field & Stream* (they're both published by Times Mirror), *Outdoor Life* continues to be an eminent hunting-and-fishing journal, with respected how-to articles, thoughtful columns, and fiction pieces.

Saltwater Sportsman
77 Franklin Street
Boston, MA 02110
Published monthly. How-to and where-to articles on saltwater game fish, with regular features on boating and new tackle and gear. As such, necessary reading for all "blue-water" anglers.

Sports Afield
250 West 55th Street
New York, NY 10019
Published monthly. The third of the triumvirate with *Field & Stream* and *Outdoor Life* (although published by another firm), *Sports Afield* can be relied on for well-written and informative articles about all varieties of fishing.

OTHER MAGAZINES

Name a geographic area or a kind of fishing, and chances are good that a magazine exists to cover that part of the world or particular interest.

In addition to the periodicals listed below, regional tabloids report "up-close and personal" on angling activities and fishing forecasts. Also, state and regional fish and game departments often publish useful "freebies." Check local newsstands and tackle shops to find out about such publications in your region.

The American Fly Fisher
c/o American Museum of Fly
   Fishing
P.O. Box 42
Manchester, VT 05254

The Atlantic Salmon Journal
c/o Atlantic Salmon Federation
P.O. Box 429
St. Andrews, NB Canada E0G
   2X0

B.C. Outdoors
202-1132 Hamilton St.
Vancouver, B.C. Canada V6B 2S2

Badger Sportsman
19 E. Main
Chilton, WI 53014

Bass Fishing
Rt. 2, Box 74B
Gilbertsville, KY 42044

Bass'n Gal
P.O. 13925
Arlington, TX 76013

B.A.S.S. Times
5845 Carmichael Rd.
Montgomery, AL 36117

The Big Game Fishing Journal
2679 Rt. 70
Manasquan, NJ 08736

Bisbee's Black & Blue Fishing
   Magazine
425 North Newport Blvd., Suite E
Newport Beach, CA 92663

Black Bass Journal
260 Crest Rd.
Edgefield, SC 29824

British Columbia Sport Fishing
   Magazine
909 Jackson Crescent
New Westminster, B.C. Canada
   V3L 4S1

Canadian Sportfishing
937 Centre Rd., Dept. 2020
Waterdown, ON Canada L0R 2H0

Crappie
5300 CityPlex Tower
2448 E 81 St.
Tulsa, OK 74137-4207

Disabled Outdoors
2052 W. 23rd St.
Chicago, IL 60608

The Fish Sniffer
Northern California Angler
   Publications, Inc.
P.O. Box 994
Elk Grove, CA 95759-0994

Fishing Collectibles Magazine
2005 Tree House Lane
Plano, TX 75023-7433

Fishing Facts
312 E. Buffalo St.
Milwaukee, WI 53202

Fishing Tackle Retailer
P.O. Box 17151
Montgomery, AL 36141

Fishing Tackle Trade News
P.O. Box 2669
Vancouver, WA 98668-2669

Fishing World
KC Publications
700 W. 47th St., Suite 310
Kansas City, MO 64112

Florida Sportsman
5901 SW 74 St.
Miami, FL 33143

Florida Wildlife
c/o Florida Game and Fresh
    Water Fish Commission
620 South Meridian St.
Tallahassee, FL 32399-1600

Fly Fishing Saltwater
Peter Van Gytenbeek
2001 Western Ave., Suite 210
Seattle, WA 98121

The Flyfisher
P.O. Box 722
Sandpoint, ID 83864

Fur-Fish-Game
2878 E. Main St.
Columbus, OH 43209

Georgia Sportsman
Game & Fish Publications, Inc.
2250 Newmarket Pkwy, Suite 110
Marietta, GA 30067

Gulf Coast Fisherman
401 W. Main, Drawer P
Port Lavaca, TX 77979

Hawaii Fishing News
6650 Hawaii Kai Drive, Suite 201
Honolulu, HI 96825

Honey Hole
P.O. Box 10399
Fort Worth, TX 76114

Hoosier Outdoors
P.O. Box 447
Cloverdale, IN 46120

Idaho Wildlife
Box 25
Boise, ID 83707

Louisiana Sportsman
P.O. Box 1199
Boutte, LA 70039

**Louisiana Woods and Waters
Magazine**
4323 Division St., Suite 106
Metaire, LA 70002

The Maine Sportsman
P.O. Box 365
Augusta, ME 04332

Marlin Magazine
330 W. Canton
Winter Park, FL 32789

Michigan Hunting & Fishing
P.O. Box 977
East Lansing, MI 48823

Michigan Out-of-Doors
P.O. Box 30235
Lansing, MI 48909

**Midsouth Hunting & Fishing
News**
2208 Central Ave.
Memphis, TN 38104

Midwest Outdoors
111 Shore Drive
Burr Ridge, IL 60521

Missouri Wildlife
c/o Conservation Federation of
    Missouri
728 W. Main
Jefferson City, MO 65101

Montana Outdoors
c/o Montana Fish, Wildlife and
    Parks
930 West Custer Ave.
P.O. Box 200701
Helena, MT 59620-0701

Muskie Hunter
P.O. Box 881
Minocqua, WI 54548

Nebraska Bass Angler
4535 29th Street
Columbus, NE 68601

New York Outdoors
51 Atlantic Ave.
Floral Park, NY 11741

New York Sportsman
P.O. Box 229
Norwich, NY 13815

Nor'east Saltwater
Recreational Publications
600 Johnson Ave.
Bohemia, NY 11716

North American Fisherman
P.O. Box 3403
Minnetonka, MN 55343

Northeast Woods & Waters
154 Grove St., Room 108
Chicopee, MA 01020

Offshore
Offshore Publications, Inc.
220-9 Reservoir St.
Needham, MA 02194

Ohio Out-of-Doors
P.O. Box 117
St. Marys, OH 45885

Ohio Sportsman
c/o Outdoor Beacon, Inc.
106 W. Perry St.
Port Clinton, OH 43452

Ontario Fisherman
85 Scarsdale Rd., Suite 100
Don Mills, ON Canada M3B 2R2

Ontario Out of Doors
35 Riviera Dr., Unit 17
Markham, ON Canada L3R 8N4

Oregon Outdoor Journal
P.O. Box 8171
Bend, OR 97708

Outdoor America
c/o Izaak Walton League
707 Conservation Lane
Gaithersburg, MD 20878-2983

Outdoor Canada
703 Evans Ave., Suite 202
Toronto, ON Canada M9C 5E9

Outdoor Notebook
R.R. 1
Lemont, IL 60439

Outdoor Oklahoma
P.O. Box 53465
Oklahoma City, OK 73152

Outdoor Women
160 White Pines Dr.
Alpharetta, GA 30201

Pacific Fisherman
23182 Alcalde, Suite K
Laguna Hills, CA 92653

Pennsylvania Angler
P.O. Box 67000
Harrisburg, PA 17106-7000

Pennsylvania Sportsman
R.D. 2, Box 457A
Farmington, PA 15437

Pennsylvania Wildlife
27 Ridge Dr.
Lititz, PA 17543

Pennsylvania Woods and Waters
P.O. Box 392
Vanderbilt, PA 15486

Salmon Trout Steelheader
c/o Frank Amato Publications
4040 SE Wister
Portland, OR 97222

South Carolina Out-of-Doors
c/o South Carolina Wildlife
    Federation
715 Woodrow St.
Columbia, SC 29205

South Carolina Wildlife
P.O. Box 167
Columbia, SC 29202

Southern Outdoors Magazine
P.O. Box 17915
Montgomery, AL 36141

Sport Fishing
330 W. Canton Ave.
Winter Park, FL 32789

Texas Fish & Game
7600 W. Tidwell, Suite 708
Houston, TX 77040

Trout
c/o Trout Unlimited
14101 Parke Long Court
Chantilly, VA 22021-1645

Virginia Wildlife
P.O. Box 11104
Richmond, VA 23230-1104

Walleye Insider
Two In-Fisherman Dr.
Brainerd, MN 56401-0999

Water, Woods & Wildlife
P.O. Box 16074
St. Paul, MN 55116-0074

**West Coast Fisherman News and
    West Coast Bass News**
3239 Monier Circle, Suite B
Rancho Cordova, CA 95742

Western Angler
350 E. Center St.
Provo, UT 84606

Western Outdoors
3197-E Airport Loop Drive
Costa Mesa, CA 92626

Western Outdoor News
3197-E Airport Loop Drive
Costa Mesa, CA 92626

Western Sportsman
P.O. Box 737
Regina, SK Canada S4P 3A8

Wild Steelhead & Atlantic
    Salmon
P.O. Box 3666
Seattle, WA 98124

Wildlife in North Carolina
512 N. Salisbury St.
Archdale Bldg.
Raleigh, NC 27611

Woods 'n' Waters
1110 W. Main St.
Perry, FL 32347-2312

Wyoming Wildlife
5400 Bishop Blvd.
Cheyenne, WY 82002

AND ACROSS THE
POND. . .

Anglophiles will also be interested in any or all of the following British magazines. They are available at some of the larger fishing tackle shops and at newsstands that carry foreign periodicals:

Coarse Fisherman

"Coarse" describes carp, pike, chub, bream, and other species that don't qualify, as trout and salmon do, as "game fish."

The Field

Although not a fishing magazine per se, *The Field* usually carries at least one article on angling per issue. Otherwise, the bill of fare includes hunting (foxhunting, or riding to hounds), shooting (which is what we Yanks call hunting), gardening, and other aspects of living the good country life.

Fly-Fishing & Fly-Tying

Well-written and handsomely photographed articles on exactly what the title describes.

Salmon, Trout & Sea-Trout

How to get the better of landlocked and sea-run members of the species of the title.

Trout & Salmon

How-to and how-about techniques and locales, with a dollop of fly-tying too.

A Collection of Favorite Fishing Books

COMPILED AND ANNOTATED BY ANGUS CAMERON

It seemed to me that the only manageable way to contribute this section of fishing books for this encyclopedia was to call in others to my assistance. The reason, of course, is that there have been so many books written on the subject in the last 500 years that no one reader can be taken as truly knowledgeable (Col. Henry Siegel's two sporting book catalogs for 1994 alone contained over 4,000 out-of-print sporting titles, with a high percentage of angling). So I have offered here a list of favorite books of eight enthusiastic and well-known anglers (plus my own list), all but two of whom have themselves written fishing books. (The non-book angler is yours truly, but perhaps I qualify because of the number of fishing books that I have edited and published.) In asking for such lists I did not say whether the books listed should be "how to" books or books of angling appreciation, nor did I limit the size of their lists. The result is that the lists run from 7 titles to as many as 43 titles. Some lists, such as Ernest Schweibert's, consist of very few contemporary titles.

I suppose one of the anglers best-read in fishing lore is Col. Henry A. Siegel. As most anglers know, the colonel publishes twice a year (in volumes "A–K" and "L–Z") *The Angler's and Shooter's Bookshelf: Out-of-Print and Rare Hunting and Fishing Books*; the two volumes together usually include from 4,000 to 5,000 titles, and they give one a good sense of what fishing pleasures lie between book covers. Indeed, the late Alfred W. Miller ("Sparse Grey Hackle" to most of us) once went the whole hog and claimed that "the best fishing is done not in water but in print." Arnold Gingrich celebrated this claim in a wonderful book called *Fishing in Print*. He wrote two others too: *The Well-Tempered Angler* and *The Joys of Trout*. In the latter he gives us a manageable list of his favorite 50 books classified under four categories. Compiled in 1973, it included "books published in the last ten years," i.e., back to 1963. Presumably, if Arnold were around now, he would perhaps have added one or two "new" books.

I too discovered that I must have a preference for books on angling published in the not-too-recent past; however, 8 of my list of 25 have been published since 1925. If I were to be, as they say, banished to a desert island and could take only one fishing book with me, it would be Negley Farson's *Going Fishing*. If I could take two, the second would be the most-recently published on my list: C.B. McCully's wonderful *A Dictionary of Fly Fishing*. My two favorite, most-used, most-thumbed-through are

unquestionably Ray Berman's *Trout* and Lee Wulff's *The Atlantic Salmon*.

The reader may wish to search these lists to see which good books he may have missed, as well as those he has discovered that are undiscovered by others. I found that I owned 21 of the 50 titles listed by Arnold Gingrich and that my list of 25 included 15 titles not included in Arnold's list. I read 19 of the 43 books listed by Ernest Schweibert. Each to his own taste, as the translation has it.

There are a number of annual catalogs that list available or out-of-print books. Besides Col. Siegel's catalogs (his address is Box 178, Goshen, CT 06756), I can think offhand of Judith Bowman's and of David Foley's catalogs (Judith Bowman Books, Pound Ridge Road, Bedford, NY 10506; and David E. Foley Sporting Books, 76 Bonny View Road, West Hartford, CT 06107).

[*Note:* Comments and publication data supplied by Mr. Cameron's contributors have been included.]

NICK LYONS (*distinguished scholar, writer, book publisher, and angler*):

Golden Days, by Romilly Fedden.

Where the Bright Waters Meet, by Harry Plunkett Greene.

A Man May Fish, by Kingsmill Moore.

A River Runs Through It, by Norman Maclean.

The Complete Fly Fisherman: The Notes and Letters of Theodore Gordon, edited by John McDonald.

Trout, by Ray Bergman.

Vermont Rivers, by W.D. Wetherall.

The Habit of Rivers, by Ted Leeson.

A Book of Trout Flies, by Preston Jennings.

Art Flick's Streamside Guide, by Art Flick.

A Modern Dry Fly Code, by Vince Marinaro.

Spring Creek, by Nick Lyons.

ED MIGDALSKI (*former professor at Yale

Oceanpgraphic Laboratory, author of numerous works on fish and fishing, angler of worldwide experience):

An Angler's Anthology, edited by Eugene Burns (Stackpole Books, 1952).

A Treasury of Fishing Stories, edited by Charles Goodspeed (A.S. Barnes, 1946).

Notable Angling Literature, edited by James Robb.

The Western Angler, Vols. I and II, by Roderick Haig-Brown (Derrydale Press, 1939).

A River Never Sleeps, by Roderick Haig-Brown.

Fisherman's Spring, by Roderick Haig-Brown.

Fisherman's Fall, by Roderick Haig-Brown.

Salus the Salmon, by Roderick Haig-Brown.

Fisherman's Luck, by Henry Van Dyke (Scribners, 1913).

Salmon Fishing in Canada, by A Resident (edited by Col. Sir James E. Alexander)(published in 1860).

A Wedding Gift, and Other Fishing Stories, by John Taintor Foote.

The Old Man and the Sea, by Ernest Hemingway.

Tales of Fishes, by Zane Grey.

Striper, by John M. Cole.

From Fish to Philosopher, by Homer Smith.

The Dry Fly in Fast Water, by George La Brante (Scribners, 1914).

Blues, by John Hersey.

Fishing the Atlantic and Pacific, by S. Kip Farrington, Jr.

A History of Fishes, by J.R. Narman and P.H. Greenwood (John Wiley, 1975).

The Complete Fly Fisherman (The Notes and Letters of Theodore Gordon)(Scribners, 1947).

Trout, by Ray Bergman (Penn Pub. Co., 1938).

Salmon of the Pacific Northwest, by Anthony Netboy.

The Compleat Angler, by Izaak Walton and Charles Cotton.

Salt Water Fishing, by Van Campen Heilner.

Tales of Fishing Virgin Seas, by Zane Grey (Grosset & Dunlap, 1925).

The Atlantic Salmon, by Lee Wulff (A.S. Barnes, 1958).

Silver Swimmers, by Richard Buck (Lyons & Burford, 1993).

A River Runs Through It, by Norman Maclean.

M.R. MONTGOMERY
(journalist and angling writer, author of The Way of the Trout*)*:

A Dictionary of Fly-Fishing: A Guide to Its Language and History, by C.B. McCully ("The best recent book on fly-fishing. . . a book for collectors—erudition with a sense of humor.").

History of Fly Fishing for Trout, by John Waller Hills (without which "no library is complete.").

An Angler's Guide to Aquatic Insects and Their Imitations for All North America, by Rick Hafele and Scott Roederer.

The Complete Book of Western Hatches: An Angler's Entomology and Fly Pattern Field Guide, by Rick Hafele and Dave Hughes.

Fly Fishing, by Viscount Grey of Fallodon (Sir Edward Grey)("No finer account of late nineteenth- and early twentieth-century British angling.").

The Rod and Line, by Hewett Wheatley (Montgomery's "favorite of the pre-scientific anglers.")(London, 1849).

ERIC LEISER *(famous fly-tyer, teacher, and author of the classic* The Complete Book of Fly Tying*)*:

Salt Water Fly Fishing, by Lefty Kreh.

Inshore Fly Fishing, by Lou Tabory.

The New American Trout Fishing, by John Merwin.

Trout, by Ray Bergman.

Fishing Widows, by Nick Lyons.

McClane's Fishing Encyclopedia, by A.J. McClane.

TED WILLIAMS *(angling and conservation writer)*:

Fishing Came First, by John Cole.

A River Runs Through It, by Norman Maclean.

Trout Magic, by Robert Traver.

Trout Madness, by Robert Traver.

Anatomy of a Fisherman, by Robert Traver.

Fisherman's Spring by Roderick Haig-Brown.

Fisherman's Summer by Roderick Haig-Brown.

Fisherman's Winter by Roderick Haig-Brown.

To Hell with Fishing, by Ed Zern.

Seasons of the Angler, by Dave Seybold.

JACK SAMSON (*angler, prolific author, former editor of* Field & Stream):

The Angler's Coast, by Russ Chatham.

A River Runs Through It, by Norman Maclean.

Salt Water Fishing, by Van Campen Heilner.

Fly Fishing Salt Water, by Lefty Kreh.

The Atlantic Salmon, by Lee Wulff.

Inshore Fly Fishing, by Lou Tabory.

Profiles in Salt Water Angling, by George Reigner.

The Sea of Cortez, by Ray Cannon.

The Practical Fly Fisherman, by A.J. McClane.

A River Never Sleeps, by Roderick Haig-Brown.

Fishing the Dry Fly, by Dermont Wilson.

Steelhead Fly Fishing, by Trey Combs.

ERNEST SCHWEIBERT
(*famous angler and writer, author of* Matching the Hatch *and the two-volume* Trout, *perhaps the definitive book on the subject*):

"Books I return to again and again"

Minor Tactics of the Chalkstream, by George E.M. Skues.

The Way of a Trout with a Fly, by George E.M. Skues.

Nymph Fishing for Chalkstream Trout, by George E.M. Skues.

Floating Flies and How to Dress Them, by Frederick Maurice Halford.

Dry Fly Entomology, by Frederick Maurice Halford.

The Flyfisher's Entomology, by Alfred Ronalds.

How to Dress Salmon Flies, by Thomas Edwin Pryce-Tannatt.

Sunshine and the Dry Fly, by John William Dunne.

The Fly Fisher and the Trout's Point of View, by Col. E.W. Hardin.

The Biology of Mayflies, by James G. Needham.

A Book of Trout Flies, by Preston Jennings.

The Dry Fly and Fast Water, by George M.L. La Branche.

Salmon and the Dry Fly, by George M.L. La Branche.

Just Fishing, by Ray Bergman.

Trout, by Ray Bergman.

A Fly Fisher's Life, by Charles Ritz.

Fishing Flies and Fly Tying, by William Fitzgerald Blades.

Salmon Fishing—A New Philosophy, by Richard Waddington.

The Practical Fly Fisherman, by Albert Jules McClane.

Trout Fishing, by Joe Brooks.

A Modern Dry Fly Code, by Vincent Marinaro.

TECHNICAL EXPOSITION

Autumns on the Spey, by The Rev. A.E. Knox.

The Angler and the Loop Rod, by David Webster.

Days and Nights of Salmon Fishing on the Tweed, by William Scrope.

Fisherman's Luck, by Henry Van Dyke.

Little Rivers, by Henry Van Dyke.

The Book of the Dry Fly, by George A.B. Dewar.

Golden Days, by Romilly Fedden.

Where the Bright Waters Meet, by

Harold Plunkett-Greene.

Fishing Dreams, by T.T. Phelps.

A Man May Fish, by T.C. Kingsmill-Moore.

A History of Fly Fishing for Trout, by Maj. John Waller Hills.

A Summer on the Test, by Maj. John Waller Hills.

A Leaf from French Eddy, by Ben Hur Lampman.

Thy Rod and Thy Creel, by Odell Shepherd.

Currents and Eddies, by William Schaldach.

Angling and Art on Scotland, by Ernest Briggs.

A River Never Sleeps, by Roderick Haig-Brown.

Fisherman's Winter, by Roderick Haig-Brown.

The Fly and the Fish, by John Atherton.

The Well-Tempered Angler, by Arnold Gingrich.

Where the Pools Are Bright and Deep, by Dana Storrs Lamb.

Fisherman's Bounty, by Nick Lyons.

ARNOLD GINGRICH (rabid angler, founder and publisher of Esquire, *author of three delightful fishing books*):

*Indicates reissue or current availability [note: in 1973]

CLASSIC

A Treatyse of Fysshinge Wyth an Angle, by Dame Juliana Berners, 1496.

A Concise Treatise on the Art of Angling, by Thomas Best, 1787.

The Book of the All-Around Angler, by "John Bickerdyke" (Charles Henry Cook), 1889.

The Art of Angling Improved in All Its Parts, Especially Fly Fishing, by Richard and Charles Bowker, 1758.

Country Contentments, by Gervase Markam, 1631.

The Fly-Fisher's Entomology, by Alfred Ronalds, 1836.

The Angler's Guide, by Thomas Salter, 1814.

The True Art of Angling, by J(ohn) S(mith), 1696.

**The Compleat Angler*, by Izaak Walton and Charles Cotton, 1676.

VINTAGE

**Salmonia, or Days of Fly Fishing*, by Sir Humphrey Davy, 1828.

A Book on Angling, by Francis Francis, 1867.

Fly Fishing, by Sir Edward Grey (Viscount Grey of Fallodon), 1899.

Dry-Fly Fishing in Theory and Practice, by Frederick M. Halford, 1889.

**A Trout and Salmon Fisherman for 75 Years*, by Edward R. Hewitt, 1950.

**The Dry Fly in Fast Water* and *The Salmon and the Dry Fly* (together in one volume), by George M.L. La Branche, 1951.

**Greased Line Fishing for Salmon*, by "Jock Scott" (D.G.H. Rudd), 1935.

**Days and Nights of Salmon Fishing on the Tweed*, by William Scrope, 1843.

The Way of a Trout with a Fly, by G.E.M. Skues, 1921.

Troutfishing from All Angles, by Eric Taverner, 1929.

MODERN

**Trout* (revised edition), by Ray Bergman, 1952.

**This Wonderful World of Trout*, by Charles K. Fox, 1963.

**The Lure and Lore of Trout Fishing*, by A.R. Grove, Jr., 1957.

The Practical Fly Fisherman, by A.J. McClane, 1953.

**The Complete Fly Fisherman (The Notes and Letters of Theodore Gordon)*, by John McDonald, 1947.

**A Modern Dry Fly Code*, by Vincent Marinaro, 1950.

**A Fly Fisher's Life*, by Charles Ritz, 1959.

Fly Tying, by Helen Shaw, 1963.

The Atlantic Salmon, by Lee Wulff, 1958.

SELECTIVE AND SUPPLEMENTAL

The Fly and the Fish, by John Atherton (Freshet Press, 1971).

Trout Fishing, by Joe Brooks (Harper & Row, 1972).

Life Story of the Fish, His Manners and Morals, by Brian Curtiss (Dover, 1961).

Fishless Days, Angling Nights, by Sparse Grey Hackle (Alfred W. Miller)(Crown Publishers, 1971).

A History of Flyfishing for Trout, by John Walker Hills (Freshet Press, 1972).

The Spawning Run, by William Humphrey (Knopf, 1970).

Fishing with Lee Wulff, edited by Edward C. Janes (Knopf, 1971).

A Book of Trout Flies, by Preston Jennings (Crown Publishers, 1971).

A Leaf from French Eddy, by Ben Hur Lampman (Touchstone Press, 1965).

The Seasonable Angler, by Nick Lyons (Funk & Wagnalls, 1970).

Fisherman's Bounty, edited by Nick Lyons (Crown Publishers, 1971).

McClane's Standard Fishing Encyclopedia, by A.J. McClane (Holt, Reinhart & Winston, 1965).

Quill Gordon, by John McDonald (Knopf, 1972).

Fly Fishing: Some New Arts and Mysteries, by J.C. Mottram (The Field Press, 1915).

An American Angler's Book, by Thad Norris (Philadelphia: 1864).

Remembrances of Rivers Past, by Ernest Schweibert (Macmillan, 1972).

Through the Fish's Eye, by Mark Sosin and John Clark (Harper & Row, 1973).

Selective Trout, by Doug Swisher and Carl Richards (Crown Publishers, 1971).

Trout Madness, by Robert Traver (St. Martin's Press, 1960).

Fishing the Dry Fly as a Living Insect (The Thinking Man's Guide to Trout Angling), by Leonard M. Wright, Jr. (E.P. Dutton, 1972).

ANGUS CAMERON (book editor, angler, and sometime writer):

The Treatise of Fishing with an Angle, anonymous (Westminster: Wyckyn de Worde, 1496)(translation available in *Quill Gordon*, by John McDonald, Knopf, 1972).

The Fisherman's Bedside Book, edited by "B.B." (Eyre and Spottiswood, 1945).

Atlantic Salmon Flies and Fishing, by Joseph D. Bates, Jr. (Stackpole Books, 1970).

Trout, 2nd edition, by Ray Bergman (Knopf, 1972)(1st edition, 1938).

Letters to a Salmon Fisher's Sons, by A.H. Chaytor (James Murray, 1925)(1st edition, 1910).

Going Fishing, by Negley Farson (Country Life Press, 1942).

Streamside Guide to the Naturals and Their Imitations, by Art Flick (G.P. Putnam's Sons, 1947).

The Well-Tempered Angler, by Arnold Gingrich (Knopf, 1965).

The Joy of Trout, by Arnold Gingrich (Crown Publishers, 1973).

Fishing in Print, by Arnold Gingrich (Winchester Press, 1974).

A Book of Trout Flies, by Preston Jennings (Derrydale Press, 1935).

Fishing in Salt Water, by Bernard (Lefty) Kreh (Lyons & Burford, 1974).

Where the Pools Are Bright and Deep, by Dana S. Lamb (Winchester Press, 1973).

Beneath the Rising Mist, by Dana S. Lamb (Stonewall Press/The Stephen Greene Press, 1979).

Green Highlanders and Pink Ladies, by Dana S. Lamb (Barre Publishers, 1971).

Woodsmoke and Watercress, by Dana S. Lamb (Barre Publishers, 1965).

Bright Salmon and Brown Trout, by Dana S. Lamb (Barre Publishers, 1964).

. . . AND THE REST OF HIS BOOKS, 1964 ET. SEQ.

The Complete Guide to Fly Tying, by Eric Leiser (Knopf, 1977).

A Modern Dry Fly Code, by Vincent Marinaro (Crown Publishers, 1970)(1st edition, 1950).

A Dictionary of Fly Fishing, by C.B. McCully (Oxford University Press, 1993).

Quill Gordon, by John McDonald (Knopf, 1972).

The Way of the Trout, by M.R. Montgomery (Knopf, 1991).

Rod and Line, by Arthur Ransome (Oxford University Press, 1980)(1st edition, Jonathan Cape, 1928).

Salmon Taking Time, by R. Righyai (Macdonald, 1965).

Inshore Fly Fishing, by Lou Tabory (Lyons & Burford, 1992).

Salmon Fishing, edited by Eric Taverner and Jock Scott (Seeley Service, 1931).

Salmon Fishing—A New Philosophy, by Richard Waddington (Scribner's, 1948).

Salar the Salmon, by Henry Williamson (1948).

The Atlantic Salmon, by Lee Wulff (A.S. Barnes, 1958).

14

ETHICS AND ETIQUETTE

The following essay is excerpted from Fishing Fundamentals *by Wade Bourne (The In-Fisherman, 1988), a highly recommended guide to freshwater angling equipment and techniques. Ethics and etiquette are an integral part of the sport, and because Mr. Bourne makes his case for that proposition so well, and with so many concrete examples, we're pleased to be able to reprint his chapter on the subject in its entirety.*

Several years ago, I traveled into a neighboring state to write a magazine story about a 77-year-old man who had fished streams all his life. He was still active and got outdoors frequently, so we drove to a creek near his farm to wade and cast for smallmouth bass.

He parked his pickup by an old country bridge, and we gathered our tackle and hiked down a path to the water. It was obvious that someone had been there ahead of us. An empty worm box, food wrappers, and soft drink cans littered the bank.

My friend didn't say anything about the litter as we went on fishing. In the next two hours he caught and released a half-dozen nice bass while I took the photographs I needed for my story. Finally we decided to head in before an approaching thunderstorm doused us.

But before we walked back up the path to the truck, the aged angler stopped and quietly picked up the cans and paper and stuffed them in his pockets. When we left, the spot was no longer marred by the leftovers of someone's thoughtlessness.

The lesson of this story is a little more complicated than it may first seem. Of course, litter spoils the natural beauty of the outdoors, and no one should leave trash on the landscape. But beyond this, the man's attitude and example of picking up someone else's mess conveyed that he was a sportsman in the truest sense. He cared enough to get involved. Even though he didn't cause the problem, it was still there, and he rectified it.

Hopefully you have this same attitude, not just about litter, but about looking after the fishing resource. Always consider fishing as a gift instead of a right. Be thankful for your opportunity to enjoy it, and do your part to preserve it. If you do this, you'll help maintain the fishery and beauty of the outdoors. You will also gain self-respect by doing what's right. When you maintain good fishing ethics, you feel better about yourself and gain more pleasure from the sport.

Obeying Fish and Game Laws

Good ethics begins with obeying fish and game laws. These laws are designed to protect fish and game populations and also to make sure that everybody has an equal chance to enjoy them.

Always buy required fishing licenses. Money from these licenses goes back to maintain and improve fishing. When you buy a license, you're actually paying your fish and wildlife agency to provide you with better fishing. When people fish without a license (if they are required to have one), they're cheating honest fishermen who buy licenses.

Be familiar with creel and length limits and always follow them. Never take more fish or smaller fish than you're supposed to. Again, limits are set to protect fish populations. If limits are exceeded, fish populations can actually be hurt beyond recovery.

Never use prohibited means of taking fish. Some methods are so effective they don't give fish a chance, and they can be taken in large numbers. This can lead to overharvesting, which is why these methods are outlawed.

And finally, if you observe others breaking fish and game laws, report them to your local wildlife officer. By doing so, you're not a snitch. Instead, you're living up to your responsibility to protect fish and game. If you saw someone breaking into a house, you'd have no qualms about calling the police. Likewise, people who break game laws are fish and wildlife thieves, and they're stealing from you and all honest sportsmen. It's your duty to report them.

Obeying Other Laws

Besides obeying fish and game laws, obey all other laws that relate directly or indirectly to fishing. Littering is the prime example. I feel littering is an almost unpardonable sin. *Never* leave trash on the shore; never toss it out of the boat or car window. Don't sink cans in the water. Don't strip old line off your reel and toss it down. Don't sail twist-off bottle caps into the bushes. Don't leave *anything* behind after a day's fishing. If you bring it with you, take it when you leave. If everybody did this, our lakes and rivers would be much cleaner and prettier. Of course, you can't control the actions of others, but you can control your own behavior, and littering is taboo.

Never go onto private land without permission. You wouldn't want somebody trespassing on your property. Instead, if you find a place you'd like to fish, ask the landowner if he'd allow you to try it. Many times he'll grant permission. But when he doesn't, respect his wishes and find another spot.

Never drive automobiles or off-road vehicles in areas where they're prohibited. These vehicles aren't allowed on many areas in order to protect fragile environments. Don't camp, cut trees, or build fires unless you're sure it's okay to do so.

Obey all boating laws. These laws are designed to protect you and other boaters. Make sure to observe "No Wake" zones. Also, while it's not a law, it's common courtesy not to run your boat too close to a nonmoving boat or to anglers fishing from the bank. Steer a wide course so you won't upset the other boat or stir up the bank angler's waters.

Other Ethical Considerations

Observing fishing, litter, trespassing, and boating laws is only the minimum in good ethics. Beyond this is a higher level of ethical behavior, one not required by law, but which separates true sportsmen from those who are ethical only when they have to be.

This is hard to define in words. The elderly angler at the beginning of this chapter didn't have to pick up someone else's litter, but he did. It may be legal to keep your limit of fish on each trip, but it's unethical to keep more than you need or to take too many fish from one small area. You should especially consider releasing trophy fish alive, unless you want to keep one for mounting. I know anglers who keep all their big fish so they can get their picture in the newspaper each week. They're more interested in building reputations as expert fishermen than in helping preserve the fishery.

This doesn't mean you shouldn't keep some fish to eat. Nor it wrong to keep that occasional trophy for mounting or for sharing with family and friends. But there are bounds beyond which keeping fish and showing off trophies is unethical. The difference has to do with excess and in placing your own considerations before that of the fishery.

This is my personal fishing philosophy, and others may disagree with it. But I think it's important to keep man's impact on nature within well-confined limits. As a fisherman, you do this but not being wasteful of fish and by not spoiling the outdoor setting.

Angling Etiquette

Part of good ethics is having good manners toward other fishermen, or in other words, maintaining good "angling etiquette."

The Golden Rule applies in fishing just as it does any other time. To paraphrase, "Do unto other anglers as you would have them do unto you." Simply be considerate of other fishermen, and try to avoid interfering with their pursuits and pleasures.

Specifically, don't crowd another angler who got to a spot first. If somebody is already fishing where you wanted to fish, let him enjoy it. Find another spot, or at least don't fish so close that you get in his way. This applies when fishing either from the bank or a boat.

Two special rules apply to boat-fishermen. One, if another angler is casting his way down a shoreline, don't circle and move ahead of him. This is like breaking line at a movie theater. Instead, leave that spot and find another bank that's vacant of fishermen. And two, if you're in a boat fishing along a bank and get close to someone fishing from shore, make a wide circle around his spot without

fishing it. He only has that one small area to fish. You have the rest of the lake.

If you're fishing in a crowd (on a bank, fishing pier, boat), avoid casting over another angler's line. If someone else hooks a fish, reel your line in so he can play the fish without tangling.

If you're launching a boat, and other fishermen are waiting in line behind you, be ready when it's your turn on the ramp. Put all your gear into the boat and undo the tie-down straps. Then you can launch the boat quickly, and you won't keep others waiting longer than necessary.

Summary on Angling Ethics and Etiquette

Being an ethical, considerate fisherman has nothing to do with how many fish you catch. In fact, I've known as few fishermen who are extremely good at catching fish, but extremely lacking in ethics. They pay little attention to fellow anglers' rights. In a word, they're selfish.

As you grow in fishing, strive to stay out of the trap of letting the end justify the means. Successful fishing entails a lot more than the number of fish you catch. It include "how" as well as "how many." In a nutshell, fish hard, but at the same time fish honorably and always with consideration for the resource and the rights of other anglers. If you do this, you'll be a beneficial addition to the fraternity of fishermen, and you'll set a good example for others to follow.*

*Copyright 1988 by The In-Fisherman® Inc. and reprinted with permission of the publisher, The In-Fisherman Inc. and the author, Wade L. Bourne. Copies of the book may be purchased directly from the author, 450 Old Trenton Rd., Clarksville, TN 37040 ($13.50, including postage and handling, as of the publication of this book).

The following essay, from Pavlov's Trout: The Incomplete Psychology of Everyday Fishing *by Paul Quinnett (Keokee Publishing, 1994), is typical of the entire book's stimulating blend of enthusiasm and erudition.*

More Curious Connections

EXCERPTED FROM *PAVLOV'S TROUT* BY PAUL QUINNETT

When I started this potpourri chapter of how we are hooked to the fishes, I thought it would take only a couple of thousand words. But, the more I researched and snooped around, the more connections I found. I'll wind things up by mentioning just a few other ways the fishes have worked their way deeply into our lives, our psyches, symbols and our souls.

ART

From *gyotaku*, the ancient Japanese art of printing inked fish on rice paper, to the wood and metal sculptures of modern artists, to the knickknacks in gift shops, fish appear everywhere in our expressions of the beauties of the natural world. The mastery of painting fish has, in the span of my lifetime alone, matured to the point that I'm not safe at large with a major credit card in certain art galleries.

RELIGION

In ancient Egypt the Moon Goddess was represented as half-fish, and was probably the forerunner of the mermaid. Although Greek in origin, the fish is the sign of Christ. "Ichthyos" was the name of a medieval hymn in which Christ is referred to as the "little fish which the Virgin caught."

Fish have proved serviceable gods; mysterious, distant, elusive. In some ways they represent our unconscious selves, the part of us we can't quite reach out and grab hold of. The Ottawas of Canada did not burn fish bones for fear the fish's spirit would leave and not return in the form of another fish. The Hurons had old men who preached to the fish to encourage them to bite, and I have extolled the fishes in this manner myself. The tribes of the Pacific Northwest greet the first salmon of the year with great tribute and praise, chanting "You fish, you fish, you are all chiefs!" The Maoris always put the first fish caught back in the water with a prayer, a practice I engaged in long before I ever began to read about the fishing rituals of aboriginal peoples.

It seems that everywhere we have depended upon the fishes for survival, we have respected them and honored them, worshipped them and placed them atop our totem poles. And now that we are ever more spiritually in need of them and the wilderness they represent, it seems the connection, at least for fishermen, is holding tighter still.

As modern totems to sport-fishing, consider fish-printed T-shirts, ties and shorts, fish handbags, fish hats, and fishing trophies.

LANGUAGE

Finny things swim through our communications on a daily basis. "Fish face!" is an unkind cut, whereas "He swims like a fish" is a compliment. Within current usage of American slang, a fish is one who has no chance of winning in a game of chance or a newcomer in a prison. A torpedo is a "tin fish." Popular phrases include "A pretty kettle of fish," "There's something fishy about this deal," and "Fish or cut bait."

SCIENCE

By the American Fisheries Society and the National Marine Fisheries Service in this country and independent ichthyologists the world over, fish are studied for their biology, their economic value, their role in the web of aquatic life, and for their own sakes. Professional books, monographs, and papers on the biology, ecology, physiology, pathology, and just about every other "ology" except psychology, run to the thousands of titles.

LITERATURE

How large the literature of fishing is, no one really knows. In the English language there are some 5,000 titles on sport-fishing and maybe 50,000 titles on ichthyology. Fishing is the most-written about of any sport, and of the fishes written about, trout get the most ink, and of trout, fly-fishing the most words. There are some 30 titles agreed upon as classics written over the last 300 years.

According to the Bible, God commanded early on that man shall have "dominion over the fishes of the sea" and, it seems, He commanded him to write about them as well. Jonah spent three days and three nights in the belly of a fish after apparently using himself as a surface popper. From the miracle of the loaves and fishes to Simon Peter going "fishing for the souls of men," angling is deeply rooted into the traditions of Western thought.

In *Hamlet*, Shakespeare wrote, "A man may fish with the worm that hath eat of a king, and eat of the fish that hath fed of that worm."

Does this mean the bard was a bait-fisherman?

The fooling and catching of a wild creature is better described in *Anthony and Cleopatra*, when the queen sings,

> *Give me mine angle—we'll to the river.*
> *There, my music playing far off, I will betray*
> *Tawny-finned fishes; my bended hook shall pierce*
> *Their slimy jaws; and as I draw them up,*
> *I'll think them every one an Antony,*
> *And say "Ah ha! Y'are caught."*

In modern times the good and great fishing writers are too numerous to mention, so let me simply promise you that if you begin with Hemingway and read through to Lee Wulff and Nick Lyons and a dozen other modern fishing writers, with a stop at John Gierich's for a beer, it will prove a delightful, thought-provoking and educational journey. Better yet, start with Father Izaak Walton and inch forward.

Now, allow me to wrap up this mackerel with a memory from a special time in my life with the fishes.

For the couple of years I lived on the shores of the Pacific Ocean in Southern California, I hunted the fishes up and down the U.S. coast and into Mexico, surf-casting, snorkeling, spear fishing, abalone hunting, and snooping around.

In those times there were days underwater when the visual pleasures of the fish's world were so powerful I would just hang there in the kelp like some human mobile and stare and wonder at the works of the deep.

"Entranced" covers the psychological effect as well as any word.

Quietly studying the fishes in an aquarium, or snorkeling among them in warm seas, or spotting a shadow glide slowly by as I stand waist-deep in a shallow bay, I have wondered if our varied connections to the beauty of fishes and the world beneath the waves take us, somehow, back to our primordial beginnings. We and the fishes are, after all, evolved from common, water-born stock, and are therefore deeply connected to one another in the far reaches of time.

Maybe, just maybe, the emotion we feel for the underwater world of the fishes is not so much that of curiosity, but of longing.[*]

*Reprint courtesy of Paul Quinnett, author of *Pavlov's Trout*, and Keokee Co. Publishing, Inc., Sandpoint, Idaho. Copyright © 1994 by Paul Quinnett

15

TELEVISION AND RADIO SHOWS

Fishing Shows on Television

Fishing shows on TV tend to fall into two categories. What can be called "personality" series focus on the host, usually a "name" fisherman (such as a longtime bass tournament champ) who is often joined by one or more guests. Together, they offer instruction about effective equipment, casting and retrieving techniques, and "fish-finding" strategy. These series may devote an entire half-hour to one geographic area and/or subject, or they may be composed in "magazine format" of two or three unrelated segments.

Then there's the "good times on the water" genre, in which the host and his guests simply chatter away (some might say "bond") while they fish, with little-to-no instruction. There used to be more of this variety of show, but instructional series have driven them off the air.

One common element between the two types of shows is country music; there's lots of pickin' and singin' as theme songs and background music. Then too, and to no one's great surprise, fishing shows of all kinds are sponsored by manufacturers of line, lures, boats, outboards, and other angling products and services.

The following weekly series aired during 1994. ESPN runs its shows on Saturday mornings as *ESPN Outdoors*, with the schedule changing somewhat in the beginning of October. Genial host Tommy Sanders introduces the shows, as well as short "entr'acte" segments on various aspects of fishing and conservation presented by editors of *Field & Stream* and *Outdoor Life* magazines and other authorities. A particularly fascinating "miniseries" came from noted bass expert Doug Hannum, who used scuba gear and underwater camera to show us the world from a fish's perspective.

Some of ESPN Outdoors' hosts: (left to right) Tommy Sanders, Jerry McKinnis, Jimmy Houston, Mark Sosin, and John Barrett. [photo courtesy ESPN]

TNN shows air on Saturdays beginning in late morning (EDT), with some repeated on Sunday nights. Although most of the series have been around for several years, others have come and gone (one such also-ran was ESPN's *Fly Fishing America*, in which an escapee from New York City's rat-race went around the country fishing and rhapsodizing about legendary locales). Which series remain on the air depends on the usual factors that determine television longevity, including but not limited to the sponsor enthusiasm and viewer approval.

Both TNN and ESPN are known to reschedule or preempt their outdoors shows when what the networks consider more important sports events are being shown "live."

For the latest on fishing on TV, check your local listings for times and channels.

Bassmasters (TNN): Presented by the Bass Anglers Sportsman Society, *Bassmasters* usually chronicles a B.A.S.S.-sanctioned fishing tournament from its opening gun to the down-to-the-wire suspense of the final weigh-in. B.A.S.S. founder and president Ray Scott at the microphone keeps things moving right along.

Bill Dance Outdoors (TNN): Bill Dance is the one in the cap with the "T" (for the University of Tennessee). A bass tournament champion, he offers straight-ahead sound and solid angling advice. Also to his credit, Dance presents the information in a way that makes the half-hour seem to whiz by.

Bill Seiff's Rod & Reel (PBS): Fresh- and saltwater fishing around the country, with Seiff's obvious enjoyment of the sport a constant wherever the episodes take place.

Canadian Sport Fishing (Prime): Italo Labignan and Henry Wasczuszak are the hosts of this fishing "travelogue" through Canada. Each episode features a province and a species, such as the one on Labrador trophy pike. (A nice feature of that particular show was Wasczuszak's detailed demonstration of the proper way to filet a pike).

Charlie West's Back Country (ESPN): A magazine-format outdoors show that frequently includes segments on freshwater fishing.

Field & Stream Legends (TNN): The magazine celebrates its centennial with a series in which its editors host celebrities on fishing (and hunting) locations. Articulate commentary enhances the colorful photography.

The Fishin' Hole (ESPN): Host Jerry McKinnis' enthusiasm comes through in every episode (so does the enthusiasm of his ever-present fishing buddy, Norman the dachshund). The wide span of angling opportunities ranges from Western pack trips to isolated trout waters to New York City's harbor (for striped bass). Each program ends with a dedication "to Dad, who always had time to take me fishing," a feeling of gratitude and generosity of spirit that permeates the series.

Fishin' with Orlando Wilson (TNN): The soft-spoken Wilson takes a reserved approach, but that may be why he's able to pack a great deal of useful information into his programs. Like other hosts, he frequently fishes with guest guides, whose phone numbers are given at the end of the show.

Fishing with Roland Martin (TNN): Martin's approach is similar to Wilson's, with an emphasis on bass tackle and techniques. Like Wilson, Martin is a noted bass tournament champion, and also like Wilson, he actively seeks advice from his guests.

Fishing University (Prime Network): Charlie Ingrim is the host (his son Hunter often joins him) of this "seminar" or "tutorial" approach. Ingrim's "down-home" Southern style is as leisurely as a hot afternoon in Alabama, but viewers can nevertheless pick up a great deal of information along the way.

Fly Fishing the World (ESPN): The format is simple and invariable: host John Barrett escorts a celebrity angler to prime waters somewhere in the world (e.g., Tom Skerritt in Alaska, Robert Wagner and Stefanie Powers in New Zealand), whereupon the celebrity catches fish. Barrett is encouraging and reverential toward his guests, the setting, and the fish, although his voice-over musings can come perilously close to poetic overkill.

Fly Fishing Video Magazine (ESPN): Husband-and-wife hosts Jim and Kelly Watt travel around the country angling for trout or salmon. One thoughtful nod to their viewers is that they always provide details about the weight and length of leaders and tippets and the patterns and sizes of whatever flies they're using.

Hank Parker's Outdoor Magazine (TNN): A magazine-format series with occasional segments on fishing and riparian conservation.

In-Fishing (TNN): *In-Fishing* magazine's publisher Al Lindner and his editors present nonstop instruction. Focusing primarily on spinning and baitcasting for bass, pike, and pickerel and muskies, the segments are have the feel of instruction at a graduate-school level: analytical, encouraging, and no-nonsense (no good-ol'-boy chatter in this classroom). Lots of useful computer graphics, especially with regard to underwater structure and cover.

A relatively recent addition to the TV curriculum is *Walleye In-Sider*, which deals exclusively with that species.

Jack DeBord's American Angler (syndicated): With limited production quality and little-to-no instruction, this show gives the impression that viewers are watching home movies of its host fishing with a guest or two.

Jimmy Houston Outdoors (ESPN): Houston's thatch of blond hair and ebullient personality (including, but not limited to, that laugh) make him the frontrunner for the title of TV's most recognizable fishing personality. There's much gleeful chuckling and chatter as Houston, alone or with a companion, fishes primarily for bass around the country, but there's also a fair amount of sharing thoughts about technique and equipment.

North American Outdoors (ESPN): This magazine-format show includes segments on fishing along with ones on hunting.

On the Fly (ESPN): A magazine-format series devoted to all forms of fly-fishing. Segments on fly-tying, casting techniques, and conservation efforts form an especially well-rounded series.

Outdoors Encounters (MSG): Another "travelogue" show that focuses on Canada. The format involves hostess Deborah Johanssen in the company of the owners of whichever fishing lodge she is visiting (one episode showed fishing for walleyes and Northern pike in Ontario). Camera technique tends toward the rudimentary, but the hostess' enthusiasm is all part of the "home video" approach.

Rod & Reel Streamside (PBS): Produced by an upstate New York PBS station, *Streamside* may lack the snazzy video effects that other series offer, but host Don Meissner more than compensates by focusing on grass-roots-level experiences. Whether it's a couple of adults having sober second thoughts about being out on a roiling Great Lake or a five-year-old girl shyly describing how she caught her first perch, the series has a captivating charm all its own.

Mark Sosin's Saltwater Journal (ESPN): Fishing (almost always fly-fishing) on the deep blue sea is the order of the day. Adept photography and the expert commentary of host Sosin help capture the excitement.

Saltwater Sportsman (ESPN): E.F. "Spider" Andreson, the publisher of *Saltwater Sportsman* magazine, hosts this series. Like the magazine, the series is good at capturing the excitement of blue-water fishing.

Sportsman's Challenge (ESPN): Host Ron Franklin and his guests take a workmanlike, almost studious approach to freshwater fishing. Good use of computer-generated graphics, such as models of lakes and underwater structures, are integrated into "live" action sequence. Frequent appearances by

Viewers old enough to remember the formative years of television are likely to recall *Gadabout Gaddis, the Flying Fisherman*. Gaddis was a pilot as well as angler, buzzing off to rivers and lakes in the U.S. and Canada. Aired on Sundays during the 1950s, the series holds the record of being TV's first fishing show.

No mention of fishing on TV should omit the role of "infomercials." Thanks to lengthy (up to 30 minutes) ad-mixtures of demonstrations and glowing testimonies, programs that tout the Flying Lure™ and Helicopter Lures™ and the Pocket Fisherman (pages 43 and 109) have led to sales in the millions.

Doug Hannum, the "Bass Professor," enhance this series.

Suzuki Great Outdoors (ESPN): The host, actor and ex-football star Dick Butkus, is joined by other celebrities (e.g., one show featured basketball coach Denny Crum and ex-footballer Paul Hornung) for male-bonding on the water. When the guys aren't commenting on the fishing action, they can always shoot the breeze about sports. There's virtually no instruction, but Butkus and the boys don't seem to care. Neither should their viewers.

Tom Miranda's Outdoor Adventures (ESPN): Sandwiched into features on less-contemplative pursuits (skydiving, mountain biking, rock climbing, and hunting, for example) are segments on fishing.

Ultimate Outdoors (ESPN): Although primarily concerned with hunting, this series, hosted by Wayne Pearson, includes occasional fishing segments. The feature on how Jimmy Houston's shows are filmed informed us that there have been times when the camera must follow up to 200 or 300 casts before a fish strikes.

Walker's Cay Chronicles (ESPN): Walker's Cay, a resort in the Bahamas, is the base for this series featuring fishing on light tackle for a variety of saltwater species. Host Flip Pallitt and the camera make the most of the lush scenery and the plethora of excellent angling opportunities in that part of the world.

The In-Fisherman Radio Show

A radio show about fishing? Why not, for if we can talk about fishing around a cracker barrel down at the tackle shop, why not over the airwaves?

More than 800 radio stations carry The In-Fisherman's radio program. Aired six times a week, the shows are on for three minutes and contain fishing tips, advice on other outdoor activities, and news of new products and environmental matters.

Regional "editions" focus on the North, South, West, and Northeast, with autumn and winter "editions" presenting items of interest to the entire country during those two seasons.

The times indicated in the following list are as of 1994, so checking your local listings regarding any changes is a sound idea. Where both AM and FM stations are indicated, the shows air at the same time on both stations unless otherwise indicated.

United States

ALABAMA

Atmore	8:20 a.m./4:20 p.m.	WASG AM 550/WYDH FM 105.9
Bessemer	7:15 A.M.	WSMQ AM 1450
Cullman	5:45 A.M./4:50 P.M.	WKUL FM 92.1
Daleville	4:35 A.M./6:30 P.M.	WXUS FM 100.5
Dothan	4:50 A.M.	WTVY FM 95.5
Florence	7:25 A.M.	WKNI AM 620
Foley	6:20 A.M.	WHEP AM 1310
Haleyville	5:55 A.M.	WJBB AM 1230/FM 92.7
Mobile	5:30 A.M.	WNTM AM 710/FM 99.9
Monroeville	7:30 A.M./3:30 P.M.	WYNI AM 930
Opelika	6:20 A.M.	WJHO AM 1400
Opp	6:15 A.M.	WOPP AM 1290
Russellville	7:50 A.M./6:30 P.M.	WJRD AM 920
Scottsboro	6:35 A.M.	WWIC AM 1050
Selma	5:30 A.M.	WMRK AM 1340/WALX FM 100.9
Sumiton	3:00 P.M.	WRSM AM 1540
Tallassee	6:55 A.M.	WTLS AM 1300
Tuscaloosa	6:20 A.M.	WSPZ AM 1150

ARKANSAS

Batesville	6:35 A.M.	KBTA AM 1340/KZLE FM 93.1
Benton	7:33 A.M. M–F/7:30 A.M. Sat	KEWI AM 690
Bentonville	6:50 A.M.	KESE FM 93.3
Cherokee Village	7:35 A.M.	KFCM FM 100.9
Corning	8:30 A.M./3:45 P.M.	KBKG FM 93.5
Eureka Springs	5:35 P.M.	KTCN FM 100.9
Fort Smith	7:10 A.M.	KFPW AM 1230/KBBQ FM 100.9
Jonesboro	6:30 A.M.	KBTM AM 1230/KJBR FM 101.9
MENA	6:35 A.M.	KENA AM 1450/FM 101.7
Newport	5:10 P.M.	KNBY AM 1280/KOKR FM 100.7
Osceola	8:35 A.M./Sat 7:35 A.M.	KOSE AM 860
Salem	7:35 A.M.	KSAR FM 95.9
Stuttgart	5:45 A.M.	KWAK AM 1240/KXDX FM 105.5
Wynne	5:50 A.M.	KWYN AM 1400/FM 92.7
Yellville	6:35 A.M./4:45 P.M.	KCTT FM 97.7

ARIZONA

Showlow	6–7 A.M./5–6 P.M.	KVSL AM 1450/KRFM FM 96.5

CALIFORNIA

Burney	7:06 A.M./Sat 7:11 A.M.	KAVA AM 1450
Lake Isabella	12:06 P.M.	KVLI AM 1140/FM 104.5
Oroville	6:23 A.M.	KORV AM 1340/KEWE FM 97.7
Ukiah	6:12 A.M.	KUKI AM 1400/FM 103.3

COLORADO

Gunnison	6:45 A.M.	KGUC AM 1490/FM 98.3
Longmont	5:30 P.M.	KLMO AM 1060
Loveland	9:12 A.M./4:12 P.M.	KLOV AM 1570
Monte Vista	6:10 A.M.	KSLV AM 1240/FM 95.3
Pagosa Springs	7:30 A.M.	KPAG AM 1400/KRQS 106.3

CONNECTICUT

Torrington	AM 6:28 P.M.	WSNG AM 610

DELAWARE

Rehoboth Beach	5:50 A.M./4:50 P.M.	WGMD FM 92.7
Selbyville	7:30 A.M.	WSBL FM 97.9

FLORIDA

Bradenton	7:20 A.M.	WBRD AM 1420
Dade City	5:30 A.M./6:30 P.M.	WDCF AM 1350
Englewood	8:15 A.M.	WENG AM 1530
Inverness	10:15 A.M./3:15 P.M.	WINV AM 1560
Lake City	6:15 A.M./3:15 P.M.	WQLC FM 102.1
Lake Worth	7:47 A.M. M–F/6:15 A.M. Sat	WLVS AM 1380
Marianna	TBA	WJAQ FM 100.9/WTOT AM 980
New Smyrna Beach	4:45 P.M.	WSBB AM 1230
Pensacola	5:07 A.M.	WOWW FM 107
Trenton	6:30 P.M./Sat 9:30 A.M.	WCWB FM 101.7
Valparaiso	6:30 A.M.	WFSH AM 1340

GEORGIA

Blue Ridge	8:35 A.M.	WPPL FM 103.9
Cleveland	8:40 A.M.	WRWH AM 1350

Cumming	7:55 A.M./4:55 P.M.	WMLB AM 1170
Dublin	7:45 A.M.	WXLI AM 1230
Eastman	9:45 A.M./4:35 P.M.	WUFF FM 97.5/AM 710
Folkston	7:30 A.M.	WOKF FM 92.5
Hazlehurst	11:45 A.M.	WVOH AM 920/FM 93.5
La Grange	5:50 A.M./5:45 P.M.	WTRP AM 620
Lyons	6:20 A.M.	WLYU FM 100.9/WBBT AM 1340
Madison	8:00 A.M.	WYTH AM 1250
St. Simons Island	7:34 A.M.	WGIG AM 1440/WOKV FM 100.7
Statesboro	7:15 A.M.	WPTB AM 850
Thomasville	7:15 & 8:15 A.M./M–F	WTUF FM 106.3/WPAX AM 1240

IOWA

Cedar Falls	8:15 A.M./5:37 P.M.	KCFI AM 1250
Clinton	6:10 A.M./5:15 P.M.	KROS AM 1340
Creston	5:25 P.M.	KSIB AM 1520/KITR FM 101.3
Dubuque	5:26 P.M.	KDTH AM 1370/KATF FM 92.9
Dyersville	6:50 A.M./3:50 P.M.	KDST FM 99.3
Elkader	6:50 A.M./3:50 P.M.	KCTN FM 100.1/KADR AM 1400
Forest City	5:20 A.M.	KIOW FM 102.3
Humboldt	6:30 A.M./10:30 P.M.	KHBT FM 97.7
Iowa Falls	5:30 P.M.	KIFG AM 1510/FM 95.3
Lemars	8:35 A.M.	KLEM AM 1410/KKMA FM 99.5
Maquoketa	4:55 P.M.	KMAQ AM 1320/FM 95.3
Muscatine	AM Drive Time A.M. 5:20 P.M.	KWPC AM 860/KFMH FM 99.7 FM
Sheldon	6:15 P.M.	KIWA AM 1550/FM105.5
Sioux Center	11:55 A.M.	KVDB AM 1090/KTSB FM 94.3
Sioux City	6:24 A.M.	KSCJ AM 1360
Spirit Lake	10:00 A.M./4:00 P.M.	KUOO FM 103.9

IDAHO

Coeur D'Alene	6:50 A.M.	KVNI AM 1080
Idaho Falls	7:30 A.M./3:30 P.M.	KID AM 590/FM 96.1
Lewiston	5:40 A.M.	KATW FM 101.5
McCall	10:00 A.M.	KMCL FM 101.1
Montpelier	4:10 P.M.	KVSI AM 1450
Pocatello	7:15 A.M.	KRCD AM 1490/FM 98.3
Salmon	9:06 A.M.	KSRA AM 960/FM 92.7
Sandpoint	5:30 A.M./3:30 P.M.	KSPT AM 1400/KPND FM 95.3

Soda Springs	AM Morning	KBRV AM 790/KFIS FM 100.1
	FM Afternoon	
St. Maries	AM 8:15 A.M.	KOFE AM 1240

ILLINOIS

Benton	4:35 P.M.	WQRL FM 106.3
Canton	4:51 P.M. M–F/6:06 A.M. Sat	WBYS AM 1560/FM 98.3
Carmi	5:55 A.M.	WROY AM 1460/WRUL FM 97.3
Decatur	6:10 A.M.	WDZ AM 1050/WDZQ FM 95.1
Fairfield	6:35 A.M.	WFIW AM 1390/FM 104.9
Freeport	5:45 P.M.	WFRL AM 1570/WXXQ FM 98.5
Lincoln	12:45 P.M.	WPRC AM 1370/WESZ FM100.1
Mt. Carmel	3:50 P.M.	WYER AM 1360/WRBT FM 94.9
Olney	7:45 A.M./2:45 P.M.	WVLN AM 740
Rockford	4:05 P.M.	WLUV AM 1520/FM 96.7
Shelbyville	Between 6:00–7:00 A.M. & P.M.	WSHY AM 1560/WT FM105.1
Sparta	7:15 A.M./4:15 P.M.	WHCO AM 1230
Sterling	5:25 A.M.	WSDR AM 1240/WSSQ FM 94.3
Streator	7:00 A.M.	WIZZ AM 1250/WSTQ FM 97.7
Watseka	6:30 P.M.	WGFA AM 1360 FM 94.1
Waukegan	6:15 A.M.	WKRS AM 1220/WXLC FM 102.3

INDIANA

Anderson	6:10 A.M.	WHBU AM 1240/WAXT FM 96.7
Corydon	8:50 A.M./4:50 P.M.	WOCC AM 1550
Crawfordsville	5:20 P.M.	WCVL AM 1550/WIMC FM 103.9
Crown Point	5:30 A.M.	WWJY FM 103.9
Elkhart	5:45 A.M.	WCMR AM 1270/WFRN FM 104.7
Jasper	8:30 A.M.	WITZ AM 990/FM 104.7
Michigan City	5:15 A.M.	WIMS AM 1420
Mt. Vernon	5:15 P.M.	WPCO AM 1590
Rushville	11:30 A.M.	WRCR FM 94.3
Sullivan	7:10 P.M.	WNDI AM 1550/FM 95.3
Tell City	7:10 A.M.	WTCJ AM 1230
Valparaiso	5:05 A.M.	WLJE FM 105.5/WAKE AM 1500

KANSAS

El Dorado	5:35 P.M.	KSPG AM 1360/KBUZ FM 99.1
Fort Scott	6:15 A.M.	KMDO AM 1600/KOMB FM 103.9
Great Bend	7:55 A.M.	KZLS FM 107.9

Hutchinson	5:45 P.M.	KWBW AM 1450/KHUT FM 102.9
Iola	9:55 A.M.	KIKS AM 1370/FM 99.3
Junction City	6:35 A.M.	KJCK AM 1420/FM 94.5
Phillipsburg	6:45 A.M./5:25 P.M. `	KKAN AM 1490/KQMA FM 92.5

KENTUCKY

Bardstown	4:45 P.M.	WBRT AM 1320/WOKH FM 96.7
Bowling Green	5:50 P.M.	WKCT AM 930/WDNS FM 98.3
Burkesville	7:35 A.M.	WKYR AM 1570/FM 107.9
Cadiz	5:50 A.M. M–F/Sat 7:40 A.M.	WKDZ AM 1110/FM 106.3
Central City	12:40 P.M.	WNES AM 1050/WKYA FM 101.9
Columbia	TBA	WAIN FM 93.5/AM 1270
Corbin	6:40 P.M.	WCTT AM 680/FM 107.3
Cynthiana	7:40 A.M.	WCYN AM 1400/FM 102.3
Danville	6:30 A.M.	WRNZ FM 105.1
Greenup	9:00 A.M. M–F	WLGC AM 1520/FM 105.7
Hardinsburg	4:30 A.M.	WHIC AM 1520/FM 94.3
Hazard	6:45 A.M.	WQXY AM 1560
Hindman	6:25 A.M./6:25 P.M.	WKCB FM 107.1/AM 1340
Liberty	9:30 A.M.	WKDO AM 1560/FM 105.5
Madisonville	5:30 A.M.	WFMW AM 730/WKTG FM 93.9
Mayfield	5:20 A.M.	WXID FM 94.7/WNGO AM 1320
Mt Sterling	6:40 A.M.	WMST FM 105.5/AM 1150
Munfordville	7:25 A.M.	WLOC AM 1150/FM 102.3
Murray	8:00 A.M./5:00 P.M.	WNBS AM 1340
Paintsville	6:45 A.M./4:15 P.M.	WKLW AM 600/FM 94.7
Pineville	6:35 A.M./4:40 P.M.	WANO AM 1230/WZKO FM 106.3
Somerset	6:30 A.M.	WTLO AM 1480

LOUISIANA

Amite	4:40 P.M.	WABL AM 1570
Franklin	6:30 A.M. M–F	KFRA AM 1390/KFMV FM 105.5
Lake Charles	varies	KAOK AM 1400
Leesville	6:00 A.M.	KVVP FM 105.5
Many	6:10 A.M.	KWLV FM 107.1/AM 1400
Minden	6:55 & 10:30 A.M.	KASO AM 1240/FM 95.3
Morgan City	7:30 A.M.	KVPO FM 105.9
Natchitoches	6:30 A.M.	KDBH FM 97.7/KNOC AM 1450
West Monroe	6:25 A.M./12:25 P.M.	KMBS AM 1310

MASSACHUSETTS

Amherst	7:23 A.M./4:45 P.M.	WTTT AM 1430/WRNX FM 100.9
Pittsfield	8:40 A.M./Sat 9:26 A.M.	WBEC AM 1420/FM 105.5

MARYLAND

Hagerstown	5:45 A.M.	WJEJ AM 1240/WWMD FM 104.7
Havre de Grace	6:32 P.M.	WASA AM 1330
Oakland	4:30 P.M.	WMSG AM 1050/WXIE FM 92.3

MAINE

Portland	6:30 A.M./P.M.	WLPZ AM 1440

MICHIGAN

Alma	7:00 P.M.	WFYC AM 1280/FM 104.9
Bad Axe	4:05 P.M.	WLEW AM 1340/FM 92.1
Cheboygan	7:25 A.M.	WCBY AM 1240/WGFM FM 105.1
Escanaba	6:16 A.M.	WCHT AM 600/WGLQ FM 97.1
Gladwin	10:30 A.M./5:30 P.M. M–F	WGDN AM 1350/FM 103.1
Grand Rapids	1:30 P.M.	WGRD AM 1410/FM 97.9
Grayling	7:30 A.M.	WGRY AM 1230/FM 101.1
Houghton	5:20 P.M.	WAAH FM 102.3
Iron Mountain	5:50 A.M./5:50 P.M.	WJNR FM 101.5
Iron River	6:25 A.M.	WIKB AM 1230/FM 99.1
Ironwood	6:30 A.M.	WJMS AM 590/WIMI FM 99.7
Jackson	4:05 P.M.	WJCO AM 1510
Kalamazoo	6:25 A.M.	WKMI AM 1360/WKFR FM 103.3
Lapeer	9:00 A.M.	WLSP AM 1530
Ludington	6:02 A.M.	WKZC FM 95.9
Marine City	6:05 A.M.	WIFN AM 1590
Marquette	6:40 A.M./5:20 P.M.	WDMJ AM 1320/WIAN AM 1240
Muskegon	7:02 A.M.	WQWQ AM 1520/FM 101.7
Newberry	8:25 A.M.	WNBY AM 1450/FM 93.7
Niles	6:45 A.M.	WNIL AM 1530/WAOR FM 95.3
Rogers City	5:30 P.M.	WMLQ FM 96.7
Saginaw	Sat between 9–10 A.M.	WSGW AM 790
Sault Ste. Marie	AM 6:35 A.M./6:05 P.M.	WKNW AM 1400
Sterling	7:40 A.M./1:40 P.M.	WSTD FM 96.9

MINNESOTA

Aitkin	4:30 P.M.	KKIN AM 930/KEZZ FM 94.3

Albany	8:35 A.M.	KASM AM 1150/FM 105.5
Alexandria	5:50 P.M.	KIKV FM 100.7
Bemidji	AM 7:25 A.M.	KKBJ AM 1360/KKBJ FM 103.7 FM
Brainerd	4:45 A.M./7:45 P.M.	WJJY FM 106.7
Crookston	11:10 A.M.	KROX AM 1260
Detroit Lakes	6:10 A.M./12:30 P.M.	KRCQ FM 102.3
Duluth	6:20 A.M.	WDSM AM 710/KZIO FM 102.5
Ely	12:15 P.M.	WELY AM 1450/FM 92.1
Fairmont	6:55 A.M.	KSUM AM 1370/KFMC FM 106.5
Fergus Falls	5:40 A.M./5:40 P.M.	KBRF AM 1250/FM 103.3
Forest Lake	6:00 A.M.	WLKX FM 95.9
Fosston	5:35 P.M.	WKCQ AM 1480/FM 107.1
Golden Valley	5:35 A.M.	KYCR AM 1570
Grand Rapids	12:50 P.M.	KOZY AM 1320/KMFY FM 96.9
Hutchinson	AM 6:45 A.M.	KDUZ AM 1260/KKJR FM 107.1 FM
Int'l Falls	6:35 A.M.	KGHS AM 1230/KSDM FM 104.1
Jackson	9:40 A.M.	KKOJ AM 1190/KRAQ FM 105.3
Litchfield	5:30 P.M.	KLFD AM 1410
Little Falls	8:30 A.M./5:45 P.M.	KLTF AM 960/KFML FM 94.1
Madison	7:20 A.M.	KLQP FM 92.1
New Prague	7:30 A.M.	KCHK AM 1350/FM 95.5
Northfield	5:20 P.M.	KYMN AM 1080
Olivia	8:30 A.M.	KOLV FM 101.7
Owatonna	5:55 P.M.	KRFO AM 1390/FM 104.9
Park Rapids	6:50 A.M./5:05 P.M.	KPRM AM 870/KDKK FM 97.5
Pipestone	9:50 P.M. M–F/Sat 8:05 A.M.	KLOH AM 1050/KISD FM 98.7
Preston	8:15 A.M.	KFIL AM 1060/FM 103.1
Princeton	5:15 P.M.	WQPM AM 1300/FM 106.1
Rochester	7:20 A.M.	KWEB AM 1270/KRCH FM 101.7
Shakopee	7:25 A.M. M–F/7:10 A.M. Sat	WKCM AM 1530
St. Cloud	6:40 P.M.	WWJO FM 98.1
St. Peter	5:45 P.M.	KRBI AM 1310/FM 105.5
Thief River Falls	6:25 A.M.	KKAQ AM 1460/KKDQ FM 99.3
Virginia	4:50 P.M.	WHLB AM 1400/WCK FM 99.9
Wadena	4:50 P.M.	KWAD AM 920 KKWS FM 105.9
Warroad	6:36 A.M./2:53 P.M.	KKWQ FM 92.5
Willmar	6:30 P.M.	KWLM AM 1340/KQIC FM 102.5
Windom	4:55 P.M.	KDOM AM 1580/FM 94.3
Winona	5:55 A.M.	KWNO AM 1230

MISSOURI

Cabool	7:50 A.M.	KOZX FM 98.1
Farmington	12:25 P.M.	KTJJ FM 98.5/KREI AM 800
Festus	5:45 A.M./5:35 P.M.	KJCF AM 1400
Louisiana	4:40 P.M.	KJFM FM 102.1
Memphis	5:31 P.M.	KMEM FM 96.7
Monett	7:10 A.M./12:10 P.M.	KRMO AM 990/KKBL FM 95.9
Osage Beach	7:40 A.M.	KRMS AM 1150/KYLC FM 93.5
Poplar Bluff	7:50 A.M.	KAHR FM 96.7
Potosi	12:30 P.M.	KYRO AM 1280
Salem	5:50 A.M./8:20 A.M.	KSMO AM 1340
Sullivan	7:05 A.M.	KTUI AM 1560/FM 100.9
Versailles	5:50 A.M.	KLGS FM 95.1
Warsaw	7:12 A.M.	KAYQ FM 97.7/KBUG FM 92.3
Waynesville	4:30 P.M.	KFBD FM 97.7/KOZQ AM 1270
Willow Springs	6:15 A.M.	KUKU AM 1330/KGAR FM 100.3

MISSISSIPPI

Greenville	varies	WGVM AM 1260/WDMS FM 100.7
Hattiesburg	6:15 A.M.	WFOR AM 1400/WHER FM 103.7
Holly Springs	8:00 A.M./1:00 P.M.	WKRA AM 1110/FM 92.7
McComb	6:20 A.M.	WAKK AM 1140/WAKH 105.7
Natchez	6:05 A.M.	KFNV FM 107.1
Picayune	4:30 P.M.	WRJW AM 1320/WZRH FM 106.3

MONTANA

Dillon	6:05 A.M.	KDBM AM 1490/FM 98.3
Glasgow	8:30 A.M.	KLTZ AM 1240/KLAN FM 93.5
Great Falls	10:03 A.M.	KMSL AM 1450/KQDI FM 106.1
Havre	6:35 A.M.	KOJM AM 610/KPQX FM 92.5
Helena	6:45 A.M./5:45 P.M.	KMTX AM 950/FM 105.3
Lewistown	7:55 A.M.	KXLO AM 1230/KLCM FM 95.9
Malta	9:23 A.M.	KMMR FM 100.1
Miles City	Between 7 & 9 A.M.	KMTA AM 1050/KMCM FM 92.5
Wolf Point	2:50 P.M.	KTYZ AM 1450/FM 92.7

NORTH CAROLINA

Black Mountain	6:48 A.M.	WAVJ AM 1350
Dunn	12:10 & 5:10 P.M.	WLLN AM 1370
Elizabeth City	5:15 A.M.	WKJX FM 96.7

Fair Bluff	TBA	WNCR AM 1480
King	7:45 A.M.	WKTE AM 1090
Monroe	3:00 P.M.	WIXE AM 1190
Murphy	AM 7:15 A.M.	WCVP AM 600/FM 95.9 FM 4:00
Roanoke Rapids	FM 6:30 A.M.	WPTM FM 102.3
Robbinsville	FM 4:00 P.M.	WCVP FM 95.9
Selma	6:45 A.M./5:45 P.M.	WBZB AM 1090
Troy	7:35 A.M.	WJRM AM 1390
Whiteville	8:45 A.M.	WTXY AM 1540

NORTH DAKOTA

Bismarck	6:55 A.M.	KBMR AM 1130/KQDY FM 94.5
Bowman	12:45 P.M.	KPOK AM 1340
Carrington	7:15 A.M.	KDAK AM 1600
Devils Lake	8:20 A.M./5:40 P.M.	KDLR AM 1240/KDVL FM 102.5
Dickinson	5:20 P.M.	KRRB FM 92.1
Grafton	4:55 P.M.	KXPO AM 1340/FM 100.9
Grand Forks	6:55 A.M./3:30 P.M.	KCNN AM 1590/KZLT FM 104.3
Hettinger	9:15 A.M.	KNDC AM 1490
Mayville	12:45 P.M.	KMAV AM 1520/FM 105.5
Oakes	8:30 A.M.	KDDR AM 1220/FM 92.3
Wahpeton	5:10 P.M.	KBMW AM 1450

NEBRASKA

Ainsworth	8:30 A.M.	KBRB AM 1400/FM 92.7
Fremont	8:15 A.M.	KHUB AM 1340/KFMT FM 105.5
Gordon	5:45 P.M.	KSDZ FM 95.5
Grand Island	9:00 A.M./1:00 P.M.	KMMJ AM 750
Holdrege	8:00 A.M./4:45 P.M.	KUVR AM 1380/FM 97.7
North Platte	6:35 A.M.	KODY AM 1240/KXNP FM 103.5
O'Neill	5:35 P.M.	KBRX AM 1350 FM 102.9
Ord	5:13 P.M.	KNLV AM 1060/FM 103.9
Plattsmouth	6:20 A.M.	KOTD AM 1000
Valentine	5:15 P.M.	KVSH AM 940

NEW HAMPSHIRE

Dover	varies	WWNH AM 1340
Keene	audio tex system/all times	INFO LINE
Lebanon	11:45 A.M./5:50 P.M.	WTSL AM 1400/FM 92.3

NEW MEXICO

Clayton	4:15 P.M.	KLMX AM 1450
Clovis	7:05 A.M.	KCLV AM 1240/FM 99.1
Gallup	Between 7 & 8 A.M.	KGAK AM 1330/KQNM FM 93.7
Las Cruces	6:51 A.M.	KOBE AM 1450
Truth or Conseq.	6:15 A.M./6:15 P.M.	KCHS AM 1400

NEVADA

Ely	6:30 A.M./6:30 P.M.	KDSS FM 92.7
Las Vegas	TBA	KNUU AM 970
Minden	12:30 P.M.	KGVM FM 99.3
Winnemucca	12:25 P.M.	KWNA AM 1400/FM 92.7

NEW YORK

Batavia	4:40 P.M.	WBTA AM 1490/WBTF FM 101.7
Brockport	7:00 A.M. M–F/Sat 7:10 A.M.	WASB 1590 AM
Canandaigua	7:45 A.M./4:13 P.M.	WCGR AM 1550/WLKA FM 102.3
Dundee	5:44 A.M.	WFLR AM 1570/FM 95.9
Ellenville	6:10 A.M.	WELV AM 1370/WWWK FM 99.3
Endwell	5:50 A.M./6:20 P.M.	WINR AM 680
Fulton	Between 9–10 A.M.	WZZZ AM 1300
Grand Island	5:45 A.M.	WHLD AM 1270
Hornell	7:30 A.M.	WHHO AM 1320/WKPQ FM 105.3
Horseheads	7:15 A.M.	WEHH AM 1590
Hyde Park	7:50 A.M.	WHVW AM 950
Jamestown	5:45 P.M.	WJTN AM 1240/WWSE FM 93.3
Riverhead	6:35 A.M./M–F	WRHD AM 1570
Rome/Utica	6:10 A.M.	WADR AM 1480/WRNY AM 1350
	5:55 A.M.	WKDY FM 102.5
Salamanca	AM 7:15 A.M./4:15 P.M.	WGGO AM 1590/WQRT FM 98.3
	FM 7:30 A.M./5:30 P.M.	
Seneca Falls	6:35 A.M.	WSFW AM 1110/FM 99.3
Springville	6:20 A.M.	WSPQ AM 1330
Ticonderoga	6:40 A.M./1:40 P.M.	WIPS AM 1250
Warsaw	8:25 A.M.	WCJW AM 1140
Watertown	6:45 A.M.	WNCQ AM 1410/WCIZ FM 97.5

OHIO

Ashtabula	5:50 A.M.	WZOO FM 102.5

Canton	AM 6:15 A.M.	WCER AM 900
Cedarville	FM 7:05 P.M.	WCDR FM 90.3
	simulcast:	WOHC FM 90.1/Chillicothe
		WCDR FM 88.1/Columbus
		WCDR FM 90.3/Dayton
		WOHP FM 88.3/Portsmouth
		WCDR FM 89.9/Richmond, IN
		WCDR FM 98.3/Wheelersburg
		WCDR FM 90.3/Springfield
Celina	5:45 A.M.	WCSM AM 1350/FM 96.7
Delaware	7:22 A.M. M–F/Sat 7:45 A.M.	WDLR AM 1550
Dover	6:40 A.M./5:30 P.M.	WJER AM 1450/FM 101.7
Elyria	5:40 P.M. M–F/Sat 7:45 A.M.	WEOL AM 930/WNWV FM 107.3
Findlay	7:40 A.M.	WFIN AM 1330/WKXA FM 100.5
Springfield	6:45 P.M.	WBLY AM 1600
Washington C.H.	6:10 P.M.	WCHO FM 105.5/WOFR AM 1250
Youngstown	10:19 A.M.	WASN AM 1330

OKLAHOMA

Alva	6:50 A.M./5:50 P.M.	KALV AM 1430
Clinton	6:45 A.M./5:10 P.M.	KSWR FM 106.9/KXOL AM 1320
Duncan	7:40 A.M.	KDDQ FM 96.7
Elk City	6:15 A.M./12:15 P.M.	KECO FM 96.5/KADS AM 1240
Enid	6:45 A.M.	KGWA AM 960/KOFM FM 103.1
Hobart	4:30 P.M. M–F/Sat 7:20 A.M./ 12:25 P.M.	WTJS AM 1420/KQTZ FM 105.9
Holdenville	4:33 P.M.	KRAF AM 1370/KXKY FM 106.5
McAlester	5:45 A.M.	KNED AM 1150/KMCO FM 101.3
Norman	7:15 A.M.	WWLS AM 640
	simulcast:	KXTD AM 1530/Wagoner
		KXOL AM 1320/Clinton
Poteau	1:05 P.M.	WPRV AM 1280/FM 92.5
Tulsa	2:00 P.M.	KAKC AM 1300/KMOD FM 97.5
Woodward	7–9:00 A.M.	KWDQ FM 102.3

OREGON

Bend	6:00 A.M.	KGRL AM 940/KXIQ FM 94.1
Coos Bay	5:20 P.M.	KYTT FM 98.7
	simulcast:	96.7/Riddle
		105.5/Tri City, Springfield, Roseburg, Brookings, Gold Beach, and Sutherlin

Eugene	7:20 A.M./5:20 P.M.	KDUK AM 1280/KLCX FM 104.7
Hermiston	5:20 P.M.	KOHU AM 1360/KQFM FM 99.3
Hood River	6:41 A.M.	KIHR AM 1340/KCGB FM 105.5
Lincoln City	8:15 A.M./4:30 P.M.	KBCH AM 1400/KCRF FM 96.7
Myrtle Creek	5:20 P.M.	KYTT FM 96.7
	simulcast:	FM 96.7/Canyonville
		FM \105.5/Winston
		FM 105.5/Harbor
		FM 107.1/Oakland
Reedsport	6:45 A.M.	KDUN AM 1030/KSYD FM 92.1
Woodburn	7:40 A.M.	KWBY AM 940

PENNSYLVANIA

Bellefonte	6:25 A.M.	WBLF AM 970
Bloomsburg	5:25 P.M.	WCNR AM 930
Emporium	8:30 A.M./4:30 P.M./M–F	WLEM AM 1250/WQKY FM 99.3
Everett	8:10 A.M.	WSKE AM 1040/FM 104.3
Greensburg	6:55 A.M.	WHJB AM 620/WSSZ FM 107.1
Kane	6:50 P.M.	WLMI FM 103.9
Lansford	7:10 A.M./12:10 P.M.	WLSH AM 1410
Lebanon	6:10 A.M./7:10 P.M.	WADV AM 940
Linesville	6:00 A.M.	WVCC FM 101.7
McConnellsburg	4:35 P.M.	WVFC AM 1530
McKeesport	12:45 P.M.	WEDO AM 810
Middletown	7:30 P.M.	WMSS FM 91.1
Milton	6:05 A.M.	WMLP AM 1380/WOEZ FM 100.9
Nanticoke	TBA	WNAK AM 730
New Castle	5:35 A.M.	WKST AM 1280
Philipsburg	12:30 P.M.	WPHB AM 1260/FM 105.9
Shippensburg	3:40 P.M.	WSHP AM 1480
Stroudsburg	6:50 A.M.	WVPO AM 840/WSBG FM 93.5
Troy	7:30 A.M./8:30 P.M.	WHGL AM 1310/FM 100.3
Warren	5:16 P.M.	WNAE AM 1310/WRRN FM 92.3
Waynesburg	7:30 P.M.	WANB AM 1580/WAWB FM 103.1

RHODE ISLAND

| Hope Valley | 7:40 A.M. | WJJF AM 1180 |

SOUTH CAROLINA

| Greer | 8:10 A.M. | WCKI AM 1300 |

| Florence | 5:50 A.M. | WMXT FM 102.1 |

SOUTH DAKOTA

Aberdeen	8:45 A.M.	KGIM AM 1420/FM 106.7
Belle Fourche	7:20 A.M.	KBFS AM 1450/FM 95.9
Brookings	5:20 P.M.	KJJQ AM 910/KKQQ FM 102.3
Huron	5:45 P.M.	KOKK AM 1210
Lemmon	1:06 P.M.	KBJM AM 1400
Mitchell	7:50 A.M./5:30 P.M.	KORN AM 1490/KQRN FM 107.3
Pierre	5:40 P.M./Sat 7:40 A.M.	KGFX AM 1060/FM 92.7
Watertown	6:00 A.M.	KWAT AM 950
Winner	4:35 P.M.	KWYR AM 1260/FM 93.7

TENNESSEE

Ashland City	varies	WQSV AM 790
Centerville	5:55 A.M./5:15 P.M.	WNKX FM 96.7/AM 1570
Clarksville	6:03 A.M.	WJZM AM 1400
Columbia	5:45 A.M.	WMCP AM 1280
Elizabethton	6:30 A.M.	WBEJ AM 1240
Fayetteville	12:20 P.M.	WEKR AM 1240
Gray	5:55 A.M./5:55 P.M.	WJCW AM 910/WKIN AM 1320
	simulcast:	WJCW AM 910/Johnson City
		WKIN AM 1320/Kingsport
Greeneville	6:15 A.M./6:15 P.M.	WSMG AM 1450
Jamestown	6:00 P.M.	WDEB AM 1500/FM 103.9
Jefferson City	AM 6:15 A.M.	WJFC AM 1480/WNDD FM 99.3
	FM 5:50 A.M.	
Morristown	7:45 A.M.	WMTN AM 1300/WMXK FM 96
Oneida	8:45 A.M./3:45 P.M.	WBNT FM 105.5/WOCV AM 1310
Pikeville	7:00 A.M./12:00 noon	WUAT AM 1110
Pulaski	6:40 A.M.	WYBM FM 92.1
Savannah	3:50 P.M.	WKWX FM 93.5
Shelbyville	6:45 A.M.	WLIJ AM 1580

TEXAS

Bay Town	6:40 A.M./6:40 P.M.	KWWJ AM 1360
Brownwood	6:20 A.M.	KXYL FM 104.1/AM 1240
Center	7:15 A.M.	KDET AM 930/KLCR FM 102.3
Columbus	5:40 & 6:10 A.M.	KULM FM 98.3

Corpus Christi	5:30 A.M.	KRYS AM 1360/FM 99.1
Denison	7:30 A.M./4:00 P.M.	KJIM AM 1500/KWSM FM 104.1
Eastland	6:45 A.M.	KEAS AM 1590/FM 97.7
Floydada	7:05 A.M.	KAWA AM 900/KFLL FM 95.3
Gatesville	7:15 P.M.	KRYL FM 98.3
Haskell	5:45 P.M.	KVRP AM 1400/FM 95.5
Hemphill	1:35 P.M.	KAWS AM 1240
Madisonville	6:50 A.M.	KMVL AM 1220
Nacogdoches	7:20 A.M.	KSFA AM 1230/KTBQ 107.7
Palestine	7:35 A.M.	KNET AM 1450/KYYK FM 98.3
Port	AM 6:50 A.M.	KZSP FM 95.3
Texarkana	8:30 A.M.	KCMC AM 740/KTAL FM 98.1
Tyler	6:40 A.M.	KDOK AM 1330/FM 92.1
Vernon	6:45 A.M.	KVWC AM 1490/FM 102.3
Wharton	varies	KANI AM 1500

UTAH

Bountiful	Between 5 & 10 P.M.	KSRE FM 106.5/KMGR AM 1230
St. George	5:55 A.M./5:55 P.M.	KSGI AM 1450
Vernal	AM 7:15 A.M.	KVEL AM 920/KLCY FM 105.9
FM 12:40 P.M.		

VIRGINIA

Big Stone Gap	7:25 A.M./4:25 P.M.	WAXM FM 93.5/WLSD AM 1220
Clarksville	8:20 A.M.	WLCQ FM 98.3
Clifton Forge	6:50 A.M./2:50 P.M.	WXCF AM 1230/FM 103.9
Hillsville	7:45 A.M.	WHHV AM 1400
Lexington	varies	WREL AM 1450
Martinsville	5:25 A.M.	WODY AM 900
Moneta	8:55 A.M.	WBLU AM 880
Rocky Mount	4:00 P.M.	WNLB AM 1290/WZBB FM 99.9
Staunton	5:43 P.M. M–F/Sat 7:11 A.M.	WTON AM 1240/FM 94.3

VERMONT

Barre	7:15 A.M.	WSNO AM 1450/WORK FM 107.1
Middlebury	5:45 A.M./5:45 P.M.	WFAD AM 1490/WGTK FM 100.9
St. Johnsbury	6:40 A.M.	WNKV FM 105.5/WSTJ AM 1340

WASHINGTON

Colville	varies	KCVL AM 1240/KCRK FM 92.1
East Wenatchee	4:35 A.M.	KYSN FM 97.7
Ellensburg	8:45 A.M.	KXLE AM 1240/FM 95.3
Forks	7:00 A.M.	KVAC AM 1490/KLLM FM 103.9
Kennewick	5:50 A.M.	KTCR AM 1340/KOTY FM 106.5
Moses Lake	7:15 A.M./12:20 P.M.	KWIQ AM 1020/FM 100.3
Oak Harbor	6:15 A.M.	KJTT AM 1110
Othello	9:25 A.M.	KRSC AM 1400
Prosser	6:55 A.M./5:55 P.M.	KARY AM 1310/FM 100.9
Quincy	11:15 A.M.	KWNC AM 1370
Walla Walla	5:50 P.M.	KNSN FM 97.1

WISCONSIN

Adams/Friendship	12:50/6:15 A.M./12:50/6:50 P.M.	WDKM FM 106.1
Amery	6:25 A.M.	WXCE AM 1260
Appleton	5:45 A.M./5:45 P.M.	WHBY AM 1150/WAPL FM 105.7
Ashland	7:35 A.M./4:30 P.M.	WATW AM 1400/WJJH FM 96.7
Beaver Dam	5:25 P.M.	WBEV AM 1430/WXRO FM 95.3
Chippewa Falls	5:15 A.M./P.M. M–F/5:15 P.M. Sat	WWIB FM 103.7/WOGO AM 680
Hartford	12:25 P.M.	WTKM AM 1540/FM 104.9
Lacrosse	5:30 & 6:30 A.M.	WQJY FM 100.1
Ladysmith	6:50 A.M.	WLDY AM 1340/FM 93.1
Madison	5:45 A.M.	WTSO AM 1070/WZEE FM 104.1
Marinette	11:50 A.M./5:50 P.M.	WMAM AM 570/WLST FM 95
Marshfield	4:35 P.M.	WDLB 1450/WLJY FM 106.5
Menomonie	8:15 A.M.	WMEQ AM 880/FM 92.1
Merrill/Wausau	5:15 P.M.	WJMT AM 730
New Richmond	12:42 P.M.	WIXK AM 1590/FM 107.1
Park Falls	7:20 A.M.	WNBI AM 980/WCQM FM 98.3
Platteville	varies	WTOQ AM 1590/WKPI FM 107.1
Port Washington	6:45 A.M.	WGLB AM 1560/FM 100.1
Portage	6:30 A.M.	WPDR AM 1350/WDDC FM 100.1
Rhinelander	7:15 A.M./5:20 P.M.	WOBT AM 1240/WRHN FM 100.3
Price Lake	5:25 P.M.	WJMC AM 1240/FM 96.3
Ripon	5:40 A.M./4:35 P.M.	WCWC AM 1600/WYUR FM 96.1
River Falls	5:30 P.M.	WEVR AM 1550 FM 106.3
Shawano	4:55 P.M.	WTCH AM 960/WOWN FM 99.3
Tomah	7:05 A.M./3:55 P.M.	WTMB AM 1460/WTRL FM 96.1
Viroqua	6:25 A.M.	WVRQ AM 1360/FM 102.3

| West Bend | 5:50 P.M. | WBKV AM 1470/WBWI FM 92.5 |

West Virginia

Grafton	5:30 P.M.	WTBZ AM 1260/FM 95.9
Martinsburg	5:50 P.M.	WEPM AM 1340/WKMZ FM 97.5
Richwood	4:30 P.M.	WVAR AM 600
W. Sulphur Spgs.	6:30 A.M.	WSLW AM 1310
Weston	7:30 A.M. M–F	WHAW AM 980/WSSN FM 102.3

Wyoming

Buffalo	4:10 A.M./4:10 P.M.	KBBS AM 1450
Cheyenne	Between 6–8 A.M./5–6 P.M.	KFBC AM 1240/KFBQ FM 97.9
Evanston	varies	KEVA AM 1240/KOTB FM 106.3
Kemmerer	6:15 A.M.	KMER AM 950/FM 94.9
Newcastle	8:45 A.M.	KASL AM 1240
Rawlins	12:30 P.M.	KRAL AM 1240/KIQZ FM 92.7

Canada

Ontario

| Marathon | 1:30 P.M./7:30 P.M. | CFNO 93.1 |

16

VACATIONS

You're stuck in traffic on the freeway, with the vista in front of you looking as bleak as Napoleon's retreat from Moscow. Or you're crammed into a tiny seat on a commuter airline that's been waiting on a fogbound runway for the past hour, and there's no way that you'll make your connecting flight home. Or you've chosen the wrong supermarket line again, this time behind a customer who seems prepared to fight to the death his right to return recyclable cans and bottles on a day that signs in the market say the store doesn't accept them.

You take a deep breath and let your mind wander.

"I'd give half my kingdom," you hear yourself muttering, "to be fishing for rainbow in Montana," or ". . . surf-casting for stripers on Martha's Vineyard," or ". . . flippin' a jig for bucketmouths in the Ozarks," or ". . . hooking into a marlin off Bimini," or—well, you get the idea.

For that matter, you don't even have to undergo a trauma to daydream that way. The weather can be lovely, whatever you do for a living can be going better than ever expected, and you can still say to yourself, "I wish I were. . . [fill-in-the-piscatory-blank].

Now, here's the beautiful part: you can do it, and it needn't even cost half your kingdom. It's called "taking a fishing vacation," and with planning, you can find yourself wetting a line in an exotic (to you) place somewhere in the world.

You've taken vacations before, but perhaps never a fishing-focused one. If not, you may need to be reminded that the choice of where and when to go involves coordinating your preferences with regard to your vacation time and destination with the kind of fishing that's available. For example, if the business you're in lets you get away only during summer months, but you've always had a yen to fish in Chile's Patagonia region, you'll be disappointed. That's because summer here in the northern hemisphere is winter down under, and the fish (and other sensible creatures) take that time off. On the other hand, fishing in Alaska or Russia or any other northern clime is a summer festival.

So, if you know where you want to go and/or the kind of fishing you want to do, get in touch with any of the travel agents listed later in this chapter. Read vacation articles and browse through ads in fishing magazines. Consult non-fishing magazines too—*Travel & Leisure* and even *Gourmet* often mention fishing opportunities in their travel articles. Take a look at books and videotapes that cover a part of the world that you've a yen to see. Write to the appropriate tourist office and, where there is one, the area's fish and game agency for information.

And if you haven't a clue about when or where you'd like to go, or you have some vague ideas but could be convinced otherwise, or your family members or Significant Other with whom you'll holiday aren't the angling types, the services of a travel agent who specializes in such holidays can help you with a destination where all involved, and especially you, will be happy as clams at high tide.

A few random yet relevant thoughts:

- No matter where you choose to go, make sure your tackle, other equipment, and clothing are in good repair. You don't want to get to the middle of Manitoba, Molokai, or Mexico to discover that the handle of your favorite rod is loose or that the soles of your fishing shoes are coming off. Check your gear in plenty of time to make repairs or to replace items.

- Fisherman who are desk-bound for most of the year should consider instituting some sort of fitness program before they go off hiking through the wilderness or spending an hour or more reeling in big-game blue-water monsters. Any kind of exercise, from a health club regimen to informal deep knee-bends and sit-ups will help. So will walking briskly to build up stamina and wind.

The next time there's an errand within walking distance, try walking instead of taking your car. You'll be better off.

- Any trip can become something of a fishing vacation. We've heard of business travelers who routinely pack a rod, reel, and tackle whenever they go someplace that's near good fishing waters ("micro" traveling rod-and-reel sets are available for just such occasions). Whenever they can find a few spare hours or even stay an extra day, they're all set to wet a line.

- Maybe the person with whom you're going to meet is a fisherman too (ask about fishing spots in his or her part of the world, and see whether the person rises to the bait). Someone we know routinely asks, and on more than one occasion has found himself holding business discussions in a bass boats and along a trout stream.

Travel Agencies

Anyone who is planning, or even just contemplating, an angling vacation would do well to consider using the services of a travel agency that focuses its attention on fishing. That's particularly important if you haven't decided on a destination: knowledgeable travel professionals can make valuable suggestions based on the kind of fishing you want to do (deep-sea, fly-fishing, etc.), your feelings about "roughing it" versus less-spartan accommodations, the time of year you want to go, and—of course—budgetary considerations. Travel agencies that focus on fishing will also be better able to help you plan what to take in the way of tackle and apparel, as well as any other items that may not occur to less-knowledgeable travel professionals.

The following agencies are among those that specialize in fishing vacation opportunities. Many tackle shops also have travel agency "arms": see the listing of catalogs beginning on page 290 for those that do.

Anglers Travel Connections
1280 Terminal Way, Suite 30
Reno, NV 89502
(800) 624-8429
fax: (702) 324-0583
Worldwide fly- and deep-sea fishing opportunities.

Arctic Adventures
19950 Clark Graham
Bale D'Urfe
Quebec, Canada H9X 3RB
(800) 465-9474
fax: (514) 457-4626
Represents four Arctic Quebec fishing establishments.

The Best of New Zealand Fly
    Fishing
2817 Wilshire Blvd.
Santa Monica, CA 90403
(800) 528-6129

fax: (310) 829-9221

Represents New Zealand lodges and farm accommodations, wilderness float trips, and helicopter fly-ins.

Dick Ballard's Fishing Adventures
140 E. Ritter
Republic, MO 65738
(800) 336-9735

Among its other destinations, bass fishing in Brazil and Venezuela.

John Eustace & Associates
Angling Tours and Travel
1445 SW 8th Ave.
Portland, OR 97225
(800) 288-0886
fax: (503) 297-3048

Worldwide destinations for the fly-fisher.

Fishing International, Inc.
P.O. Box 2132
Santa Rosa, CA 95405
(800) 950-4242
fax: (707) 539-1320

A program of worldwide freshwater and saltwater angling destinations. The firm's brochure, "International Fishing Journal" and its newsletter supplement, "International Fishing News," may be the largest and most handsomely produced of all such travel agency literature.

The Fly Shop
4140 Churn Creek Road
Redding, CA 96002
(800) 669-FISH

This firm's catalog contains an intriguing section on domestic and international fly-fishing vacations.

Frontiers International Travel
100 Logan Rd.

Wexford, PA 15090
(800) 245-1950

Bass fishing in Venezuela and Brazil, among other holiday opportunities.

The Global Flyfisher
2849 W. Dundee Rd., Suite 132
Northbrook, IL 60062-2501
(800) 531-1106
fax: (708) 291-3486

The shop's catalog contains a wide selection of books and videos on fishing vacations, as well as a travel service.

Off The Beaten Path
109 East Main Street
Bozeman, MT 59715
(800) 445-2995

"Customized" fishing vacations throughout the Rocky Mountain states, along with dude ranching, hiking, rafting, skiing, and other pastimes.

Owenoak International
88 Main Street
New Canaan, CT 06840
(800) 426-4498
fax: (203) 972-3235

"Customized" vacations for salmon and brown trout in Ireland.

Professional Adventures
800 S. Michigan
Seattle, WA 98108
(800) 633-3085
fax: (206) 763-4016

Worldwide vacations, featuring salmon fishing in Russia.

Reel Women Fly Fishing
Adventures
P.O. Box 20202
Jackson, WY 83001

(307) 733-2210
fax: (307) 733-8655.

Spring and summer trips of four, five, or six days to Montana's "classic" trout rivers, the South Fork of Idaho's Snake River, and lake fishing spots in Wyoming's Wind River Mountains. February and March are spent bone-fishing in the Bahamas.

Trek International Safaris
P.O. Box 19065
Jacksonville, FL 32245
(800) 654-9915

Fishing trips in Alaska, Montana, and Central and South America. A $15 club fee includes a subscription to the firm's monthly newsletter.

OTHER AGENCIES

Angler Adventures
P.O. Box 872
Old Lyme, CT 06371
(203) 434-9624
fax: (203) 434-8605

Frontiers International
P.O. Box 959
Wexford, PA 15090
(800) 345-1950
fax: (412) 935-5388

Rod & Reel Adventures
3507 Tully Rd.
Modesto, CA 95356
(800) 356-6982
fax: (209) 524-1220

Wide World Sportsman, Inc.
P.O. Box 787
Islamorada, FL 33036
(800) 327-2880
fax: (305) 664-3692

Travel Books and Videos

These books and videos will be of interest to anyone planning to fish in the states, regions, or countries listed below. Since the selection is by no means exhaustive, and since new books and videos are published or released every month, you'll want to consult tackle shops, bookstores, and libraries for other titles, especially with regard to specific angling methods (e.g., fly-fishing, deep-sea) and the species of fish you hope to encounter in your travels.

BOOKS

U.S. STATES

The Complete Alabama Fisherman, by Mike Bolton and Tom Bailey (Seacoast Books, 1990).

Chris Batin's Twenty Great Alaska Adventures, by Chris Batin (Alaska Angler, 1991).

Fishing Arizona, by Guy J. Sagi (Golden West Publishing Co., 1992).

Fishing California, by David P. Colby (Sabertooth Pub., 1991).

The Colorado Angling Guide, by Chuck Fothergill and Bob Sterling (Stream Stalker, 1987).

Delaware Bay Fishing Guide: Delaware Edition, by D.H. Olsen and B.E. Straub (Vayu Press, 1991).

Florida Freshwater Fishing Guide, by Max Branyon (Tribune, 1987).

Florida Saltwater Fishing Guide, by Max Branyon (Tribune, 1988).

Georgia Fishing Digest, edited by Andrew Ard (Pisces Press, 1992).

Modern Hawaiian Gamefishing, by Jim Rizzuto (University of Hawaii Press, 1977).

Idaho's Top Thirty Fishing Waters, edited by Lewis Watson (Outdoor Digest, 1989).

Fishing Northern Illinois' Top 20 Lakes, by Jack Laasch et al. (Fishing Hot, 1989).

Fishing Southern Illinois, by Art Reid (Shawnee Books, 1986).

Watermark Guide to Fishing Kansas, by George Stanley (Watermark Press, 1991).

One Hundred Northern Lower Michigan Lakes, by Tom Huggler (Friede Publications, 1993).

The Angler's Guide to Twelve Classic Streams in Michigan, by Gerth E. Henrickson (University of Michigan Press, 1994).

Michigan Trout Streams: A Fly-Angler's Guide, by Bob Linsenman and Steve Nevala (The Countryman Press, 1993).

Fishing Minnesota, by Greg Breining (Greg Lindner, ed.)(North Word, 1993).

Angler's Guide to Montana, by Michael S. Sample (Falcon Press, 1992).

AMC Guide to Freshwater Fishing in New England, by Brian R. Kologe (AMC Books, 1991).

Delaware Bay Fishing Guide: New Jersey Edition, by D.H. Olsen and B.E. Straub (Vayu Press, 1991).

New Hampshire Fishing Maps, by Donald Wilson and Charlton Swasey (DeLorme Maps, 1993).

Fishing in New Mexico, by R. Titus Piper (University of New Mexico Press, 1989).

San Juan River Chronicles, by Steven J. Meyers (Lyons & Burford, 1994).

Good Fishing in Western New York, edited by C. Scott Sampson (The Countryman Press, 1992).

The following other books on New York State are also published by The Countryman Press:

Good Fishing in the Catskills, by Jim Capossela et. al. (1992)

Good Fishing in the Adirondacks, edited by Dennis Aprill (1993).

Good Fishing in Lake Ontario and Its Tributaries, by Rich Giessuebel (1992).

North Carolina Fishing Digest, edited by Laura Bierce (Pisces Press, 1992).

Fishing in Oregon, by Dan Casali and Madelynne Diness (Flying Pencil, 1989).

Pennsylvania Fishing Guide (by regions), by Jim McCracken (Recreational Guides, 1988).

Pennsylvania Trout Streams and Their Hatches, by Charles R. Meck (The Countryman Press, 1993).

Glory Holes: An Expert's Guide to Tennessee's Best Fishing, edited by Jacki Reeser (J.T. Publishing Co., 1985).

Fishing Texas, by Russell Tinsley (Shearer Pub., 1988).

Fishing Vermont's Streams and Lakes: A Guide to the Green Mountain State's Best Trout and Bass Waters, by Peter F. Cammann (The Countryman Press, 1992).

Virginia Fishing Guide, by Bob Gooch (University Press of Virginia, 1992).

Virginia Trout Streams: A Guide to Fishing the Blue Ridge Watershed, by Harry Slone (The Countryman Press, 1994).

Washington State Fishing Guide, by Stan Jones (Jones Pub. Co., 1984).

Fish Wisconsin, 2nd edition, by Dan Small (Krause Publications, 1993).

The Wyoming Angling Guide, by Chuck Fothergill and Bob Sterling (Stream Stalker, 1986).

U.S. REGIONS

Fishing the Southeast Coast, by Donald Millus (Sandlapper Pub. Co., 1989).

Greatest Fishing Locals of North America, by Ken Schultz (Outlet Book Co., 1991).

North America's Freshwater Fishing Book, by Mike Rosenthal (Scribner's/Macmillan, 1989).

OTHER COUNTRIES

The Canadian Fishing Trip: A Guidebook, by John Harschutz (Barker & North, 1993).

Angler's Guide to Baja California [Mexico], by Tom Miller (Baja Trail, 1987).

At the Water's Edge: A Fisherman's Progress Around Britain, by Benjamin Perkins (Godine, 1989).

Game Angler in Ireland and *Sea Angler in Ireland,* both by K. Whelan (Country House ER, 1991).

The Best Fishing in Scotland, by Lewis-Ann Garner (Lochar Press, 1991).

European Fishing Handbook, by Claus Frimodt (Van Nostrand Reinhold, 1989).

Whether you're a fly-fisher planning a vacation or an armchair angler who likes to daydream, you'll savor planning or contemplating the vacations described in *The Travelling Angler* by Ernest Schweibert (Doubleday, 1991). The 20 locales suggested by this well-respected fishing author and commentator pretty much cover the globe: North America (especially America's storied trout waters), Chile and Patagonia in South America, Europe (with an emphasis on the British Isles and Ireland), New Zealand, and—for the truly intrepid—Bhutan. The paperback's a real passport to pleasure.

Chris Hole, a retired naval office and active painter and photographer, set out from his native Australia on two around-the-world fly-fishing safaris, one for each hemisphere. *Heaven on a Stick* (Kangaroo Press/Seven Hills Distributors, 1993) chronicles his adventures. Hole writes with the same passion for fly-fishing that he confesses to and with the same clarity and attention to detail that his accompanying watercolors convey. In the process the reader shares experiences that include Tasmania, Zimbabwe, and Patagonia, and on the northern trek, England, Iceland and Greenland, Labrador, the Rocky Mountains, British Columbia, and Christmas Island.

The National Parks system offers many angling opportunities, about which *The National Parks*

Fishing Guide by Robert Gartner (Globe Pequot, 1990) provides all the guidance you'll need. Gartner catalogs all 125 parks throughout the U.S. and its territories in terms of location, access, fishing (with tips on tackle and bait and refreshingly candid assessments of the quality of the fishing), licenses, maps, camping, and where to get further information.

Included in *Gene Kilgore's Ranch Vacations* (John Muir Publications, 1991) are 16 resorts that specialize in fly-fishing. They range in location from Maine to Alaska to New Mexico and in cost and style from modest to deluxe. If you're also interested in a horseback holiday, many of the guest ranches featured in the book also offer fishing (tackle as well as tack, as it were).

Getting a handle on all the good bass fishing waters in America is a daunting chore, but Ed Lusch takes a number of giant steps in that direction in his *American Bass Angling Guide* (Frank Amato Publications, 1990). Lusch describes some 500 lakes, rivers, and reservoirs, limiting himself to 10 per state. Among other valuable data, the book contains suggestions on appropriate lures and bait and, where available, sources for further information.

Northeastern surf-fishermen who don't know about *Striper Hot Spots* by Frank Daignault (Globe Pequot, 1993) will want to correct that deficiency before the next full moon. The author pinpoints 100 locations from Maine to New Jersey, then offers counsel on the best times to fish, recommended methods, the species in addition to striped bass that are available, and even non-fishing activities in the area.

VIDEOS

[The featured species and/or locales are given where they are unclear from the video's title.]

The following videos by Jim and Kelly Watt, hosts of the ESPN TV fly-fishing series, are available from The Global Flyfisher and other tackle shops.

Alagnak Acrobatics (Alaska salmon)

Kings of Ayakulik (Alaska salmon)

Alaskan Sockeye

Belize—A Fly Fishing Fantasy (bonefish and tarpon)

Costa Rica—Fly Fish Paradise (sailfish)

Montana Trout (brown and rainbow)

South Island Browns (brown and rainbow trout on New Zealand's South Island)

Argentina Trout (brown, brook, and rainbow trout)

Utah's Green River Trout (browns, rainbows, and cutbows)

San Juan and Delores Trout (browns, rainbows, and cutbows)

Big Horn River (brown and rainbow trout in Montana)

Atlantic Salmon (Atlantic salmon on Russia's Kola Peninsula)

Washington Monster Trout (rainbows)

Joe Buterac Steelhead Guide (in Washington State)

Venezuela Tarpon and Bonefish

Olympic Treat (brown and rainbow trout in Calgary, Alberta)

British Columbia Steelhead and Trout

Tarpon—The Silver King (Florida Keys)

Silver Creek and Cousin Downunder (brown and rainbow trout in Idaho and New Zealand)

Isla Mujeres (sailfish and marlin in Mexico)

Tarpon, Snook and Guapote (Costa Rica)

Iliaska Rainbows and Grayling (Alaska)

Mexico's Bonefish and Dorado (Cancún)

Florida Tarpon and Bonefish (Florida Keys)

Lee's Ferry Trout (Arizona rainbows)

African Sailfish and New York Striped Bass

Stillwater Lakes Trout (Washington and northeast Canada)

Washington's Yakima River (trout)

Colorado's Gunnison River (trout)

Mirimichi Atlantic Salmon (New Brunswick)

Trout in Patagonia (rainbow and brown trout in Argentina)

Oregon's Wood and Williamson Trout

The producers of the *Walker's Cay Chronicles* TV series have issued five instructional videos that highlight well-known saltwater locales:

Costa Rica Sailfish

Everglades Tarpon

Redfish/Sharks (shark fishing in the Bahamas and redfish, snook, and tarpon in the Florida Everglades)

Bonefish (Florida Keys and Bahamas)

The Flats (Florida Keys and Walker's Cay in the Bahamas)

Lee Wulff's legacy includes these videos that feature exotic destinations:

To Ecuador for Marlin (striped marlin and Pacific sailfish)

Three Trout to Dream About and Minipi's Discovery (brook trout in Newfoundland's Minipi Basin)

Giant Tuna Small Boat (bluefin tuna in Newfoundland)

Soliliquy to a Salmon and the Atlantic Salmon (Newfoundland)

Two In-Fisherman videos explore the delights of Canadian sport-fishing:

Big Fish Ontario

Fishing Canada Hot Spots

Australian golf ace Greg Norman acts as host on four videos, two on freshwater and two on saltwater fishing. They're set, not surprisingly, Down Under and in New Zealand, where "The Shark" is joined by representatives of several American fishing magazines.

The Ultimate Sportfishing Adventure (Clear Water Big Fish series):

Vol. 1, "Jungle Bass/Tasmanian Trout."

Vol. 2, "New Zealand Trout/Top End Barra."

Vol. 3, "Cairns Black Marlin/Great Barrier Reef Sailfish/Bay of Islands Striped Marlin."

Vol. 4, "Madang Blue Marlin/Saltwater Fly Rodding at Seven Spirit Bay/Madang Dog Tooth on Fly."

From SwiftCurrent, the producers of the ESPN series *On the Fly*, comes *Fly Fishing Belize*, with Stu Apte (60 min.).

Fan of the series will be pleased to learn that the thirteen 1994 shows are also available. Their magazine format includes domestic and foreign on-location segments that qualify as travel videos. Consult your dealer, or phone (800) 331-6483.

The Colorado Division of Wildlife (via Colorado Outdoors Videos) produced a tempting trio of 30-minute videos. *Colorado Trout Fishing* points out some of the state's best rivers and streams for browns, brooks, rainbows, and cutthroats. *Colorado Warm Water Fishing* explores the lake and reservoir homes of bass, crappies, walleyes, Northern pike, and channel catfish. *Colorado Fishing Hot Spots* focuses on such places as high-altitude lakes, plains reservoirs and, of course, the Rio Grande.

Further Information

U.S. STATES

The following state travel agencies will furnish general tourist material, and, when specifically requested, can often provide detailed information about fishing vacation opportunities. However, people who inquire about fishing are frequently directed to state wildlife agencies, which you will find listed on pages 258–261.

Alabama Bureau of Tourism and Travel
532 S. Perry St.
Montgomery, AL 36104
(800) ALABAMA

Alaska Division of Tourism
Box E
Juneau, AK 99811
(907) 465-2010

Arizona Office of Tourism
1100 West Washington
Phoenix, AZ 85007
(602) 542-TOUR

Arkansas Dept. of Parks and Tourism
One Capital Mall
Little Rock, AK 72201
(800) 643-8383

California State Office of Tourism
1121 L St., Suite. 103
Sacramento, CA 95814
(800) 862-2543

Colorado Tourism Board
1625 Broadway, #1700
Denver, CO 80202
(800) 433-2656

Connecticut Tourism
210 Washington Street
Hartford, CT 06106
(203) 566-3948

Delaware Tourism Office
99 Kings Hwy., Box 1401
Dover, DE 19903
(800) 282-8667

Florida Dept. of Commerce Division of Tourism
107 W. Gaines St.
Tallahassee, FL 32399
(904) 488-8230

Georgia Tourist Division
P.O. Box 1776
Atlanta, GA 30301
(404) 656-3590

Hawaii Visitors Bureau
P.O. Box 8527 HVB
Honolulu, HA 96815
(808) 923-1811

Idaho Travel Council
700 West State Street
Boise, ID 83720
(800) 635-7820

Illinois Bureau of Tourism
310 S. Michigan Avenue
Chicago, IL 60604
(312) 814-4732

Indiana Dept. of Commerce Tourism Development Division
1 North Capitol, Suite 700
Indianapolis, IN 46204-2288
(317) 232-4124

Iowa Dept. of Economic Development
200 E. Grand Ave.
Des Moines, IA 50309
(800) 345-IOWA

Kansas Dept. of Travel and Tourism
400 W. 8th, 5th floor
Topeka, KS 66603
(913) 296-2009

Kentucky Dept. of Travel Development
P.O. Box 2011
Frankfort, KY 40602
(800) 225-TRIP

Louisiana Office of Tourism
P.O. Box 94291
Baton Rouge, LA 70804-9291
(800) 33-GUMBO

Maine Publicity Bureau
97 Winthrop Street
Hallowell, ME 04347
(207) 289-2423

Maryland Office of Tourist Development
217 E. Redwood St.
Baltimore, MD 21202
(800) 543-1036

Massachusetts Office of Travel and Tourism
100 Cambridge St.
Boston, MA 02202
(617) 727-3201

[photo courtesy Minnesota Tourism]

Michigan Travel Bureau
P.O. Box 30226
Lansing, MI 48909
(800) 248-5700
(See Figure 1)

Minnesota Office of Tourism
375 Jackson St.
St. Paul, MN 55101
(800) 657-3700

Mississippi Division of Tourism
P.O. Box 22825
Jackson, MS 39205
(800) 927-6378

Missouri Division of Tourism
P.O. Box 1056
Jefferson City, MO 65102
(314) 751-4133

Dept. of Commerce, Travel Montana
1424 9th Ave.
Helena, MT 59620
(800) 541-1447

Nebraska Travel & Tourism
P.O. Box 94666

Lincoln, NE 68509
(800) 228-4307

Nevada Commission On Tourism
Capitol Complex
Carson City, NV 89710
(800) NEVADA-8

New Hampshire Office of Vacation Travel
P.O. Box 856
Concord, NH 03301
(603) 271-2666

New Jersey Division of Travel and Tourism
20 West State St., CN 826
Trenton, NJ 08625
(800) 537-7397

New Mexico Tourism & Travel Division
1100 San Francisco Dr.
Santa Fe, NM 87503
(800) 545-2040
(See Figure 2)

New York State Division of Tourism
One Commerce Plaza
Albany, NY 12245
(800) CALL-NYS

North Carolina Division of Travel and Tourism
430 N. Salisbury St.
Raleigh, NC 27611
(800) VISITNC

North Dakota Tourism Promotion
Liberty Memorial Building
State Capitol Grounds
Bismark, ND 58505
(800) 437-2077

[photo courtesy New York State Commerce Dept.]

Ohio Office of Travel and Tourism
P.O. Box 1001
Columbus, OH 43266-0101
(800) BUCKEYE

Oklahoma Tourism and
    Recreation Dept.
500 Will Rogers Bldg.
Oklahoma City, OK 73105
(800) 652-6552

Oregon Tourist Division
775 Summer St, NE
Salem, OR 97310
(800) 547-7842

Pennsylvania Bureau of Travel
    Development
416 Forum Building
Harrisburg, PA 17120
(800) VISIT-PA

Rhode Island Tourist Division
7 Jackson Walkway
Providence, RI 02903
(800) 556-2484

South Carolina Division of
    Tourism
Box 71
Columbia, SC 29202
(803) 734-0218

South Dakota Division of Tourism
P.O. Box 600
Pierre, SD 57501
(800) 843-1930

Tennessee Tourist Development
P.O. Box 23170
Nashville, TN 37202
(615) 741-2158

Texas Division of Tourism
P.O. Box 12728

Austin, TX 78711
(800) 888-8839

Utah Travel Council
Council Hall, Capitol Hill
Salt Lake City, UT 84114
(800) 538-1030

Vermont Travel Division
134 State Street
Montpelier, VT 05602
(802) 828-3236

Virginia Division of Tourism
1021 E. Cary St.
Richmond, VA 23206
(804) 786-4484

Washington State Tourism
101 General Administration Blvd.
Olympia, WA 98504
(800) 544-1800

Travel West Virginia, Dept. of
    Commerce
State Capitol Complex
Charleston, WV 25305
(800) CALL WVA

Wisconsin Tourist Information
P.O. Box 7970
Madison, WI 53707
(800) 432-TRIP

Wyoming Travel Commission
I-25 and College Drive
Cheyenne, WY 82002
(800) 225-5996

U.S. TERRITORIES

Puerto Rico Tourism Co.
11 E. Adams St.
Chicago, IL 60603
(312) 922-9701

Other offices in Dallas, Los Angeles,
New York, and Miami.

U.S. Virgin Islands Tourist
    Information Office
343 S. Dearborn St.
Chicago, IL 60604
(312) 416-0180
Other offices in Los Angeles, Miami,
New York, and Washington, DC

FOREIGN COUNTRIES

These national tourist
offices are the primary sources
of international fishing holiday
information. Consulates in
major American cities can also
furnish information about visa
requirements and currency
restrictions.

Although it's out of alpha-
betical order, let's begin with
Canada. Whether you're after
Atlantic salmon in the Maritime
Provinces, or smallmouth, pickerel, and muskies in Ontario's
Lake of the Woods complex, or
steelheads and salmon along the
Pacific coast, our neighbor to
the north offers a wide range of
fishing opportunities.

Inquiries to any or all of the
provincial tourist offices and
wildlife agencies will elicit tanta-
lizingly handsome brochures that
contain very helpful information.
These offices and agencies can
also assist prospective visitors to
get in touch with lodges, camps,
guides, and outfitters.

CANADA

Alberta Tourism Vacation Counselling
3rd floor, City Centre Building
10155 102 St.
Edmonton, Alberta T5J 4L6
(800) 661-8888

Alberta Energy/Forestry Lands and Wildlife
9920 108 St.
Edmonton, Alberta T5K 2M4
(403) 427-3590
(See Figure 3)

Tourism British Columbia
Parliament Buildings
Victoria, British Columbia V8V 1X4
(800) 663-6000

Fish and Wildlife Branch
Ministry of the Environment, Lands and Parks
810 Blanchard St.
Victoria, British Columbia V8V 1K5
(604) 387-9740

Travel Manitoba
Dept. 20, 7th floor
155 Carlton St.
Winnipeg, Manitoba R3C 3H8
(800) 665-0040

Department of Natural Resources
1995 St. James St.
Winnipeg, Manitoba R3H 0W9
(204) 945-6784

Tourism New Brunswick
P.O. Box 12345
Fredericton, New Brunswick E3B 5C3
(800) 561-0123

Mt. Assiniboine Provincial Park, British Columbia. [photo courtesy Tourism B.C.]

Newfoundland and Labrador
Department of Tourism and Culture
P.O. Box 8730
St. John's, Newfoundland A1B 4K2
(800) 563-6353

Northwest Territories Tourism
P.O. Box 1320
Yellowknife, N.W.T. X1A 2L9
(800) 661-0788

Nova Scotia
Department of Tourism and Culture
P.O. Box 456
Halifax, Nova Scotia B3J 2R5
(800) 341-6096

Nova Scotia Department of Lands and Forests
P.O. Box 698
Halifax, Nova Scotia B3J 2T9
(902) 424-5935

Ontario Travel
Queen's Park
Toronto, Ontario M7A 2R9
(800) ONTARIO

Ministry of Natural Resources, Fisheries Branch
Queen's Park
Toronto, Ontario M7A 1W3
(416) 314-2225

Prince Edward Island
Department of Tourism, Parks and Recreation, Visitors Services Division
P.O. Box 940
Charlottetown, P.E.I. C1A 7M5
(800) 565-0267

Tourisme Quebec
C.P. 20 000
Quebec (Quebec) G1K 7X2
(800) 363-7777

Ministère du Loisir, de la Chasse et de la Peche
150 Saint-Cyrille Blvd. Est
Quebec (Quebec) G1R 4Y1
(418) 643-3127

Tourism Saskatchewan
1919 Saskatchewan Drive
Regina, Saskatchewan S4P 3V7
(800) 667-7191

Tuna fishing in Nova Scotia. [photo courtesy Tourism Nova Scotia]

Tourism Yukon
P.O. Box 2703
Whitehorse, Yukon Y1A 2C6
(403) 667-5340

As for the rest of the world, some countries offer far more fishing opportunities than others. Great Britain, Ireland, Germany, Panama, Belize, Mexico, Bermuda, Argentina, and New Zealand are among the countries that encourage angling vacations, and their tourist offices are helpful in that regard (both Britain and Ireland, for example, offer detailed brochures). Where no tourist office is given, contact a consulate of the country in which you are interested.

Although some countries don't immediately come to mind when you think of fishing, there's often sport to be found if you make an effort to find out (assuming you're not using the services of a travel agent who specializes in fishing vacations). In the best of all worlds, tourist office and consulate personnel have firsthand knowledge or can put you in touch with someone who has. Otherwise, seek out the names and addresses of the country's fishing federation, its fish and game commission, and/or one or two fishing magazines.

Foreign countries, especially those in Europe, have little of the unrestricted freshwater fishing that the U.S. and Canada have. You'll need to obtain permission from landowners or other holders of the riparian rights to streams and rivers. The right to fish is usually rented out according to the beat system: a "BEAT" is an exclusive stretch of water, the ownership of which can be bought and sold (several British rock stars invested in such rights along the Test, the Itchen, and other legendary trout streams and salmon rivers. . . and have seen the value increase). Some hotels own beats and will accommodate guests, while fishing clubs occasionally grant temporary guest membership. . . all for a fee. Then too, you should be aware that renting a beat doesn't give you and your traveling companions unrestricted license to fish to your collective heart's content. Restrictions as to number of "rods" limits the number of people permitted to fish at one time.

And while you're making inquiries, don't forget to ask about open and closed seasons, daily limits, licenses and where to get them, and whether any particular type of fishing or equipment is restricted.

ANGUILLA

Anguilla Tourist Information Office
271 Main Street
Northport, NY 11768
(800) 553-4939

ARGENTINA

Argentina Tourist Information
330 W. 58 St., Suite. 6K
New York, NY 10019
(800) 722-5737
Consulates in Baltimore, Chicago, Houston, Miami, and New Orleans.

ARUBA

Aruba Tourism Authority
521 Fifth Ave.
New York, NY 10175
(212) 557-1614

AUSTRALIA

Australia Tourist Commission
2121 Ave. of the Stars
Los Angeles, CA 90067
(213) 552-1988

also:

489 Fifth Ave.
New York, NY 10017
(212) 687-6300
Consulates in Chicago, Honolulu, Houston, and San Francisco.

AUSTRALIA 20c

AUSTRIA

Austria National Tourist Office
500 N. Michigan Ave., Ste. 544
Chicago, IL 60611
(312) 644-5556

also:

4800 San Filipe St.
Houston, TX 77056
(713) 850-8888

3440 Wilshire Blvd.
Los Angeles, CA 90010
(213) 380-3309

500 Fifth Ave.
New York, NY 10110
(212) 944-6880
Consulates in Atlanta, Boston, Chicago, Cleveland, Denver, Detroit, Honolulu, Houston, Los Angeles, Miami, New Orleans, New York, Philadelphia, St. Paul, San Francisco, San Juan, and Seattle.

BAHAMAS

Bahamas Tourist Information
Office
1950 Century Blvd. N.E.
Atlanta, GA 30345
(404) 633-1793

also:

875 N. Michigan Ave.
Chicago, IL 60611
(312) 787-8203

3450 Wilshire Blvd.
Los Angeles, CA 90010
(213) 385-0033

150 E. 52 St.
New York, NY 10022
(212) 758-2777
Consulates in Miami and New York.

BARBADOS

Barbados Tourism Authority
800 Second Ave.
New York, NY 10017
(800) 221-9831

BELGIUM

Belgian Tourist Office
745 Fifth Ave.
New York, NY 10151
(212) 758-8130
Consulates in Atlanta, Chicago, Houston, New York, and Los Angeles.

BELIZE

Belize Tourist Board
421 Seventh Ave.
New York, NY 10001
(212) 568-6011

BOLIVIA

Consulates in Miami, New York, and San Francisco.

BONAIRE

Bonaire Government Tourist
Office
444 Madison Ave., Suite 2403
New York, NY 10022
(800) 826-6247

BRAZIL

Brazil Tourism Authority
551 Fifth Ave., Suite 210
New York, NY 10165
(212) 916-3200
Consulates in Atlanta, Chicago, Dallas, Houston, Los Angeles, Miami, New Orleans, New York, and San Francisco.

BERMUDA

Bermuda Department of Tourism
310 Madison Ave.
New York, NY 10017
(212) 818-9800

also:

Bermuda Game Fishing
  Association
P.O. Box HM 1306
Hamilton HM FX Bermuda

CAYMAN ISLANDS

Cayman Islands Department of
  Tourism
420 Lexington Ave., Suite 2733
New York, NY 10170
(212) 682-5582

CHILE

Consulates in Boston, Houston, Los
Angeles, Miami, New York, San
Francisco, and Wheatridge
(Colorado).

[photo courtesy Bermuda Dept. of Tourism]

COLOMBIA

Colombian Govt. Tourist Office
140 E. 57 St.
New York, NY 10022
(212) 688-0151
Consulates in Boston, Chicago,
Houston, Los Angeles, Miami,
Minneapolis, New Orleans, New
York, San Francisco, Southfield
(Michigan), St. Louis, and Tampa.

COSTA RICA

Costa Rica National Tourist
  Bureau
1101 Brickell Ave.
Miami, FL 33131
(305) 358-2150
Consulates in Chicago, Lockport
(Buffalo, NY), Los Angeles, Miami,
New Orleans, New York, San Diego,
and San Francisco.

CURAÇAO

Curaçao Tourist Board
400 Madison Ave., Suite 211
New York, NY 10017
(800) 332-8266

DENMARK

Scandinavian Tourist Board
655 Third Ave.
New York, NY 10017
(212) 949-2333

also:

150 N. Michigan Ave., Ste. 2110
Chicago, IL 60601
(312) 726-1120

8929 Wilshire Blvd.
Los Angeles, CA 90211
(213) 854-1549

Consulates in Chicago, Cleveland, Honolulu, Houston, Los Angeles, Miami, New Orleans, New York, Philadelphia, San Francisco, and Seattle.

DOMINICA

Caribbean Tourism Organization
20 E. 46 St.
New York, NY 10017
(212) 682-0435

DOMINICAN REPUBLIC

Dominican Republic Tourist
    Information Center
485 Madison Ave.
New York, NY 10022
(212) 826-0750

ECUADOR

Consulates in Baltimore, Boston, Chicago, Dallas, Houston, Los Angeles, Nashville, New Orleans, New York, San Francisco, and Seattle.

EL SALVADOR

Consulates in Detroit, Houston, Los Angeles, Miami, New Orleans, New York, and San Francisco.

FRANCE

French Government Tourist
    Office
9401 Wilshire Blvd.
Beverly Hills, CA 90212
(213) 212-2661

also:

645 N. Michigan Ave.
Chicago, IL 60611
(312) 337-6301

P.O. Box 58610
Dallas, TX 75258
(214) 742-7011

610 Fifth Ave.
New York, NY 10020
(212) 757-1125

Consulates in Boston, Chicago, Detroit, Houston, Los Angeles, New York, San Francisco, and Washington, DC

FRENCH WEST INDIES

French West Indies Tourist Board
610 Fifth Ave.
New York, NY 10020
(212) 757-1125

GERMANY

German Tourist Office
440 S. Flower St., Ste. 2230
Los Angeles, CA 90071
(213) 688-7332

also:

747 Third Ave.
New York, NY 10017
(212) 308-3300

Consulates in Atlanta, Boston,

Chicago, Detroit, Houston, Los Angeles, Miami, New Orleans, New York, San Francisco, Seattle, and Washington, DC

GREAT BRITAIN

British Tourist Authority
551 Fifth Ave.
New York, NY 10176
(212) 986-2266

also:

2580 Cumberland Pkwy.
Atlanta, GA 30339
(404) 432-9635

875 N. Michigan Ave., Suite 3320
Chicago, IL 60611
(312) 787-0490

River Tay, Scotland
[photo courtesy British Tourist Authority]

2305 Cedar Maple Plaza
Dallas, TX 75201
350 S. Figueroa St., Ste. 450
Los Angeles, CA 90071
Consulates in Atlanta, Boston,
Cleveland, Dallas, Houston, Los
Angeles, New York, and San
Francisco.

GREECE

**Greek National Tourist
 Organization**
645 Fifth Ave.
New York, NY 10022
(212) 421-5777

also:

168 N. Michigan Ave.
Chicago, IL 60601
(312) 782-1084

611 W. Sixth St.
Los Angeles, CA 90017
(213) 626-6696
Consulates in Atlanta, Boston,
Chicago, New Orleans, New York,
and San Francisco.

GUATEMALA

**Guatemala Tourist Information
 Office**
501 Fifth Ave.
New York, NY 10017
(212) 370-0550
Consulates in Chicago, Coral Gables
(Florida), Houston, Los Angeles, New
Orleans, New York, and San
Francisco.

HONDURAS

Honduras Tourist Office
1140 Fremont Ave.
South Pasadena, CA 91030
(800) 327-1225
Consulates in Chicago and Los
Angeles.

HUNGARY

IBUSZ Tourist Office
630 Fifth Ave., Ste. 2455
New York, NY 10111
(212) 582-7412

ICELAND

Scandinavian Tourist Board
655 Third Ave.
New York, NY 10019
(212) 949-2332
Consulates in Atlanta, Boston, Los
Angeles, Miami, Minneapolis, New
York, Norfolk (Virginia), Portland
(Oregon), San Francisco, and Seattle.

IRELAND

Irish Tourist Board
757 Third Ave.
New York, NY 10017
(212) 418-0800
Consulates in Boston, Chicago, New
York, and San Francisco.

ISRAEL

Israel Government Tourist Office
5 S. Wabash Ave.
Chicago, IL 60603
(312) 782-4306

also:

4151 S.W. Freeway
Houston, TX 77027
(713) 850-9341

6380 Wilshire Blvd.
Los Angeles, CA 90048
(213) 658-7462

420 Lincoln Road
Miami Beach, FL 33139
(305) 673-6862

350 Fifth Ave.
New York, NY 10118
(212) 560-0620

220 Montgomery St.
San Francisco, CA 94102
(415) 775-5462

3514 International Dr., NW
Washington, DC 20008
(202) 364-5699
Consulates in Atlanta, Boston,
Chicago, Houston, Los Angeles,
Miami, New York, Philadelphia, and
San Francisco.

ITALY

**Italian Government Tourist
 Office—ENIT**
500 N. Michigan Ave.
Chicago, IL 60611
(312) 644-0990

also:

630 Fifth Ave.
New York, NY 01011
(212) 245-4822

360 Post St.
San Francisco, CA 94108
(415) 392-5266

Consulates in Boston, Chicago, Detroit, Houston, Los Angeles, Newark (New Jersey), New Orleans, New York, Philadelphia, and San Francisco.

JAMAICA

Jamaica Tourist Board
36 S. Wabash Ave.
Chicago, IL 60603
(312) 346-1546

also:

8411 Preston Rd.
Dallas, TX 75225

3440 Wilshire Blvd.
Los Angeles, CA 90010
(213) 384-1123

1320 S. Dixie Hwy.
Coral Gables, FL 33146
(306) 665-0557

866 Second Ave.
New York, NY 10017
(212) 688-7650

MEXICO

Mexican Ministry of Tourism
233 N. Michigan Ave., Ste. 1413
Chicago, IL 60601
(312) 565-2785

also:

2707 North Loop West
Houston, TX 77008
(713) 880-5153

10100 Santa Monica Blvd.
Los Angeles, CA 90067
(213) 203-8151

405 Park Ave., Ste. 1203
New York, NY 10022
(212) 755-7212

MOROCCO

Moroccan National Tourist Office
20 E. 46 St.
New York, NY 10017
(212) 557-2520

THE NETHERLANDS

Netherlands Board of Tourism
355 Lexington Ave.
New York, NY 10017
(212) 370-7364

also:

605 Market St., Rm. 401
San Francisco, CA 94105
(415) 543-6772

NEW ZEALAND

New Zealand Tourist and
Publicity Office
10960 Wilshire Blvd.
Los Angeles, CA 90024
(213) 477-8241

also:

630 Fifth Ave.
New York, NY 10111
(212) 586-0060

1 Maritime Plaza
San Francisco, CA 94111
(415) 788-7404

NORWAY

Scandinavian Tourist Board
655 Third Ave.

New York, NY 10017
(212) 949-2333

Consulates in Chicago, Houston, Los Angeles, Minneapolis, New York, and San Francisco.

PANAMA

Consulates in Atlanta, Baltimore, Beverly Hills, Boston, Burbank, Chicago, Dallas, Detroit, El Paso, Houston, Los Angeles, Mobile (Alabama), Montgomery (Alabama), New Orleans, New York, Norfolk (Virginia), Portland (Maine), Portland (Oregon), Rochester (New York), Sacramento, San Diego, San Francisco, San Juan, and Seattle.

PARAGUAY

Consulates in Dallas, Huntington Beach (California), New Orleans, New York, and San Francisco.

PERU

Consulates in Chicago, Houston, Los Angeles, Miami, New York, Paterson (New Jersey), and San Francisco.

POLAND

Polish Travel Bureau, Inc.—Orbis
500 Fifth Avenue
New York, NY 10036
(212) 391-0844
Consulates in Chicago and New York.

PORTUGAL

Portuguese National Tourist
Office
548 Fifth Ave.
New York, NY 10036
(212) 354-4403
Consulates in Boston, Honolulu,
Houston, Los Angeles, Miami,
Newark (New Jersey), New Bedford
(Massachusetts), New Orleans, New
York, Philadelphia, Providence
(Rhode Island), and San Francisco.

RUSSIA

Intourist
630 Fifth Ave.
New York, NY 10111
(212) 757-3884
Consulates in San Francisco and
Washington, DC

SOUTH AFRICA

South Africa Tourist Corp.
9465 Wilshire Blvd. Ste. 721
Beverly Hills, CA 90212
(213) 275-4111
also:
307 N. Michigan Ave.
Chicago, IL 60601
(312) 726-0517

747 Third Ave.
New York, NY 10017
(212) 838-8841
Consulates in Chicago, Houston, Los
Angeles, and New York.

SPAIN

National Tourist Office of Spain
845 N. Michigan Ave.
Chicago, IL 60611
(312) 944-0215
also:
5805 Westheimer
Houston, TX 77056
(713) 840-7411

8383 Wilshire Blvd.
Los Angeles, CA 90211
(213) 658-7188

665 Fifth Ave.
New York, NY 10022
(212) 759-8822
Consulates in Boston, Chicago,
Houston, Los Angeles, Miami,
New Orleans, New York, and San
Francisco.

ST. BARTHELEMY

French West Indies Tourist Board
610 Fifth Ave.
New York, NY 10020
(212) 757-1125

ST. CROIX

See U.S. Virgin Islands
under "U.S. Territories"

ST. JOHN

See U.S. Virgin Islands
under "U.S. Territories"

ST. KITTS–NEVIS

St. Kitts-Nevis Department of
Tourism
414 East 75 St.
New York, NY 10021
(800) 582-6208

ST. LUCIA

St. Lucia Tourist Board
820 Second Ave.
New York, NY 10017
(212) 867-2950

ST. MAARTEN

St. Maarten Tourist Office
275 Seventh Ave.
New York, NY 10001
(212) 989-0000

ST. THOMAS

See U.S. Virgin Islands
under "U.S. Territories"

SWEDEN

Scandinavian Tourist Board
150 N. Michigan Ave.
Chicago, IL 60601
(312) 726-1120
also:

655 Third Ave.
New York, NY 10017
(212) 949-2333

Consulates in Chicago, Houston, Los
Angeles, Minneapolis,
New York, and San Francisco.

SWITZERLAND

Swiss National Tourist Office
104 S. Michigan Ave.
Chicago, IL 60603
(312) 641-0050

also:

608 Fifth Ave.
New York, NY 10020
(212) 757-5944

250 Stockton St.
San Francisco, CA 94108
(415) 362-2260

TORTOLA

British Virgin Islands Tourist
Board
370 Lexington Ave., Suite 313
New York, NY 10017
(212) 696-0400

TRINIDAD AND TOBAGO

Trinidad and Tobago Tourist
Board
25 West 43 Street
New York, NY 10036
(800) 232-0082

TURKS AND CAICOS

Turks and Caicos Tourist Board
P.O. Box 594023
Miami, FL 33159
(800) 241-0824

URUGUAY

Uruguay Tourist Bureau
341 Lexington Ave.
New York, NY 10022
(212) 755-1200

Consulates in Chicago, Miami,
Newark, New Orleans, San Francisco,
and Santa Monica (California).

VENEZUELA

Consulates in Baltimore, Boston,
Chicago, Houston, Coral Gables
(Florida), New Orleans, New York,
Philadelphia, San Francisco, and
Santurce (Puerto Rico).

17

GUIDES

Hiring a Guide: How to Do It and What to Expect

BY JACK FRAGOMENI

Life is a series of expectations. Some are great, some small, some fulfilling, and some disappointing. We live our lives striving to achieve our expectations (or the expectations of others) and most of us fall somewhat short of a perfect score. Many of us are fortunate enough to live up to many of our expectations with help from mentors or other persons whose experience we can benefit from. Unfortunately some of us are left to fend for ourselves, doing the best we can. If this sounds like a metaphor for fishing—it is (substitute the word "fishing" for "life" and the word "guide" for "mentor"). In life, we don't always have the option of choosing our mentors, but in fishing we usually do have the option of choosing our guides. Helping you to do so is the purpose of this essay.

Let me begin by saying I have many years of experience as both a guide and client, and I strongly believe there are many benefits of fishing with a guide on unfamiliar water. Although most of my fishing experience has been with a fly rod (I have done a fair amount of spin-fishing too), this essay is not limited to how to find and hire fly-fishing guides. The topics to be discussed are applicable to all types of waters and styles of fishing.

Why hire a guide?

The answer is very simple: A guide knows something you don't know. Basically the guide's job is to show you where the fish are, get you there and back safely, make sure you know and observe the laws and regulations of the waters you're going to fish, and help you to do whatever is necessary to catch fish. How the guide does this will vary with the angler and the angler's skill as well as the guide and the guide's skill.

Your job as client is to go fishing, learn something, have a great time, and leave with some long-lasting memories. Be aware, however, that you and the guide are not the only determining factors in this equation. Weather and water conditions play very important roles as well—and so do the fish.

In order to perform the job at hand, a guide may assume many roles. They can be: teacher, by showing you new fishing tactics, techniques, and equipment, or by helping you to improve your casting; historian, by giving you local historical and geographical information; and, in many instances, philosopher, fishing guru, and general all-around friend.

A guide's knowledge, manner, and presentation is a matter of personal style, and all guides have a style of their own. It is important to understand that you are hiring a guide primarily for his or her knowledge, expertise, and experience, just as you would hire any other professional provider of service. But personality and style also play important roles in deciding which guide to hire.

Another reason for hiring a guide is to gain access to good waters. Not only do guides usually know the most productive spots to fish, but they also usually know the best places to enter the water, whether by boat or on foot. Some guides have access to private waters or easier private access to public waters. I have access to a couple of trout ponds on private lands that are not only great places to bring a client who is just a beginner in the sport, but have produced some spectacular fishing. I also have some private access points to public waters that otherwise would be inaccessible to anglers who have limited mobility. My friend and guiding partner, Bob Hesse, has some drift boat access points that most other guides on the upper Delaware River don't have.

So how do you find a guide to hire?

This question is not so easily answered, but here are some tips. First, there is no substitute for experience. If you have none of your own, use someone else's. The most reliable information often comes from people whose opinions you trust. If you don't know someone who can help you, ask other fishermen who have fished the waters in which you're interested to recommend a guide. Be sure to say that you want a guide who specializes in the type of fishing you're interested in doing (fly-fishermen if you are going to fly-fish, spin-fishermen if you are going to spin-fish, etc.—you wouldn't go an ophthalmologist to treat acne). This is an important consideration because although there are hundreds of great fishing guides out there, many of them are neither qualified nor choose to be versed in the style of fishing you're interested in doing.

Local chapters of fishing groups such as Federation of Fly Fishers, Trout Unlimited, or Bass Anglers Sportsman Society are good sources of information. So are fly-fishing or bait tackle shops both in your home area and in the area where you want to fish. Most parts of the country have at least one fly shop, tackle shop, or a sporting goods store that carries fishing equipment. Ask whether the proprietor, sales clerks, or customers have been to your water of interest and if so, could they recommend a suitable guide. Not only can the shop often provide you with the name of guide or outfitter, but they usually can provide you with suitable equipment and literature.

With regard to shops in the area where you are going, they can also be especially good places to get your terminal tackle; the people who work in the shop or the anglers who stop in usually know what artificials are working best on the water at that time. (I will occasionally consult with George Schlotter from the Battenkill Angler's Nook, whose shop I sometimes guide out of, regarding the latest water conditions and hatches when I have been away from the Battenkill for a week or more.)

Other sources of information are computer on-line services such as CompuServe, America Online, and GEnie; advertisements in fishing magazines; and phone calls to the editors of the magazines and to outdoor writers whose columns appear in newspapers in your area as well the destination area. Also contact local chambers of commerce and the departments of tourism or fish and wildlife in the area or the state where you plan to fish. Catalog stores such as L.L. Bean, Orvis, Thomas & Thomas, and Bass Pro Shop have lists of recommended guides or excursion packages to choose from. Once again, ask about guides who specialize in the type of fishing you're interested in doing.

Okay, now that you've got the name of a prospective guide, what's next?

Several matters should be discussed and understood before you hire the guide. As in all personal dealings, don't ignore your instincts. Your initial conversation will often reveal any potential personality conflicts with the guide. This isn't to say that either of you is necessarily a bad person, but it's best to minimize chances of potential disaster. It's common sense.

Basic points that should be understood and agreed upon are:

QUALIFICATIONS

Most states require that a professional guide have a considerable amount of training and knowledge of the sport to be licensed. Applicants must meet a number of objective criteria before being issued a license to guide in that state. These criteria typically include Red Cross First Aid, CPR, and Water Safety certifications, as well as the successful completion of a written exam administered by the state. Most guides who use power boats for angling (Florida Keys flats guides and Great Lakes charter boat guides, for example) must have their U.S. Coast Guard Captain's license as well. Guides who use drift boats on National Park lands and on other places like as the upper Delaware River system are subject to additional licensing and permits from the federal government.

Ask the prospective guide whether he or she is properly licensed on the water you're going to fish. But keep in mind that proper licensing doesn't necessarily mean that the guide is the right one for you, as all guides are not created equal.

FEES

What does the guide charge for his or her services, and what are acceptable methods of payment (cash, personal check, or traveler's check)? Are there separate charges for flies, lures, use of equipment, etc.? If you'll be fishing with a friend, is there an extra charge for a second angler (although most guides charge a flat rate whether it's one angler or two)? Is a deposit required, and if so, what is the accepted amount?

HOURS

Are the charges for half-day or full day? What is considered a half-day and what is considered a full day? Here is a point where guides may differ. Some will consider eight hours of fishing a full day, while others may consider more or less time a full day depending on prevailing conditions.

Don't hesitate to ask such questions. It is far more awkward for the guide to surprise the angler after the day's fishing than to answer a question before. Most guides will make sure that the angler is informed of all conditions and charges and is given a generous amount of fishing time (as conditions will allow), but guides are human and subject to erring occasionally, so it is your responsibility as the paying client to make sure you understand and agree upon all points for your trip.

EQUIPMENT

Most anglers prefer to use their own equipment, but circumstances won't always allow it. If this is the case, then will the guide be able to supply tackle and flies or lures or bait? If so, is there any extra charge (most guides do not charge extra or charge only a minimal fee)?

Even if you do bring your own equipment, there are still questions to be asked. What are the appropriate-sized rods to bring? What type and size of flies or lures would be best for the situation? What clothing is appropriate for the weather likely to be encountered?

CONDITIONS

How have the fishing conditions been, and what is the guide's policy for dealing with inclement weather? Surprisingly, these are important questions that anglers seldom ask, but that guides will always answer. Reputable guides, who rely on repeat clients, seldom give inaccurate reports for the sake of a day's work.

Anglers often schedule a day or two of fishing with a guide in the event of an opening during a business trip or on a non-fishing family vacation. Such people are at the mercy of prevailing water and weather conditions. Guides are very resourceful and usually can offer exciting fishing alternatives when the game fish of preference are unavailable or uncooperative. Most guides will not charge the client for a day not fished due to inclement weather or other uncontrollable factors, and they usually prorate the fee for similar situations that may occur during a fishing day.

Any deposit that has been paid is usually nonrefundable, but it often can be applied to a day of fishing on a later date. As for cancellations, please be aware that it is a common courtesy to notify the guide as soon as possible if you must cancel a fishing day. Not only is neglecting to do so inconsiderate, but it prevents the guide from rebooking the date or dates and thus deprives the guide of a day's pay or more.

Another important question is whether the fishing will be catch-and-release, or will you be allowed to keep some fish? Many guides, myself included, practice strict catch-and-release with a few exceptions. An increasing number of modern fishermen subscribe to the same policy, so it's usually a moot point, but there are also anglers like to keep a fish for dinner or for mounting if it's trophy-sized. If keeping fish is an important issue, make sure it is agreed upon beforehand.

Is it a boat trip or a walking trip? An obvious question, but nonetheless one that needs to be asked. Depending on the waters to be fished or if the angler has any physical restrictions, I may use a boat, a canoe, or walking as the mode of transportation. If you have any health conditions that would limit your activities or that could arise during the day's fishing, tell the guide during your initial conversation. The guide could then make necessary arrangements for access to the water, alter the day's strategy for fishing sites, or arrange for facilitating equipment for you.

Meals

Are food and beverages provided? If so, will it be a shore lunch or a box lunch? Can the guide accommodate any specific dietary considerations? If not, you would have to bring your own food and/or beverage?

Guides vary widely on this aspect of service. Options range from nothing to eat or drink to a formal shore lunch with tablecloth, linen napkins, hors d'oeuvres, fine wines, and exotic entrées and desserts. (Dave and Kim Egdorf of Western Alaska Sportfishing and Curt Collins of Bighorn Cast and Blast Outfitters are among the masters of fine outdoor cuisine.)

Can you bring alcoholic beverages? Aside from the obvious reasons of health and safety for not bringing them, a few other reasons are not so obvious. While you're fishing under a hot sun, an ice-cold beer can be very refreshing, but alcohol will make you dehydrated much sooner than you would be by drinking nothing at all. The same kind of dehydration can occur in cold weather, and it will also contribute to hypothermia.

Most guides will leave it up to their clients as to their beverages of choice, but few guides (especially when they're sober) enjoy having to babysit drunk or sick anglers. In no way am I on a soapbox preaching temperance, but what I am saying is if you're going to drink alcohol, save the drinking for the end of the day. I often sit around with the anglers at the end of a fishing trip and enjoy reviewing the events of the day with a cold beer or a flask of brandy.

INSTRUCTION

Most guides are very competent in one or more styles of fishing. But guides don't need to know a lot about your fishing style of preference to fulfill the requirements of their jobs as defined earlier in this essay. Experienced fly-fishermen can have a great day of fishing with a guide who knows very little about fly-fishing but can put the angler over feeding fish. The same can be true for experienced spin-fishermen with a fly-fishing guide. Yet it makes for a more enjoyable and fulfilling day if the guide knows as much or more than you do about the style of fishing you're going to do. If you are a novice or intermediate fisherman (I assume you are by virtue of the fact that you are reading this—unless you're an expert angler or guide who wants to see if I know what I'm talking about), ask the guide whether he or she can provide instruction if you think it would be necessary or helpful or both. Some guides charge a different fee for an instructional outing. This will vary from guide to guide.

During your initial conversation, give the guide an honest assessment of your fishing skill. Overstating your ability can make for an unpleasant day for everyone involved. Remember to leave your ego at home. The vast majority of guides are eager to help you in every way possible to make your fishing trip a great one and to help you to become a better angler.

Nevertheless, a few of my past clients (a very small percentage) who claimed more ability and experience than they actually had were unpleasantly surprised to find that they were in over their heads—literally and figuratively. One angler, who was downstream from where I was teaching his wife to cast, fell into a sharp drop-off alongside an eddy that I had warned him about. He informed me, as I helped him out of the water, that he didn't

know what an eddy was. Needless to say, I kept him close by me for the rest of the day and spent quite a bit of time working with him on his "expert" casting. Many of my clients have been better served by being provided with instruction for part of the day rather than a frustrating day of flogging the water, not catching fish because they couldn't present a fly properly, or, in that client's case, drying off.

Always be open to suggestions from guides. Part of their job is to provide important information, and they are usually very eager to do so. Negative criticism and taunting are not parts of the repertoires of the vast majority of guides. They genuinely enjoy helping the angler. This is a rewarding aspect of the job.

After the decision of which guide to hire, the only preparation left for your trip is to read as many books and articles and watch as many videotapes as you can about the type of fishing you're going to do. The preparation and anticipation of a fishing trip can be nearly as much fun as the fishing itself.

When the day of your trip arrives, there are a few things to keep in mind while fishing with your guide. If you're sharing the guide with another angler (most likely a friend, I hope—you could be opening Pandora's box if you're with an angler you've never met), expect to share the guide's attention or, in some cases, the fishing time. In some situations, only one angler can fish at a time. Two novice fly-rodders bonefishing from a skiff with a flats guide in the Florida Keys is a prime example. Fishing time can be shared several ways, two of which are arbitrary time periods (the anglers alternate half-hour fishing periods, for example) or fish casted to (you and your partner alternate fish to cast over regardless of the outcome). Agreeing on the method of sharing fishing time with your partner before getting on the water will avoid problems throughout the day. Besides, you're there to fish, not to argue.

Most situations allow both anglers to fish simultaneously, and under these conditions you and your partner will have to share the guide's time. Be considerate of your fishing partner. If you are the more-experienced angler, be prepared for the guide to spend a little more time helping your partner. Under these circumstances, I usually will put the more-experienced angler on the more challenging water (which usually holds the bigger fish) and spend a bit more time helping the less-experienced angler. More-experienced anglers often prefer to be on challenging water and left to their own devices. This brings to mind an experience I had guiding a corporate CEO and his wife, he a very experienced fly-fisherman and she a novice. He went downstream to fish the water I mapped out for him with a designated meeting time and place. As I worked with his wife, an unpredicted lightning storm came in from nowhere. I had to react quickly, as these storms tend to be violent. My responsibility was clear: I had to get the wife to safety without unnecessary alarm. She was understandably concerned about her husband's safety, but I assured her he would know what to do. I knew that there was a log cabin near where he should have been fishing and that he should have seen it from the water. The only problem was that the land was heavily posted and the landowner could be very unpleasant to some fishermen. Luckily the angler saw the cabin and waited out the storm on the porch without incident (the owner was not at home).

Although the angler came out of the storm safely, he had trespassed, but I'm sure the circumstances allowed this to be an understandable exception. This leads me to a very important point: Any warnings or instructions the guide gives you should, with very few exceptions, be followed. Guides, who have a legal and moral responsibility to their clients, have authority over the people in their charge. They also have to deal with local landowners and fishermen, by whom they are held accountable for their clients' actions. If a guide places any restrictions on your range of walking or fishing (not walking above the high-water mark, for example), it is incumbent on you to comply with the instructions. Reputable guides would never restrict a client's activities without good reason. Don't hesitate to ask for a reason, but your compliance is a must.

That holds especially true on a charter boat, where the captain has command of the vessel and the anglers have a legal responsibility to obey any and all reasonable orders.

When you have completed the day's fishing comes the matter of payment. Most guides prefer to be paid in cash or traveler's checks, but this matter should be determined at the time of hiring. If you have had an enjoyable day, don't be hesitant about showing your appreciation by tipping the guide. Ten to twenty percent is a fair amount, depending on the guide's effort and how enjoyable the experience has been. Don't judge the guide's performance solely by the number of fish you have taken, as many factors that are beyond the guide's control can influence this aspect of the trip.

There is no great mystery to hiring a guide. Common sense and courtesy are as important in this situation as they are in our everyday personal and business dealings. By asking the correct questions up front, agreeing on the conditions, and making the necessary preparations, you will have laid the proper groundwork for an enjoyable fishing experience.

When he isn't guiding, Jack Fragomeni performs as a jazz guitarist around the country and teaches courses in jazz guitar fly-fishing at The College of St. Rose in Albany, New York.

Guiding Light

Think you might want to become a professional guide? The Western Rivers Professional Guiding School could help you decide. It certainly offers a comprehensive curriculum in its 9-day course held in early June at the school's Jackson Hole, Wyoming, "campus" (the course is repeated later in that month).

Instruction includes lectures on "Clients and Fishing Guides" given by a psychologist, on first aid by a Red Cross representative, and on "Recreational Liabilities" by the staff. There are also field trips led by a geologist ("Evolution of the Rocky Mountains and River Systems"), a naturalist ("Identifying Nature"), and the school's staff ("Entomology").

Students spend the rest of the course receiving instruction in fly casting and how to teach it, and then applying what they have learned during five days of camping and fishing.

Tuition includes instruction, accommodations, meals, and fees.

Contact: Western Rivers Professional Guide School, Box 766, Wilson, WY 83014, phone: (800) 654-0676.

18

TOURNAMENTS

An Introduction to Fishing Tournaments

BY ANTHONY J. BALLAY

Some people are more competitive than others. Some fishermen are more competitive than others. And at some time a fisherman wants to know how good he is in regard to other fishermen. This wondering can sometimes be put into practice as simply as one friend versus another to see who will buy lunch after the outing. Or it can be as complex as wondering who will be crowned the Bassmaster's Classic Champion when all the sport's heavy hitters gather each year in August.

This competitive nature can manifest itself at many levels. It can be between a father and his son. It can be between a couple of friends. It can be a more formal affair, as when a couple of fishermen get together and form a fishing club. Some fishermen get even more serious and compete in semi-professional touring circuits. It is at this level where entry fees and the prize money go up. The most talented and some of the most competitive fishermen compete on the national pro touring level, the "major leaguers" of competitive fishing.

People fish competitively for many species of fish. Carp, crappie, panfish, walleye, and bass all have a following. However, the most sought-after fish, in terms of numbers of tournament fishermen, is the largemouth, or black bass.

BASS TOURNAMENTS

My father and I were preparing to fish an Indiana B.A.S.S. [Bass Anglers Sportsman Society] Federation tournament when my brother-in-law, Scott, asked why we were doing so much hook-sharpening and line-changing. Scott is a good bass fisherman, but he has never fished a bass tournament. I started out with an answer about preparation that led from one aspect to another until I finally figured that it may be clearer to explain a tournament from start to finish.

To begin with, there are many different circuits that you can compete on. All having different levels of competition and different formats. The circuit that I fish is the Indiana B.A.S.S. Chapter Federation. This particular circuit has draw tournaments where all anglers pay an entry fee and then are divided into two groups: those who have boats and those who do not. The names of the boaters are put in one basket and the names of the non-boaters are put in another basket, and at the pre-tournament meeting the names are drawn out one at a time and paired up to be partners.

Not all circuits are draw events. Many tournaments and even some entire circuits are composed of teams of a boater and non-boater who want to fish together. These types of tournaments are referred to as "buddy tournaments."

A pre-tournament meeting is usually held the day before the tournament. In most circuits attendance is mandatory for all participants. At this meeting the tournament director draws names for partners (if it's a draw tournament), determines the positions that the competitors will leave the starting line in, and goes over all the pertinent rules that apply to that particular tournament. He will also answer any questions the anglers may have.

Some of the general rules the tournament director covers concern such matters as the number and size of fish that make up a limit, whether the use of life jackets during the tournament is mandatory (most tournaments, especially B.A.S.S.-sanctioned events, require all participating anglers to have their life jackets on any time the boat's engine is running), and what time the check-in will take place. The director may also make certain sections of the lake or reservoir off-limits to fishermen. He and his assistants have the final say in the interpretation of the rules.

At this pre-tournament meeting you will meet with your partner after your names have been drawn and discuss where you will fish during the tournament. You will also want to share any information you have learned during pre-fishing. If one partner has more intimate knowledge of the body of water, he may be able to help with suggestions of lure choices and popular colors to use.

The question of who will control the boat and at what time during the day you will switch off should be discussed at this time, and not when you get on the water.

Another important item to make plans for where you will meet your partner the next day. The last thing you may want to consider is what color truck and boat your partner has, but it will be easier to find out now than trying to find him and his rig in the dark at four in the morning. Especially if the tournament has 350 men all trying to find their partners, you will be better off having a designated spot to meet. Many anglers meet at a restaurant where they can have breakfast and get further

acquainted before they begin their day. After the pre-tournament meeting, most anglers have their dinner and try to get as much rest as they can. The next day will start early and last a long time. The night before is not the time to be sharpening hooks and putting line on your reels. These things should be done before you even leave for the tournament.

The morning of the tournament comes early, so being organized with your equipment will allow you to concentrate on other important things. The first thing is to find your partner at the designated spot and time. Load all the gear into the boat and get in line to launch the boat. Usually while you are in line, someone from the tournament will check to see that your live-well is empty, then will issue you a piece of paper that lets the tournament people know you have been checked.

The non-boater (the fisherman who doesn't own the boat) usually drives the tow vehicle to back the boat down into the water. Most boaters would rather trust a stranger with their truck than with their boat. If you're the non-boater, this is not the time to let the boater know that you can not back a trailer down a ramp. At this level of competition, most fishermen are familiar with boats and ramps, but if you are not, there are other fishing circuits where you can learn these skills.

Launching boats prior to the start of a bass tournament. [photo courtesy Anthony J. Ballay]

Once all boats are on the water, the tournament director will take a position where he can start the boats out at the take-off time. The boaters will usually get into a fairly organized line to help with the take-off. Some tournaments use a shotgun start where boats are lined up abreast and the tournament director fires off a shotgun. Other tournaments use a number system in which the tournament director calls out numbers and gives the participants time to clear the take-off area before the next number is told to start off.

When your number is called you take off with all the power your boat can muster and head to the area that you and your partner have agreed upon. Most anglers want an early take-off position so that they can get to the spot they want to fish before any one else gets there. The first angler on the spot customarily gets the right to fish the area. However, sportsmanship and consideration for fellow anglers and a little common sense seems to let everyone fish where they want. If an angler wants to sit on a spot that he believes holds fish, he must anchor his boat there. Then other anglers must stay at least 50 yards away from his boat.

Most tournaments last between six and eight hours. During your time on the water, you will try to fish efficiently and quickly. This kind of fishing is quite a bit different from tossing out the cane pole and watching the bobber until it goes under. Different seasons warrant different techniques and locations. You will want to have put your plan of action together before you get on the water; the precise kinds of rods, reels, and tackle that you will use will depend upon what level you fish.

As the day goes on, you will want to make sure you can be at the check-in area at the set time. If you have fish to weigh in, make sure you are there early. There will be a check-in boat at the prescribed area that was discussed at the pre-tour-nament meeting. Make sure the official has you checked in as being on time, because being late will cost you penalties that are assessed in pounds and ounces.

Since you have invested so much money and time in this tournament, now is not the time to make frivolous errors. Once I was with my father fishing a tournament on the Ohio River. His partner ran 30 miles downriver to the locks where they fished all day. My father's boater partner had a big bass in the live-well that had a good chance to win big bass that day. He and my father allowed themselves enough time to get back, based on how long it took them to get there in the morning. However, during the runback that afternoon they had to endure barge traffic and the huge swells that barges can make. During a frenzied run back up the river, with the boat sometimes coming out of the water as it crossed barge wakes and contended with pleasure boat traffic, the boat ran out of gas! Fortunately, they got gas and did make it back to the weigh-in in time, where my dad's partner did cash a nice check for big bass. The point is, be prepared and expect the unexpected when fishing tournaments.

Most tournaments provide the anglers with weigh-in bags in which you can put your catch and take it up to the scales. The weigh master (usually the tournament director or one of his assistants) will drain off all the water and weigh the fish. He will call out the weight, which is recorded by someone on the staff. You will then be presented with a weigh slip that you will sign and your partner will also sign as witness. The fish are then released back into the lake.

At this point, you can relax because you have to wait for all the other anglers to weigh-in. This is now a good time to talk with other fishermen to see how they did. Find out what lures they used to catch their fish and at what locations they fished. Ask what they did that worked best and what didn't work. Get a general feel for what worked compared to how you fished. Did your game plan agree with what the majority of the other anglers did, or was it 180° away from their thinking? Remember the bottom line: Who caught more fish?

After all the anglers have weighed in their catches, the tournament crew puts the results in order and determines who is in what place. In my Indiana Federation tournaments, the top 5 places get plaques, the top 25 get money prizes, and the top 50 finishers get points that add up for the "classic," or year-end finals.

After the awards presentation, everyone stows their gear and heads home. Hopefully, you came away a little more experienced in one aspect or another. Even though this is competitive fishing, having fun is still what this is all about.

I have just described what a fishing tournament encompasses, and a lot of people may be thinking that they cannot or do not want to do all that just to fish in a tournament. Well, and here comes the really nice part about fishing competitively, bass fishing tournaments come in all shapes and sizes.

You recall that I described the circuit that I was fishing in as the Indiana B.A.S.S. Federation circuit. That's only one of many circuits all over the U.S. A "circuit" is created by an organization or a group of fishermen who want to put together and run a series of organized tournaments that usually lead up to a classic.

Anglers can compete at different levels of competition. One of the levels commonly chosen is the club level, the grass roots level of bass fishing. The fishing club is one of best places to learn about bass fishing, since a club is in essence a small circuit.

Most clubs hold a series of tournaments on lakes that are close to home. These collective lakes are known as the "tournament trail." At the end of the year, the club fishermen fish in a final tournament. That's the classic, which traditionally has very nice prizes of items, money, and/or trophies for the top finishers. Also customary at the end of the year is a club awards banquet where accolades are bestowed upon the most successful anglers.

Prize time at an awards dinner. [photo courtesy Anthony J. Ballay]

There are many ways to find a fishing club. A local bait and tackle shop would know of clubs in your locale and can introduce you to members who come in to buy tackle. A guide on your favorite lake may be able to hook you up with a club that he knows of or the guide may already be a member. One surefire way to find a club is to call B.A.S.S., who will let you know what clubs are in your area.

Fishing clubs come in all shapes and sizes. Some are very competitive. Some are family-oriented. Others are looking to be community-oriented, while others want to promote conservation. To find out what a club offers, you must attend one of its meetings. See how the membership greets you, and watch how the members conduct themselves. If you like what you see, then ask to submit an membership application.

The club level is where anglers do not have to show up in a $30,000 bass rig with all the bells and whistles, every rod and reel ever made, and the confidence that they can take first place. Clubs are the testing grounds for fishing. They are the perfect place to learn new skills and techniques. This is where you can talk to people who enjoy the same things you do. If you are thinking about buying a new reel or rod, someone in the club may have one that you can try before you go out and spend the money. Maybe you will like the reel and maybe you won't, but at least you will get to try it out before you commit yourself.

Club members are usually willing to let a fellow angler use a bait that is really getting hit on that day, if they have more than one. However, an angler has to have some basic lures of his own. A tackle box with some lures in each basic group is good for starters. Some top-waters, some bottom-bouncers, and some lures that run in-between (like crankbaits and spinnerbaits) should be the minimum for the beginning club angler. He should have at least a couple of fishing rods: a bait- or spin-caster and a spinning rod should cover most situations. As the fisherman becomes more knowledgeable about different techniques and develops as an angler, his tackle and rods and reels will grow with his needs.

A boat is not a necessity to join a club. In fact, the beginning angler will find it better to fish as a non-boater, because that's the way to fish with anglers who have more experience. Many things can be learned and refined at the club level, including such skills as backing boats down ramps, reading and interpreting hydrographic maps, and using depth-finders and other electronics.

Another bonus of fishing as a non-boater is learning a new technique from every boater that you fish a tournament with. Almost every fisherman has one technique in which he has real confidence, and this is usually his strongest asset. Fishing with this person is an opportunity to learn the how's and why's of what he is doing. If this fisherman is using a technique that you are familiar with, you can still profit from him because he may have some subtle variations on this technique or he may emphasize a different aspect of the technique that you had previously not seen.

You can get by and be competitive with only a handful of techniques at the club level. A top-water pattern such as "walking the dog" with a Zara spook, slow-rolling a spinnerbait, and fishing soft plastic baits like worms and lizards can keep you in the hunt in a fishing club tournament.

As you progress onward and fish more competitive circuits such as The Midwest Bass Association, The Rusty Hook, or any state B.A.S.S. Federation circuit, you will need more and varied techniques in order to be competitive at that more advanced level. Also at this level are numerous tournaments that are sponsored by bass clubs to benefit charitable organizations such as the Muscular Dystrophy Association, The Leukemia Foundation, and The Make a Wish Foundation. These open tournaments will draw some of the best local and regional anglers around.

When you feel that you can aggressively compete with the competition at this regional circuit level, there is only one more move to make. That is up to the touring professional level.

There are two major organizations at this pro level of bass competition. One is Operation Bass' Red Man Circuit, and the other is B.A.S.S. Invitational and Top 100 circuit.

Operation Bass' Red Man circuit holds six qualifying events in 22 different divisions. These divisions are primarily composed of geographic areas based on Red Man's theme of close-to-home tournaments for the working man. For example, the Hoosier division fishes in Indiana, and the 'Bama division fishes in Alabama. You can enter a Red Man tournament as either a boater or non-boater. The top finishers in each division earn the right to fish in one of six regional tournaments. The top finishers in each of the regional tournaments then qualify for the All-American, the grand finale for all the competitors on the Red Man trail.

The recent 10th anniversary of Red Man All-American had the largest purse ever. The total purse for the event was $212,000 with a minimum payout of $1,000 per man. The lucky winner of the 55-man field took home $100,000.

The B.A.S.S. circuit holds qualifying events under two circuits: the B.A.S.S. Invitationals, of which there are six tournaments; and the Top 100, with four tournaments. The top 20 pro anglers from the Top 100 tournaments and the top 15 anglers from the Invitational tournaments then qualify for the Bassmaster's Classic. The cash and prizes for the Classic add up to $200,000.

B.A.S.S. also conducts a premier tournament open to all B.A.S.S. members. It's the Bassmaster BP MegaBucks®, a six-day elimination tournament that has a total payout of $474,000.

The touring professionals fish at the pinnacle of the competitive fishing mountain. At this level, fishermen are masters of many techniques and their variations. They can differentiate extreme subtleties in conditions and techniques, and they know when to use each variation to help them catch bigger stringers of fish.

These anglers have all the rods and reels they need for special situations and techniques. In fact, at this level, manufacturers of fishing equipment seek out these professional fishermen for their input to help in the research and development of their products. This relationship manifests itself in the form of sponsorships, a handy arrangement because at this level most pros need sponsors to compete. The use of the latest up-to-date equipment together with cash remuneration is essential for these touring pros to stay on the circuit. For example, a pro who is fishing the B.A.S.S. circuit will compete in ten events that are each roughly a week long. The events are all over the country, from Chesapeake Bay to Texas. The pro will probably pre-fish each tournament for another week, in order to get a feeling for the lake or river and where the fish are holding. The competitor's bills add up very quickly when you account for the gas for the boat and the tow vehicle, lodging, food, and (of course) a fishing license for each state he fishes in. This is just a small portion of the expenses that a touring pro brings upon himself, so it is easy to see how sponsorship is essential to sustaining a pro career.

One of the nice things about competitive fishing is that you can make it as competitive or as social as you like. You can compete with friends or at the club level or at regional circuits or go on national tour—it is up to you. Bass clubs are starting up all over, and more and more circuits are developing at the regional level.

One of the best magazines today on the market that is just for tournament anglers, *Midwest Tournament Angler*, is intended for competitive anglers who live in Arkansas, Illinois, Indiana, Kentucky, and Missouri. The magazine features all the tournaments in these states: when and where they are, who is eligible to compete, and all the pertinent questions that need to be asked are all answered in this comprehensive magazine. It also has feature articles on techniques and tactics for the tournament angler, as well as columns written by some very well-known pro anglers.

Midwest Tournament Angler
4717 West Main St.
Belleville, IL 62223
(618) 227-1044

Other recommended magazines are B.A.S.S.'s *Bassmaster* and *B.A.S.S. Times*, *Bassin'*, and *Bass Fishing*. Their addresses can be found on pages 150–152.

WALLEYE TOURNAMENTS

Like bass tournaments, walleye tournaments are big-time affairs. Anglers fish for big purses, using special boats that are designed for large open water. Walleye anglers at this level have numerous techniques to take walleye from varied bodies of water ranging from rivers to the Great Lakes.

Walleye anglers fish out of deeper draft boats than do bass fishermen, primarily because they fish larger and more open bodies of water. Their boats can be made from aluminum just as easily as they can be made from fiberglass. Walleye boats usually have a large motor to get them around the lake, as well as a smaller inboard combustion engine for trolling. Some walleye boats are also equipped with two trolling motors, one front and one rear; these allow more precise trolling passes with regard to staying on a breakline, as well as maintaining the desired speed.

Walleye anglers are allowed to use live bait as well as artificial lures during the tournament. This rule allows them to have an extremely varied arsenal of tips, tricks, and techniques. Depending on the seasonal pattern and weather, pro walleye anglers will fish with jigs, rigs, slip-bobbers, crankbaits, downriggers, and even side-planners.

The In-Fisherman magazine organizes the Professional Walleye Trail™. Familiarly known as the PWT, it's the big circuit for the premier walleye anglers. The purses are great: $162,000 for 1995, including a new Big Walleye Pot. The PWT has

been run in a pro-am format: a professional fisherman in the front of the boat and an amateur in the back. During a three-day tournament each amateur gets to fish with three different professionals drawn from the best in the sport. The pros provide the boat and gear, and they're the ones who decide when, where, and how the pair will fish. Amateurs are eligible to win top prizes that often include fully-rigged walleye tournament boats.

However, the PWT organizers announced in 1994 that, beginning in 1996, the tournament series will adopt an invitational format. The top 90 pros who fish the entire 1995 circuit will automatically be invited to compete in 1996, with the balance of the field made up of rookies and one-time pro anglers.

For more information on the Professional Walleye Trail, contact The In-Fisherman, Two In-Fisherman Dr., Brainerd, MN 56401-0999; phone: (218) 829-0620.

CARP TOURNAMENTS

The carp is not a fish known for being fine table fare, but a group of fisherman specifically target this fish. They enjoy the fight that the carp puts up when it is caught. Carp are thick-bodied and can easily weigh over 25 pounds. They make line-burning runs when hooked and do not tire easily.

Although not known as a tournament fish, most carp tournaments are held on smaller lakes and ponds, to hold down the amount of rough fish in that body of water. These tournaments are usually small affairs, with participants who are usually people who live on the lake or in the area.

One feature about a carp tournament that is quite different from most other tournaments is that the fish are not returned to the water to fight again. Also, many carp tournaments are not line-and-pole affairs. Quite often carp tournament "anglers" can use spears and/or bows and arrows.

Most often a bow and arrow is used to harvest the carp. The arrow is specially modified with a fiberglass shaft and a screw-off head with wire barbs that keep it from backing out once the fish is hit. The arrow also has a hole in the very end so that fishing line can be tied on and used to retrieve the fish. Another feature of the bow is that a reel can be mounted on the bow so the angler can reel in the fish after it has been shot.

Winning a carp tournament requires having the most pounds and ounces of all the competitors. However, most people feel that they have won if a large quantity of rough fish have been removed from the lake.

Since carp tournaments are typically small local affairs, prizes tend to be donated items such as dinner at the local diner or gift certificates to local businesses.

PANFISH TOURNAMENTS

Competitive angling for panfish is usually a small-scale affair. Panfish are the perfect size for smaller anglers to handle, and by their very size and sheer numbers lend themselves to children's tournaments. Some of the most entertaining and emotionally intense competitive anglers are not even old enough to drive to the tournament!

Panfish tournaments tend to be shorter in length than most other kinds of tournaments, three or four hours being considered a long one. However, these tournaments are more of an event than a mere contest of catching fish. Most contain a number of activities that often include a casting contest, a barbecue, a raffle of fishing-related products, and the awards presentation.

Awards at these tournaments include trophies for different species of bluegill or sunfish, the total weight of fish caught, the total cumulative length of fish caught, and the heaviest fish caught. These categories can be many and varied depending on how many the tournament officials want to give out.

Other awards at these tournaments can include hats, shirts, rods and reels, tackle boxes, and tackle, and anything and everything that the tournament officials can convince people and businesses to donate.

These tournaments are supposed to be very fun events that try to teach young anglers some technical skills along with sportsmanship. Young anglers can thus develop a love for the outdoors and a healthy respect for nature. And since almost everyone seems to come away a winner in some respect or another, these smaller panfish tournaments may be a stepping-stone to a more competitive level of tournament angling.

CRAPPIE TOURNAMENTS

Crappie tournaments are panfish tournaments that have come up into the big leagues. They are in all respects like the big bass tournaments except that fishermen seek out crappies instead of bass.

The biggest and probably the best-known tournament for this species is the Crappie-a-thon, which holds events on some of the larger impoundments around the Midwest. Places like Kentucky Lake in Kentucky, Monroe Reservoir in Indiana, and Lake Clinton in Illinois all host Crappie-a-thon tournaments.

Crappie tournaments have an entry fee that is not as high as that of other tournaments. Anglers customarily fish in two-person teams from a boat that can be launched anywhere on the lake or reservoir. Certain tournaments have hourly weigh-ins for the biggest fish caught during that hour.

There are also prizes for fish that have been previously been caught and tagged. In Crappie-a-thon tournaments some tagged fish are worth thousands of dollars. If that fish is caught while the angler is using a sponsor's product, that fish is also eligible for contingency prize money that could add up to additional thousands of dollars.

The weigh-in at a crappie tournament is a pounds-and-ounces affair for a limit of fish. The heaviest limit of fish indicate the first-place team, with subsequent weights taking the following places until all the ranking places have been filled.

Competitive crappie anglers need a full complement of tricks and techniques in order to be competitive. They also have to possess a certain amount of tools to do the job.

Most competitive crappie anglers have a couple of rods rigged and ready for use at any given time. These rods are usually spinning rods; however, sometimes casting and even modified fly rods are pressed into service, depending on the technique that is being used.

Other basic tools include the type of baits. Crappie tournament permit both live bait and artificial lures. A good crappie angler will use both types of baits, depending on the conditions at the time. Live bait usually means minnows. Artificial baits are mostly small jigs, but sometimes small spinnerbaits and even ultra-light crankbaits are used.

Most anglers start looking for their crappies by using jigs or artificial lures and targeting the more aggressive fish. If the fish are inactive or if the angler feels that there are more crappies in the area, he may change to live bait and use a **CRAPPIE RIG.** That rig has a weight or sinker on the bottom or terminal end of the line. About 6 inches above is a small hook, and then further up another 12 inches is another hook. This rig is then attached to a snap swivel on the line. The advantage of this rig is that you can cover two separate depths of water with live bait at one time.

Another popular method involves a long rod, such as a fly rod that has been modified with a spinning reel instead of a fly reel and with a jig tied onto the line. The angler usually uses this technique when there is some timber or brush in the water. As the angler moves from brush to tree, he uses the long pole to reach deep inside the cover and lower his jig down to fish that may be holding in the center of the cover.

One of the nice aspects of a crappie tournament is that the competitors tend to help novices or even more-experienced anglers who are having a hard time boating fish that day. It is nothing for competing anglers to tell you what color jig is producing fish for them and share information about what depth or structure or cover they have been finding their fish on. I have heard of anglers who, after catching their limit, put a novice on the spot that they have just left. This is not the rule in competitive fishing, but it shows that even though anglers are competitors they are still fellow anglers. This camaraderie seems to be more prevalent at crappie tournaments than at any other competitive fishing events that I have seen.

For information on the subject, consult *Crappie Magazine*, 5300 CityPlex Tower, 2448 E 81 St., Tulsa, OK 74137-4207.

Anthony J. Ballay is an accomplished tournament and recreational fisherman based in Whiting, Indiana.

Major Tournament Circuits

Bass

Bassmaster® Tournament Trail (1995 competition days unless otherwise indicated):

TOP 100™ TOURNAMENT TRAIL ($271,200 payout per event)
Lake St. Clair, Mt. Clemens, Michigan (near Detroit)

AUGUST 27-30, 1994
weigh-in: Metro Beach, Metro Park Marina
Connecticut River, Hartford, Connecticut

SEPTEMBER 21-24, 1994
weigh-in: Riverside Park
Lake Norman, Mooresville, North Carolina (near Charlotte)

OCTOBER 19-22, 1994
weigh-in: River City Marina
Lake Seminole, Bainbridge, George (near Tallahassee, Florida)

FEBRUARY 22-25
weigh-in: Earl May Boat Basin Park
Wheeler Lake, Huntsville, Alabama

MARCH 8-11
weigh-in: Ditto Landing Marina
Mississippi River, Moline/Rock Island, Illinois

MAY 17-20
weigh-in: Sunset Park, Potters Lake

$474,000 BASSMASTER BP MEGABUCKS®:
Lake Murray, Columbia, South Carolina

MARCH 20-25, 1994
weigh-in: Lake Murray Public Access Park (Lexington side of Lake Murray Dam)

Bassmaster® Central Invitational Tournament Trail:

$190,000 TEXAS BASSMASTER CENTRAL INVITATIONAL
Lake Livingston, Onalaska, Texas

NOVEMBER 3-5, 1994
weigh-in: Lakeside Marina and Campground

$190,000 TEXAS BASSMASTER CENTRAL INVITATIONAL
Sam Rayburn Reservoir, Jasper, Texas

FEBRUARY 16-18
weigh-in: Twin Dikes Marina

$190,000 OKLAHOMA BASSMASTER CENTRAL INVITATIONAL
Grand Lake, Afton, Oklahoma

APRIL 6-8
weigh-in: Shangri La Marina

$190,000 MISSOURI BASSMASTER CENTRAL INVITATIONAL
Lake of the Ozarks, Lake of the Ozarks, Missouri

MAY 11-13
weigh-in: Lake of the Ozarks State Park, Grand Glaize Beach Marina

Bassmaster® Eastern Invitational Tournament Trail:

$190,000 MARYLAND BASSMASTER EASTERN INVITATIONAL
Potomac River, Charles County, Maryland (near Washington, DC)

SEPTEMBER 15-17, 1994
weigh-in: Smallwood State Park

$190,000 SOUTH CAROLINA BASSMASTER EASTERN INVITATIONAL
Lake Santee Cooper, Manning, South Carolina (near Charleston)

OCTOBER 13-15, 1994
weigh-in: Sen. John C. Land III Boating and Sportfishing Facility (Log Jam Landing), Summerton, South Carolina

$190,000 GEORGIA BASSMASTER EASTERN INVITATIONAL
Lake Lanier, Suwanee, Georgia (near Atlanta)

DECEMBER 1-3, 1994
weigh-in: Holiday Marina

$190,000 VIRGINIA BASSMASTER EASTERN INVITATIONAL
Buggs Island Lake, South Hill, Virginia

APRIL 26-29
weigh-in: North Bend Park, Boydton

$230,000 B.A.S.S. MASTERS CLASSIC®
Greensboro, North Carolina

AUGUST 3-5

*Weigh-in at a 1994 U.S. Invitational
Bass'n Gal tournament.
[photo courtesy Bass'n Gal]*

1994 Bass'n Gal Tournament Trail:

BASS'N GAL TEXAS INVITATIONAL (EARLY BIRD SEASON OPENER)

Toledo Bend Lake, Hemphill, Texas

OCTOBER 27-28, 1994
weigh-in: Frontier Park Marina

BASS'N GAL TEXAS INVITATIONAL

Lake Sam Rayburn, Jasper, Texas

MARCH 16-17, 1995
weigh-in: Twin Dikes Marina

BASS'N GAL SOUTH CAROLINA INVITATIONAL

Santee-Cooper Lake System, comprising Lake Marion and Lake Moultrie, Eutawville, South Carolina

MAY 4-5, 1995
weigh-in: Rocks Pond Campground and Marina

BASS'N GAL ALABAMA INVITATIONAL

Coosa River (Lake Neely Henry), Gadsden/Rainbow City, Alabama

JUNE 22-23
weigh-in: Gadsden City Docks

BASS'N GAL U.S. INVITATIONAL (OKLAHOMA)

Lake Tenkiller, Cookson, Oklahoma

AUGUST 18-19, 1995
weigh-in: Elk Creek

$100,000 DELCO VOYAGER/BASS'N GAL CLASSIC STAR XIX WORLD CHAMPIONSHIP

(location to be announced)

SEPTEMBER 25-30, 1995

WALLEYE

The 1995 schedule of The In-Fisherman® Professional Walleye Trail™:

LOWRANCE/MARINER EASTERN PRO/AM

Lake Erie

APRIL 26-28
weigh-in: De Rivera Park, Put-In-Bay, Ohio

STARCRAFT/DODGE MIDWEST PRO-AM

Mille Lacs, Minnesota

MAY 27-29
weigh-in: Myr Mar Marina, Garrison, Minnesota

MINNKOTA/STREN MIDEAST PRO/AM

Lake Winnebago, Wisconsin

JUNE 29-JULY 1
weigh-in: Pioneer Inn, Oshkosh, Wisconsin

LUBRIMATIC/DAIWA WESTERN PRO/AM

Lake Oahe, South Dakota

AUGUST 3-5
weigh-in: Oahe Lodge, Pierre, South Dakota

G. LOOMIS/POWERBAIT PROFESSIONAL WALLEYE TRAIL CHAMPIONSHIP

Lake Huron

SEPTEMBER 7-9
weigh-in: Northport Marina, AuGres, Michigan

The 1995 schedule of the Shimano® World Billfish Series, offshore fishing for giant black and blue marlin:

FEBRUARY

MARLIN WORLD CUP

Black River, Mauritius, Indian Ocean

MARCH

TAHITIAN INTER-ISLAND BILLFISH TOURNAMENT

Tahiti, French Polynesia

AUGUST

USVI OPEN ATLANTIC BLUE MARLIN TOURNAMENT

St. Thomas, U.S. Virgin Islands

SEPTEMBER

BISBEE'S/BILLFISH FOUNDATION COSTA RICA CHALLENGE

Flamingo Bay, Costa Rica

OCTOBER

BISBEE'S BLACK & BLUE MARLIN JACKPOT TOURNAMENT

Cabo San Lucas, Baja California, Mexico

For further information, contact Shimano® World Billfish Series, 425 North Newport Blvd., Suite E., Newport Beach, CA 92663; phone: (800) 322-1763; fax: (714) 650-7822.

Blue-Water Tournaments

Blue-water fishing tournaments, especially those that focus on billfish, take place throughout the world. Almost all have a limit on number of boats that compose the field, with the exact amount of prize money based on the number of participants.

Approximately 90% of the following events can be counted on to repeat every year, while those that don't often resurface after a year or so of inactivity. The most accurate and timely source of information are the tournament directors, whose phone numbers are given. Prospective spectators for weigh-ins and award ceremonies might also contact the chambers of commerce or visitor tourist bureaus in the appropriate locales.

Additional up-to-date information about particular tournaments (and saltwater tournaments in general) appears in *Bisbee's Black & Blue Fishing Magazine*, 425 North Newport Blvd., Suite E., Newport Beach, CA 92663; phone: (800) 322-1763; fax: (714) 650-7822.

See also the "International Tournament Calendar" that appears in each issue of the IGFA's *The International Angler*: International Game Fish Association, 1301 E. Atlantic Blvd., Pompano Beach, FL 33060; phone: (305) 941-3474; fax: (305) 941-5868.

Note: "modified release" means each tournament establishes its own restrictions with regard to minimum weight and number of fish that can be boated.

MID-ATLANTIC REGION

JANUARY

GEORGIA TEAM ANGLER'S CLASSIC

Milledgeville, GA
(404) 683-8680

FEBRUARY

"FIELD OF DREAMS" OPEN STRIPER CLASSIC

Buford, GA
(404) 683-8680

JUNE

ANNUAL SOUTH JERSEY SHARK TOURNAMENT

Cape May, NJ
modified release
(609) 884-2400

JULY

SOUTH JERSEY BLUE MARLIN INVITATIONAL

Cape May, NJ
modified release
(609) 884-2400

OAK BLUFF MONSTER SHARK TOURNAMENT

Martha's Vineyard, MA
modified release
(508) 533-2707

OCEAN-VIKING SHOWDOWN

Cape May, NJ
modified release
(609) 884-2400

WHITE MARLIN INVITATIONAL TOURNAMENT

Beach Haven, NJ
modified release
(609) 492-1000

AUGUST

MARTHA'S VINEYARD BIG GAME FISHING CLASSIC

Martha's Vineyard, MA

billfish release; tuna and mako minimum weight
(508) 533-2707

WHITE MARLIN OPEN

Ocean City, MD
modified release
(410) 289-9229

OVERNIGHT TUNA BILLFISH TOURNAMENT

Montauk, NY
modified release
(516) 668-5052

BLOCK ISLAND ANNUAL BILLFISH INVITATIONAL

Block Island, RI
(401) 884-4100

OCEAN CITY OVERNIGHT BILLFISH TOURNAMENT

Ocean City, NJ
release
(609) 398-3356

MONTAUK MARINE BASIN— FISH UNLIMITED'S NORTHEAST

Montauk, NY
kill/release
(516) 349-3474

MID-ATLANTIC $500,000

Cape May, NJ
modified release
(609) 884-2400

PIRATE'S COVE BILLFISH TOURNAMENT

Mantes, NC
modified release
(919) 473-3700

FALMOUTH OFFSHORE GRAND PRIX FISHING TOURNAMENT

Falmouth, MA
modified release
(508) 888-0207

GREATER MYRTLE BEACH OPEN

Myrtle Beach, SC
kill
(803) 238-0485

SEPTEMBER

LABOR DAY CANYON CLUB CLASSIC

Cape May, NJ
modified release
(609) 884-2400

PIRATE'S COVE WHITE MARLIN RELEASE TOURNAMENT

Mantes, NC
modified release
(919) 473-3700

SOUTH JERSEY TOURNAMENT OF CHAMPIONS

Cape May, NJ
modified release
(609) 884-2400

U.S. OPEN KING MACKEREL TOURNAMENT

Southport, NC
kill
(919) 457-5787

OCTOBER

STINGRAY BOAT 1000 KING MACKEREL CLASSIC

Myrtle Beach, SC
kill
(803) 238-0485

FLORIDA

YEAR-LONG

METROPOLITAN SOUTH FLORIDA FISHING TOURNAMENT

10 southern Florida counties
kill/modified release
(805) 376-3698

JANUARY

ANNUAL CHEEKA LODGE PRESIDENTIAL SAILFISH TOURNAMENT

Islamorada
(305) 664-4651

BUCCANEER CUP INVITATIONAL SAILFISH RELEASE TOURNAMENT

Buccaneer Yacht Club, Singer Island

HOLIDAY ISLE SAILFISH TOURNAMENT

Islamorada
(305) 664-2321

OLD PORT YACHT CLUB ANNUAL SPORTFISHING TOURNAMENT

North Palm Beach, FL
modified release
(407) 626-2280

INVITATIONAL GOLD CUP TEAM TOURNAMENT

Sailfish Club of Florida, Palm Beach, FL

release

(407) 844-0206

APRIL

ANNUAL MIAMI BILLFISH TOURNAMENT

Miami

contact:

P.O. Box 530551

Miami Shores, FL 33153

JULY

GRANDE COC TARPON TOURNAMENT

Boca Grande, FL

release

(813) 964-0568

BUD LIGHT KING MACKEREL TOURNAMENT

Pensacola, FL

weigh-in

(904) 932-5726

BAY POINT INVITATIONAL

Panama City, FL

kill/modified release

(904) 235-6911

SEPTEMBER

STUART SAILFISH CLUB JUNIOR ANGLER TOURNAMENT

Stuart, FL

billfish release; all others kill

(407) 286-9373

DESTIN FISHING RODEO

Destin, FL

kill/release

(904) 837-6734

KEY WEST MARLIN TOURNAMENT

Oceanside Marina, Key West, FL

kill/modified release

(305) 296-7586

NOVEMBER

FT. LAUDERDALE SEMI-ANNUAL BILLFISH TOURNAMENT

Bahia Mar Yaching Center, FL

release (except non-billfish)

fax: (305) 728-9465

MARATHON SMALLBOAT BILLFISH TOURNAMENT

Marathon, FL

release

(305) 743-2795

WORLD CLASS ANGLER SAILFISH TOURNAMENT

Marathon, FL

release

(305) 743-6139

ISLAMORADA SAILFISH TOURNAMENT

Islamorada, FL

release

(305) 664-9452

KEY LARGO SAILFISH SHOWDOWN

Key Largo, FL

(305) 451-5875

DECEMBER

STUART SAILFISH CLUB LIGHT TACKLE SAILFISH TOURNAMENT

Stuart, FL

release

(407) 286-9373

TEXAS

JULY

TEXAS INTERNATIONAL FISHING TOURNAMENT

Port Isabel/South Padre Island, TX

kill/catch-and-release

(210) 943-8438

CALIFORNIA

AUGUST

SAN DIEGO INTERNATIONAL LIGHT TACKLE TOURNAMENT

San Diego, CA

modified release

(619)223-4607

CHANNEL ISLANDS INVITATIONAL BROADBILL TOURNAMENT

Oxnard, CA

kill/release

(805) 488-3684

CHANNEL ISLANDS INVITATIONAL BROADBILL/MARLIN TOURNAMENT

Oxnard, CA

kill swordfish/release marlin

(818) 889-3820

TIM TATE MEMORIAL LADIES TOURNAMENT

Newport Beach, CA

tag/release

(714) 673-6316

SEPTEMBER

HOAG HOSPITAL 552 TOURNAMENT

Newport Beach, CA

tag/release

(714) 750-4288

UNITED COAL FISHERIES FOUNDATION (NORTH VS. SOUTH)

Newport Beach, CA

tag/release

(714) 846-8259

MASTER ANGLER BILLFISH TOURNAMENT

Newport Beach, CA

tag/release

(714) 673-6316

LOS PESCADORES MARLIN TOURNAMENT

Newport Beach, CA

tag/release

(714) 642-6482

NOVEMBER

CATALINA GOLD CUP

Catalina Island, CA

kill/release

(805) 485-7777

BAJA CALIFORNIA

JANUARY

SAILFISH TAG AND RELEASE TOURNAMENT

Ixtapa, Mexico

contact:

Mrs. Judy Franish

93 Cutter Dr.

Watsonville, CA 95076

OCTOBER

CABO SAN LUCAS GOLD CUP

Cabo San Lucas, Mexico

kill/release

(805) 485-7777

BISBEE'S BLACK & BLUE MARLIN JACKPOT TOURNAMENT

Cabo San Lucas, Mexico

kill/release

(800) 322-1763

"FOR PETE'S SAKE"

Cabo San Lucas, Mexico

kill/release

(619) 560-4727

HAWAII

SEPTEMBER

OKOE BAY RENDEZVOUS

Kailua-Kona, HI

tag and release

(808) 322-2010

BAHAMAS

JANUARY

BIMINI INTERNATIONAL LIGHT TACKLE BONEFISH TOURNAMENT

Bimini

Contact:

Bimini Big Game Club

P.O. Box 523238

Miami, FL 33152

FEBRUARY

MID-WINTER WAHOO TOURNAMENT

Bimini

contact:

Bimini Big Game Club

P.O. Box 523238

Miami, FL 33152

BIMINI INTERNATIONAL LIGHT TACKLE BONEFISH TOURNAMENT

Bimini

contact:

Bimini Big Game Club

P.O. Box 523238

Miami, FL 33152

MARCH

ANNUAL BACARDI RUM BILLFISH TOURNAMENT

Bimini

contact:

Bimini Big Game Club

P.O. Box 523238

Miami, FL 33152

APRIL

NORTH ABACO BAHAMAS BILLFISH CHAMPIONSHIP

Walker's Cay

contact: Bahamas Billfish

Championship

P.O. Box 343

Dania, FL 33004

JULY

LATIN BUILDERS FISHING TOURNAMENT

Bimini
release (500-lb. minimum)
(305) 593-6803

NOVEMBER

THE WAHOO (ALL WAHOO) TOURNAMENT

Bimini
contact: Bimini Big Game Club
P.O. Box 523238
Miami, FL 33152

CAYMAN ISLAND AC LIGHT TACKLE TOURNAMENT

Grand Cayman, British West Indies
contact: Donna Sjostrom
P.O. Box 30280
SMB, Grand Cayman, BWI

BERMUDA

JULY

THE SEAHORSE ANGLERS CLUB ANNUAL BILLFISH TOURNAMENT

Hamilton, Bermuda
release (500-lb. minimum)
(809) 292-7272

CARRIBEAN

AUGUST

INTERNATIONAL BILLFISH TOURNAMENT

San Juan, Puerto Rico
modified release (300-lb. minimum)
(809) 722-0477

SEPTEMBER

U.S.V.I. OPEN ATLANTIC BLUE MARLIN TOURNAMENT

St. Thomas, U.S. Virgin Islands
modified release (500-lbs. or more)
(809) 774-2752

AUSTRALIA

AUGUST

SHERATON TOWNSVILLE GAME FISHING TOURNAMENT

Townsville, N. Queensland
modified release
(077) 725053

SEPTEMBER

THE FOSTER'S BILLFISH CLASSIC

Dunk Island, Queensland
tag and release
61-18-796 608

OCTOBER

LIZARD ISLAND BLACK MARLIN CLASSIC

Lizard Island, Great Barrier Reef, Queensland
tag and release
61-75-374 105

NOVEMBER

NISSAN BILLFISH BONANZA

Hamilton Island, Great Barrier Reef, Queensland
kill and tag
61-18-769 608

MARCH

CALTEX BILLFISH SHOOTOUT

Port Stephens
tag and release
61-18-769 608

NEW ZEALAND

JANUARY

FITZROY ONE BASE TOURNAMENT

Auckland
contact:
**Auckland Sportfishing Club
P.O. Box 6115, Wellesley St.
Aukland**

FEBRUARY

WAITANGI WEEKEND TAG AND RELEASE CONTEST

Whangaroa
contact:
Whangaroa Big Game Fishing Club
R.D. 1, Kaeo

FOSTER'S FYRAN WEST COASTERS TOURNAMENT

contact:
Foster Bay Fishing Club
2 Foster Bay, Huia

NEW ZEALAND OPEN NATIONAL GAMEFISH TOURNAMENT

contact:
New Zealand Big Game Fishing Council
P.O. Box 93, Whangarei

SHARK TOURNAMENT

Whakatane
contact:
Whakatane Big Game Fishing Club
P.O. Box 105, Whakatane

MARCH

NEW ZEALAND OPEN NATIONAL GAMEFISH TOURNAMENT

Paeroa
contact:
New Zealand Angling and Casting
   Association
P.O. Box 171, Paeroa

APRIL

EASTER WEEKEND TOURNAMENT

Te Kaha
contact:
Te Kaha Sport Fishing Club
P.O. Box 173, Opotiki

TROUT TOURNAMENT

Whakatane
contact:
Whakatane Big Game Fishing Club
P.O. Box 105, Whakatane

INDIAN OCEAN

JUNE

THE MARLIN WORLD CUP

Black River, Mauritius
(230) 68 36 843

AFRICA

FEBRUARY

INTERNATIONAL BILLFISH TOURNAMENT

Malindi, Kenya
contact:
Secretary
Malindi Sea Fishing Club
Box 364
Malindi, Kenya

NOVEMBER

NORMAN MATTHEWS MEMORIAL TOURNAMENT

Malindi, Kenya
contact:
Secretary
Malindi Sea Fishing Club
Box 364
Malindi, Kenya

EUROPE

JANUARY

ANNUAL COD-FESTIVAL

Helsingborg, Sweden
contact:
Hans Elmroth
Box 75
310 10 Vaxtorp, Sweden

NOVEMBER

ANNUAL LAX-CUP VATTERN INTERNATIONAL TROLLING TOURNAMENT

Karlsborg, Sweden
contact:
Granviks Herrgard AB
54600 Karlsborg, Sweden

AN INTERVIEW WITH CHRISTOPHER PARKENING

Christopher Parkening, the noted classical guitarist, has been an avid and skillful fly-fisherman since the tender age of six. Accomplishments during his teens included spending a summer as a guide when he was 15, and, four years later, winning the Western U.S. All-Around Casting Championship.

In a magazine advertisement for an album released in 1993, Parkening referred to his passion for fly-fishing. Hmm, the author of this book mused, perhaps the guitarist would care to reflect on connections between his vocation and avocation.

What began as a conversation about similarities between music and fishing led into Parkening's sharing the story of a memorable tarpon tournament.

Ultimate Fishing Guide: Are there any similarities between fishing and music, guitar or otherwise?

Christopher Parkening: Rhythm is certainly one element. Casting a fly effectively requires establishing a very definite rhythmic pattern. By the same token, the pause in the back cast while the rod is loaded with the line is perhaps the equivalent of a musical rest.

UFG: How about between fishing and performing on the concert stage?

C.P.: Both require discipline and hard work. Also, it's a matter of controlling your emotions, of channeling whatever stage fright you might experience (and no matter how experienced a musician might be, he or she can get stage fright) into positive energy.

UFG: "Stage fright" in fishing?

CP: Sure. There are moments of anxiety, "butterflies" when I'm casting to a six-foot tarpon. Being aware that one false move on my part or a bad cast can spook the fish is a very similar feeling to the stage fright that concert musicians sometimes experience. The only cure is to pray and simply get on with the task.

UFG: You've fished all over the world, both fresh and salt water. What's your most exciting experience?

CP: Early in June of 1987 I took part in the Gold Cup Tarpon Tournament, the "Wimbledon" of saltwater fly-fishing competitions. It's a five-day invitational event for 25 fishermen, held off Islamorada, Florida. I almost didn't compete; at the last minute another fellow found that he couldn't get away from business commitments, and I was fortunate enough to be invited to substitute. The competition was pretty heady company, including Billy Pate, the world record-holder, and many other fishing legends. Harry Spear, my friend who was my guide for the tournament, assured me that our chances to win would be slim, "so let's just have fun."

Tournament rules required a 12-pound-test tippet and 12 inches of 100-pound shock tippet. I used Harry's rod and reel, and he had an assortment of his favorite flies.

On the very first day, we started fishing at about 7:00 A.M. We spotted a laid-up [lying still] tarpon just under the surface of the water. I made a good cast, and the fish struck immediately. After a long fight of about 1½ hours with much travail and apprehension (not to mention perspiration), we landed our first fish, a 131-pound monster.

However, my luck didn't hold, and I caught only two release fish on the second day. Nevertheless, my first day's catch kept me in first place.

Fishing ended each day at 3:00 P.M., after which contestants had up to two hours to return to the weigh-in dock (you could keep on playing anything that you hooked before 3:00 as long as you weighed in by 5:00). At 2:30 on the third day, Harry spotted a laid-up tarpon facing away from us. Casting ahead of the fish, I got it to turn around. I quickly made another cast, and the tarpon took my fly.

Ninety minutes later, the fish was still on my line. When it was close enough to the boat, Harry used his gaff, but he missed. The fish took off, and I played it for another 10 minutes. Harry's second try caught only a scale. He was slightly more successful on his third attempt, getting a top layer of skin. That presented a problem, because the gaff hook was certainly not in deep enough to pull in the fish.

There was no time for a fourth try. Just as Harry had gaffed the fish, my shock tippet broke. Harry jumped overboard into chest-deep water and followed the fish away from the boat, using an emergency technique jokingly called "walking a poon."

"Get him!" Harry yelled. I jumped into the water too, grabbing for the tarpon's tail, but without success. "Get the hand gaff," Harry instructed, and I waded back to the boat (losing my tennis shoes in the muddy bottom) and found the tool.

No matter how hard I tried, I couldn't capture the tarpon. Only when the fish opened its mouth and gills did I find a way. Thrusting my left hand and forearm into the gills and out the mouth, I grabbed my left wrist with my right hand and clutched my arm to my chest. The tarpon responded to my hammerlock by thrashing around like a crazed alligator.

When Harry and I did managed to get the fish into the boat, I discovered how its gills and mouth had taken their toll: All the way up to my elbow, my left arm looked as though it had been slashed with razor blades.

The tournament's daily weigh-in period ended at 5:00 P.M. That gave us only 12 minutes to race back to the dock. We barely made it in time, but when we did, my tarpon was measured at 136½ pounds, the fourth largest in Gold Cup history.

That put me *way* in the lead. It also put pressure on me. What had begun as "let's just have fun" was shaping up to be an entirely different proposition.

The fourth day saw me hook into 10 tarpon without landing any of them. Only at the very end of the day was I able to land two modest-sized fish, which we released since neither would have enhanced my score.

Nevertheless, I was still holding a slight lead when Harry and I set out on the final day of the tournament. We headed toward a spot called Oxfoot Basin, among other things a notorious haunt of big sharks. The weather could hardly have been less cooperative: windy, cloudy, and blustery, the worst possible conditions for catching tarpon.

My fishing started off as bad as the weather. No sooner had we settled in when Harry spotted three tarpon moving in a line from our left to our right. I cast to the lead fish,

Chris Parkening (right) and guide Harry Spear.
[photo courtesy Christopher Parkening]

but when I failed to compensate for the wind coming from the opposite direction, my fly landed right on the lead tarpon's back, spooking all three fish.

Some 20 minutes later, four other tarpons appeared, coming from right to left. The wind had shifted 180° too, and this time I took it correctly into account. My fly landed one foot in front of the lead tarpon, and the fish struck.

The fight started out as a repeat of the third day, another hour-and-a-half battle with a 100+-pound fish. But then that became the least of it.

As with the third day's tarpon, Harry was unable to gaff this fish on his first two attempts. He succeeded on his third try, but as he pulled, the fish pulled harder. Losing his balance, Harry was yanked overboard and dragged—without exaggeration—for 40 yards away from the boat. The scene looked like some sort of surrealistic version of Cyprus Gardens' aquacade water-skiing show, with Harry refusing to relinquish his grip on the gaff.

Then I realized that the situation was anything but funny. Harry was not standing in chest-high water, but was being pulled down to a depth of 12 feet, and right in the middle of "Shark Alley."

Harry came up for air, kicking frantically and with both hands still on the gaff. Moreover, the red bandanna he wore around his neck had become wedged in his mouth. As he reached the surface, instead of getting a gulp of much-needed oxygen, he got nothing, for the tarpon jerked him back underwater. For several long moments I saw nothing. Then the tarpon jumped perhaps 20 yards further away, followed by Harry who was still hanging onto the gaff. This time he was able to get a good breath, and he screamed for me to bring the boat over to him.

I started the motor, in the process accidentally letting my fly line, which was still attached to the tarpon, wrap around the propeller shaft. That, however, was not my primary concern. Getting to Harry was. Thank the Lord, I did so before he drowned or met up with a shark.

Somehow I helped pull Harry and the still-gaffed tarpon into the boat. The entire episode, from hook-up to landing, had taken more than two hours.

"There is still plenty of time to fish," Harry reflected when he had caught his breath. He moved us to a likely spot called Nine Mile Bank, where I hooked three fish, but landed none.

Back at the final weigh-in, my tarpon registered 115 pounds, and my good fortune held. What had started as a "let's just have fun" tarpon tournament debut ended in a Gold Cup victory and the memory of a lifetime.

19

COOKERY

ost species of fish are delectable, and for whatever reason the ones we catch seem to taste best of all. Although there are scores of excellent fish cookbooks, no fishing guide would be complete without a few words on the subject. The following section was prepared by Norton Wolf and Joan Lipton, two accomplished cooks who share with us their approach to "Fish Cookery."

Fish Cookery

Fish cookery is *not* recipes. It is *the cooking process* itself. It's how to be sure that the river, lake, or ocean beauties you catch and cook will always glow with delicious fresh taste and delicate texture.

Here are the three principles of fish cookery:

1. Never overcook. Fish meat is fragile, muscle fibers are short, and fat content is low.
2. Cook just to the point at which muscle proteins begin to thicken—the moment they turn from transparent to opaque.
3. When cooking goes beyond this point, moisture and tenderness dry out, and texture either toughens or falls apart.

THE OPAQUE TEST

Insert a skewer (or fork) into the thickest part of the fish. When the meat in the center is just start-ing to turn from transparent to opaque, that's it! Your fish will finish cooking on your plate and be perfectly done when you serve it, either hot or cold.

A HANDY TIMING GUIDE

According to the Canadian Department of Fisheries, lay the fish on its side and measure it at its thickest point. Figure cooking time at *10 minutes per inch* of thickness, whether it's a fillet, steak, or whole fish, or whether you're broiling, frying, sautéing, baking, etc. For poaching in a pot, the 10 minutes begin when the water starts to boil.

The seven most popular cooking techniques:

OVEN BROILING

The top of the fish is nicely seared, while the meat inside remains tender and moist. Excellent for steaks or fillets of salmon, trout, swordfish, halibut, red snapper, sea bass and stripers, cod, and the like.

PREPARATION

Lightly brush your fillet, steak, or whole cleaned fish with olive oil. Place it (skin-side down) in a shallow ovenproof pan or foil tray. Add white wine to cover half the thickness of the fish.

BROILING

Broil at HIGH setting, close to the flame or coils, until the wine is *almost* evaporated. Remove the fish from the pan with a spatula. It should be opaque. If it's underdone, just add ¼ inch of wine or water and cook another minute or so.

VARIATIONS

If you like the top blackened Cajun-style, sprinkle the fish with paprika before you broil. You can also mix fish stock and/or your favorite marinade (French, Italian, Oriental, etc.) with the white wine. And adding a bit of orange juice gives you an even richer sauce.

OVEN POACHING IN FOIL

Chefs call it *en papillote* ("in paper"), but it's even better and easier in aluminum foil—superb for any fish you've been steaming in a poacher, because it's cooking in its own rich natural juices. Excellent for larger fish: salmon, bass, pike, cod, mackerel.

PREPARATION

Place your fish (fillet, steak, or whole cleaned) on a lightly buttered sheet of heavy-duty aluminum foil. (Olive oil can be used instead of butter, especially if the fish is to be served cold.) Sprinkle with a touch of salt and pepper. Make a pouch by wrapping the fish loosely in the foil, crimping the ends and edges to form a tight seal.

POACHING

Place in a preheated oven and cook for 25 minutes at 375° F. Open the foil and use the Opaque Test for doneness. Remove the fish from the foil, put it on your plate, and top with its own aromatic juices.

OPTIONS

(1) Try a touch of dill, fennel, or tarragon. (2) Chinese style: a little soy sauce, ginger, black beans, and scallions. (3) After you open the foil, set the fish close under a high broiler for a minute, to give it what chefs call "a little finish."

OUTDOOR GRILLING

Caution #1: Whether your grill is charcoal, gas, or electric, *fish are too fragile to cook directly on the widely spaced bars of the grill.* Grill whole fish in a special fish basket; grill fillets or steaks on a special perforated rack. A double-sided "hamburger" grill is also excellent for turning your fish without damage.

Caution #2: If you use charcoal, do not use a liquid fire starter. Fish absorb the petroleum aroma.

PREPARATION

Dress the fish lightly with olive oil, salt, and pepper—and give it an hour or so in your favorite marinade, if you like. (If you're grilling a whole fish, make three crosswise cuts in the skin on both sides, to keep it from blistering.)

GRILLING

For charcoal, wait until the coals are covered with white ash. For gas or electric, preheat for 5 minutes. For a whole fish, place it gently in the fish basket, then on the hot grill. For fillets and steaks, place them on the perforated rack, then on the hot grill.

TIME

Roughly 5–8 minutes each side. . . .*BUT!* You know that fish vary greatly in texture, muscle density, and thickness. So rely on the Opaque Test to be sure your fish is done to a turn.

SAUTÉING

This is every European chef's specialty. What's special (so they say) is their sauce with its secret ingredients handed down for 200 years. You, however, have a big advantage: your fish was caught just hours, maybe minutes, ago.

PREPARATION

Sautéing is usually done with one or more thin fillets, lightly sprinkled with salt and pepper.

SAUTÉING

Put about 2 tablespoons each of butter and olive oil in a saucepan, and bring the pan up to medium heat (when the butter and oil become golden). Cook the fish until it's lightly browned, then give it the Opaque Test for doneness.

VARIATIONS

In the preparation stage, you can brush the fish lightly with flour, or dip it in egg yolk, or add a little lemon juice or chopped onions or shallots and/or parsley, or add your favorite herbs and spices—or all of the above. Be as creative as you like, just so long as you don't overcook.

FRYING

While fried fish is as American as Mom's Apple Pie, it's been getting a bad rap lately, mostly because of folks who think fried means *fat*. Well, if your cooking heat is too low, oil tends to soak into the coating. But at "smoke-point" heat (375° F), fried fish is crispy dry outside and juicy tasty inside.

PREPARATION

Dredge pieces of fish of the same size and thickness in flour, cornmeal, or cracker dust, mixed with a light sprinkle of salt and pepper.

DEEP FRYING

Heat olive oil or a good vegetable oil to the "smoke-point" (about 375° F). Gently put in the fish and leave it until it's golden brown.

OVEN FRYING

Heat your oven to 500° F and lay your fish on a lightly oiled cookie sheet; bake until it's crisp and golden.

POACHING IN A POT

This is the traditional way to poach fish. One of its great by-products is a large quantity of fish stock—extremely valuable if you're into chowders, fish soups, or linguine with clam sauce (but that's another kettle of fish).

PREPARATION

Place the whole, nicely cleaned fish in a pot (or a poacher) in enough cool liquid (water or water with a glass or so of white wine) to cover the fish. Slowly bring the liquid to a boil—and then quickly turn the heat down to a gentle simmer. *Do not let the fish boil.* If it does, move the pot to a cool burner, then back on the hot burner at a somewhat lower setting.

ENHANCEMENTS

The addition of a few herbs and spices is a nice bonus, as are a few carrots and small onions.

BAKING A WHOLE STUFFED FISH

This cooking method allows the rich flavors and aromas of your favorite stuffings to permeate both the kitchen and the inner fisherman. Ingredients range from spices to herbs, from mushrooms to seafood, from grapes to nuts—you name it.

PREPARATION

Lightly salt the interior of the fish and stuff it firmly. Close up the edges with skewers and light cooking string. Oil the skin and put the fish on a lightly oiled pan. Bake at 450° F, allowing 10 minutes per inch of thickness, measured *after* you stuff the fish.

ENHANCEMENTS

You may want to sprinkle the fish lightly with breadcrumbs, cornmeal, or flour; salt; pepper; herbs; etc. You can, of course, bake half a fish, a fillet, or a steak, using the same method (but without the stuffing).

FREEZING YOUR CATCH

The magic word is "glaze." A glaze is a thin film of ice that protects your delicate fish from freezer burn and oxidation. And it's very simple to do. Put a single layer of fish (whole, fillets, or steaks) on a sheet of aluminum foil—and put it in the freezer. When your fish are cold, dip them in ice water. Put them back in the freezer for 10 minutes or so (they'll freeze very quickly). Take them out and dip them in ice water again—then back into the freezer. When the glaze forms (you can't miss it), put your frozen fish in individual plastic bags, or wrap each piece separately in aluminum foil.

When you're ready to *unfreeze* and cook, let your fish thaw out *gradually—in the refrigerator*. If you thaw at room temperature, fast-melting ice crystals can damage the delicate muscle cells, texture, and flavor of your beautiful fish.

If you're in a real hurry, you can go to Plan B: Cook your fish frozen, using the Canadian Method, allowing 20 minutes per inch of thickness, instead of 10.

A FAMOUS FRENCH TROUT

"Never with butter. Never with almonds." So said a great *pêcheur-chef*. Always, he said, you take a fine fat trout, fresh from the stream, gutted

and scaled. Then you take a frying pan and rinse it out with flaming wine vinegar. You make it very hot on the fire, and then you put in this mixture: 1 cup of olive oil and 3 cups of water, which you let boil very fast. Then you add a few tied branches of thyme, 2 crushed juniper berries, and some pepper. When you're down to ½ inch of boiling liquid, put in your fine fat trout. Do not turn it; just cover the pan and let it continue to boil for 1 minute; then turn down the fire, let it cook very gently for 3 minutes—and serve. *C'est magnifique*!

Joan Lipton and Norton Wolf, who are active in civic and cultural projects, live and cook in New York City.

Cookbooks

Countless cookbooks contain at least one chapter's worth of recipes for fish. Browsing through your bookshelf or a friend's, or in your local bookshop or library will open your eyes to the variety of approaches to the subject. However, the following volumes deserve special mention:

The L.L. Bean Game and Fish Cookbook, by Angus Cameron and Judith Jones (Random House, 1983).

A well-respected outdoors editor and writer and an equally celebrated cookbook editor teamed up to write what is the definitive guide to game-fish cookery. Cameron's angling anecdotes add a delightful dimension.

Jane Brody's Good Seafood Book, by Jane Brody with Richard Flaste (Norton, 1994).

The author, nationally known for her weekly column on health matters in *The New York Times*, presents more than 200 low-fat recipes. She also offers advice on selecting, cleaning, preparing, and storing fish.

Fish Cookery, by Russ Lockwood (Lyons & Burford, 1993).

An easygoing style contributes to the book's "user-friendly" feeling.

Gray's Fish Cookbook, by Rebecca Gray with Cintra Reeve (GSJ Press, 1986).

Published under the aegis of *Gray's Sporting Journal* magazine, this book presents a "menu" approach: recipes for each fish entrée is accompanied by recipes for other appropriate side dishes and a dessert.

365 Ways to Cook Fish and Shellfish, by Charles Pierce (HarperCollins, 1993).

Many of the recipes in this spiral-bound (for easier handling) book can be easily adapted to suit other species of fish.

Wade a Little Deeper, Dear: A Woman's Guide to Fly Fishing, by Gwen Cooper and Evelyn Hass (Cortland Library/Lyons & Burford, 1989).

The chapter entitled "Fish in the Pan and Other Ways, Too" is chock-full of tasty recipes.

A shore lunch in Canada's Northwest Territories. [photo courtesy Northwest Territories Tourism]

Preserving the Flavor

Preserving the flavor of freshly-caught fish begins when the fish is landed. That means keeping your catch cool, whether in a traditional wicker creel lined with moist grass or leaves, or in one of the canvas or linen "Arctic coolers" that retain moisture and coolness after being immersed in a stream or lake.

What to do with your catch once you return to camp or home depends on when you plan to use it. If you plan to cook it either the day of or the day after capture (the so-called "stream-to-skillet" syndrome), remove the fish's gills, then slit the stomach from tail to below the gills and remove the lungs, intestines and kidneys. Thoroughly dry the belly cavity and the outside. Keep the cleaned fish cool, iced if possible, but not frozen.

Fish that are to be transported should not be cleaned, but packed in ice cubes in a Styrofoam™ cooler. Water produced by melting ice needs to be removed frequently.

Some species that are to be cooked whole must be scaled, a messy but inescapable chore. First rinse the entire fish in cold water, and then place it on a cutting board. Hold the fish down by its head with one hand. Working from tail to head, scrape off all its scales with a serrated scaler, then rinse again in clean cold water. Because scaling is an untidy job, pick a location away from other people and one that requires the easiest amount of cleaning up afterwards.

Slicing a fish into fillets requires a very sharp thin knife. Using a cutting board and working from head to tail, cut through the flesh all along the backbone, beginning just behind the gills. Don't cut into the spine. Using the flat of the knife's blade, pry the meat away from the bone. Repeat the process on the other side of the fish so that you have two fillets.

If you choose to skin a fillet, place it on the cutting board skin-side down. Cut down to the skin at the fillet's tail end. Holding the skin firmly with your fingers, slice the flesh away from the skin while pulling the skin away with your "holding" hand.

Preparing a fish into steaks requires no more than cutting vertically through the backbone. The thickness of each slice depends on your preference, although 1-inch wide is something of a standard.

Recipes

Although this chapter wasn't intended to be a cookbook, a number of friends clamored to be allowed to pass along favorite recipes:

BLUEFISH CORN CHOWDER

(SERVES 6–8)

1½ pounds bluefish cut into large chunks

4 strips diced bacon

4 tablespoons chopped onion

2 cups peeled and diced potatoes

1 quart milk

¼ teaspoon sage

salt and pepper to taste

2 cups cream-style canned corn

chopped fresh parsley as garnish

Brown the bacon in a large pot. Add the onion and cook for another 5 minutes, until the onion is transparent but not browned. Add the bluefish, potatoes, milk, sage, salt, and pepper. Simmer gently for 10–12 minutes, or until the fish and potatoes are done. Add the corn and simmer for another 2 minutes.

Serve garnished with parsley. Slices or hunks of your favorite bread are handy to clean the bottom of the soup bowl.

GRILLED TROUT

(SERVES 4)

4 trout

salt and pepper to taste

½ cup unsalted butter

2 lemons, one for juice and the other cut into quarters

Preheat broiler to highest setting. Melt the butter and add the juice of one lemon.

Make two or three diagonal cuts in the sides of the trout with a sharp knife. Sprinkle trout inside and out with salt and pepper.

Place the trout in a heat-proof dish and brush with the butter. Broil for 5 minutes close to the heat source, then move further away from the heat and continue cooking for another 2–4 minutes. Turn the fish and cook the other sides until the skin is brown and the flesh tender and moist.

Serve basted with the cooking juices and garnish with the lemon quarters.

BAKED FISH WITH FENNEL

(SERVES 6)

2 pounds fillets of striped bass (or flounder or halibut)

1 tablespoon vegetable oil

½ cup dry white wine

juice of one lemon

salt and pepper

3 tablespoons chopped fresh parsley

¾ cup chopped fennel leaves

Preheat oven to 400° F.

Rinse and pat dry the fillets. Coat a large baking dish with some of the oil.

Place the fillets in the dish, covering them with wine and lemon juice and adding salt and pepper to taste. Sprinkle the parsley and fennel over the fillets.

Cover the dish with a sheet of aluminum foil that has been oiled on the underside. Bake for 15 minutes.

From Great Fishing Tackle Catalogs of the Golden Age.
[courtesy Nick Lyons Books]

20

FIRST AID

First Aid for the Ailing Angler

BY LAURENCE I. BURD, M.D.

In the best of all worlds, accidents and injuries while fishing would be as rare as bad weather and empty creels. But, as inevitable as rainstorms and blank days, at some point in our angling careers we find ourselves either in need of first aid or in a position where administering it to a buddy or to ourselves becomes necessary.

If you're not familiar with the following basic outdoors first aid, take the time to learn it. And even if first aid is second nature (perhaps through your participation in Scouting or the Red Cross), you might still want to review the material. In either case, please bear in mind that the following advice is not meant to be a substitute for care from trained emergency personnel or a physician whenever, in your judgment, a situation warrants such professional attention.

FISHHOOK PUNCTURES

Injuries caused by fishhooks are undoubtedly the most common wounds suffered by fishermen. The wound might be the result of a hook's sudden release from a log or another place where the hook was snagged, or from trying to removing a hook from a fish's mouth once the fish has been landed. Or the culprit might be a misguided cast, or a gust of wind carrying the hook where it doesn't belong

(that's why wearing a cap and sunglasses is recommended, whatever the weather). But whatever the reason, you're hooked.

Once a hook enters the skin, you've got to make an initial determination whether the hook can be removed on the spot or whether professional medical assistance is in order. If more than one barb of a treble hook is involved, if the hook is caught near the patient's eye, or if there is severe pain or the combination of a tingling sensation plus a gentle motion (suggesting that the hook is near a tendon, nerve, or bone), seek medical assistance. But first, apply an antiseptic to the affected area, then stabilize and protect the hook so it will not catch on another object or part of the body during the patient's trip to the emergency room or doctor's office.

If, however, the hook moves freely in the skin and the pain is bearable, you can work at removing the hook on the spot. First remove all clothing from the surrounding area, then clean the skin with soap and water. Cut the line from the hook, and if the hook is part of a lure, detach it from the lure if possible. If the offending hook is part of a treble hook, remove the other hooks if you can, or at least crimp down their barbs.

Removing a hook when the point and barb are exposed is the simplest to do: clip off or crimp down the barb, then pull the hook out the way it came. If you clip off the barb, take care to shield everyone's eyes from any bits of flying metal.

Just as often, however, the hook's point and barb will be buried in flesh. In that case, the most common removal technique is called the push-through method. Using your fingers or a pair of pliers, push the hook shank forward along the path of the hook's curve until the tip and barb emerge. Then clip off or crimp down the barb, and retract the hook through its entry point.

Another technique is called the line method. Slip a piece of monofilament line or, in a pinch, a shoelace under the bend of the hook so the line rests between the embedded portion of the hook and the hook's eye. With gentle downward pressure on the hook eye toward the skin, the line will loosen the barb so that end can be extracted through the entry point.

Once the hook is out, the affected area should again be washed with soap and water. Since ointments may seal in dirt and bacteria, the wound should be left open to drain with only a simple dressing as a cover. However, a dirty or rusty hook or one on which live bait had been used requires an application of antibiotic powder. If the area becomes red or inflamed, see a doctor as soon as possible. The same advice applies, of course, if you are unable to remove the hook.

SCRAPES, CUTS, AND OTHER WOUNDS

Fishhooks aren't the only causes when it comes to fishing-related wounds. We're never too old to scrape our knees or elbows, some fish have sharp scales and spines, and even the most experienced anglers don't always handle knives and scalers with the respect the tools deserve.

In the case of any bleeding, the affected area should be elevated as high as possible and then cleansed with soap and water. After being sure that all dirt and debris are gone, firmly press a sterile compress against the wound to control the bleed-ing. The process may take as long as 10 or 15 minutes, and may have to be repeated until the bleeding stops.

Then apply sterile gauze dressing, but not in such a way to close the wound completely; a wound that is prevented from draining well is liable to become infected. Use antiseptic cream sparingly to keep the dressing from sticking to the wound, but not so much that the wound cannot drain.

Some wounds will be unable to be cleaned thoroughly, and some puncture wounds will not drain. They call for professional medical attention, and antibiotics will be needed while the patient is being transported.

People who handle fish frequently often get nicks and scrapes on their hands. The tiny wounds then become infected with the bacteria *Erysipelothrix insidiosa*, resulting in a red, tender, and warm area which within a week will surround the wound. An antibiotic, either penicillin or erythromycin, is the proper treatment.

MUSCLE STRAIN AND BACK PAIN

Muscle strain, the consequence of injury to tissue that connects muscle to bone (the tendon) or bone to bone (the ligament), results from sudden stretching or twisting or from a blunt injury like a fall. An allied problem is back pain, which may come from overusing muscles that surround and support the spinal column, as well as from sudden strain to those muscles. A more serious form of back injury happens when the segments between the vertebrae weaken and the cushioning material within these segments herniates out and puts pressure on nerves, a condition known as a herniated disc.

Strains happen to fishermen in any number of ways. Anglers who do a great deal of casting may experience strain in their shoulders, elbows, or wrists. Sudden falls on a boat deck in rough seas or slipping while wading a stream or portaging a canoe may stretch muscles and produce tendon injuries. Back pain is often the result of long periods of standing or sitting, especially to people who slouch or otherwise demonstrate poor posture habits, or from bending or lifting heavy objects.

In the case of strains, relief comes from applying ice to the affected area for about 30 minutes at a time every 2 hours. Use a compress or ice pack, since ice placed directly on the skin may produce frostbite. After 24 to 48 hours, switch to a heating pad or hot water bottle (heat increases blood flow and promotes healing). Ointments and creams such as Ben-Gay produce a superficial skin reaction that feel warm, but they do little good in reaching deeper tissue. To relieve pain, take an analgesics like Tylenol® or ibuprofen in the amount of one or two tablets every 4 to 6 hours. If pain continues, the patient should consult a doctor, especially with regard to back pain and nerve compression.

The best prevention is preparedness. Like any sport, fishing requires being in good shape. That means conditioning, and a person who does not exercise regularly is the most likely to suffer strains and pulls. Concentrate on flexibility exercises rather than developing power. Fatigue is another element: the more tired we become, the more susceptible to injury we become.

Of particular interest to anglers with lower back problems are the back-support belts described on page 137. These people may also want to consider using chairs that have backs.

NEAR DROWNING

Someone in your fishing party may fall overboard or lose his balance while wading. A worst-case scenario is that the person will take water into his lungs, in which event you will have to cope with the possibility of drowning.

The first step is, obviously, to remove the victim from the water as rapidly as possible. Unless the situation is otherwise clear, be careful to treat the person as if he has a neck injury by stabilizing the victim's head, as further movement may cause injury to the spinal column.

After removing any debris from the victim's mouth with your fingers, begin mouth-to-month resuscitation. Pinch the victim's nose closed and breathe into his mouth until his chest rises. A child's nose and mouth should both be covered by your mouth. Repeat at a rate of 12 times per minute, or every 5 seconds, for an adult and 20 times, or every 3 seconds, for a child.

Feel for a pulse on the neck or in the groin. If none is discernible, you will have to add chest compression. Holding your arms straight, place both hands palms down with one on top of the other flat against the victim's breastbone. Depress the victim's chest about $1\frac{1}{2}$ to 2 inches, and then release, repeating once a second for an adult and 80 to 100 times a minute for a child. Whenever possible, two people should work together, one performing the mouth-to-mouth breathing once for every five of the other person's chest compressions. If only one person is performing this cardiopulmonary resuscitation, give two breaths after every 10 chest compressions. Continue until help arrives, then make sure the victim is taken to a medical facility even if he appears fully recovered. Water can damage lung tissue, and the full consequences of the episode may take time to become evident.

The possibility of drowning is greatly reduced through preparation and common sense. Everyone who fishes should know how to swim, and even though you have that skill, wearing a life vest or inflatable apparatus makes good sense. Be aware that wet decks, slippery rocks, and other poor footing situations increase the chance of losing one's balance and falling into the water. And statistics show that alcohol consumption and the poor judgment that often results is an avoidable yet recurring factor in more boating and fishing mishaps than people would like to admit.

MOTION SICKNESS

Our sense of balance comes from a portion of the middle ear called the labyrinth. The motion of a boat, particular on choppy seas or windswept water, upsets fluid in the labyrinth and disturbs our equilibrium. The resulting nausea, vomiting, and a sense of discomfort and fatigue is best known as motion (or sea-) sickness.

Some people are predisposed to motion sickness no matter how large the boat or how calm the water. Certain factors can also affect even the most resolute sailors, such as an ear injury or infection, emotional turmoil, exposure to fumes from a boat engine's exhaust, and excessive consumption of alcohol or tobacco.

The onset of motion sickness may be forestalled by focusing on a single point on the horizon: keep your eyes straight ahead and move your body as little as possible. Splashing cold water on your face and exposing yourself to cool fresh air may also help. Vomiting may provide some relief, at least temporarily.

A number of medications are recommended for motion sickness. The more common ones include meclizine (sold as Antivert® or Bonine®) 25 mg or dimenhydrinate (Dramamine) 50 mg. These should be started prior to encountering rough seas, and may be taken two to four times a day. Astemizole (Hismanal®) 10 mg is another in this class, but with less of the side effect of drowsiness, and it can be taken once daily.

Scopolamine, which can be applied as a skin patch worn behind the ear (sold as Transderm Scōp®), lasts for 3 days. You should be aware, however, that its side effects can include blurred vision, drowsiness, and a dilated pupil on the side on which the patch is worn.

SUNBURN

Exposure of the skin to the sun's ultraviolet radiation (UVR), especially in the UV-B spectrum, causes dilation of the skin's blood vessels. We call it sunburn, which in the most debilitating cases can result in a second-degree burn with accompanying blistering.

Sunburn is of particular concern to fishermen; water reflects from 10% to 30% of UVR, while—ice-fishermen, please note—snow or ice reflects as high as 85%. With regard to weather conditions, wind, heat, water, and atmospheric moisture all augment the sun's effect. So does the time of day (UVR is most intense from 10 A.M. to 2 P.M.), and altitude (the higher, the more intense).

Other factors that determine severity are the duration of exposure, and a person's skin thickness and pigmentation. Moreover, certain medications increases the risk of sunburn by causing photosensitivity: these include drugs that contain sulfa; tetracycline antibiotics; thiazide diuretics; and tranquilizers in the phenothiazine class.

Adequate protection begins by wearing the right kind of clothing. Light-colored fabrics reflect the sun, while darker hues absorb UVR. To guard against burning, wear long-sleeved shirts and long pants, as well as a broad-brimmed hat to protect your head, face, and the back of your neck. You'll also want to be aware that any water-soaked material will absorb rays, while thin fabrics like T-shirt material let rays pass through.

However, since some portion of your skin will inevitably be exposed, sunscreens are highly recommended. They come in lotion or cream form; most absorb UVR, although some act as reflectors. Sunscreens are graded according to their sun-protecting factor, abbreviated as SPF and ranging from 2 to 50, with the higher numbers indicating greater protection. Which strength to use depends on your complexion and the sun's strength. Individuals who tan easily but never burn may use preparations with an SPF of 8 or less. Those with more sensitive skin should use an SPF of 10 or higher, while fair-skinned individuals, those with a family history of skin cancer, and anyone who will be on the water or in snow at high altitudes should begin with an SPF of 15, which blocks out 95% of the sun's rays, and probably go higher (many dermatologists recommend never using anything below 15 under any circumstances).

One of the more popular chemicals in sunscreens is para-aminobenzoic acid (PABA). Individuals who find they have a skin sensitivity to PABA will prefer products sold under the names Shade, Piz-Buin, Solbar, Uval, and Ti-Screen.

Whichever sunscreen you use, apply it a half-hour before exposure to the sun. Unless you use a water-resistant preparation (for example, Aloegator 40, Pre-Sun 29, Solbar 50, and Sundown 30), you'll need to reapply it after you go swimming or when you perspire.

Sunblocks offer total protection. You can make a preparation from zinc oxide, titanium dioxide, zinc, talc, kaolin, red ferric oxide, and a benzophenone. Benezophenone is particularly effective in screening out light in the Ultraviolet A spectrum, widely considered to be the radiation responsible for skin wrinkling and aging. This preparation is also commercially available as glacier cream, highly recommended to protect the burn-prone areas of the nose, lips, and eyelids. Like sunscreens, sunblocks need to be reapplied after swimming and perspiration.

Mild sunburns can be treated with cold compresses and such painkillers as aspirin or Tylenol®. Skin moisturizers may also help, but they must be of the non-sensitizing variety (for example, Vaseline Intensive Care®), since topical anesthetics that contain benzocaine may cause allergic reactions. Aloe vera, an ancient but effective remedy, will soothe the skin and promote healing. A more severe sunburn, but one with no blistering, may call for a stronger analgesic like ibuprofen (found in Advil®) or a topical steroid cream.

Blistering is a more serious matter, one that calls for taking the patient to a medical facility. On the way, the affected areas should be cleansed and wrapped in sterile dressings, with the patient given fluids and analgesics.

HYPERTHERMIA

Without being aware of the possibility, an angler may become the victim of heat exhaustion, an elevation of body temperature that results from dehydration. Symptoms include dizziness, confusion, nausea, diarrhea, and a body temperature as high as 105° F.

Preventing hyperthermia begins with maintaining adequate hydration. Drink plenty of fluids: at least 3 quarts a day, and 4 or 5 if you're being even moderately active. Coffee, tea, and especially alcohol should be used in moderation if at all, since all are natural diuretics that work to deprive the body of fluid. Stick to water whenever possible, although excessive perspiration may require restoring your body's minerals with such electrolyte-enhanced drinks as Gatorade, Squincher, or Bodyfuel.

Hand in hand with maintaining adequate

hydration is dressing properly. Wearing layers of clothing makes sense, so you can shed layers as the temperature and/or humidity rises. Plastic, rubber, or other fabrics that do not allow perspiration to escape should be avoided.

With regard to treating hyperthermia, the goal is to reduce the patient's body temperature to its normal 98.6° F as quickly as possible. Determining temperature is a job for a rectal thermometer, since feeling a person's skin is not an accurate method. Move the patient into a cool spot and remove his or her clothing. If ice is available, apply it in ice packs, never directly to the skin. If ice is unavailable, use the coolest water available. Never use alcohol as a coolant. Then once the patient is alert, rehydration in the form of cool (not cold) water and/or electrolyte-enriched fluids should be started.

Rarer than heat exhaustion is heatstroke, which can be permanently disabling due to the destruction of vital organs and the disruption of the body's chemical mechanisms. Symptoms include low blood pressure leading to seizures or shock, bleeding, and temperature elevations as high as 115° F. Once the patient is made as comfortable as possible, move him to the nearest medical facility without delay.

HYPOTHERMIA

Cold weather can cause as many problems as hot weather. Hypothermia, which is one of them, occurs when the body temperature drops below the normal 98.6° F. People who ice-fish and those who wade run the risk of sudden immersion in cold water. They should be especially careful, since heat loss caused by a plunge into cold water occurs more than 20 times more rapidly than loss caused by exposure to air of the same temperature. This heat loss is made even more dangerous by wet clothing and also by wind, as anyone who has been exposed to a severe wind-chill factor can attest.

Hypothermia symptoms are related to the severity of the condition. Mild hypothermia (a body temperature between normal and 95° F) involves shivering, increased heart rate, a desire to urinate, and slight muscle incoordination. Symptoms of moderate hypothermia (between 95° F and 90° F) include greater loss of coordination, weakness, drowsiness, confusion, and/or slurred speech. A severe condition (below 90° F is characterized by considerable confusion, vision loss, and often a coma and reduction of vital signs that seem tantamount to death.

Treatment begins by removing all wet clothing, then insulating the patient with blankets to raise the body temperature. A sleeping bag is a good alternative, or it can be used in conjunction with blankets (so can another person's huddling with the patient). Applying well-insulated hot water bottles is useful, but encouraging the patient to move around or otherwise exercise is not. If the patient is conscious, encourage him to drink warm fluid. Alcohol, which allows heat to dissipate by dilating blood vessels, does not belong on the menu. Finally, the patient should be moved to a warm environment, and, if symptoms indicate severe hypothermia, to professional medical assistance.

Preventing hypothermia begins with dressing correctly. Wearing layers of clothing allows the warm air of body heat to be trapped, while polypropylene and silk undergarments "wick" moisture away from the body. Mittens and hats and quilted outer garments are made for cold weather, and for a reason—they work. And while you're at it, avoid dehydration and fatigue, both of which make us more susceptible to the rigors of cold weather.

FROSTBITE

Frostbite occurs when tissue freezes, which happens when the temperature drops to 28° F. The effect causes blood vessels to go into spasms and blood flow to be affected, so that tissue does not receive adequate oxygen or nutrients.

People who smoke, drink alcohol, have poor circulation, or had previous cases of frostbite are among the most susceptible. Poorly fitting or constricting clothing and footwear have also been implicated.

Symptoms include numbness, itching, and often a "pins and needles" tingling. Although the skin feels hard to the touch, it will yield unless frozen solid.

As with burns, the severity of frostbite is classified according to the severity of tissue damage. First-degree frostbite is characterized by numbness, redness, and swelling. A second-degree injury shows a small amount of blistering, with further blistering marking a third-degree injury.

Treatment is a relatively simple matter: gradually warming the patient, a process that can take up to an hour. Do not apply heat directly to the affected area, or else a burn will occur. Protect the thawed skin with fluffy bandages, and if there are blisters, leave them alone. An analgesic will comfort the patient, who should be transferred to a medical facility if the situation warrants.

Preventing frostbite is a matter of wearing warm clothing that doesn't cut off circulation. If possible, keep out of severe wind-chill factor weather. Keep bare hands and other exposed skin away from metal, and avoid standing or sitting in one position for prolonged amounts of time.

CHILBLAINS

If frostbite occurs from exposure to cold air, chilblains comes from prolonged exposure to cold water. As with frostbite, people who smoke, drink alcohol, have poor circulation, or had previous cases of chilblains are most susceptible. The affected individual will complain of numbness and a burning and/or tingling sensation in the toes, foot, or fingers. The affected limb first appears red and then mottled. Poor circulation encourages infection and blistering, and occasionally gangrene can set in.

Treatment begins with drying and then warming the affected extremity, followed by transporting the patient to a medical facility as quickly as possible.

Prevention involves wearing waterproof and well-fitting boots or shoes.

LIGHTNING

Although the odds of being struck by a bolt of lightning are low, between 200 and 400 Americans are nevertheless victims of such bolts from the blue.

Typically, someone struck by lightning is rendered unconscious and experiences difficulty in breathing. In many cases, the force of the impact throws the victim over a distance. Cardiac arrest may occur in the most serious cases, while less-severe injuries include ruptured eardrums and/or temporary blindness. Clothing may catch on fire, and metal jewelry and belt buckles may overheat. Sunburst or fern-like patterns may appear on the victim's skin.

A victim who stops breathing should receive cardiopulmonary resuscitation immediately (see "Near Drowning" above). The CPR should last until help arrives, as there have been cases where victims had paralysis of their breathing for as long as 30 minutes and yet still made full recoveries. A victim who has been thrown to the ground may have sustained a spinal injury, in which case the spinal area should be immobilized to prevent further trauma.

To avoid being hit by lightning, avoid high-risk situations. Being on or in the water greatly increases the odds of being hit, as does holding such metal objects as a fishing rod, a ship's mast, or an umbrella. Anyone in a wide open space during a thunderstorm becomes the focus of electrical conduction, so stay away from clearings if you're on land, and crouch down close to the ground. Groups of people should spread out. Anyone in the woods should seek shelter near a clump of small trees, always staying away from the tallest tree in the area.

And as for that bit of folklore about lightning never striking in the same place twice. . . don't believe it for an instant.

SNAKEBITES

While hiking through the woods or climbing over a rocky area, an unlucky angler may encounter every woodsman's nightmare: a venomous snake. And if provoked, even if it only perceives it has been provoked, the snake will bite.

At this point the question to answer is whether or not the snake is of the venomous or nonvenomous variety. The U.S. has two varieties of venomous snakes: the pit viper and the coral snake. In the pit viper family are the rattlesnake, copperhead, and cottonmouth (sometimes called the water moccasin).

The copperhead and cottonmouth are found in all areas of the country except the Pacific coast. Rattlesnake species vary according to locale, with timber rattlers found in the Northeast and Central regions and the Eastern diamondback and pygmy rattlesnakes in the Southeast. The latter variety is also found in the Southwest along with the massasauga, northern black-tailed, prairie, sidewinder, Mojave western diamondback and red diamondback rattlesnakes. Massasauga, timber, and prairie rattlesnakes are found in the Central region. Along the Pacific coast are the northern Pacific, southern Pacific, Great Basin rattlesnake, western diamondback, red diamondback, sidewinder, and Mojave rattlesnakes.

Coral snakes are found predominantly in the Southeast and Southwest.

Five characteristic features of rattlesnakes make them easy to identify: the triangular shape of their head, hinged fangs, a single row of scales on their underbelly, vertical elliptical pupils like cat's eyes, and a rattle on the tail. Coral snakes have round pupils and red, black, yellow, or white bands encircling their body. The bite of both venomous and nonvenomous snakes can be identified by rows of teeth marks. A rattlesnake bite can be identified by two or four fang marks at the front of a row.

Signs of envenomization (transfer of poison) are rare because most bites do not break the skin or too little venom has been injected to cause any harm. However, if signs do occur, this is a medical emergency.

Signs of pit viper envenomization include swelling and burning of the skin at the site of the bite, which may occur within 5 to 10 minutes. Within an hour the victim may experience numbness and tingling of the lips, scalp, and face. Muscle twitching of the mouth and eyes can be seen within 90 minutes. There is often a rubbery or metallic taste noted within that same period of time. Within 2 hours there can be nausea, vomiting, sweating, and weakness. Between 6 and 10 hours are the more severe life-threatening signs and symptoms: these include increased bleeding, bruising at the site of the bite, difficulty breathing, and vascular collapse.

Victims of coral snakes show very little local reaction. Weakness and numbness of the extremity are the first signs to occur, usually within 90 minutes. Salivation and drooling, as well as twitching, nervousness, drowsiness, and giddiness will be seen within 1 to 3 hours. Death from heart and lung failure follows soon after.

The definitive therapy for a snakebite is antivenin. The victim should be taken to a medical facility so that therapy can be instituted as soon as possible. If at all possible, the snake should be killed and brought along so the proper identification can be made and the proper type and amount of antivenin can be administered. It is imperative that the person who carries the snake's head be aware that a secondary bite can happen by reflex action up to 1 hour after the snake is dead.

The patient must immediately become calm and must be treated in a calm manner because panic only accelerates the onset of symptoms from envenomization. If the bite occurred on an arm or leg, that extremity should be immobilized and maintained below the level of the victim's heart. An attempt can be made to delay absorption of venom by the use of elastic bands applied 4 to 6 inches above and below the area of the bite. These should be applied over ¼-inch-thick gauze pads and applied in such a way to avoid constriction of the circulation.

Although the idea of the use of incisions to apply suction has been popularized, this technique is beneficial only if done within 5 minutes after the bite. Incisions should be made by an experienced person (if possible), using a sterile razor directly over the fang marks. The incisions should be made in a parallel fashion ¼ to ⅛ inch long and deep. Suction should be applied with a rubber suction cup found in snakebite kits. One's mouth should be used only as a last resort since this method is sure to introduce infection. Then the wound area should be washed and cleaned, and a prophylactic antibiotic administered.

An Extractor suction device (Sayer Products,

Box 188, Safety Harbour, FL 34695) will allow the removal of venom without an incision.

The optimum way to deal with snakebites is preventative. Don't put your hands into cracks and crevices. Walk in well-lit areas or use a flashlight. Wear boots that are ankle-high or even taller. And never travel alone in snake-infested country.

INSECT BITES

MOSQUITO BITES

Few of us have escaped mosquito bites, but fewer of us know the best ways to avoid attracting the female of the species, whose saliva causes the itching and scratching. The easiest and most effective method is to cover exposed skin areas, with nylon a particularly effectively fabric. Avoid aftershave lotion or perfume.

The most effective mosquito repellents contain deet (Permanone), DMP, and Indalone. They are sold under the brand names Cutter, OFF, Repel, and 6–12. Liquid repellent may be applied directly to the skin, while sprays can be used on clothing. You'll need to reapply the repellent after bathing, swimming, or perspiring, or if you spend much time under windy conditions.

An Avon cosmetic product called Skin So Soft has as a side effect the ability to repel many species of insects, including mosquitoes.

If you are bitten, apply a cold compress. Some people have a sensitivity reaction that may call for corticosteroid prescribed by a physician.

BEE AND WASP STINGS

Honey bees, bumblebees, yellow jackets, wasps, and hornets all possess stingers that introduce venom into their victim.

You'll know when you've been stung by the pain, burning, and itching that immediately occurs.

Ice should be immediately applied. Adolph's meat tenderizer can be mixed with water into a paste and applied for about 15 minutes; the papain in the tenderizer will lessen the sting's effect. Several commercial products containing anti-inflammatory agents are also available.

People with a hypersensitivity to insect venom may develop serious reactions that usually happen immediately, although in some cases the reaction may take several hours to occur. Raised red lesions on the skin are accompanied by a swelling of the tongue, wheezing, and other difficulty in breathing, nausea, vomiting, and eventual collapse. Anyone who experiences a severe reaction should immediately be given epinephrine; bee sting kits containing this chemical are available and should be essential gear for anyone so afflicted.

The good news is that bees and other stinging insects will seldom attack unless provoked, so a live-and-let-live attitude will usually carry the day. Just to be on the safe side, however, avoid after-shave lotion or perfume, both of which attract stinging insects.

TICK BITES

The most common tick-borne illness in the U.S. today, and certainly the most notorious, is Lyme disease. It comes from spirochete organisms transmitted by the bite of deer ticks, pinhead-sized creatures that frequent tall grass and attach themselves to prospective victims. Their bite gives a tell-tale sign of a red bull's-eye skin eruption that measures about 2 inches around the place of the bite and takes from 3 to 30 days to show. The disease then spreads quickly through the bloodstream of the patient, who may complain of overwhelming fatigue, headaches, sore muscles, chills, and fever. If an antibiotics treatment is not immediately begun, Lyme disease will become chronic,

manifesting itself as arthritis or heart or neurological problems.

Currently a vaccine against Lyme disease is in its trial stages and is not yet commercially available. Until it is, the wisest course is to dress defensively. If you're heading for Lyme disease country (primarily New England, Wisconsin, Minnesota, Wyoming, northern California, and Oregon), wear a long-sleeved shirt, long pants with cuffs tucked into boot tops, and a hat. A liberal use of insect repellent containing deet (Permanone) sprayed on your clothing can be effective.

A daily self-examination for the presence of ticks should become part of your schedule.

The tick usually attaches itself for 24 hours before passing along the disease. If you spot a tick, grasp it near its mouth part with a pair of tweezers and slowly pull it off. Do not put kerosene, mineral oil, alcohol, or Vaseline® on the tick or burn it off with a match; all these maneuvers may cause the tick to release infected fluid and contaminate the victim. However, if after pulling the tick off you see that a portion of its mouth remains, applying any of the above substances will encourage the remains to drop off without harm to the person.

PLANT RASH

Poison ivy, poison oak, and poison sumac all produce urushiol, a resin in the sap that causes an allergic reaction when it comes in contact with human skin. The resin can stick to clothing, bedding, and pet hair, thus increasing the likelihood of contagious infection. It can also travel in the smoke of burning leaves.

Some people have a natural immunity to these plants. Those of us who aren't so lucky will break out in a rash within a week to 3 weeks after initial contact. The area will become an angry red, and the sufferer will experience intense itching.

Scratching the rash only spreads the infection. Calamine lotion, however, is useful to reduce the discomfort. Pramoxine hydrochloride (Prax cream or lotion) is preferable to topical antihistamines and local anesthetics, since the latter may cause sensitization. Some people find relief in a tepid bath with baking soda. Oral antihistamines such as terfenadine (Seldane®) may be helpful as well. In the case of severe reactions, a physician may recommend corticosteroid therapy.

Being able to recognize poison ivy, poison oak, and poison sumac is necessary to avoid the plants. Wearing long-sleeved shirts and long pants reduces the chance of contact. You might also want to consider a commercial preparation called Ivy Shield that seems to be effective.

The allergic reaction will not occur if the resin is removed within 10 minutes after contact, so if you think you've tangled with a noxious weed, head for soap and water. Techu wash, a mixture of alkane and alcohol that should be rubbed in for 2 minutes and then rinsed and reapplied, seems to work well in many cases, but only if used immediately after exposure.

The following additional advice will go a long way to insure a safe and healthy fishing trip:

A first aid kit should be as much a part of your fishing gear as any rod and reel. If you don't want to invest in a ready-made kit (many are commercially available), you can easily assemble one of your own. Basic items include:

scissors, tweezers, hemostat, cutting pliers

antiseptic soap (e.g., Phisohex or Phisoderm)

antiseptic ointment (e.g., bacitracin or povidone-iodine)

4" × 4" sterile gauze pads

bandages: adhesive variety in various sizes; butterfly

triangular cloth for sling

ACE bandage for sprains

water-resistant adhesive tape

medication for motion sickness (meclizine or dimen-hydrinate [Dramamine])

analgesics: Tylenol® or ibuprofen

antacids: TUMS, Mylanta, or Mylicon

antidiarrheal medication: Lomotil, Pepto-Bismol

skin rash: calamine lotion, hydrocortisone cream

dry lips: lip balm

antihistamines: Benadryl®; Seldane®

antibiotics: ampicillin

a first-aid manual

for insect-infected areas: a bee sting kit, Adolph's meat tenderizer

for long periods in intense sun: aloe vera

for extremes of temperature: a rectal thermometer

Tetanus shots or boosters should be kept current.

Someone in your party should be experienced in cardiopulmonary resuscitation (CPR), including mouth-to-mouth resuscitation. Your local Red Cross chapter can help you find a place to learn. Also valuable is a working knowledge of bandaging and splinting, and transporting injured individuals.

Trips to unfamiliar destinations should be planned in detail. Gear should include maps and a compass, and escape routes should be outlined in the event of a flash flood or a forest fire. Inform appropriate local authorities, such as forest rangers or marina officials, of your itinerary and anticipated times of departure and return. Where practicable, carry a two-way radio or portable phone in case of emergency.

Laurence I. Burd, M.D., who practices medicine in Chicago, fishes throughout the Midwest, the Rocky Mountains, and Florida.

21

CATCH-AND-RELEASE

As with so many other angling innovations, Lee Wulff is credited with enunciating the "catch-and-release" philosophy: A good game fish is too valuable to be caught only once. Add to that notion the dwindling amount of fishable waters and the corresponding lessening number of "keepable" fish, and you begin to understand why more and more anglers recognize the wisdom of the catch-and-release philosophy.

There are, however, circumstances where reasonable minds differ over whether keeping fish is always a bad idea. Take, for example, a stream where stocked fish thrive to the point of overpopulation or a pond where panfish teem. In such instances, and especially when fishermen plan to consume what they keep, many anglers find what one wag termed "catch and reheat" perfectly acceptable.

Two excellent and thorough discussions of the philosophy's pros and cons can be found under "Catch and Release" in *The Illustrated Encyclopedia of Fly-Fishing* by Silvio Calabi (Henry Holt, 1993) and in *The Complete Guide to North American Freshwater Game Fish* by Henry Waszczuk and Italo Labignan (Key Porter Books, 1992).

Anyone who plans to release fish that might otherwise be kept should know the proper way of releasing them:

1. Using barbless hooks makes releasing a far simpler and faster procedure than used barbed hooks. Accordingly, either use ready-made barbless hooks or crimp down the barbs on hooks that have them.

2. The process of releasing begins the moment a fish is hooked. Land or boat the fish as quickly as possible, but without being any rougher than necessary. Don't drag the fish through underwater rocks or stumps or onto the bank, if possible. The slime that covers a fish's body is a protective coating that can easily be removed through contact with land, the bottom of a boat, or human hands. With regard to the last, wetting your hands or putting on a pair of wool gloves before you handle any fish reduces the likelihood of damage to the fish's protective slime.

    Some fishermen don't use nets because they feel that nets rub away this slime. If, however, you plan to use a net, be aware that one with a shallow cotton bag made of tiny knots or fine mesh is preferable to one with a deep bag and thick abrasive knots. Even better for a fish is a "cradle" net onto which the fish is slid and held just below the surface of the water.

3. Keep the fish in the water as much as possible. In addition to being the creature's natural medium, water supports a fish's organs in a reduced gravitational way that air or land does not. Turning a fish onto its back tends to reduce its struggling, while cradling (but not squeezing) in both your hands causes the least harm. However, the lower jaw of a bass is strong enough so you can use

your thumb and forefinger as pincers to lift and hold a fish that way.

4. Avoid handling a fish's gills, sensitive breathing apparatus that can be easily damaged. Be particularly careful, too, of its eyes, fins, and the end of its tail. A large fish can be safely held just in front of its tail, but only as long as you hold it gently as well as firmly.

 Billfish, like marlin and swordfish, can be safely lifted by their bills.

 A word about safety to anglers: Carelessly handling some species is an invitation to human injuries. Special pliers that hold open the mouths of sharp-toothed fish like pike are valuable tools, as are long "de-hooking" pliers that can grasp and remove lures that end up far down into a fish's throat.

 Bluefish are particularly vicious, known to attack anglers when boated. Regardless of the weather, many fishermen routinely wear reinforced gloves when dealing with bluefish.

5. If you or someone else want to photograph your catch, plan the shot in advance and keep your camera handy so no one wastes time fumbling for equipment and position. Whoever is holding the fish out of water should support it under its belly with one hand while grasping its tail with the other hand.

6. If you can't remove the hook easily with your fingers, use a hemostat, long-nosed pliers or a hook-removing tool. If the hook still won't come out or if removing it will cause irreparable damage, snip the line or leader as close to the hook as possible and leave the hook in the fish. In less time than you think, the hook will work itself free, be dissolved by the fish's digestive acids, or become encased in tissue. In any event, the fish will survive.

7. Tossing any fish back into the water, especially one that is "all played out," increases the possibility of permanent injury. Instead, cradle the fish under water until it is strong enough to swim away under its own power.

8. However, a fish that remains worn-out requires special attention. Hold its face into the current or, if no current, move the fish back and forth to force water through its gills. Continue to do so until the revived fish swims away under its own power.

9. Despite your best efforts, there will be occasions when a fish will not survive the catch-and-release procedure. Rather than allowing it to suffer, dispatching the fish with one or more sharp blows to its head is by far a greater kindness.

Landing Equipment

NETS

The "classic" fly-fishing net is composed of a net bag attached to a wooden frame about the size of a tennis racket. Its advantages are portability and maneuverability, especially under circumstances where the fisherman hasn't much room to work. Nets are customarily attached to the back of the angler's vest by means of a quick-release snap, although some vests have built-in pockets that act as a sort of scabbard.

Nets intended for catch-and-release use have shallow bags so that fish will be less likely to become injuriously entangled.

Even kinder are **CRADLES**, pieces of canvas or another fabric attached to two long handles. The fish is maneuvered onto the cradle, which is then lifted out of the water. Cradles work well for large fish, especially salmon and many of the saltwater game fish.

Whether fresh- or saltwater, fishing from a pier or a boat calls for nets with a long handle. The "hardware" is usually aluminum tubing, with handles between 4 feet and 8 feet. Models with adjustable handles that telescope within that range have the advantage of versatility. Nets used in boats tend to have deep bags, which tend to tangle less than shallower lengths.

GAFFS

A **GAFF** looks like a barbed fishhook that has been straightened out and mounted onto a long pole. Some gaff hooks have sharp points, although plunging a gaff into a fish's body in order to land it is practiced less frequently than it once was.

Instead, a gaff with blunt tip and barb will be thrust into a fish's mouth, then twisted until the barb catches into a gill. Sharks, billfish, and other large species can be landed in this fashion in a relatively uninjured condition.

TAILER

Most commonly used in salmon fishing, this device is a loop mounted onto a pole. The angler maneuvers the loop around the fish's tail, then tightens the noose until the fish is secured and can be pulled into shore.

HARDWARE

The "Hook Out" hook remover is a pair of pliers especially designed to remove fishhooks. Its 90° handle keeps your hands from obscuring your sight of the spring-operated, nonslip jaws.

22

OUTDOOR SHOWS AND EXPOSITIONS

Fishing/outdoors/sportsmen shows or expositions are often billed as antidotes to the winter "blahs." Those that take place between October and March certainly live up to that promise, and the ones held during the rest of the year aren't too bad either.

You'll get that "locked in a candy store" feeling as soon as you enter. Booths display arrays of new and old products, with spokespeople for manufacturers on hand to answer questions. Dealers' booths sell things. Lodges and outfitters tempt passersby with videos of vacation opportunities. Most shows feature casting, fly-tying, and other demonstrations by experts, and many have door-prize raffles of tackle or trips.

Anyone who doesn't leave with a couple of shopping bags full of brochures isn't trying very hard. . . shows and expositions are a wonderful way to learn about the state-of-the-art of whatever kind of fishing you're interested in.

Shows are arranged by month, based on the schedule of previous shows. Check with the venues for specific dates.

Note: The words "sportsmen" and "outdoors" usually indicate hunting as well as fishing.

JANUARY

OREGON INTERNATIONAL SPORTSMEN'S EXPOSITION

Oregon Convention Center, Portland, Oregon

MIDWEST FLY SHOW

Inland Meeting and Exposition Center, Westmont, Illinois

THE MEADOWLANDS SPORTSMEN'S SHOW

Byrne Arena, East Rutherford, New Jersey

NEW YORK BOAT SHOW

Javits Convention Center, New York, New York

Exhibitors include fresh- and saltwater fishing craft and tackle shops.

DENVER SPORTSMEN'S SHOW

Colorado Convention Center, Denver, Colorado

INTERNATIONAL SPORTSMEN'S EXPOSITION

CAL-EXPO, Sacramento, California

GARDEN STATE OUTDOOR SPORTSMEN'S SHOW

Raritan Center Exposition Hall, Edison, New Jersey

FLY FISHING BOOK AND TACKLE FAIR

Harris Convention Center, Camp Hill, Pennsylvania

GREATER PHILADELPHIA SPORT TRAVEL & OUTDOOR SHOW

Fort Washington Exposition Center, Philadelphia, Pennsylvania

EUGENE BOAT AND SPORTSMEN'S SHOW

Lane County Fairgrounds, Eugene, Oregon

NATIONAL FLY FISHING SHOW

World Trade Center, Boston, Massachusetts

THE FLYFISHING SHOW

Garden State Exposition Center, Somerset, New Jersey

FEBRUARY

SEATTLE INTERNATIONAL SPORTSMEN'S EXPOSITION

The Kingdome, Seattle, Washington

EASTERN FISHING & OUTDOOR EXPOSITION

The Centrum, Worcester, Massachusetts

NATIONAL SPORTFISHING & OUTDOOR EXPO

Nassau Coliseum, Uniondale (Long Island), New York

EASTERN SPORTS & OUTDOORS SHOW

State Farm Show Complex, Harrisburg, Pennsylvania

PACIFIC NORTHWEST SPORTSMEN'S EXPOSITION

Portland Expo Center, Portland, Oregon

GART SPORTS DENVER INTERNATIONAL SPORTSMEN'S EXPOSITION

Currigan Convention Center, Denver, Colorado

NORTHEAST LIGHT TACKLE EXPO

Wilton High School Field House, Wilton, Connecticut

GREAT LAKES FISHING & OUTDOOR EXPOSITION

Buffalo Convention Center, Buffalo, New York

SPORTSMAN'S SHOW

Jaffa Mosque, Altoona, Pennsylvania

MARCH

WORLD FISHING & OUTDOOR EXPO

Rockland Community College Field House, Suffern, New York

INTERNATIONAL SPORTSMEN'S EXPOSITION

San Mateo County Expo Center, San Mateo, California

TORONTO SPORTSMEN'S SHOW

Coliseum Building, Toronto, Ontario

NATIONAL CAPITOL FLY FISHING SHOW

University of Maryland at College Park, College Park, Maryland

APRIL

FLY FISHER'S SYMPOSIUM

Seven Springs Mountain Resort, Champion, Pennsylvania

SEPTEMBER

FLY FISHING CONVENTION

Currigan Convention Center, Denver, Colorado

NOVEMBER

INTERNATIONAL FLY TYERS SYMPOSIUM

South Jersey Expo, Pennsuaken, New Jersey

NATIONAL FLY FISHING SHOW

Miami, Florida

2 3

ORGANIZATIONS AND ASSOCIATIONS

Although fishing has the reputation of being a solitary pursuit, fishermen as a species tend to be gregarious. At the very least, they enjoy the company of like-minded souls, the better to trade true-life adventures and swap ideas.

Then too, when confronted with environmental issues that demand solutions, fishermen understand that a unified front is the best way to achieve their goals. Nowhere is this more evident than in those organizations that include political action on environmental issues.

A letter or phone call eliciting membership information will result in brochures and other literature that includes, in some cases, a complimentary copy of the group's magazine or newsletter.

American Littoral Society
Building 18
Sandy Hook
Highlands, NJ 07732
(908) 291-0055

The American Littoral Society is a national nonprofit organization that encourages a better understanding of aquatic environments and acts as a public interest advocate for marine and shore protection. Among its activities is the Baykeeper Program, a citizen watchdog effort for the New York/New Jersey harbor estuary system, with water-quality monitoring, urban outreach initiative, and a hotline for environmental emergencies. Members receive a newsletter and a quarterly publication, *The Underwater Naturalist.*

Atlantic Salmon Federation
P.O. Box 429
St. Andrews, New Brunswick
 EOG 2X0 Canada
(506) 529-4581

The Atlantic Salmon Federation is a conservation group involved in preserving salmon waters along the Atlantic coast and in its riparian waters. Among its activities are supporting innovations such as satellite rearing stations, where newborn salmon are able to be "imprinted" by what will become their native waters (something that rearing in a centralized hatchery does not permit).

Bass Anglers Sportsman Society
 (B.A.S.S.)
5845 Carmichael Rd.
Montgomery, AL 36117
(205) 272-9530

As the name suggests, this group—the largest of the fishing organizations—is devoted to bass fishing in all its forms. Among its activities are producing and promoting tournaments throughout the U.S., publishing *Bassmaster* magazine, and producing the *Bassmasters* TV series on TNN. B.A.S.S. is also actively involved in conservation efforts.

Bass'n Gal
P.O. Box 13925
Arlington, TX 76013
(817) 265-6214

Among the stated purposes of Bass'n Gal are bringing together women anglers, improving its members' fishing skills, encouraging conservation programs, and promoting the sport of fishing. The organization also puts on a series of tournaments, the results of which are reported in *Bass'n Gal* magazine and shown on the *Bass'n Gal* TV series on ESPN.

Federation of Fly Fishers
P.O. Box 1595
Bozeman, MT 59771
(406) 585-7592

Federation of Fly Fishers is composed of nearly 300 clubs divided into 10 regional councils throughout the U.S., Canada, and abroad. There are, additionally, FFF members who do not belong to clubs. Activities include fly-fishing and fly-tying clinics, conservation and educational projects, fishing promotion programs, and regional and international conclaves. Membership includes a subscription to *The Flyfisher* magazine.

Fish Unlimited
P.O. Box 1073
Shelter Island Heights, NY 11965
(516) 749-FISH

Fish Unlimited is a national federation of local chapters composed of members who are dedicated to protecting, preserving, and perpetuating fin and shellfish and their respective environments. Among the organization's targets are toxic chemical dumping and such indiscriminate fishing practices as drift nets and unsound harvesting.

The organization also has an active tag-and-release program by which data on fishes' migratory habits are made available to interested parties.

Future Fisherman Foundation
1033 N. Fairfax St.
Suite 200
Alexandria, VA 22314
(703) 519-9691

This educational arm of the American Sportfishing Association offers programs with classroom materials and teacher workbooks that encourage the sport of fishing. The group's well-regarded "Hooked on Fishing—Not on Drugs"™ program has achieved notable results.

International Game Fish Association
1301 E. Atlantic Blvd.
Pompano Beach, FL 33060
(305) 941-3474
fax: (305) 941-5868

The IGFA encourages the study of game fish and acts as a repository for such data. Best known for maintaining and publishing world records for saltwater, freshwater, and fly-fishing catches, the organization also promulgates guidelines for ethical fishing practices. Its International Library of Fishes is one of the world's most comprehensive collections of books, film, art, and artifacts.

The IGFA is a good source for information about fishing clubs too: its membership computer lists (at present writing) 250 domestic and 462 foreign clubs.

Izaak Walton League of America
1401 Wilson Blvd., Level B
Arlington, VA 22209
(703) 528-1818

Established in 1922, the Izaak Walton League promotes involvement in environmental protection efforts. Its projects include political activities and public education on the local and national levels.

Outdoor Writers Association of America
2017 Cato Avenue, Suite 101
State College, PA 16801
(814) 234-1011

Formed in 1927, the OWAA is a nonprofit international organization that represents more than 2,000 professional communicators who report on outdoors subjects. The group conducts meetings and conferences, publishes a monthly newsletter, offers student scholarships, promulgates standards of professional ethics, and acts as a liaison with the outdoor industry and commercial interests.

Theodore Gordon Flyfishers
24 East 39 Street
New York, NY 10156
(212) 689-1155

Founded in 1962 by a group of conservation-minded fly-fishermen (including Ed Zern, Lee Wulff, and Ernest Schweibert), TGF is primarily focused on the Catskills, Delaware Valley, and other natural resources adjacent to the greater metropolitan New York area, although it also participates in national and worldwide environmental efforts. Membership activities include bimonthly luncheons that feature noted speakers, social evenings, weekend outings, and an annual exposition and dinner. *Gordon Quill* is its newsletter.

Trout Unlimited
501 Church St.
Vienna, VA 22180
(703) 281-1100
(800) 834-2491

The nation's largest coldwater environmental and conservation organization, TU is active in retaining and/or restoring fishing venues, as well as encouraging public awareness and participation in environmental efforts. Membership includes a subscription to *Trout* magazine.

State Wildlife Agencies

State wildlife/fish and game agencies are the most authoritative sources of information on such subjects as fishing license requirements, open seasons, limits on the number of fish that can be kept, and any other restrictions.

State Aquatic Resource Education Program contacts are there to provide up-to-date material on fishing opportunities and conservation efforts on a statewide, regional, and local basis.

Alabama Department of Game and Fish
64 North Union Street
Montgomery, AL 36130
(205) 832-6300
Contact for Aquatic Resource Education Program:
C. Jack Turner (205) 242-3628

Alaska Department of Fish and Game
P.O. Box 3-2000
Juneau AK 99802
(907) 465-4100
Contact for Aquatic Resource Education Program:
Jon Lyman (907) 465-6186

Arizona Game and Fish Department
2222 West Greenway Road
Phoenix, AZ 85023
(602) 9422-3000
Contact for Aquatic Resource Education Program:
Bill Powers/Doug Thornburg
(602) 789-3229/3240

Arkansas Game and Fish Commission
P.O. Box 1650
Mountain Home, AR 72653
(501) 223-6351
Contact for Aquatic Resource Education Program:
Jeryl Jones/Sloan Lessley (501) 223-6385/297-8053

California Department of Fish and Game
1416 Ninth Street
Sacramento, CA 95814
(916) 445-3531
Contact for Aquatic Resource Education Program:
Bob Garrison/Elena Scofield
(916) 323-7215/653-9843

Colorado Division of Wildlife
6060 Broadway
Denver, CO 80216
(303) 297-1192
Contact for Aquatic Resource Education Program:
Robin Knox/Jim Satterfield (303) 291-7362/7232

Connecticut Department of Environmental Protection
165 Capitol Avenue
Hartford, CT 06115
(203) 556-5599
Contact for Aquatic Resource Education Program:
George Babey/Tom Bourret (203) 566-2287/663-1656

Delaware Division of Fish and Wildlife
P.O. Box 1401
Dover, DE 19901
(302) 556-5599
Contact for Aquatic Resource Education Program:
Gary Kreamer/Nanci Rolli (302) 653-2882/739-4506

Florida Game and Freshwater Fish Commission
620 South Meridian Street
Tallahassee, FL 32301
(904) 488-1960
Contact for Aquatic Resource Education Program:
Scott Hardin/Mark Trainer/Phil Chapman (904) 488-4068

Georgia State Game and Fish Department
205 Butler Street SE
Atlanta, GA 30334
(404) 656-3530
Contact for Aquatic Resource Education Program:
Chris Martin (404) 918-6418

Hawaii Division of Aquatic Resources
1151 Punchbowl Street
Honolulu, HI 96813
(808) 548-4000
Contact for Aquatic Resource Education Program:
Randy Honebrink (808) 587-0111

Idaho Fish and Game Department
P.O. Box 25
Boise, ID 83707
(208) 334-5159

Contact for Aquatic Resource Education Program:

Julie Scanlin (208) 334-2633

Illinois Department of Conservation

Fish and Wildlife Resources Division

524 South Second Street

Springfield, IL 62706

(217) 782-6302

Contact for Aquatic Resource Education Program:

Larry Dunham (217) 290-3223/232-4080

Indiana Department of Natural Resources

607 State Office Building

Indianapolis, IN 46204

(317) 232-4080

Contact above office for Aquatic Resource Education Program.

Iowa Department of Natural Resources

Wallace State Office Building

Des Moines, IA 50319

(515) 281-5385

Contact for Aquatic Resource Education Program:

Barbara Gigar (515) 747-2200

Kansas Fish and Game Commission

Box 54A, RR2

Pratt, KS 67124

(316) 672-5911

Contact for Aquatic Resource Education Program:

Steve Stackenhous/Roland Stein (316) 627-5911

Kentucky Department of Fish and Wildlife Resources

1 Game Farm Road

Frankfort, KY 40601

(502) 564-3400

Contact for Aquatic Resource Education Program:

Lonnie Nelson (502) 564-4762

Louisiana Department of Wildlife and Fisheries

P.O. Box 15570

Baton Rouge, LA 70895

(504) 925-3617

Contact for Aquatic Resource Education Program:

Paul Jackson (318) 491-2585

Maine Department of Inland Fisheries and Wildlife

Station 41, 284 State Street

Augusta, ME 04333

(207) 289-2221

Contact for Aquatic Resource Education Program:

(freshwater) Lisa Kane/Bob Williams (207) 287-3303/3128

(marine) Elaine Jones/Peter Dumont (207) 624-6550

Maryland Department of Natural Resources

Tawes State Office Building

Annapolis, MD 21401

(301) 974-7947

Contact for Aquatic Resource Education Program:

Janet Greenfield/Cindy Grove (800) 688-FINNS

Massachusetts Division of Fisheries and Wildlife

100 Cambridge Street

Boston, MA 02202

(617) 727-3180

Contact for Aquatic Resource Education Program:

Gary Zima (508) 792-7270

Michigan Department of Natural Resources

P.O. Box 30028

Lansing, MI 48909

(517) 373-1220

Contact for Aquatic Resource Education Program:

Dr. Ned Fogel/Starr Jurney (517) 373-1280

Minnesota Department of Natural Resources

500 Lafayette Road

St. Paul, MN 55155

(612) 296-6157

Contact for Aquatic Resource Education Program:

Linda Ericson-Eastwood (612) 297-4919

Mississippi Department of Wildlife Conservation

P.O. Box 451

Jackson, MS 39205

(601) 961-5315

Contact for Aquatic Resource Education Program:

Libby Hartfield/Martha Cooper (601) 354-7303

Missouri Department of Conservation

P.O. Box 180

Jefferson City, MO 65102

(314) 751-4115

Contact for Aquatic Resource Education Program:

Don Heard/Cindy Borgwordt (314) 751-4115 ext. 295

Montana Department of Fish,
Wildlife and Parks
1420 East 6th Street
Helena, MT 59620
(406) 499-3186
Contact for Aquatic Resource
Education Program:
Kurt Cunningham/Mark Sweeny
(406) 444-1267

Nebraska Game and Parks
Commission
P.O. Box 30370
Lincoln, NE 68503
(402) 464-0641
Contact for Aquatic Resource
Education Program:
David Hagengruber (402) 332-
3901

Nevada Department of Wildlife
P.O. Box 10678
Reno, NV 89520
(702) 784-6214
Contact for Aquatic Resource
Education Program:
Kim Toulouse (702) 688-
1500/1893

New Hampshire Fish and Game
Department
34 Bridge Street
Concord, NH 02201
(603) 271-3421
Contact for Aquatic Resource
Education Program:
Laura Ryder/Kelle MacKenzie
(603) 271-3212

New Jersey Division of Fish,
Game and Wildlife
401 East State Street, CN 402
Trenton, NJ 08625
(609) 292-9410

Contact for Aquatic Resource
Education Program:
Paul Tarlowe/Larry Sarner (908)
637-4125/(609) 748-2031

New Mexico Game and Fish
Department
Villagra Building
Santa Fe, NM 87503
(505) 827-7835
Contact for Aquatic Resource
Education Program:
Don MacCarter/Dan Shaw/Ti
Piper (505) 827-7901/867-
4661

New York State Division of Fish
and Wildlife
50 Wolf Road
Albany, NY 12233
(518) 457-5690
Contact for Aquatic Resource
Education Program:
Karen Edelstein/Bruce Matthews
(607) 255-2834/9370

North Carolina Wildlife
Resources Commission
512 North Salisbury Street
Raleigh, NC 27611
(919) 733-3391
Contact for Aquatic Resource
Education Program:
Celeste Westcott/Randy Cotton
(919) 733-7123

North Dakota Fish and Game
Department
100 North Bismarck Expressway
Bismarck, ND 58501
(701) 224-2180
Contact for Aquatic Resource
Education Program:
David Jensen (701) 221-6322

Ohio Fish and Game Division
Fountain Square
Columbus, OH 43224
(614) 265-6300
Contact for Aquatic Resource
Education Program:
Jim Wentz (614) 265-6544

Oklahoma Department of Wildlife
Conservation
P.O. Box 53465
Oklahoma City, OK 73152
(405) 521-3851
Contact for Aquatic Resource
Education Program:
Colin Berg (405) 521-4603

Oregon Department of Fish and
Wildlife
Box 59
Portland, OR 97850
(503) 229-5551
Contact for Aquatic Resource
Education Program:
Bill Hastie/John Yaskovic (503)
867-4741/229-5410 ext. 413

Pennsylvania Fish Commission
P.O. Box 1673
Harrisburg, PA 17105
(717) 787-6593
Contact for Aquatic Resource
Education Program:
Kim Mumper/Carl Richardson
(717) 657-4518

Rhode Island Division of Fish and
Wildlife
Washington County Government
Center
Wakefield, RI 02879
(401) 789-3094

Contact for Aquatic Resource
Education Program:
Christine Dudley (401) 789-0281

**South Carolina Wildlife and
Marine Resources
Department**
P.O. Box 167
Columbia, SC 29202
(803) 758-0020
Contact for Aquatic Resource
Education Program:
**Don Winslow/Hope Collier (803)
734-3964**

**South Dakota Department of
Game, Fish and Parks**
445 East Capitol
Pierre, SD 57501
(605) 773-3387
Contact for Aquatic Resource
Education Program:
Steven Kirsch (605) 733-5511

**Tennessee Wildlife Resources
Agency**
P.O. Box 40747
Nashville, TN 37204
(615) 741-1431
Contact for Aquatic Resource
Education Program:
Deborah Patton (615) 781-6538

**Texas Parks and Wildlife
Department**
4200 Smith School Road
Austin, TX 78744
(512) 479-4800
Contact for Aquatic Resource
Education Program:
Steve Hall (512) 389-4568

**Utah Division of Wildlife
Resources**

1596 West North Temple
Salt Lake City, UT 84116
(801) 533-9333
Contact for Aquatic Resource
Education Program:
Phil Douglass (801) 538-4717

**Vermont Department of Fish and
Wildlife**
103 South Main
Waterbury, VT 05676
(802) 828-3371
**Contact for Aquatic Resource
Education Program:**
Mark Scott (802) 241-3700

**Virginia Department of Game and
Inland Fisheries**
P.O. Box 11104
Richmond, VA 23230
(804) 257-1000
Contact for Aquatic Resource
Education Program:
Anne Skalski (804) 367-1000

**Washington Department of
Fisheries**
115 General Administration Blvd.
Olympia, WA 98504
(206) 753-6623
Contact for Aquatic Resource
Education Program:
**(freshwater) Mike O'Malley (206)
586-5508**
**(marine) Rich Kolb/Donna Van
Kirk (206) 902-2260/2261**

**West Virginia Division of Natural
Resources**
1800 Washington St. E.
Charleston, WV 25305
(304) 348-2771

Contact for Aquatic Resource
Education Program:
**Gordon Robertson/Art Shomo
(304) 558-2271**

**Wisconsin Department of Natural
Resources**
P.O. Box 7921
Madison, WI 53707
(608) 266-2121
Contact for Aquatic Resource
Education Program:
**Carole Lee/Theresa Stabo (608)
266-2272**

**Wyoming Game and Fish
Department**
5400 Bishop Blvd.
Cheyenne, WY 82002
(307) 777-7631
Contact for Aquatic Resource
Education Program:
Jake Hohl (307) 777-4543

Other
Contacts

Puerto Rico
Aileen Velazco (809) 725-8619

Washington, DC
**Adel Gordon/Ira Palmer (202)
433-8124/404-1151**

24

OPPORTUNITIES FOR WOMEN, YOUTH, AND THE DISABLED

Fishing and Women

There was a time when fishing was considered a male bastion and escape. Fishing was how the man of the family could get out of the house for a while, away from the "little woman" and the kids. It was also a way to enjoy the company of other men in a particularly masculine way; in this pre-"Iron John" era, men sat around campfires and got in touch with their inner feelings by draining a bottle of rye, not beating on a tom-tom.

And when hubby wasn't out on the lake or along a stream, he bonded with the boys down at the local tackle shop, which in those days was as much a male haunt as the barbershop or pool hall.

Even learning to fish was considered a masculine rite of passage. Dad or Gramps taught Junior. As for Mom and Sis, if they were involved at all, their role was to clean and cook what the men brought home.

That's hardly the case now.

According to industry statistics, some 20 million women fish, a number that accounts for 33% of the fishing licenses in the country. They spend $128 million each year on tackle and related goods (freshwater gear outweighs saltwater equipment and apparel by some 8 to 1), again a one-third segment of the market.

Industry response has taken a decidedly femi-

nine turn over the past decade. Tackle shop catalogs offer items specifically intended for women, from rods with thinner handles (to fit smaller hands) to boots, waders, vests, and other apparel designed and cut along the lines of the female figure.

Nor must Mom or Sis wait for Dad or Gramps to extend a mentoring hand. Fishing schools offer classes that cater exclusively to women, who tend to experience far less embarrassment and anxiety than when they're part of coed groups. There are also entire organizations and programs that welcome women into a universal sisterhood which claims as its spiritual founder Dame Juliana Berners, a fifteenth-century English cleric who wrote the earliest fishing treatise in the English language.[*]

RECOMMENDED READING

Uncommon Waters, edited by Holly Morris (Seal Press, 1991), is an anthology of women's writings about fishing. Its essays, fiction pieces, and poetry cover the range of fishing techniques. Some speak to a sense of empowerment; the granddaughter of Ernest Hemingway writes insightfully in that regard. All reflect the sense of curiosity, self-fulfillment, and unalloyed pleasure that the sport affords.

---

[*]Despite its old-boy network of upper-class pursuits, Britain's angling population has always included women. One of this century's most celebrated fly anglers was Queen Elizabeth, the Queen Mother. She instructed Prince Charles and many of her other royal relatives in the sport, and until well into her eighties she regularly fished the streams and rivers of her native Scotland.

Two excellent fly-fishing primers contain advice about fishing in general that anyone—regardless of gender—will find useful:

Joan Wulff's Fly Fishing: Expert Advice from a Woman's Perspective (Stackpole Books, 1991), written by the most influential spokeswoman for that branch of fishing, is now something of a textbook in its field. The information on equipment, technique, and attitude is illustrated by many instructive personal anecdotes, and if that weren't enough, the book concludes with a modernized text of the first printed version of Dame Juliana Berners' seminal "Treatise of Fishing with an Angle."

Wade a Little Deeper, Dear: A Woman's Guide to Fly Fishing by Gwen Cooper and Evelyn Haas (Cortland Library/Lyons & Burford, 1989) takes the sensible position that the fishing should be taken no more (or less) seriously than it deserves to be taken. Toward that goal, the authors serve up information about tackle, technique, and tactics, as well as a chapter of recipes (useful after times when fish are biting) and one on what to do when they aren't biting (e.g., bird-watching, panning for gold, nature walks).

REEL WOMEN FLY FISHING ADVENTURES

Reel Women Fly Fishing Adventures was formed by Christy Ball and Lori-Ann Murphy, two women whose other credits include guiding in Idaho and Wyoming and instructing in Orvis' "Women Only" program (Murphy served as the fly-fishing consultant on the movie *The River Wild*). Their firm escorts women on spring and summer trips of four to six days to Montana's "classic" trout rivers, the South Fork of Idaho's Snake River, and lake fishing spots in Wyoming's Wind River Mountains. February and March find Ball, Murphy,

Reel Women's Christy Ball and Lori-Ann Murphy.
[photo courtesy Reel Women]

and their clients bonefishing in the Bahamas. Groups are limited in size to insure maximum comfort and attention.

The women also continue to teach as part of Orvis' "Women Only" program in Manchester, Vermont, and their "home waters" in Jackson Hole, Wyoming.

Contact: Reel Women Fishing Adventures, P.O. Box 20202, Jackson, WY 83001; phone: (307) 733-2210; fax: (307) 733-8655.

BASS'N GAL

Bass'n Gal was formed to bring together women who want to improve their fishing skills and become more involved in conservation efforts. The competitive spirit is served by a series of tournaments. For information, contact: Bass'n Gal, P.O. Box 13925, Arlington, TX 76013; phone: (817) 265-6214.

"BECOMING AN OUTDOORS-WOMAN" WORKSHOPS

A 1990 conference at the University of Wisconsin—Stevens Point centered around the topic of "Breaking Down the Barriers to Participation of Women in Hunting and Angling." Hearing about the conference, a number of women asked Christine

Bagging fish at the 1993 Classic Star Women's World Championship. [photo courtesy Bass'n Gal]

Thomas, associate professor of resource management and one of the participants, whether the conference would include the chance for them to learn basic skills in one or both of the sports.

Encouraged by the inquiries, Dr. Thomas created the "Becoming an Outdoors-Woman" workshop program, a weekend-long seminar that offered lectures and hands-on training in hunting, fishing, and woodcraft and camping skills.

The success of the first weekend led to considerable written and word-of-mouth publicity, which in turn attracted other women who wanted to attend future sessions. It also attracted support in the form of equipment and funding from field-sports-related corporations and other organizations.

Other workshops followed, word spread further, and now "Becoming an Outdoors-Woman" workshops are held across the country and in Canada. Under the aegis of state wildlife sport and/or conservation agencies, they offer participants the opportunity to choose from a varied menu of subjects. All are presented by instructors who have been selected for their enthusiasm and patience.

Workshops were scheduled during 1995 in the following states: Alabama, Alaska, Arkansas, California, Colorado, Florida, Georgia, Indiana, Iowa, Kansas, Kentucky, Louisiana, Minnesota, Mississippi, Missouri, Montana, Nebraska, New Jersey, New Mexico, New York, North Dakota, Ohio, Oklahoma, Oregon, South Dakota, Tennessee, Texas, Vermont, Wisconsin. In Canada: Manitoba.

For further information, contact Dr. Christine Thomas, College of Natural Resources, University of Wisconsin, Stevens Point, WI 54481; phone: (715) 346-4185.

Instructor and participant at a "Becoming an Outdoors-Woman" workshop. [photo courtesy University Graphics and Photography/University of Wisconsin—Stevens Point]

Fishing and Youngsters

Since fishing is a sport that can be enjoyed throughout a lifetime, it's a good idea to introduce youngsters to its delights at as young an age as possible.

The exact age depends on the child's attention span and coordination skills. Five or six is not too young for most youngsters to hold a short pole or drop line, then keep an eye on the bobber at the end of the line (however, baiting the hook and casting the line might have to be the responsibility of the accompanying adult). Seven- or eight-year-olds are usually capable of using spin-casting rod-and-reel tackle and appropriate lures.

Parents, camp counselors, and others who have taught youngsters stress that gearing the length of the outing to a child's attention span is crucial. Look for the first signs of restlessness, and call it a day before boredom sets in. However, some children may want to stop for a while and do something else (like taking a walk), and then begin fishing again. Having room to roam is useful, and that's why fishing from a shoreline or a pier or dock makes more sense than from a rowboat or another small and contained area.

Nothing succeeds like success, and a youngsters' enthusiasm for fishing is in direct proportion to the number of fish that they catch. The size of the fish or the fight it puts up doesn't matter. What's important is number of times the bobber jiggles, and even more important is the number of fish that are landed. Select the part of a pond, lake, or bay where you know that perch, bluegill, or other easy-to-attract species congregate, and you're more than halfway there.

Fishing helps develop a sense of self-sufficiency. Accordingly, allow older youngsters to do as much for themselves as they can safely manage. That includes putting worms or other live bait on the hook; handling worms, crickets, and leeches as bait encourages youngsters to overcome any queasiness about touching any such "yucky" creatures. Backlash snarls and hooks snagged in rocks or logs or caught on overhanging branches are all part of the game, and to the extent that youngsters are able, they should learn to make their best effort at independent problem-solving before they seek assistance.

Adults should never forget their function as role models. That means a demonstration as well as a lecture about what constitutes a good fisherman. Qualities that you'd like to see in a young fisher-

man—patience, awareness of surroundings and respect for nature, courtesy to other anglers, knowledge and observance of rules and laws, and a sense of what constitutes safety—are learned by copying how *you* behave.

Across the generation gap on a Montana trout stream. [Harley Hettick photo courtesy Travel Montana Dept. of Commerce]

RECOMMENDED READING

Several books and other publications will make the task of a parent or mentor much easier. One is *Fly Fishing with Children: A Guide for Parents* by Philip Brunquell, M.D. (The Countryman Press, 1993). No matter what kind of equipment—bait-casting, spinning, or just a drop line off a pier—you have in mind for your child, the author's approach to the sport of fishing makes wonderful sense. Written by a father of a young fisherwoman, the book helps parents and mentors introduce youngsters to the technical side of selecting and using appropriate tackle (remember that little hands can seldom cope with adult-size equipment), and safety tips. Just as important, if not more so, is the emphasis on building and nurturing the spiritual bond between parent/mentor and child that should arise from their shared experience. Then too, the author suggests ways to focus a youngster's attention to his or her environmental responsibilities. And because Dr. Brunquell teaches pediatrics and neurology at the University of Connecticut Medical School, his advice of helping physically disabled children to fish fills a real void in the literature.

Another good book on the subject is Jim Arnosky's *Flies in the Water, Fish in the Air: A Personal Introduction to Fly Fishing* (The Countryman Press, 1992), an engaging guide aimed at young adults.

Saltwater Adventure in the Florida Keys: An Introduction to Fishing for Kids by Jacky Robinson (White Heron Press, 1995) is a fictionalized account of a transplanted city boy whose uncle teaches him about saltwater fishing. By following the youngster's education, young readers learn about types of tackle, fly-tying, marine biology and behavior, and even something about adolescent human behavior too. A glossary and a fill-it-out-yourself journal enhance the captivating story line. [White Heron Press, P.O. Box 468, Islamorada, FL 33036; phone/fax: (305) 664-8108.]

TACKLE

Many tackle manufacturers offer products aimed at attracting the junior market.

Zebco's line of "hot" rods and spin-casting reels come in fluorescent colors. Its dinosaur-inspired "Fishasaurus Rex" package contains "Castasaurus" practice plugs, while Donald Duck, Mickey Mouse, and Snoopy appear on tackle boxes, tote bags, plastic bobbers, and yet another line of rods and spin-casting reels.

Berkley's Nibbler® and Wildfire™ kits are equally child-friendly. The former features a 2-foot, 6-inch telescopic rod, and the latter a two-piece 4-foot, 6-inch rod; both kits contain appropriate spin-casting reels and terminal tackle.

Among other items for youngsters, Bass Pro Shop carries kiddie-size T-shirts, caps, and flotation vests. And for hours off the water, toy bass boats (one a tournament model) and trucks to haul them give young fishermen a taste of what lies ahead.

Another company that is active in fishing for youngsters is Rubbermaid, the manufacturer of tackle boxes (among other products for households and the outdoors). Its free booklet titled *Pro Series Tips* includes articles on conservation, worm-fishing, and even kids and fishing.

Contact: Rubbermaid Inc, Specialty Products Division, 1147 Akron Rd., Wooster, OH 44691; phone: (216) 264-6464; fax: (216) 287-2052.

Rubbermaid and B.A.S.S. collaborate in their Rubbermaid®-Bassmaster® CastingKids™ program. *CastingKids™* is its magazine, and *Fishing and Our Environment* is an activity book aimed at young fishermen. For information about this program, contact: Bass Anglers Sportsman Society, 5845 Carmichael Rd., Montgomery, AL 36117; phone: (205) 272-9530.

HOOKED ON FISHING—NOT ON DRUGS™

Statistics bear out the indisputable fact that youngsters who participate in sports have very little time and less inclination to become involved in self-destructive activities. Sport-fishing is no exception, as the Future Fisherman Foundation's "Hooked on Fishing—Not on Drugs"™ program demonstrates. A supplementary, interdisciplinary drug-prevention effort for young people in grades K–12, the program uses fishing to focus students' attention on strategies toward building self-esteem, life skills, civic values, better relationships with family and community, and a sense of stewardship toward aquatic resources.

The materials for the program include a parent's guide that outlines ways to introduce children to the sport (amplifying many of the points made at the beginning of this section), all the while helping to create lines of communication among family members. A teacher's guide contains lesson plans, suggestions for parental and community involvement, and a comprehensive "Aquatic Resources Education Curriculum" (from which, quite frankly, fledgling fishermen of any age can benefit).

The Department of the Interior's U.S. Fish and Wildlife Service is a partner in this program. So is the American Sportfishing Association, which helps to fund the Foundation's administrative costs and allows the Foundation to adapt its *Teacher's Guide*, the "Aquatic Resources Education Curriculum," and student manuals into "Hooked on Fishing—Not on Drugs"™ lessons.

For information about this valuable program, contact Sharon Rushton, Future Fisherman Foundation, P.O. Box 10693, Fort Smith, AK 71917; phone: (501) 484-0051; fax: (501) 484-0905.

Finally, the following essay, which appeared in The New York Times Magazine's "About Men" column, has much to say about fishing and young-sters, whether they are parents or children.

Just a Walleyed Optimist

BY JAMES GORMAN

A few weeks ago, my 3-year-old son and I caught a 32-inch, 10-pound striped bass. We were fishing, with a young friend, on a spit of land that juts out into the Hudson River a couple of miles below the Tappan Zee Bridge. I put a bloodworm on the hook and cast it out into the water with an ounce-and-a-half sinker. Fifteen minutes later, we were hauling in Moby Dick. Everyone on the pier came by to congratulate us, admire the fish, take our picture, and measure and weigh the prize.

We brought the fish home to clean and cook. Daniel, the 3-year-old, danced around it with a stick in classic *Lord of the Flies* fashion. Filleted, marinated briefly in soy sauce, and cooked on the grill, the bass had the delicious flavor of really fresh fish, with the added piquancy of the Hudson's PCBs. My son ate it with as much gusto as he displayed in describing the killing that produced the banquet. "It was still alive! My daddy killed it with his knife!" I felt like Hawkeye, La Longue Carabine, Fishslayer—raising up a young'un to live by his wits and a well-honed blade.

The transmission of fishing knowledge from father to son is a tradition to many families. In its purest saltwater form, the exercise of this tradition insures that the son learns to fish for flounder at the turn of the tide and to follow the terns for bluefish. He learns, if his family is of the freshwater persuasion, where trout hide in a stream and how to smoke a cigar and change flies while standing chest-deep in a cold stream with leaky waders and black flies biting him around the eyes without ever saying more than, "Kinda buggy out here."

In some families, this tradition is adulterated, and the pursuit of fish becomes an inculcation in class bias. The son learns that if you don't fish with a fly rod, preferably in cold, clear running water, you are a low-rent, no-class lout engaging in a prac-tice one notch above throwing dynamite into a salmon pool, and your father not only didn't go to Princeton, he probably jacklights deer for fun.

Or, from the other end of fishing society, the boy is taught that any so-called man who diddles a bit of feather on a prissy wire hook and then makes sure the itty-bitty trout he catches are all right before he lets them go is a snobby, soft-handed, overdressed Orvis clone who wouldn't know a walleye from a wahoo or bunker from bunkum and who, if he ever had the grit to kill and clean a fish, would probably insist on washing his hands before he ate his lunch of Brie and Black Forest ham on French bread with honey mustard.

And then there are the families that don't catch anything. There are more of these than anyone realizes. I grew up in this tradition. I learned that things do not always come to those who wait, that no lure is guaranteed to catch fish, and that, if at first you don't succeed, the same thing may well happen the next time. When I was a child, my father and I went fishing every opening day of the trout season for about 10 years. We never caught a fish. I don't mean that we usually didn't catch a fish, or that we hooked fish and almost netted them, or that we caught the wrong kind of fish. I mean we never caught anything.

I don't know whether it was my desire or my father's perseverance (I now know that 5 A.M. is earlier for fathers than it is for sons) that kept us going, but by the end it was another case of the Vietnam syndrome. We had spent too much time, too many years, endured too much heartbreak (well, disappointment) to just give up and admit that it had all been a horrible mistake. Eventually what happened was that I learned to fish on my own and then taught him (this is my version of the story, of course, but then that's the whole point of being a writer).

I'm sure the whole experience sounds like the old joke (one of my father's favorites) in which a child keeps asking his dad questions about the sun, moon, and stars and the nature of the universe. Each time the father replies, "I don't know." Finally,

the boy starts to ask another question, but stops, saying "Never mind!" The father, indignant, insists: "Ask! Ask! How else are you going to learn?"

Except that I never said, "Never mind." I was so excited on the morning of every opening day that I was awake hours before the appointed time. By rights I should have learned hopelessness. But it didn't happen, at least not with fishing. As regards life in general, I see little hope for the human race and count both Dean Swift and Mark Twain as sentimental Pollyannas. But every time I go fishing, I am transformed. The deep optimism that lurks in my soul emerges. I know, every time I cast out a line, whether it has a size 14 Adams at the end of it or a live eel on a hook, that I will catch fish. I have been known, on fishing trips, to fish all day, from long before breakfast to long after dinner, for days in a row. I get skunked sometimes like everyone else. But I never learn. I'm a believer.

But that's the way I want my son to grow up. I don't much care if he rebels against my general dyspepsia and ends up viewing the human race as the crown of creation, but if he turns out to be a fishing pessimist I'll be devastated.

But you see the problem. Dad and boy never catch fish; boy grows up to love fishing. Fine. Dad and boy catch fish the first time out—huge fish. What happens then? I have broke with tradition, deviated from a time-honored path, and made my father look bad to boot. When I told him about the event, he said: "Now you've ruined him. He's going to think this is what happens whenever you go fishing. I brought you up the right way." He was kidding, of course, sort of, just as I am when I claim that I taught him to fish.

I hope he's wrong. Danny is still an optimist. He fishes off the porch with string. (We live on land.) At night when he goes to bed, he talks about catching a big fish the next day. He is completely convinced that we will catch a big one the next time we go fishing. I've been so busy the past couple of weeks and the weather hasn't been good, so we haven't gone again yet. But we will, and we will catch a fish. I have no doubt whatsoever.*

*Copyright © 1994, James Gorman. Reprinted with permission from *The New York Times*. Distributed by New York Times Special Features/Syndication Sales.

Fishing for the Disabled

Thanks to the work of a growing number of individuals, groups, and organizations, barriers to spending a day on the water are dropping for physically and emotionally challenged anglers.

The following organizations offer general advice and assistance:

Disabled Boaters and Campers News
HBS News Co.
P.O. Box 173
Lyons, IL 60534
Disabled Outdoors Magazine
2052 W. 23rd St.
Chicago, IL 60608

Coalition to Promote Accessible Outdoor Recreation
12974 S. Kevin Ln.
Sapulpa, OK 74066
Fish Hawk Enterprises
P.O. Box 9157
North St. Paul, MN 55109

Information Center for Individuals With Disabilities
20 Park Plaza
Boston, MA 02116

National Association of Handicapped Sportsmen
RR 6
P.O. Box 25
Centralia, IL 62801

National Handicapped Sports and Recreation Association
1145 19th St., NW
Washington, DC 20036

Physically Challenged Access to the Woods (PAW)
P.O. Box 357
Empire, CO 80438

Physically Challenged Sportsman's Association
30006 Louisiana Ave.
Cleveland, OH 44109

Information on access to fishing areas are addressed in the following publications:

Accessible Fishing—A Planning Handbook, available from New Mexico Natural Resources Department, Management and Development Division, Suite 129, Villagra Building, Santa Fe, NM 87504.

Guidelines for the Design of Barrier-Free Recreational Boating and Fishing Facilities, available from States Organization for Boating Access, P.O. Box 25655, Washington, DC 20007.

Barrier-Free Fishing, available from Dr. Richard Chenowith, Department of Landscape Architecture, University of Wisconsin—Madison, Madison, WI 53706.

A number of states have handicapped sportsmen associations; consult your state's fishing and game commission and/or state conservation agency for addresses.

For information on instruction, consult:

Disabled Outdoor Experiences
Box 567
Jackman, ME 04945
Fishing Has No Boundaries

Amerifish Corporation
P.O. Box 175
Hayward, WI 54843

Fish Hawk Enterprises
P.O. Box 9157
North St. Paul, MN 55109

New York Sportfishing and Aquatic Resources Education Program
Department of Natural Resources
8 Fernow Hall
Cornell University
Ithaca, NY 14853

In addition to further references to the above topics, sources of such equipment as motor-driven reels, rod holders, casting systems, and outdoor-adapted wheelchairs appear in the excellent pamphlet, *Go Fish! Developing Fishing Programs for Therapeutic Recreation*. Compiled by Bruce E. Matthews, Director of the New York Sportfishing and Aquatic Resources Education Program, the pamphlet is available from the NYSAREP, Department of Natural Resources, 8 Fernow Hall, Cornell University, Ithaca, NY 14853; phone: (607) 255-2814.

A chapter titled "The Disabled Child" is included in *Fly Fishing with Children: A Guide for Parents* by Philip Brunquell, M.D. (The Countryman Press, 1993).

25

FISHING INSTRUCTION AND SCHOOLS

I n the best of all worlds, we learn to fish through the instruction of a kindly and encouraging mentor, perhaps a relative or a friend who has the savvy, time, and patience to show us the ropes. For those of us whose universe doesn't include such a person, instruction is no further away than one of the many fishing schools through the U.S. and Canada.

Courses range from half-day seminars to four- or five-day stints. Instruction in fly-fishing predominates, and group lessons can handle from six to a dozen or more students. Most schools supply tackle, although students are free to use their own rods and reels.

The syllabus of a full-fledged course typically begins with such "classroom" matters as an introduction to tackle and other equipment, entomology (with an eye toward matching the hatch), "reading" the water, conservation (such as catch-and-release), and safety procedures (especially with regard to wading). Casting lessons take place on dry land or on the bank of a pond or a snag-proof stretch of stream. This aspect of the course stresses fundamentals, although an instructor will offer more advanced techniques for students who are ready for them. Courses usually end with students being given an opportunity to put what they've learned into practice on a nearby stream or lake.

Perhaps even more than at golf or tennis schools, adult novice anglers tend initially to be very self-conscious, as if a back cast's snagging a tree branch or a roll cast's churning a placid pool into a froth is somehow the most heinous crime than any athlete can commit. It's therefore a good thing that fishing instructors overflow with patience and encouragement. To the extent group situations allow individual attention, teachers routinely can be counted on to work as long it takes to iron out a student's particular problem.

Tuition varies widely, based on the course's duration, time of year, and number of students in the group. If the course you choose is some distance from where you live, you must remember to factor in the cost of transportation and accommodations, although some schools have "package" arrangements with regard to lodging.

In addition to the following schools, many tackle shops offer individual and group instruction, and in disciplines other than fly-fishing. Ask at shops in your area. If proprietors or salespeople are unable to provide instruction, they can usually and easily find someone else to teach you. Local chapters of such organizations as Trout Unlimited and Bass Anglers Sportsman Society (B.A.S.S.) are other good places to inquire.

L.L. Bean
Freeport, ME 04032
(800) 341-4341
Seminars conducted at the company's Maine location.

Al Caucci Flyfishing
RD 1, Box 102
Tannerville, PA 18372
(717) 629-2962
On the West Branch of the Delaware River. Caucci also conducts programs on the Missouri River in northwestern Montana during July and bonefishing on Andros in the Bahamas in November and in March.

The Florida Keys Fly Fishing
School & Outfitters
P.O. Box 603
Islamorada, FL 33036
(305) 664-5423
Weekend sessions once a month (January, February, March, April, May, July, October, and December) conducted by the folks who produce the ESPN TV series, *Walker's Cay Chronicles*.

Murray's On The Stream Fly
Fishing Schools
P.O. Box 156
Edinburg, VA 22824
(703) 984-4212
Instruction is held on streams in the Shenandoah Valley of Virginia.

Orvis
Manchester, VT 05254
(802) 362-3434
Courses conducted at the Vermont location, as well as at many of Orvis' approved lodges throughout the country.
According to the company's cata-

log, *The Orvis Fly-Fishing School*, a 60-minute video, takes the viewer through the "complete course of instruction" given at Orvis' school.

Joan Wulff Fishing School
Beaverkill Road
Lew Beach, NY 12753
(914) 439-4060
Highly recommended by those who have studied fly-fishing from this doyenne of the sport.

Other Schools

Jack Dennis Flyfishing School at
Teton Pines
Box 362-A
Jackson, WY 83001
(800) 443-8616

Flyfishing Outfitters
Box 310-1, RD 1
Benton, PA 17814
717) 925-2225

Kaufmann's Fly Fishing
Expeditions
P.O. Box 23032
Portland, OR 97223
(503) 639-6400

Letort Ltd.
P.O. Box 417
Boiling Springs, PA 17007
(717) 258-3010

Vermont Bound
HCR 34 Box 28
Killington, VT 05751
(800) 639-3167

College and University Programs

There are schools of fish, and there are schools—that is, colleges and universities—that grant degrees in general commercial fishing and fisheries and marine biology.

GENERAL FISHING AND FISHERIES

Alaska, University of, Fairbanks

Arkansas, University of, Pine Bluff

Colorado State University, Fort Collins

Humboldt State University (California State University), Arcata

Idaho, University of, Moscow

Iowa State University, Ames

Minnesota Twin Cities, University of, Minneapolis

Mississippi State University, Starkville

Ohio State University, Columbus

Oregon State University, Corvallis

Rhode Island, University of, Kingston

Sheldon Jackson College, Sitka, AK

Tennessee Technological University, Cookeville

Texas A&M University, Galveston

Unity College, Unity, ME

Washington, University of, Seattle

MARINE BIOLOGY

Alabama, University of, Tuscaloosa

Auburn University, Auburn, AL

Bemidji State University, Bemidji, MN

Brown University, Providence, RI

California State University, Long Beach

California, University of, Santa Cruz

College of Charleston, Charleston, SC

Eckerd College, St. Petersburg, FL

Fairleigh Dickinson University, Teaneck, NJ

Florida Institute of Technology, Melbourne

Hampton University, Hampton, VA

Jacksonville University, Jacksonville, FL

Long Island University, Southampton College, Southampton, NY

Miami, University of, Miami, FL

New England University, Biddeford, ME

Nicholls State University, Thibodaux, LA

North Carolina, University of, Wilmington

Rhode Island, University of, Kingston

Roger Williams College, Bristol, RI

Pennsylvania, University of, East Stroudsburg

Savannah State College, Savannah, GA

South Carolina, University of, Coastal

South Carolina, University of, Columbia

Southwest Texas State University, San Marcos

Southwest Louisiana, University of, Lafayetteville

Stockton State College, Pomona, NJ

Tampa, University of, Tampa, FL

Texas A&M University, Galveston

Troy State University, Troy, AL

Virgin Islands, University of the, Charlotte Amalie, St. Thomas

Western Washington University, Bellingham

Source: *Cass and Birnbaum's Guide to American Colleges*, 16th edition (HarperCollins, 1994).

Fishing Courses

Some colleges and universities include sport-fishing "how to" courses in their curricula. Extensive research failed to unearth anything approaching a master list of such enlightened institutions. However, what scientists call anecdotal evidence, much of it gained through an Internet fly-fishing network inquiry, revealed that the following schools offer fishing courses. Some are given for credit (usually as part of the physical education department), while others are noncredit courses in continuing education programs. In the spirit of "you should have been here on the lake last week," there were also tales about once-flourishing courses that disappeared due to lack of interest or loss of instructors.

Boise State University, Boise, ID
College of St. Rose, Albany, NY
Colorado State University, Fort Collins
State University of New York, Purchase
Pennsylvania State University, College Park
Portland Community College, Portland, OR
University of Texas at Arlington, Arlington
University of Wisconsin—Steven's Point, Steven's Point
Western State College, Gunnison, CO

In addition, members of fishing clubs at the University of Indiana and at Purdue University meet in friendly intercollegiate competition for the Minnow Bucket trophy.

Many people who were questioned added that many other schools are "out there," but they couldn't remember which ones. Anyone who is able to contribute such names and addresses for future editions of this book is cordially invited to send the information to *The Ultimate Fishing Guide*, c/o Reference Department, HarperCollins Publishers, 10 East 53 Street, New York, NY 10022-5299.

One such course is taught at the College of St. Rose in Albany, New York, by Jack Fragomeni, who wrote Chapter 17 of this book on guides and guiding.

Fly-Fishing 101

BY JACK FRAGOMENI

Several years ago, 1987 to be exactly, in a moment of enlightenment I decided to approach the chairman of the physical education department at the small private college in upstate New York where I am an adjunct faculty member. Although the school is basically a conservative liberal arts institution (an oxymoron if there ever was one), the administrators of the physical education and natural sciences divisions decided that a fly-fishing course would be a worthwhile offering. I will spare you the details of the credit justification and the other mundane particulars of the acceptance of PED154—Fly Fishing, but suffice it to say it was no mean feat. To the best of my knowledge, no other college offered a course of this kind for credit (except possibly Joe Humphrey's course at Penn State), and college administrators are often reluctant to offer unprecedented courses.

I felt proud in accomplishing the noble task of bringing the gospel of fly-fishing to the heathen water of academia, and I fantasized about becoming a great disciple delivering inspirational lectures and demonstrations that would bring the spirit of Theodore Gordon to these young piscatory

pagans. However, as the reality of the situation became clear, I began to feel like the proverbial dog that chases the car—only this time he catches it and asks "*now* what do I do?" Up to that point I had taught only weekend courses at a local fly-fishing shop with five or six people, and I had done several one-on-one instructional outings as a guide—but never a 14-week course with 25 students.

After this initial panic, I settled down to write the course outline. The abundance of information that could be included in a comprehensive syllabus made me realize that there was too much material for only one semester, and I saw that I had to limit the number of topics as well as the details. That was when I began seeing myself not as a cross between Izaak Walton and St. Paul the Apostle, but more like Mr. Peepers with waders.

I decided to present the course as an introduction, one that would provide a solid foundation in the rudiments of fly-fishing by focusing on the basics of casting, elementary aquatic entomology, artificial flies, equipment, knot-tying, and habitat analysis. The course material would be designed for, but not limited to, fly-fishing for trout, although several videos would expose the students to angling methods for such other species as tarpon, bass, and steelhead.

Colleges bring to mind lecture halls, libraries, laboratories, and other trappings of the academic environment. Lecture halls often tend to be solemn settings for pontificating, platitude-preaching pundits, and libraries and labs can be as somber as the lecture halls. This is as it should be: higher education is not to be taken lightly. However, I felt that presenting my material in a less-pedantic way would be consistent with the subject. I wanted the course to be fun as well as informative.

In keeping with the yin and yang of these classroom presentations, some topics are first discussed in a formal academic manner and then expounded upon in a lighter fashion. My reasoning is somewhat devious as I feel that the juxtaposition of the serious and the funny is not only entertaining, but it can be a learning aid. During a lecture on the life cycle of the mayfly one semester, I tried to demonstrate the process using the Stanislavski method: I became the mayfly. The class' response was enthusiastic, to say the least, and the technique proved very effective, as everyone in the classroom that day answered that question correctly on the final exam. My performance also left a lasting impression; an older gentleman who was enrolled in the class asked whether I minded if he incorporated my "method" into his lectures; he was a biology professor at a local university who was taking my course to learn to fly-fish. My subsequent demonstrations the rest of that semester became a bit more conservative.

Teaching 25 students how to cast a fly line properly can prove to be a daunting task. The problem isn't so much with the student you're working with—it's keeping the other 24 from falling asleep.

The deceptively simple solution came to me in the middle of a false-casting demonstration: a contest. That saw the birth of the NFL—the National Flycasting League. The class was split into two teams that competed against each other in feats of fly-rod prowess. The individual events involved various obstacles that challenged the contestants' casting skills, requiring both distance and accuracy as well as ingenuity in problem-solving to score points. While administering a faculty performance evaluation, the chairman of the natural science department was so impressed by the students' enthusiasm and casting proficiency that he authorized the purchase of four complete fly-rod combos to be used in the course (the chairman, an avid angler, was aware how fishing

can enhance a person's well-being).

Then there were the field trips. I use the past tense here, as there is now only one field trip. During the first two semesters that the course was given, I took the class fishing at a local pond. Loaded with smallmouth bass and panfish, the pond is located just outside the city limits in an attractive wooded area and is bound on one side by a well-traveled street. Students stood along the parts of the bank that allowed for back casts and tried their hands at catching fish on a fly. Many students caught a fish or two, but some had problems removing hooks, and many made back casts that became hung up on foliage or street lamps. I was doing a lot of running around helping solve these dilemmas, and the task proved to be somewhat unnerving. I finally decided not to continue this trip when a student was nearly spooled by a passing Toyota that she caught on her back cast.

The field trip that's part of the "new and improved" Fly Fishing 101 is a day's outing to the Orvis Company's rod factory and the American Museum of Fly Fishing, both in Manchester, Vermont. Orvis' Mary Ann Kendall has been most accommodating and has provided interesting and informative perspectives into the creating of the high-quality bamboo and graphite rods made there. Don and Alanna Johnson of the Museum have been equally accommodating in giving us tours of the many historical displays, the 3,000+-volume library, and the collection of more than 1,100 rods and 900 reels, many of which belonged to such noted and avid anglers as ex-Presidents Eisenhower, Carter, and Bush, and actors Jimmy Stewart and Robert Redford. One of the most impressive artifacts is a book of snelled wet flies used by President John Quincy Adams.

The fly-fishing course has become very popular over the years. It's one of the first courses to be closed due to capacity enrollment. Several students who have taken the course went on to purchase their own equipment which I've seen them use on a few of the local trout streams. I take satisfaction in knowing that the course has provided an opportunity for students to learn the rudiments of the noble sport of fly-fishing, and that I may have played a part in starting them on a life-long exploration of it.

[With Professor Fragomeni's kind permission, here are topic suggestions for his course's term paper (although any other topic that relates to fly-fishing is acceptable), followed by the final exam (exam answers on pages 277–278)]:

Suggested Topics for Term Papers

Historic Anglers	Topics
Theodore Gordon	Trout Unlimited
Dame Juliana Berners	Nature Conservancy
Lee Wulff	Types of Streams
Mary Orvis Marbury	Brown Trout
Izaak Walton	Rainbow Trout
Art Flick	Brook Trout
Vincent Marinaro	Atlantic Salmon
John Atherton	Pacific Salmon
Ernie Schweibert	Bamboo rods

Sierra Club

Acid rain

Battenkill (River)

Fly-tying

Catch-and-release fishing

Federation of Fly Fishers

Atlantic Salmon Federation

Final Exam

1. What are the 3 reasons for false-casting?
2. Describe one situation in which you should use the roll cast.
3. What type of cast should you use when fishing with a dry fly?
4. Name the 4 types of aquatic insects found in most trout streams and briefly describe their life cycles.
5. Name the 4 types of flies used in trout fishing and what they imitate. List 2 names of flies used for each.
6. What are the 2 factors that influence the hatching of aquatic insects?
7. What are the 3 types of lies found in trout waters? Briefly describe each type and what purpose they serve.
8. What are the correct knots to use for the following situations?

    Attaching the leader to the connector.
    Typing the tippet to the leader.
    Tying the fly to the leader.
9. Describe the correct way to release a fish back to the water.
10. What do the following line abbreviations mean?

    DT-5-F
    WF-9-F/S
    L-6-S
    ST-12-F
    WF-7-ST
11. Which fly line listed in Question 10 would be most suitable for trout fishing with a dry fly?
12. What are 2 different materials used in rod-building (2 types of fly rods)? Name one advantage of each material.
13. What are the 2 types of fly reels?
14. What are the 2 types of drag systems used in fly reels?
15. What are the 2 styles of chest waders?
16. What are the parameters of the overhead cast? (in clock hours)

17. What are the 3 styles of soles found on wading boots?

18. Which type soles would you use for the following:

    Streams and other waters with slippery-rock bottoms.
    Heavier flows with icy conditions.
    Lake shores and ocean surf with sandy bottoms.

19. Name 3 important wading accessories.

    Identify the following line tapers:

    —————===============————-

    -=============————-

    —————————

20. What is the correct X classification for the following tippet diameters?

    .007
    .010
    .004

21. What is the correct tippet size for the following hook sizes?

    12
    16
    22
    8

22. What is a correct hook size for the following tippet sizes?

    4X
    3X
    6X
    5X

23. List 2 reasons for using neoprene waders.

24. List 3 ways the sport of fly-fishing can improve the quality of your life.

Answers to PED154— Fly Fishing Final Exam

1. Lengthen line.
   Dry off the fly.
   Change direction.

2. When an overhead cast is impossible; e.g., when foliage is very close behind you.

3. Overhead cast [false-casting is acceptable]

4. Mayflies: nymph[ra] dun[ra] spinner
   Caddis flies: larva[ra] pupa[ra] adult
   Stoneflies: nymph[ra] adult
   Midge flies: larva[ra] pupa[ra] adult

5. Dry fly: imitates adult aquatic insects (Adams, Elk Hair Caddis, etc.)
   Wet fly: imitates emerging mayfly dun (Light Cahill wet, Hendrickson wet, etc.)
   Streamer: imitates baitfish (Mickey Finn)
   Nymph: imitates nymphal stages of mayflies and stoneflies (Pheasant Tail Nymph, Breadcrust, etc.).[*Teacher's Note:* Doesn't apply to midges or caddis flies—I don't get too advanced as the course is introductory level; I keep to a more traditional use of the terms and don't include imitations such as emergers, transitionals, etc.]

6. Water temperature
   Length of daylight reaching stream bed

7. Shelter lie: offers protection from predators and strong currents (under-cut banks, blowdowns in water).
   Feeding lie: usually shallower, flatter-surfaced water with a good concentration of insects floating downstream—fish expend less energy feeding (tail of a pool, along a current seam, etc.).
   Prime lie: offers both protection and good food concentration (riffle, current seam, etc.)

8. Perfection loop
   Blood (barrel) knot or surgeon's knot
   Clinch or improved clinch knot, Duncan Loop, Uni-knot, etc.

9. Wet your hands and gently hold the fish facing upstream in slower-moving water, supporting it with one hand under the belly and the other hand around the fish just in front of the tail. Let the fish swim away under its own power.

10. Double-taper—5 weight—Floating line.
    Weight-forward—9 weight—Sinking-tip line.
    Level—6 weight—Sinking line.
    Shooting head—12 weight—Floating line.
    Weight-forward—7 weight—Sinking-tip line.

11. a. (DT-5-F)

12. Graphite: superior sensitivity, very forgiving to casting flaws, relatively inexpensive, lightweight.

   Bamboo: superior craftsmanship, aesthetic, delicate presentations.

13. Single action and Multiplier.

14. Click-pawl drag and disc drag.

15. Stocking-foot waders and boot-foot waders.

16. 10 A.M. to 1 P.M. (or 10 P.M. to 1 A.M. if you're a night person).

   [*Teacher's Note:* ha-ha!]

17. Lug soles; felt soles; and studded or cleated soles.

18. Felt soles.

   Studded or cleated soles.

   Lug soles.

19. Brimmed hat, wading belt, wading staff, polarized sunglasses, etc.

   Double-taper

   Weight-forward, or single-taper

   Level line

20. 4X

   1X

   7X [*Note:* Subtract the diameter from .011 to get the X classification.]

21. 3X

   5X or 6X

   7X or 8X

   2X or 3X [*Note:* Divide hook size by 3 to get approximate tippet size.]

22. 12

   8 or 10

   18

   14 or 16 [*Note:* Multiply tippet size by 3, the opposite of Question 22.]

23. Superior insulation, good mobility, superior flexibility, easy streamside repairs, lightweight, streamlined for less wading drag, etc.

24. [*Teacher's Note:* This is a "cake" question—no wrong answers. . . although I've gotten some real doozies.]

26

A MIXED CREEL: MOVIES, SONGS, POEMS, QUOTATIONS, COLLECTIBLES, AND OTHER MISCELLANY

Creels'N'Reels, or Role-Casting

Name the movies in which fishing plays anything from a major to a minor part (answers on page 280):

1. Robert Redford's adaption of the Norman Maclean novella starring Tom Skerritt, Craig Sheffer, and Brad Pitt (and the film that was also praised for attracting considerable attention to fly-fishing).

2. Spencer Tracy portrays Hemingway's aging angler.

3. Spencer Tracy again, this time as a newspaperman trying to outfox heiress Myrna Loy (the scene in which Tracy, who claimed to be an expert fly-fisherman, demonstrates his lack of skill is worth the price of admission—or videotape rental).

4. Rock Hudson is another angling "expert" whom Paula Prentiss forces to enter a fishing tournament.

5. Walter Matthau and Jack Lemmon, the two curmudgeons of the title, trade hot insults while ice-fishing in Minnesota.

6. Henry Fonda bonds with his grandson (played by Doug McKeon) as they fish for a lunker named Walter.

7. Roy Scheider, Richard Dreyfuss, and Robert Shaw star in the Steven Spielberg horror movie that changes perspective about who (or what) is after whom.

8. Meryl Streep plays a fly-fishing guide who leads her family to defeat whitewater rapids and bad guys.

9. John Cazale is the Corleone brother who is given a lead sinker while out fishing on Lake Tahoe (and who ends up sleeping with the fishes).

10. James Stewart is a lawyer who postpones a fishing trip to represent Ben Gazzara in a murder case, in the film based on a novel by noted fishing author Robert Traver.

11. Jack Nicholson takes his fellow patients on a fishing trip (no, "Nurse Ratchet" doesn't refer to a reel's drag mechanism).

12. Roger Bowen plays the colonel with trout flies on his hat and a fly-tying vise on his desk in this Korean War comedy.

13. Frank Langella goes fly-fishing while wearing a business suit in this flick that starred Ellen Barkin and Laurence Fishburne.

14. The title character, the prototypical barefoot-boy-with-rod-of-cane, was played by Jackie Coogan, Mickey Rooney, and Ron Howard in three versions.

Answers to "Creels'N'Reels" Movie Quiz

(on page 279)

1. *A River Runs Through It* (1992)
2. *The Old Man and the Sea* (1958)
3. *Libeled Lady* (1936)
4. *Man's Favorite Sport?* (1963)
5. *Grumpy Old Men* (1994)
6. *On Golden Pond* (1981)
7. *Jaws* (1975)
8. *The River Wild* (1994)
9. *The Godfather, Part II* (1974)
10. *Anatomy of a Murder* (1959)
11. *One Flew Over the Cuckoo's Nest* (1975)
12. *M*A*S*H* (1970)
13. *Bad Company* (1995)
14. *Huckleberry Finn* (1931), *The Adventures of Huckleberry Finn* (1939), and *Huckleberry Finn* (1975)

Tackle Collectibles

Attics, yard sales, and other sites of buried treasures sometimes reveal antique rods, reels, lures, and other angling artifacts of a bygone era. Coming across something of interest in this fashion is often the first step to becoming a collector, but even if your search draws a blank, any number of dealers will be happy to help you get started.

Some collectors concentrate on bamboo rods produced by Dickerson, Gillum, and other "classic" rod-makers. Some enjoy collecting an example of every reel made in a particular series. Still others specialize in such esoterica as commercially-inspired lures (e.g., a spoon in the shape of a Schlitz beer bottle, circa 1950).

To read up on the subject, try *Coykendall's 2nd Sporting Collectibles Price Guide*, by Rolf Coykendall, Jr. (Lyons & Burford, 1994); *Fishing Tackle Antiques and Collectibles: Reference and Evaluation*, by Karl T. White (Holli Enterprises, 1992); *Collectors Guide to Antique Fishing Tackle*, by Silvio Calabi (Book Sales Inc., 1989); and *Identification and Value Guide to Old Fishing Lures and Tackle*, by Carl F. Luckey (Books Americana, 1991).

Another source of information are the displays at the American Museum of Fly Fishing in Manchester, Vermont. The museum also publishes such useful books as *A Treasury of Reels* by Jim Brown (American Museum of Fly Fishing, 1990).

As for dealers, many collectors highly recommend Len Codella's Heritage Sporting Collectibles, 22A Third St., Turners Falls, MA 01376; phone: (413) 863-3151; fax (413) 863-2123. Another established dealer is J. Garman, 316 Hartford Rd., Manchester, CT 06040; phone: (203) 643-2401. Other dealers can be found by their advertisements in fishing magazines, especially in the classified sections under "Rods and Reels" or "Tackle."

Ask too at your local tackle shop. Someone may be able to point you in the direction of a collector in your area who'll be only too pleased to share his or her knowledge. Even better, there may be a collectors' club too.

Like so many waterfowl paddling their way around lakes and ponds, flipper-footed fishermen are propelling themselves out on the water. They're using float tubes and belly boats, as inflatable flotation craft are more popularly known. It's the equivalent of wading in streams, a way to get out to where fish are, and, in many instances, a way to get away from back-cast-snagging foliage.

Float Tubes and Belly Boats

BY DOUG TUCKER-ECCHER

The variety of inflatable fishing rafts is tremendous. To determine which device will work best for you, several criteria must be evaluated: how much will the device be used; under which fishing conditions will it most often be used (small ponds, larger reservoirs, or running water); the size of the boat with regard to ease of inflation and deflation, space required for storage, and ease of transportation; available accessories; and cost.

And speaking of cost, the price of flippers and waders (which anglers wear while using these craft) must also be taken into account.

The most basic boats consist of a rubber truck inner tube that is covered with a nylon shell. A seat in the center of the boat that is attached to the shell

supports the angler's weight. Most boats also have a backrest, a smaller inner tube inflated in a zippered pocket on top of the shell back.

Although the original float tubes were round, most boats today have a more square shape. The shell is made so that more of the inner tube is at the boat's rear. Such additional rear buoyancy allows the angler to float in a more level fashion. It also prevents waves from splashing over the back of the tube, and it facilitates movement through the water. Basic boats retail from $50 to $250.

The next major evolution in float tubes came with the introduction of U-shaped boats. Virtually all have a lightweight polyurethane bladder that replaces the heavier inner tube. These U-shaped craft are more expensive ($200–$400) than their circular counterparts.

Any or all of the following features may be included, depending on the manufacturer and model. Each feature affects the boat's cost.

single, double, or triple stitching that reinforces the shell seams; extra-heavy zippers; nylon weight

side accessory pockets

stripping apron

Velcro® rod holders

adjustable seat

oversized main tube for people weighing over 250 pounds

fleece fly patch

backpack straps

anchor

lightweight blades (they reduce overall boat weight by about 50%)

Fishellaneous

The U.S. Fish and Wildlife Service predicts that the number of recreational fisherman in the

U.S. will increase by 90% over the next 40 years (cited in *Field & Stream,* March 1994).

The oldest largemouth bass ever recorded was 24 years old when he finally went to hawg heaven. Caught by Mark Lenegar on June 23, 1992, in Mariaville Lake, outside of Schenectady, New York, the bass measured 23 inches and weighed 6.78 pounds.

Lenegar, who caught the fish three times that morning, finally decided to keep it. He reported the tag number to the Department of Environmental Conservation (DEC), which confirmed the fish's history; the senior citizen had been tagged in 1980 when it was determined to have been at least 11 years old. To be certain, an otolith from the fish was sent to a research specialist. The expert declared Lenegar's bass to be the Methuselah of the species, by far the oldest on record (by 6 years).

[As reported in Nick Karas' "Outdoors" column, *New York Newsday*, March 7, 1993.]

For the past several years, the following states have designated one or more days in June to be "Free Fishing Days," when no licenses are required. The dates vary from year to year, and some restrictions and regulations apply. For details about this year, check with your fish and wildlife or conservation department:

Alabama; Arizona; Arkansas; California; Colorado; Connecticut; Delaware; District of Columbia; Florida; Georgia; Idaho; Illinois; Iowa; Kansas; Kentucky; Louisiana; Maine; Maryland; Massachusetts; Michigan; Minnesota; Missouri; Nevada; New Hampshire; New Jersey; New York; North Dakota; Ohio; Oklahoma; Oregon; Pennsylvania; Rhode Island; South Carolina; South Dakota; Tennessee; Texas; Utah; Vermont; Virginia; Washington, West Virginia; Wisconsin.

A survey conducted between 1990 and 1992 revealed that Thursdays are the most popular—or at least the most populous—days for fishing. 1.3% of Americans' leisure time on that day is spent fishing, as compared to 1.2% of leisure time on Saturdays and 1.1% on Sundays.

With regard to frequency, another survey indicates that among all people age seven or older who play a sport more than once a year, 31% freshwater anglers admitted to fishing 110 or more days a year, 38% between 25 and 109 days, and 30% between 6 and 24 days.

As for saltwater, the numbers were 23%, 39%, and 39%, respectively.

Only exercise walking, softball, and soccer ranked above freshwater fishing in the first category.

Some six years ago, a commercial for Britain's Yellow Pages telephone directory showed an elderly chap calling secondhand bookshops in an effort to track down a copy of an out-of-print book, *Fly Fishing* by J.R. Hartley. When the fellow finally locates one, the clerk asks the chap's name. "J.R. Hartley," is the answer.

The title and author were figments of some advertising copywriter's imagination, and there was a great public outcry when people who bombarded booksellers for the book learned of the hoax.

One enterprising publishing house came to the rescue. It hired a writer and a fishing expert to collaborate on the purported memoirs of an octogenarian angler. The result: a best-seller that spawned a sequel.

Fly Fishing by J.R. Hartley was published in this country by HarperCollins in 1993.

You can hang a memorable catch on your wall even after releasing it. Mike Mahoney, a Billings, Montana, artist, will turn your photograph of any varieties of trout, salmon, grayling, and char into a life-size watercolor portrait on tag paper. Even if the fish escaped your camera, Mahoney can replicate it through your description. The painting will also include a line about the fish's vital statistics and when and where you caught it. The charge is approximately $400 (and possibly more for fish in excess of 32 inches, if you should be so lucky!) plus shipping.

Trout Portraits, P.O. Box 1502, Billings, MT 59103-4564; phone: (800) 353-0055.

The *Angling Report* is a monthly newsletter that promises "bias-free" information to help us make better informed decisions with regard to travel agents, outfitters, guides, and lodges throughout the world. The emphasis is on fly-fishing and light-tackle saltwater fishing in the Rocky Mountain states and Alaska, Canada, and Latin America. Claiming no commercial affiliations, the newsletter includes subscriber reports that may or may not suggest "stay-away" conclusions. The annual $39 subscription will get you the newsletter, a hotline telephone number for up-to-date Rocky Mountain stream reports, and other information.

The Angling Report, 9300 S. Dadeland Blvd., Suite 605, Miami, FL 33156-2721; phone: (305) 670-1918.

Landing (Inter)Nets and Other Cyberspace Byways

Tens of thousands of fishing enthusiasts are out there to correspond with. All you need is a computer, a modem, and the willingness to join one of the information superhighway networks.

Among Internet's USENET bulletin boards is "alt.fishing", "rec.outdoors.fishing", "rec.outdoors.flyfish", and, in an E-mail vein, "FLYFISH.listserv".

By the time this book ends up in your hands, many other networks are likely to be created. Need a guide? Just place a message on existing network bulletin boards.

In the CD-ROM and software area:

FLYbase offers an interactive program concerning entomological information based on geographic area and time of year. Included are hatch charts, patterns, and average fishing conditions. Your own observations can be recorded, and some "stream-specific" databases are available. FLYbase requires an IBM-compatible and uses 1.6 megabytes of memory; the cost is about $75, plus shipping.

FLYbase, Tom Dewey & Associates, P.O. Box 672, Coudersport, PA 16915; phone: (814) 274-7981.

Packaged in a replica of a tackle box, Gone Fishin™ simulates a day's fishing on Lake Ontario's Bay of Quinte. Among the game's elements to be taken into account are fish behavior, weather, and water temperature over 20 "hot spots" along 50 miles of shoreline. If that sounds daunting, be advised that you'll have 30 lures to choose from. Available for IBM/compatibles.

AMTEX Softwear Corporation, P.O. Box 572, Belleville, Ontario K8N 5B2 Canada; phone: (800) 810-7345.

HyperComplete Angler's program includes a reference library of flies, a compendium of patterns for tying them, and a journal in which to record relevant data about your fishing experiences. HyperComplete Angler will run on any Macintosh using System 7.0, including the Powerbook; IBM-compatible PCs need Windows 3.1 or higher, a Super VGA card, and a Windows-compatible mouse. The price is about $40.

HyperComplete Angler, Dunworth & Hagen Co., 998 Centre St., Boston, MA 02130; phone: (617) 983-9260.

Fish Fax isn't exactly a computer program, but it's close enough to that category to be mentioned in the same breath. The service faxes its subscribers timely data on fly-fishing in Yellowstone Park, Montana, and parts of Idaho, plus a column containing useful information.

The material is faxed out on Tuesday evenings each week between the beginning of June and mid-September. For the $25/season service, subscribers also receive a booklet that contains maps of relevant rivers and streams. All you need is a fax machine or a computer capable of receiving faxes.

FISH FAX, 500 S. Higgins, Missoula, MT 59808; phone: (800) 654-1136; fax: (406) 523-5221.

Learning Fly Fishing, an entry-level CD-ROM tutorial on the subject, covers such expected areas as tackle, flies, knots, casting, and fishing. It also has an extensive glossary, a section on species of fish associated with fly-fishing, and a section giving the sport's history (including, however, the erroneous statement that the word "angling" came from fishermen holding rods at a 45-degree angle. . . sorry, folks, but "angle" refers to a hook).

The first of a series of fishing CD-ROMs, Learning Fly Fishing, which retails for $49.95, will be followed by others on bass, saltwater fishing, and teaching youngsters.

For further information: EE Multimedia Productions, 1455 West, 2200 South, Suite 100, Salt Lake City, UT 84119; phone: (800) 826-6810; fax: (801) 973-0184.

In the fun 'n' games department, there's Bassin' Black Bass with Hank Parker, an interactive game that works on Super Nintendo systems. Lots of fishing spots and realistic fish movements teach players about the sport while they play.

Hot-B USA, Inc., 1255 Post St., Suite 1040, San Francisco, CA 94109; phone: (415) 567-9501.

The TNN Bass Tournament of Champions comes in versions for Super Nintendo and SEGA Genesis. Players select the lake and weather conditions, then compete against tournament "pros." If you're not landing lunkers right away, you can change tackle and bait (you're given $100 play money to spend on additional rods and lures at a TNN Bass Pro Shop). There's even a tournament ladder to earn your way up toward the "Classic." *The Ultimate Fishing Guide*'s resident games-player gave the game a high rating for its graphics and challenges.

Not surprisingly, it's available through Bass Pro Shop.

Singing Scales

Goin' Fishin' is a collection of "classic" country and novelty fishing songs by such a mixed bag of singers as Bing Crosby, Bobby Bare, Tennessee Ernie Ford, Andy Griffith, and the Austin Lounge Lizards. The CD retails for about $15 and the cassette about $11, both plus shipping.

Fish Head Productions, P.O. Box 281, Marengo, IL 60152; phone: (815) 568-FISH.

Tag-and-Retain

Once upon a time, when hopping around the planet was less a routine occurrence than it now is, travelers adorned their luggage with decorative decals and stickers that commemorated memorable destinations.

Steamer Trunk Collection has revived that practice with its Rod Case Memory Decals. More than U.S. 150 rivers are available, together with handsome graphics. Others, as well as saltwater sites, are on the way. The cost is $2 apiece.

Steamer Trunk Collection, 51 Chestnut Grove Rd., Shippensburg, PA 17257.

Ye Olde Angling

History is well served by the efforts of Ken Reinard, the Colonial Angler. Wearing Ben Franklin-look-alike garb, Reinard uses as tackle only his own replicas of eighteenth-century angling gear, from silk line to handmade hooks with flies tied according to centuries-old patterns.

For information about The Colonial Angler's program of demonstrations and lectures, contact Kenneth Reinard, 905 Hannah Rd., Lititz, PA 17543; phone: (717) 738-1815.

I Whistle a Happy Tuna

If you enjoy puns, here are some fish- and fishing-inspired song titles. If you don't enjoy puns, skip(jack) ahead:

Hit the Road, Amberjack
Somewhere Over the Salmo gairdneri
If They Asked Me, I Could Fight a Brook
You Stepped Out of a Bream
When Sunfish Get Blue
Get Me to the Perch on Time
Sweet Pike from Betsy
Salmon 'Chanted Evening
While Trolling Through the Park One Day
The graduation march for a school of fish:
Pompano and Circumstances.
. . . and on the end of the line: Schubert's lieder

Along with accounts of jackalopes and other fabulous critters, American Western lore gave rise to tales of fur-bearing fish. The legends arose during the 1930s, when people reported sighting the results of (1) a hair tonic spill into a Rocky Mountain stream; or (2) several randy male trout paying a midnight visit to a mink farm.

Quotations of an Angling Nature

Angling will prove to be so pleasant, that it will prove to be like virtue, a reward to itself.

ISAAK WALTON, THE COMPLEAT ANGLER

It was an employment for his idle time, which was then not idly spent, a rest to his mind, a cheerer of his spirits, a diverter of sadness, a calmer of unquiet thoughts, a moderator of passions, a procurer of contentedness.

ISAAK WALTON ON A FRIEND'S DEVOTION TO FISHING

Solomon in his proverbs sayeth that a glad spirit maketh a flowering age, that is to say, a fair age ad long, and since it is so, I ask this question, "What are the means and causes which lead a man into a merry spirit?" Truly in my best judgement, it seems that they are good sports and honest games. . . and therefore, I will now choose among four good sports and honorable pastimes—to wit, among hunting, hawking, fishing and fowling. The best, in my simple judgement, is fishing, called angling with a rod and a line, and a hook.

DAME JULIANA BERNERS, "TREATYSE OF FYSSHINGE WYTH AN ANGLE," FROM THE BOOK OF ST. ALBANS

If an angler catches fish, surely there is no man merrier in his spirit than he is in his spirit. Thus have I proved, according to my purpose, that the sport and game of angling is the true means and cause that brings a man into a merry spirit.

DAME JULIANA BERNERS, "TREATYSE OF
FYSSHINGE WYTH AN ANGLE," FROM
THE BOOK OF ST. ALBANS

———

Some circumstantial evidence is very strong, as when you find a trout in the milk.

HENRY DAVID THOREAU

———

Some men fish all their lives without knowing it is not really the fish they are after.

HENRY DAVID THOREAU

———

Time is but the stream that I go a-fishing in. I drink at it; but while I drink I see the sandy bottom and detect how shallow it is. Its thin current slides away, but eternity remains. I would drink deeper; fish in the sky, whose bottom is pebbly with stars.

HENRY DAVID THOREAU

———

Beauty without grace is the hook without the bait.

RALPH WALDO EMERSON, BEAUTY

———

"They're a funny fish," I told him. "They aren't here until they come."

ERNEST HEMINGWAY, TO HAVE AND
HAVE NOT

———

Give a man a fish, and you feed him for a day. Teach a man to fish, and you feed him for a lifetime.

CHINESE PROVERB

———

I went out to the hazelwood,
Because a fire was in my head,
And cut and peeled a hazel wand,
And hooked a berry to the thread;
And when white moths were on the wing,
And moth-like stars were flickering out,
I dropped the berry in a stream
And caught a little silver trout.

WILLIAM BUTLER YEATS, THE SONG OF
WANDERING AENGUS

———

"It's certain there are trout somewhere
And maybe I shall take a trout
If but I do not seem to care."

WILLIAM BUTLER YEATS, THE THREE
BEGGARS

———

Fish die belly-upward and ride to the surface; it is their way of falling.

ANDRÉ GIDE

———

No human being, however great, or powerful, is ever so free as a fish.

JOHN RUSKIN

———

The gods do not deduct from man's allotted span the hours spent in fishing.

ATTRIBUTED TO A BABYLONIAN PROVERB

———

Overwork, n. A dangerous disorder affecting high public functionaries who want to go fishing.

Ambrose Bierce, The Devil's Dictionary

Fly fishing may be a very pleasant amusement; but angling or float fishing I can only compare to a stick and a string, with a worm at one end and a fool at the other.

Attributed to Samuel Johnson

That hook I love that is in compass round
Like to the print that Pegasus did make.
With horned hoofe upon Thessalian ground;
His shank should neither be too short nor long,
His point not over-sharp, nor yet too dull:
The substance good that may endure from wrong;
His needle slender, yet both round and full,
Made of the right Iberian metal strong,
That will not stretch nor break at every pull,
Wrought smooth and clean without crack or knot
And bearded like the wild Arabian goat.

John Dennys, "Hooks," from Secrets of Angling (1613)

This sort of angling, with its concomitants, is the most gentle, ingenious, pleasant and profitable part of the innocent recreation of angling; to the perfect accomplishment of which is required not only good affection and frequent practice, but also diligent observation and considerable judgment; yea, some rules and directions too, especially in the choice of materials and mixing of colors for flies.

Robert Howlett, "On Artificial Fly-Angling," from The Angler's Sure Guide (1706)

Bait the hook well: this fish will bite.

Shakespeare, Much Ado About Nothing (Act II, Scene 3)

Give me mine angle—we'll to the river.
There, my music playing far off, I will betray
Tawny-finned fishes; my bended hook shall pierce
Their slimy jaws; and as I draw them up,
I'll think them every one an Antony,
And say "Ah ha! Y'are caught."

Shakespeare, Antony and Cleopatra (Act II, Scene 5)

T'was merry when
You wagered on your angling, when your diver
Did hang a salt fish on his hook, which he
With fervency drew up. . .

Shakespeare, Antony and Cleopatra (Act II, Scene 5)

A man may fish with the worm that hath eat of a king, and eat of the fish that hath fed of that worm.

Shakespeare, Hamlet (Act IV, Scene 3)

Nothing is so clean as a fish.

Welsh proverb

The bigger the river, the bigger the fish.

Portuguese proverb

The biggest fish he ever caught were those that got away.

Eugene Field, Our Biggest Fish

Fish must swim thrice—once in the water, a second time in the sauce, and a third time in the wine in the stomach.

JOHN RAY, ENGLISH PROVERBS

———

All fish are not caught with flies.

JOHN LYLY, EUPHUES

———

You must lose a fly to catch a trout.

GEORGE HERBERT, JACULA PRUDENTUM

———

If you swear, you will catch no fish.

ENGLISH PROVERB

———

Of all the world's enjoyments
That ever valued were,
There's none of our employments
With fishing can compare.

THOMAS D'URFEY, PILLS TO PURGE
MELANCHOLY

———

Still he fishes that catches one.

THOMAS FULLER, GNOMOLOGIA

———

When the wind is in the East,
Then the fishes bite the least;
When the wind is in the West,
Then the fishes bite the best;
When the wind is in the North,
Then the fishes do come forth;
When the wind is in the South,
It blows the bait in the fish's mouth.

OLD ENGLISH PROVERB

———

The trout. . . must be caught with tickling.

SHAKESPEARE, TWELFTH NIGHT (ACT
II, SCENE 5)

———

No taking of trout with dry breeches.

CERVANTES, DON QUIXOTE

———

Come live with me and be my love,
And we will some new pleasures prove
Of golden sands, and crystal brooks,
With silken lines, and silver hooks.

There will the river whispering run
Warmed by thy eyes, more than the sun.
And there the enamored fish will stay,
Begging themselves they may betray.

When thou will swim in that live bath,
Each fish, which every channel hath,
Will amorously to thee swim,
Gladder to catch thee, than thou him.

If thou, to be so seen, be loath,
By sun or moon, thou darkenest both,
And if myself have leave to see,
I will not need their light, having thee.

Let others freeze with angling reeds,
And cut their legs with shells and reeds,
Or treacherously poor fish beset,
With strangling snare, or windowy net.

Let coarse bold hands from slimey nest
The bedded fish in banks out-wrest,
Or curious traitors, sleave-silk flies
Bewitch poor fishes' wandering eyes.

For thee, thou needest no such deceit,
For thou thyself are thine own bait;
That fish, that is not catch'd thereby,
Alas, is wiser far than I.

JOHN DONNE, THE BAIT

———

The fishers also shall mourn, and all they that
cast angle into the brooks shall lament, and they
that spread nets upon the waters shall languish.

ISAIAH 19:8

———

Canst thou drawest out leviathan with a fish-hook?
Or press down his tongue with a cord?
Canst thou put a ring in his nose?
Or bore a jaw through with a hook?

JOB 41:1-2

———

For he was astonished, and all that were with
him, at the draught of the fishes which they had
taken.

LUKE 5:9

———

Simon Peter saith unto them, I go a-fishing.
They say unto him, We also go with thee. They
went forth, and entered into a ship immedi-
ately; and that night they caught nothing.

JOHN 21:3

———

Lord, give me grace to catch a fish so big that
even I, when talking about it afterwards, shall
have no cause to lie.

ANONYMOUS

———

27

MAIL-ORDER HOUSES AND TACKLE SHOPS

Mail-Order Tackle Shop Catalogs

Angler's Covey
917 W. Colorado Ave.
Colorado Springs, CO 80905
(800) 753-4746

Remarkably comprehensive for its relatively small size, this catalog presents essential tackle, accessories, clothing, and reference material for fly-fishing.

Angler's Workshop
P.O. Box 1044
Woodland, WA 98674
(206) 225-9445
fax: (206) 225-8641

Components for rod-building and fly-tying, as well as ready-made fresh- and saltwater tackle.

The Bass Pond
P.O. Box 82
Littleton, CO 80160-0082
(800) 327-5014
fax: (303) 730-8932

The imaginative catalog of a firm that's devoted to a fast-growing fly-fishing sub-specialty. Mailings also include a very useful newsletter.

Bass Pro Shops
1935 S. Campbell
Springfield, MO 65898-0123
(800) BASS-PRO

One of the giants of the retail tackle world, Bass Pro Shops issues a huge (400+ pages) general catalog, plus specialty and sale mailings. The store itself, with its fish tanks and demonstration areas, is a major draw for anglers from all over the country.

Dan Bailey's Fly Shop
P.O. Box 1019
Livingston, MT 59047
(800) 356-4052

A major "player" in the western fly-fishing game, Dan Bailey's offers an authoritative catalog to match. It includes a particularly attractive display of flies, and it includes a listing of vacation opportunities.

L.L. Bean, Inc.
Freeport, ME 04033-0001
(800) 221-4221
fax: (207) 797-8867

This venerable store has achieved the status of an outdoors institution, with its own "house-brand" tackle and accessories (almost exclusively fly-fishing) and its "classic" styles of clothing and footwear.

Cabela's
812 13th Avenue
Sidney, NE 69160
(800) 237-4444

Cabela's is a large mail-order house specializing in freshwater fishing. Its comprehensive and eminently browseable catalog displays a large line of tackle, accessories, and clothing. After years of including fly equipment in its omnibus catalog, Cabella's began a separate and quite complete offering in 1994.

Captain Harry's Fishing Supply
100 NE 11th St.
Miami, FL 33132
(800) 327-4088

This catalog is a complete offering of saltwater (including big-game fishing) tackle and accessories.

Choice Collections
6109 Remount Road
North Little Rock, AR 72118
(800) 532-2767

A slim catalog offers what's indicated to be a select number of baitcasting, spinning and fly rods, lures, accessories, and clothing. The firm annotates its choices in a chatty and enlightening text.

Cold Spring Anglers
P.O. Box 129
Carlisle, PA 17013-0129
(800) 248-8937
fax: (717) 245-2081

This catalog lists standard fly-fishing and tying items, but with helpful accompanying explanatory captions. There's also information on guided fishing opportunities along Pennsylvania's limestone spring creeks.

English Angling Trappings
P.O. Box 8885
New Fairfield, CT 06812
(203) 746-4121
fax: (203) 746-1348

Its no-frills fly-fishing catalog isn't as awe-inspiring as the firm's name might imply. The catalog has a nice chatty and useful style.

Feather-Craft Fly Fishing
8307 Manchester Road
P.O. Box 19904
St. Louis, MO 63144
(800) 659-1707
fax: (314) 963-7876

The chatty tabloid-style newsletter catalog gives lots of advice about fly-fishing tackle, accessories, and fly-tying material products, both popular and hard-to-get.

Fishing Creek Outfitters
RD 1, Box 310-1
Benton, PA 17814
(800) 548-0093

Helpful descriptions of fly-fishing essentials. The firm's fishing school includes one-day beginner's and intermediate programs, and there are guided trips around the eastern Pennsylvania area.

Flies Away Publishers
2124 Nevada
Liberal, KS 67901
(800) 556-9359

Obviously inspired by the J. Peterman Company catalog's exotic wearables (and affected copywriting), this offering of two dozen or so selected fly-fishing items nevertheless picks up on some of the best that's available.

Flyfisher's Paradise
2603 East College Ave.
State College, PA 16801
(814) 234-4189
fax: (814) 238-3686

A selection of fly-fishing essentials: tackle, accessories, tying equipment, and books and videos. There's also a page about fishing opportunities in the State College area.

The Fly Shop
4140 Churn Creek Road
Redding, CA 96002
(800) 669-FISH

A slim catalog with the usual fly-fishing essentials, but also with an intriguing section on domestic and international vacations.

Gander Mountain
P.O. Box 248
Wilmot, WI 53192-0248
(800) 558-9410
Fax: (800) 533-2828

Better known for its outdoors clothing and camping gear, Gander Mountain now offers a limited but essential selection of freshwater bait-fishing and fly-fishing tackle and accessories.

The Global Flyfisher
2849 W. Dundee Rd., Suite 132
Northbrook, IL 60062-2501

(800) 457-7026
fax: (708) 291-3486

Billing its merchandise as "essentials for the traveling flyfisher," this catalog contains a limited but select choice of products. There is, however, a wide and varied collection of books and videos on fishing vacations, as well as a travel service.

Gorilla and Sons
Box 2309
Bellingham, WA 98227
(800) 246-7455
fax: (800) 647-8801

A competitively-priced selection of freshwater and saltwater baitfishing and flyfishing products in a well-illustrated full-color catalog.

The Hook & Hackle Company
7 Kaycee Loop Road
Plattsburgh, NY 12901
(518) 561-5893
fax: (518) 561-0336

This no-frills catalog presents fly-fishing essentials. Its prices are as competitive or better than most other firms.

K & K Flyfisher's Supply
8643 Grant
Overlook Park, KS 66212
(800) 795-8118
fax: (913) 341-1252

Fly-fishing essentials presented in a well-illustrated catalog with a friendly feel.

Kauffman's Streamborn
P.O. Box 2303
Portland, OR 97223
(800) 442-FLY

An important fly-fishing force in the Pacific Northwest, Kauffman's issues a suitably authoritative and hand-somely-illustrated catalog of tackle and accessories.

Kettle Creek Tackle Shop
HCR 62, Box 140
Renovo, PA 17754
(717) 923-1416
fax: (717) 923-1420

Phil Baldacchino bills his Kettle Creek Tackle Shop as "Pennsylvania's largest, most complete fly shop." The no-frills catalog features a nice line of largely economically-priced items. A telephone phone service offers information about local stream conditions.

Madison River Fishing Company
109 Main Street
P.O. Box 627
Ennis, MT 59729
(800) 227-7127
fax: (406) 682-4744

Fly-fishing items from the heart of "Yellowstone Country" in a comprehensive catalog. The firm's services include instruction as well as guiding through parts of Montana.

Murray's Fly Shop
P.O. Box 156
Edinburg, VA 22824
(703) 984-4212
fax: (703) 984-4895

A nice "homey" but selective catalog with an emphasis on trout and bass fishing in the Shenandoah Valley area of Virginia. Murray's also arranges guided trips through the region, as well as some international fresh- and saltwater trips.

Muskie Fever
P.O. Box 32011

Minneapolis, MN 55432
(800) 458-1205

A slim but thorough listing of tackle, accessories, books, and everything else for the muskelunge set, this catalog sometimes includes helpful essays on tackle manufacturing and use.

Netcraft Fishing Tackle
2800 Tremainsville Road
Toledo, OH 43613
(800) NETCRAFT
customer service: (419) 472-9826
fax: (419) 472-8058

The catalog, which has a homespun 1940s-graphics look, offers primarily baitcasting, although there is some saltwater and fly-fishing tackle, and marine equipment too. Its prices are toward the reasonable side of the scale.

Offshore Angler
1935 S. Campbell
Springfield, MO 65898-0140
(800) 663- 9131

The saltwater "arm" of Bass Pro Shop, the catalog contains an ample selection of tackle, accessories, and clothing for inshore, offshore, and surf-fishing.

On The Fly
3628 Sage Dr.
Rockford, IL 61111
(815) 877-0090

A whopping 120 pages long at the latest count, this catalog may be the largest in the fly-fishing part of the world. The lack of illustrations doesn't matter, because the items are well described. So are the books and videos. The "how-to" knot-tying drawings that are interspersed throughout the booklet lend a nice (and useful) touch.

Orvis
Route 7A
P.O. Box 798
Manchester, VT 05254-0798
(800) 541-3541
fax: (703) 343-7053

Top-of-the-line own-label tackle, accessories, and clothing marketed as part of an upscale "outdoors" lifestyle. Orvis has retail stores in Boston, Chicago, Chestnut Hill (Pennsylvania), Houston, Jackson Hole (Wyoming), Manchester (Vermont), New York City, Philadelphia, Roanoke (Virginia), San Francisco, Skokie (Illinois), Tysons Corner (Virginia), and Williamsville (New York). There are three stores in England: London, Harrogate (Yorkshire), and Stockbridge (Hampshire). In addition, more than 100 tackle shops across the country are "authorized dealers."

Outer Banks Outfitters
Highway 70 East
P.O. Box Drawer 500
Beaufort, NC 28516
(800) 682-2225
fax: (919) 728-6988

A mixed bag of saltwater fishing and marine supplies, from rods and reels to bathing suits to such electronic gear as radios and autopilots.

Pennsylvania Outdoor Warehouse
1508 Memorial Avenue
Williamsport, PA 17701
(800) 441-7685
fax: (717) 322-5281

A comprehensive color-illustrated catalog with an unusual format: the tackle, accessories, etc., are on one side; turn the catalog over and you'll find 22 pages of fly-tying material on the other side.

Fred Reese's Trout Shop
220 Thompson St.
Jersey Shore, PA 17740
(717) 398-3016

A "no-frills" fly-fishing and fly-tying catalog with brief but helpful descriptions of products. The store offers information on Pine Creek Valley and other regional trout waters.

The Surfcaster
P.O. Box 1731
Darien, CT 06820-1731
(800) 551-SURF
fax: (203) 831-0307

As the name suggests, items for saltwater lure- and fly-throwers, with helpful photos and line drawings.

Urban Angler Ltd.
118 East 25 Street, 3rd floor
New York, NY 10010
(212) 979-7600
fax: (212) 473-4020

Nestled in a Manhattan office building, this fly-fishing firm issues a well-annotated catalog of choice tackle, accessories, clothing, and fly-tying material. Supplementary newsletters are turning it into something of a mini-magazine.

Westbank Anglers
P.O. Box 523
Teton Village, WY 83025
(800) 922-3734

A handsome full-color fly-fishing catalog with particularly clear photographs of a wide range of fresh- and saltwater flies. Its inset photos focus on the Jackson Hole region, "home water" to this company.

Specialty Catalogs

Angler's
4955 East 2900 North
Murtaugh, ID 83344
(800) 657-8040

A catalog full of such gift items as jewelry, T-shirts, stationery, calendars, and signs, primarily of interest to fly-fishing enthusiasts.

Angler's Expressions
P.O. Box 3136
Boise, ID 83703
(800) 634-3313
fax: (208) 343-9414

A limited selection of stationery, mugs, jewelry, and other gift goods, as well as prints and other sporting art.

Barlow's Tackle Shop
Box 830369
Richardson, TX 75080
(214) 231-5982
fax: (214) 690-4044

A comprehensive selection of plastic worms, lures, fly-tying, and rod-building supplies, all for the do-it-yourself set.

Blue Ridge Rod Company
P.O. Box 6268
Annapolis, MD 21401
(410) 224-4072
fax: (410) 573-0993

Fly rod blanks and components and rod-building tools.

Hagen's
Rte. 2, Box 82
Mitchell, SD 57301
(800) 541-4586
fax: (605) 996-8946

A "component catalog" for the do-it-yourselfer, the publication contains all the fixings to make jigs, spoons, spinners, and other lures.

Jann's Sportsman's Supplies
P.O. Box 4315
Toledo, OH 43609
(800) 346-6590
fax: (419) 536-9443

Another catalog for handy hobbyists: components to build rods, mold jigs and other lures, and tie flies.

Terminal Tackle Co.
P.O. Box 427
Kings Park, NY 11754
(516) 269-6005

Primarily saltwater in orientation, this catalog offers hooks, swivels, sinkers, leaders, and everything else that belongs at the "business end" of a line.

Other Mail–Order Houses

Fly Fisher's Paradise
2603 E. College
State College, PA 16801
(814) 234-4189

Frontier Anglers
P.O. Box 111
Dilon, MT 59725
(800) 228-5263

Henrickson Rod Company
3825 Hollow Creek
Benbrook, TX 76116
(800) 933-7637
fax: (817) 738-0609

Henry's Fork Anglers
P.O. Box 487
St. Anthony, ID 83445
(208) 558-7525

Hunters Angling Supplies
1 Central Square
New Boston, NH 03070
(800) 331-8558

International Angler
504 Freeport Rd.
Pittsburg, PA 15215
(800) 782-4222

Marriott's Fly Fishing
2700 W. Orangethorpe
Fullerton, CA 92633
(800) 367-2299 (California)
(800) 535-6633 (elsewhere)

Swallow's Nest
2308 6th Ave.
Seattle, WA 98121
(800) 676-4041

Tackle Stores

In the course of the compilation of the following roster, one aspect of the research became clear: Manufacturers of fly-fishing equipment are not at all reluctant about sharing the names and locations of dealers who sell their products. On the other hand, makers of other kinds of tackle are not at all so forthcoming.

Someone familiar with the industry suggested the reason: Unlike fly tackle manufacturers (who sell directly to dealers), makers of other types of gear sell to wholesalers, who then distribute the goods to retail outlets. These outlets include general sporting goods stores, hardware stores, and other multi-ware retailers; the "middleman" wholesalers aren't keen about their competitors discovering the names and locations of places where they too might sell their products.

In addition to the following state-by-state, municipality-by-municipality list, you can check telephone directory classified pages (under "Fishing Tackle," "Sporting Goods," or "Bait Shops") for other shops in whatever city or town you're interested.

Other places to find fishing tackle are the sporting-goods sections of Wal-Mart, Kmart, Target, and similar chains. Most contain well-stocked shelves and racks of rods, reels, and other fishing tackle. Seldom, however, will you find the kind of technical information and the knowledge about local fishing spots that you will get from tackle shops.

U.S. CITIES

ALABAMA

Birmingham: Angler's Paradise
Birmingham: Mark's Outdoor
   Sports

Huntsville: The Fisherman's
   Choice
Huntsville: Fred's Custom Roads
   & Flies
Northport: Woods & Water
Jasper: Riverside Company
Jasper: Sportsman's Center

ALASKA

Anchorage: McAfree's Fly Shop
Anchorage: Gary King's Sporting
   Goods
Anchorage: Mountain View Sports
   Center
Anchorage: The Rod and Reel
Fairbanks: Alaska Fly Shop
Ketchikan: Alaska Wilderness
   Outfitting
Kodiak: Cy's Sporting Goods &
   Outfitters

ARIZONA

Eagar: X Diamond Fly Shop
Flagstaff: Flagstaff Rod & Tackle
Marble Canyon: Lees Ferry
   Anglers
Phoenix: Canyon Creek Anglers
Phoenix: Fisherman's Choice
Scottsdale: Fisherman's Line
Tempe: Arizona Fly Fishing
Tempe: Arizona Outdoors
Tucson: Tight Lines Flyfishing

ARKANSAS

Fayetteville: Bancroft & Tabor
Fayetteville: Southern Sporting
   Goods
Fort Smith: The Woodsman

Hot Springs: Fly Best Fly Fishing
Centers
Little Rock: Arkansas Rod & Reel
Little Rock: Fly Best Fly Fishing
Centers
Little Rock: Gene Lockwood
Sports
Little Rock: Ozark Angler
Mountain Home: Blue Ribbon
Flies
Stuttgart: Mack's Sports Shop

CALIFORNIA

Albany: Fish First!
Arcata: Time Flies Tackle Shop
& Guide Service
Arnold: White Pines Outdoors
Bakersfield: Bigfoot
Mountaineering
Beaumont: Pappy's Bait & Tackle
Belmont: The Caddis Fly Shop
Bishop: Brock's Sporting Goods
Bishop: Culver's Sports & Spirits
Bridgeport: Ken's Sporting Goods
Burney: Vaughan's Sporting
Goods & Fly Shop
Chico: Chico Fly Shop
Chico: Powell Fly Shop
Citrus Heights: Fly Fishing
Specialties
Compton: Rainbow Bait & Tackle
Eureka: Eureka Fly Shop
Fair Oaks: Wilderness Exchange
Fall River Mills: Rick's Lodge Fly
Shop
Fall River Mills: Shasta Angler
Fremont: Angler's Bait and Tackle
Fresno: Herb Bauer Sporting
Goods

Fullerton: Bob Marritt's Fly
Fishing Store
Gridley: Butte Creek Outfitters
Half Moon Bay: Hill Top Grocery
& Fishing Supply
Irvine: East Fork Fly Fishing
Store
La Canada: Sport Chalet #2
Lafayette: Fly Fishing Outfitters
Larkspur: The Selective Angler
Los Altos: The Midge Fly Shop
Los Angeles: New York Hardware
Trading Co.
Los Angeles: Sport Chalet #12
Los Gatos: Upstream Flyfishing
Mammoth Lakes: Hope It Floats
Mammoth Lakes: Kittredge Sport
Shop
Mammoth Lakes: Trout Fitter
Marina Del Rey: Sport Chalet
#11
Modesto: E. Crosby
Tobacconist/Outfitter
Modesto: Sierra Anglers Fly Shop
Montclair: Sports Chalet
Napa: Sweeney's Sports
Nevada City: Nevada City Anglers
Oxnard: Sport Chalet #14
Pleasant Hill: Creative Sports
Redding: The Fly Shop
Redding: Hollister's Bait & Tackle
Redwood City: Herb & Jim's
Sports Shop
Ridgecrest: High Sierra Fly Fisher
Riverside: Riverside Ski & Sport
Sacramento: American Fly
Fishing Co.
Sacramento: Broadway Bait Rod
& Gun
Sacramento: Kiene's Fly Shop

Salinas: Monterey County
Petroleum
San Bruno: The Ultimate Fly
Shop
San Diego: Stroud Tackle
San Francisco: Fly Fishing
Outfitters
San Franciso: Hi's Tackle Box
San Francisco: Orvis
San Francisco: San Francisco
Flyfishers Supply
San Francisco: Sullivan's Sport
Shop
San Jose: Reed's Sports Shop
San Rafael: Western Sports Shop
Santa Barbara: Hook Line &
Sinker
Santa Clara: Cope & McPhetres
Santa Clarita: Sports Chalet #10
Santa Fe Springs: Sav-On Tackle
Santa Rosa: King's Western
Angler
Sonoma: Sportsmen
Headquarters
Soquel: Ernie's Casting Pond
Spring Valley: Bob's Bait &
Tackle
Stockton: Knowls
Thousand Oaks: Malibu
Fish'n'Tackle
Torrence: Huber's Hackle Heaven
Truckee: Mountain Hardware
Truckee: Tourist Liquor &
Sporting Goods
Van Nuys: Fisherman's Spot!
West Hills: Sport Chalet #15
West Sacramento: Keith
Warkentine
Yreka: Don's Sporting Goods

COLORADO

Alamont: Willow Fly Anglers
Antonito: Cottonwood Meadows Fly Shop
Aspen: Mark Justin Outdoors Guide & Outfitters
Aspen: Oxbow Outfitters
Aspen: Pomeroy Sporting Goods
Aurora: Alpine Anglers
Basalt: Frying Pan Angler
Basalt: Taylor Creek Angling Services
Boulder: Front Range Anglers
Boulder: Gart Bros. Sporting Goods
Boulder: McGuckin Sporting Goods
Breckenridge: Breckenridge Outfitters
Breckenridge: Mountain Angler Ltd.
Canon City: Royal Gorge Anglers
Colorado Springs: Angler's Covey
Colorado Springs: Broadmore Sporting Classics
Colorado Springs: C/S Angler
Creede: Ramble House
Denver: Executive Angler
Denver: The Flyfisher Ltd.
Denver: Gart Bros. Sporting Goods
Denver: The Trout Fisher
Englewood: Complete Angler
Englewood: Royal Stevens Ltd.
Englewood: Uncle Miltie's Tackle Box
Estes Park: Estes Angler
Evergreen: Blue Quill Angler
Fort Collins: Longs Drug Store
Fort Collins: Gart Bros. Sporting Goods
Fort Collins: Rocky Mountain Fly Shop
Fort Collins: St. Peters Fly Shop
Frisco: Columbine Outfitters
Glenwood Springs: Roaring Fork Anglers
Grand Junction: Big Creek Fly Shop
Hayden: Dry Creek Anglers
Lake City: Dan's Fly Shop
Lake City: The Sportsman
Lakewood: Colorado Angler
Littleton: Anglers All
Longmont: St. Vrain Angler
Loveland: Bob's Fly Tying Specialties
Meaker: Elk Creek Lodge
Meredith: Fryingpan River Ranch
Montrose: Cimarron Creek
Pueblo: T & M Sporting Goods
South Fork: Rainbow Lodge & Grocery
Steamboat Springs: Buggywhip's Fish & Float Service
Steamboat Springs: Straightline Products
Tabernash: Nelson Fly & Tackle Shop
Vail: Gart Bros. Sporting Goods
Vail: Vail Rod & Gun Club

CONNECTICUT

Berlin: Mickey Finn's
Bolton: Hop River Fly Shop
Bozrah: Colonial Sports
Bristol: Fall Mountain Sports
Bristol: Quiet Sports
Brookfield: Saltwater Angler
Cornwall Bridge: Housatonic Meadows Fly Shop
Cos Cob: Sportsman's Den
Danbury: Valley Angler
Darien: Complete Angler
Darien: The Surfcaster
East Lyme: New England Wilderness
East Norwalk: Fisherman's World
Greenwich: Rudy's Tackle Barn
Hamden: Mill River Fly Shop
Litchfield: Wilderness Shop
Manchester: Joe Garman
New Hartford: Classic & Custom Fly Shop
Norwalk: Bait Shop, Inc.
Norwalk: Fisherman's World
Norwalk: Scott Moss Gun & Tackle
Old Saybrook: Angler's Ark
Old Saybrook: North Cove Outfitters
Old Saybrook: Rivers End Tackle
Old Saybrook: Ted's Bait & Tackle
Preston: The Fish Connection
South Winsor: Clark & Clark
Stratford: Stratford Bait & Tackle
Vernon: A & B Sport
Voluntown: Mike's Bait & Tackle
Waterford: Hillyer's Tackle

DELAWARE

Rehobeth: Old Inlet Bait

FLORIDA

Apopka: Bitter's Bait & Tackle
Big Pine Key: Sea Boots Outfitters
Casselberry: Duncan's Bait & Tackle

Crystal River: The Fly Shop at
  Leisure Time Travel
Fort Lauderdale: Fly Shop of Fort
  Lauderdale
Fort Lauderdale: L.M.R. Fly Shop
Fort Lauderdale: Outdoor
  Outfitters
Fort Pierce: White's Tackle Shop
Islamorada: H.T. Chittum & Co.
Islamorada: Florida Keys Fly
  Fishing School & Outfitters
Islamorada: World Wide
  Sportsman
Jupiter: Tropical Outfitters
Key West: H.T. Chittum
Key West: The Saltwater Angler
Kissimee: Midway Bait & Tackle
Lakeland: Village Trader
Marathon: Tournament Bait &
  Tackle
Melbourne: Ammo Attic
Miami: A Fisherman's Paradise
Miami: Aquarius Rod & Reel
Miami: Captain Harry's Fishing
  Supply
Miami: Gold Coast Fisherman
  Supplies
Miami: Iggie's Bait & Tackle
Miami: Ocean Marine
Miami: River Marine Supply, Inc.
Miami: Watson Island Fuel &
  Fishing Supplies
North Fort Myers: Lehr's
  Economy Tackle Shop
North Miami: Charlie Richter's
  Fly Shop
North Palm Beach: Lott Bros.
Naples: Everglades Angler
Orlando: Bitter's Bait & Tackle
Orlando: Scotty's Bait & Tackle

Orlando: Tim's Tackle Box
Orlando: Tackle Plus
Panama City: Bell Tackle Co.
Panama City: Cogburn Clothing
Panama City: Half Hitch Tackle
Punta Gorda: Shallow Waters
  Outfitters & Fly Shop
Sarasota: Angler's Image
Stuart: C. Foster Marine Supplies
Stuart: Southern Angler
Tallahassee: Kevin's Guns &
  Sporting Goods
Tampa: Tampa Sports Unlimited
Titusville: The Fly Fisherman
Umatilla: Eustis Outdoor Shop
Vero Beach: Back Country
West Palm Beach: Kleiser's Sport
  Shop
Winter Park: Downeast Orvis
Winter Park: Sports Unlimited

GEORGIA

Albany: Franklin's South Sports
  Center
Atlanta: Atlanta Flyfishing
  Outfitters
Atlanta: Bass Pro Shop
Atlanta: Classic Angler Fly
  Fishing
Atlanta: Fish Hawk
Atlanta: Great Atlantic Boating
  Supply
Atlanta: Hammond's Pro Bass
Atlanta: Pro Bass Shop of
  Gwinnett
Augusta: Augusta Sporting Goods
  Co.
Bogart: Franklin Sports
Conley: Conley Bait & Tackle
Conyers: Conyers Sports & Boats

Riverdale: Riverdale Sports &
  Boats
Sylvester: Jack's Bait & Tackle
Smyrna: Adventure Outdoors
  Inc.
Smyrna: The Bait Shop
Stockbridge: Charlie's Fish 'N
  Tackle
Thomasville: Stafford's

IDAHO

Ashton: Three Rivers Ranch
Boise: The Benchmark
Boise: Intermountain Arms &
  Tackle
Boise: The Ultimate Angler
Boise: Silver Creek Outfitters
Boise: Stonefly Angler
Boise: Streamside Adventures
Coeur d'Alene: Cast Away Fly
  Shop
Grangeville: Raw Bros. Sporting
  Goods
Idaho Falls: Jimmy's All Season
  Angler
Island Park: Henry's Fork Anglers
Ketchum: Lost River Outfitters
Ketchum: Silver Creek Outfitters
Lewiston: Twin Rivers Anglers
McCall: Lick Creek
Meridian: Intermountain Arms &
  Tackle
Pocatello: Jimmy's All Season
  Angler
Salmon: Salmon Angler
Sandpoint: Pen Oreille Sport
  Shop
St. Anthony: Henry's Fork Anglers
Stanley: McCoy's Tackle Shop
Swan Valley: South Fork Lodge

Twin Falls: Blue Lakes Sporting
 Goods
Wendell: Simerly's

ILLINOIS

Alton: The Great River Road Bike
 & Fly Shop
Bannockburn: Roaring Fork
 Outfitters
Barrington: Saturday Morning
 Company
Carbondale: The Wildlife Refuge
Chicago: Dan's Tackle Service
Chicago: Eddie Bauer Sports
 Shop
Chicago: Orvis
Elk Grove: Swanson Bros. Tackle
Geneva: Riverside Sports
Glen Elyn: Fly & Field
Highland: Jerry's Tackle Shop
Morton Grove: Ed Shirley and
 Sons Sports
New Lenox: F & L Supply
Northfield: Trout and Grouse
Oakbrook: Eddie Bauer Sports
 Shop
Peoria: Sideside Worm Ranch
Rockford: On The Fly
Skokie: Orvis Old Orchard
Villa Park: American Fishing
 Stores
Winthrop Harbor: The Outdoor
 Sports Shop

INDIANA

Bloomington: J.L. Waters & Co.
Fort Wayne: Jorgenson's
Greenwood: The Outdoorsman
 Sports Shop

Griffith: Blythe's Sports Shop
Huntington: Broadway Bait &
 Tackle
Indianapolis: Flymasters of
 Indianapolis
Indianapolis: Southside Bait &
 Tackle
Indianapolis: That Place in
 Clermont
Indianapolis: White River Bait &
 Tackle
Morseville: Tackle Service Center
Noblesville: Schwartz's Bait &
 Tackle

IOWA

Cedar Rapids: Fin & Feather
Davenport: Winborn Sporting
 Goods
Des Moines: Second Avenue Bait
 House
Iowa City: Fin & Feather

KANSAS

Olathe: The Gun Shop
Overland Park: K & K Flyfishers
 Supply
Wichita: Backwoods

KENTUCKY

Lexington: Dave's Tackle Box
Lexington: The Sporting
 Tradition
Louisville: Bullfrog Creek
Louisville: Lac Loon Fly Fishing
 Specialty Shop
Paintsville: Wayne's Tackle Box

LOUISIANA

Baton Rouge: Favaro's Rod &
 Reel Repair Shop
Baton Rouge: Spillway Sportsman
 Inc.
Baton Rouge: The Sports Shop
Baton Rouge: Sports Unlimited
Bossier City: Bass' Bait & Food
 Mart
Chainette: Hook & Line
Jefferson: Southern Sporting
 Goods
Kenner: Sports Unlimited
Metairie: Chag's Sporting Goods
Metairie: Puglia's Sporting Goods
New Orleans: Professional Sport
 Shop
New Orleans: Southern Safaris
 Inc.
Shreveport: Clearwaters Rod &
 Fly Shop

MAINE

Auburn: Dag's Bait Shop
Bangor: Eddie's Flies & Tackle
Belfast: Outdoor Sportsman
Brewer: Ron's Gun & Sports
 Shop
Brewer: Van Raymond Outfitters
Cape Neddick: Eldredge Bros.
 Sporting Goods
Caribou: Country Sports
Dover-Foxcroft: Cahill Sporting
 Goods
Ellsworth: Willeys Sport Shop
Freeport: L.L. Bean
Fort Fairfield: Maverick's
 Sporting Goods
Houlton: Brown's Trading Post

Kennebunkport: Port Fly Shop
Kittery: Kittery Trading Post
North Jay: Robb's Fly Shop
Norway: Woodsmans Sporting Goods
Presque Isle: Roy's Army & Navy Store
Rangeley: Rangeley Region Sports Shop
Saco: Saco Bay Tackle
Veazie: Hachey's Rod & Reel
West Bath: Hoskin Enterprises
Windham: Bibeau's Fly Shop
Winthrop: D.L. Fleury's Sporting Goods

MARYLAND

Annapolis: Angler's Sport Center
Baltimore: The Fisherman's Edge
Baltimore: The Fishing Shop
Baltimore: T.G. Tochterman & Sons
Baltimore: Wayne Grauer
Bethesda: Eddie Bauer Sports Shop
Bethesda: King River Fly Fishing Shop
Frederick: The Rod Rack
Gaithersburg: Angler & Archer
Gaithersburg: Hudson Trail Outfitters
Ellicott City: Wolf's Sporting Adventure
Monkton: On The Fly
Mt. Airy: Crosswind All Outdoors
Rockville: Angler & Archer
Temple Hills: Holiday Sports
Thurmont: Thurmont Sporting Goods
Towson: Seth's Sports Shop

Westernport: North Branch Fly Shop

MASSACHUSETTS

Barre: Flagg's Flies & Tackle
Boston: Orvis
Boston: Stoddard's
Cambridge: Roach's Sporting Goods
Edgartown: Larry's Tackle Shop
Fall River: Bucko's Parts & Tackle Service
Falmouth: Eastman's Sport & Tackle
Framingham: Lew Horton's Sports Shop
Leominster: Lanza's Fly Fishing Shop
Nantucket: Bill Fisher Tackle
Pembroke: Henry Weston Outfitters
Pittsfield: Dick Moon's Sporting Goods
Salem: Lake 'n' Surf Sport Shop
Seekonk: Thompson's Sport Shop
West Brighton: Tight Lines
Townsend: Squannacook River Outfitters
Waltham: Bear's Den Bait & Tackle
Wayland: Wayland Orvis Shop
Westfield: B.G. Sporting
Wichendon: Outdoor Endeavors
Worcester: Lower Forty Outfitters

MICHIGAN

Ada: Thornapple Orvis Shop
Ann Arbor: MacGregor's Outdoors, Inc.

Baldwin: Ed's Sports Shop
Baldwin: Johnson's Pere Marquette Lodge
Bay City: Hexagon Rod & Fly Shop
Benzonia: Backcast Fly Shop
Berrien Springs: Open Season Sporting Goods
Clare: Jay's Sporting Goods
Clarkston: The Hairy Hook
Farmington: The Benchmark
Ferndale: Geake & Sons
Flint: Hick's Tackle
Gaylord: Alphorn Sport Shop
Grand Rapids: Al & Bob's Sports
Grayling: Fly Factory
Grayling: Gates AuSable Lodge
Kalamazoo: Angling Outfitters
Linwood: The Fly Shop at Frank's
Marquette: Lindquist's Outdoor Sports
Monroe: LaJinness Bait & Tackle
Okemos: M. Chance Fly Fishing Specialties
Redford: B-17 Fly Tackle Ltd.
Rockford: Michigan River Outfitters
Roscommon: Dan's Fly Shop
Southfield: Riverbend Sports Shop
St. Claire Shores: Michi-gun & Tackle
Traverse City: Countrysport
Traverse City: Troutsman
Williamsburg: Streamside Orvis

MINNESOTA

Blane: Capra's Sporting Goods
Fridley: Trail's End Bass Pro Shop

Fridley: The Fly Angler
Finley: Thorne Bros. Custom Rod
Lake Elmo: Bob Mitchell's Fly
   Shop
Minneapolis: B & D Bait &
   Tackle
Minneapolis: Burger Brothers
Minneapolis: Tackle Plus of
   Minnesota
Minneapolis: Thorne Brothers
   Fishing Specialty Store
Plymouth: Stamina Fishing Tackle
Richfield: Rodcraft
Rochester: B & M Bait & Tackle
Rochester: Lake Country
Rochester: Paint Creek Outfitters
St. Paul: Joe's Sporting Goods
Vadnais: Lake Outfitters
Walker: Reed's Sports Shop

MISSISSIPPI

Greenville: Sportsman, Inc.
Jackson: Brown's Bass Angler
   Shop
Jackson: Fireside Fly & Field
Jackson: Shorty's Southern
   Angler
Jackson: Surplus City USA

MISSOURI

Cape Girardeau: Chapman
   Outfitters
Columbia: Pucketts Sportsman's
   Outfitter
Columbia: Wilson's Fly Shop
Dexter: Chrisman Outfitters
Independence: Rainbow Fly &
   Outfitting
Lebanon: Larry's Sporting Goods

Lebanon: Reading's Fly Shop
Lebanon: Spring View Fly Shop
Springfield: Bass Pro Shop
Springfield: Metropolitan Rod &
   Reel
Springfield: Ozark Custom Rod &
   Fly
St. Louis: Feather-Craft Fly
   Fishing
St. Louis: Frontenac Outfitters
St. Louis: Outdoors, Inc.
St. Louis: Paul's Bait & Tackle
St. Louis: T. Hargrove Flyfishing

MONTANA

Billings: Rainbow Run Fly Shop
Billings: Scheels Sport Shop
Bozeman: Mama's Cache Fly
   Shop
Bozeman: Montana Troutfitters
Butte: Fish on Fly & Tackle
Butte: Fran Johnson's Sport Shop
Choteau: Battle Creek Lodge
Clinton: Rock Creek Fisherman's
   Mercantile
Dillon: Tom Tollett's Frontier
   Anglers
Emigrant: Big Sky Flies and
   Guides
Emigrant: *Hubbards* Yellowstone
   Lodge
Ennis: Madison River Fishing Co.
Ennis: The Tackle Shop
Fort Smith: Big Horn Trout Shop
Fort Smith: Bighorn Angler
Fort Smith: Quill Gordon Fly
   Fishers
Gardiner: Parks' Fly Shop
Glacier National Park: Trail &
   Creek Outfitters

Great Falls: Sheels Sport Shop
Great Falls: Wolverton's Fly Shop
Hamilton: Fishaus Tackle
Havre: Bing 'n' Bob's Sports
   Shop
Hardin: Bighorn Fly & Tackle
   Shop
Helena: Montana Fly Goods
Livingston: George Anderson's
   Yellowstone Angler
Livingston: Dan Bailey's Fly Shop
Livingston: Montana's Master
   Anglers
Melrose: Montana Trophy Angler
Missoula: Grizzly Hackle
Missoula: Missoulian Angler
Missoula: Miller Barber's
   Streamside Anglers
Ronan: Ronan Sports & Western
Sheridan: Harman's Fly Shop
Twin Bridges: Four Rivers Fishing
   Co.
West Yellowstone: Blue Ribbon
   Flies
West Yellowstone: Bob Jacklin's Fly
   Shop
West Yellowstone: Bud Lilly's
   Trout Shop
West Yellowstone: Madison River
   Outfitters
Whitefish: Lakestream Fly Shop

NEBRASKA

Elmwood: Sam's Inlet Bait &
   Tackle
Norfolk: Outdoors Unlimited
Omaha: Backwoods Equipment
Omaha: The Outdoor Enthusiast
Sidney: Cabela's

NEVADA

Fallon: Sportsman's Paradise
Las Vegas: Clear Water Flyfishing
Reno: Mark Fore & Strike
  Sporting Goods
Reno: Reno Fly Shop
Roundhill: Trout Creek Flies
Sparks: Gilly

NEW HAMPSHIRE

Antrim: Place in the Woods
Colebrook: Ducret's Sporting
  Goods
Errol: L.L. Cote
Gorham: Gorham Hardware &
  Sports Center
Hookset: Steve's Sportsmen's Den
Hudson: Merrimack River
  Outfitters
Jaffray: Pelletier's Sports Shop
Laconia: Paugus Bay Sporting
  Goods
Lyme: Lyme Angler
Manchester: Wildlife Taxidermy
  Sport
New Boston: Hunter's Angling
  Supplies
North Conway: North Country
  Angler
Rochester: Fox Ridge Outfitters
Salem: American Angling
  Supplies
West Lebanon: Mink Brook
  Outfitters
Wolfeboro: Lakes Region Sports

NEW JERSEY

Bernardsville: Gatto International
  Sport

Bordentown: Sportsmen's Center
Bound Brook: Effinger Sporting
  Goods
Brielle: Brielle Bait & Tackle
Brielle: The Reel Seat
Brielle: MV Tackle
Chadwick: Chadwick Bait &
  Tackle
Clinton: Oliver's Orvis Shop
East Tom's River: The Hook
  House
Forked River: Forked River Bait &
  Tackle Shop
Forked River: Mud Hole Custom
  Tackle
Garfield: S. Meltzer & Sons
Hackettstown: Angling Around
Jackson: Jackson Sporting Goods
Jersey City: Har Lee Rod
Lakewood: Shenandoah Boating
  Bait & Tackle
Ledgewood: Ramsey Outdoor
  Sports
Long Branch: Steven's Bait &
  Tackle
Neptune City: The Sportsman's
  Shed
Newton: Simon Peter Sport Co.
North Plainfield: Ray's Sport
  Shop
Northfield: Campbell Marine, Inc.
Normandy Beach: Bait 'N Tackle
  Shop
Paramus: Ramsay Outdoor Stores
Point Pleasant: Captain Bart's
  Custom Tackle
Point Pleasant: Fishermen's
  Supply
Point Pleasant: Reel Life Bait &
  Tackle

Point Pleasant Beach: Kevin
  Brogan's Custom Tackle
Ramsey: Ramsey Outdoor Store
Red Bank: The Fly Hatch
Red Brick: Pell's Fish & Sport
Seabright: Giglio'a Bait & Tackle
Sea Isle City: Gibson's Tackle Box
Seaside Park: Betty & Nick's Bait
  & Tackle
Seaside Park: Dolphin Bait &
  Tackle
Ship Bottom: Fisherman's
  Headquarters
South Amboy: Fred's Tackle Shop
Summit: The Angler
Summit: Valley Tackle
Surf City: Bruce & Pat's Bait &
  Tackle
Tom's River: Sportsman's Trading
  Post
Waretown: Captain Crunch's Bait
  & Tackle

NEW MEXICO

Albuquerque: Charlie's Sporting
  Goods
Albuquerque: Los Pinos Custom
  Rods
Albuquerque: Los Ranchos Gun
  & Tackle
Navajo Dam: Abe's Motel & Fly
  Shop
Navajo Dam: Rizuto's Fly Fishing
Santa Fe: High Desert Angler
Taos: Los Rios Anglers

NEW YORK

Albany: Adventure Out

Albany: Taylor & Vadney
   Sporting Goods
Albion: The Oak Orchard Fly
   Shop
Amagansett: Lure & Feather Co.
Amagansett: The Tackle Shop
Amity Harbor: Bob's Bait &
   Tackle
Amityville: Bargain Bilge
Amityville: Combs Bait & Tackle
Aqurbogue: Warren's Tackle
   Center
Babylon: Augie's Custom Tackle
Babylon: Captree Bait & Tackle
   Shop
Babylon: Lo Man Outdoor Store
Batavia: Batavia Marine &
   Sporting Supplies
Bayport: Captain T's Bait &
   Tackle
Bay Shore: Willie K. Bait & Tackle
Bedford Hills: The Bedford
   Sportsman
Briarcliff Manor: North State Bait
   & Tackle
Brooklyn: Bernie's Fishing Tackle
Brooklyn: Sheepshead Bay Bait &
   Tackle
Bronx: Fleiss City Island Bait &
   Tackle
Bronx: Jack's Bait & Tackle
Buffalo: Big Catch Bait & Tackle
Buffalo: Fish Tale Bait & Tackle
Buffalo: G & R Tackle
Center Moriches: B & B Tackle &
   Sports
Cochecton: Joe McFadden's Fly &
   Tackle
Cold Spring Harbor: H & M
   Powles Bait & Tackle

Cortland: Cortland Line Factory
   Company Store
Cross River: Sportsman's Shack
Deposit: West Branch Angler &
   Sportsman's Resort
Derby: Dave's Bait & Tackle Shop
East Hampton: Dixon's Sporting
   Life
East Hampton: Mrs. B's Bait &
   Tackle
East Rockaway: Skippy's Bait &
   Tackle
Elmira: Dick's Clothing &
   Sporting Goods
Elmira: J & M Sporting Center
Farmingdale: Edelman's
Flushing: Pro Fishing Tackle
Freeport: Donart
Freeport: Sea Isle Sports Center
Gloversville: B & D Lures
Hampton Bays: Altenkirch
   Precision Outfitters
Hampton Bays: Blue Water Tackle
Hamburg: Water Wizard Tackle
   Co.
Haverstraw: Matt's Sporting
   Goods
Hancock: West Branch Angler
Howard Bay: Crossbay Bait &
   Tackle
Hudson Falls: B & M Sports
Huntington Station: Campsite
   Sports Shop
Huntington Station: Four Winds
   Bait & Tackle
Keene Valley: The Mountaineer
Kings Park: Terminal Tackle Co.
Lake Mohegan: Mohegan
   Sportsman

Lindenhurst: Lindenhurst Bait &
   Tackle
Little Neck: The Practical Fly
   Shop
Livingston Manor: Fin, Fur &
   Feather Sports Shop
Lynbrook: Beckmann's Tackle
Margaretville: Del-Sports
Mexico: Oswego Outfitters
Middletown: Bob Lounsbury
   Sporting Goods
Miller Place: Complete Angler
Millerton: Taconic Sports &
   Camping Center
Montauk: Freddie's Bait & Tackle
Montauk: Gone Fishing Marina
Montauk: Montauk Marine Basin
Montauk: Johnny's Tackle Shop
Mt. Kisco: The Frugal Flyfishers
New Rochelle: Hudson Park Bait
   & Tackle
New York City (Manhattan):
   Capitol Tackle
New York City (Manhattan): Eddie
   Bauer
New York City (Manhattan):
   Custom Tackle, Ltd.
New York City (Manhattan): Orvis
New York City (Manhattan):
   Paragon Sporting Goods
New York City (Manhattan):
   Sportsman's World
New York City (Manhattan):
   Urban Angler
New York Mills: D & D Sports
Niagara Falls: Wild Life Sports
Northport: Bowman's Sporting
   Goods
North River: North Country
   Sports

North Tonawanda: Rainbow
  Sports
Oakdale: J & H Sports Center
Olean: Whitetail Country Sports
  World
Patchogue: Bargain Bilge
Patchogue: J & J Sports
Pelham: Al's Tackle
Phoenicia: The Tackle Shack
Pine Bush: Esopus School of Fly
  Fishing
Plattsburgh: The Blue Goose
Point Lookout: Scotty's Fishing
  Station
Poughkeepsie: Don's Tackle
  Service
Pulaski: The Portly Angler
Pulaski: Whittaker's Sports Store
  & Motel
Pulaski: Yankee Fly & Tackle
Rexford: Brookwood, Inc.
Riverhead: Edward's Sports
  Center
Riverhead: Shane's Marine
Rochester: Carl Coleman's Fly
  Shop
Rochester: Eastsdie Hunting &
  Fishing
Rochester: Panorama Outfitters
Rome: Woods 'n Water
Roscoe: Beaverkill Anglers
Roscoe: Donegal, Inc.
Saranac Lake: Blue Line Sports
  Shop
Scaneateles: The Royal Coachman
Seaford: Lon Wanser Fishing
  Tackle
Selden: Warren's Archery &
  Fishing
Shinhopple: Al's Wild Trout Ltd.

Shirley: Smith Point Bait
Slotesburg: Davis Sports Shop
Spencerport: Coleman's
Staten Island: Fred's Bait &
  Tackle
Staten Island: Great Kills Bait &
  Tackle
Staten Island: Michael's Bait &
  Tackle
Syracuse: The Troutfitter
Tonawanda: American Sportsman
  Center, Inc.
Vestal: Dick's Clothing &
  Sporting Goods
Walden: Thruway Sports
Wantagh: Causeway Bait &
  Tackle
Waterloo: Les Maynard's Fly
  Shop
White Plains: R & R Sports
  Center
Williamsville: Orvis
Wilmington: Hungry Trout Fly
  Shop
Yonkers: J & A Sportsmen Center

NORTH CAROLINA

Asheville: Hunter Banks Co.
Boone: High Country Fly Fishing
Burnsville: Young's Mountain
  Adventures
Cary: Mountain Meadows
Cary: Nature's Own Sportsman
Charlotte: Jesse Brown Outdoors
Charlotte: Great Outdoor
  Provision Co.
Chandler: Sportsman's Pro Shop
Cherokee: One Feather Fly &
  Tackle Shop

Clinton: Hook, Line & Sinker
  Bait & Tackle
East Garner: Variety Pic-up #24
Goldsboro: Four Seasons Sports
Highlands: Main Stream
  Outfitters
Linville: Paul & Fay Hughes
  Store
Morehead City: Henry's Tackle &
  Sporting Goods
Morgantown: Table Rock Angler
Raleigh: Bayleaf USA Bait &
  Fishing Tackle Store
Raleigh: Great Outdoor Provision
  Co.
Raleigh: Woods & Water Tackle
  Shop
Whittier: Outpost

OHIO

Addyston: Outdoor Products
Ashland: Fin-Feather-Fur
Bainbridge Township: Pine Lake
  Fly Shop
Boardman: Boardman Fly
  Fisherman
Brunswick: Brunswick Gun &
  Tackle
Chagrin: Pine Lake Fly Shop
Chagrin Falls: Valley Angler
Cincinnati: A & S Sports
Cincinnati: Afield
Cincinnati: Fishermen's Pro
  Shop
Cincinnati: Relo Sporting Goods
Cincinnati: Sportsman's Edge
Cincinnati: Streamside Outfitters
Cleveland: American Sportsman
  Shop

Cleveland: Angler's Mail
Cleveland: Atlantic Gun & Tackle
Cleveland: Backpacker's Shop—
    Ohio Cave
Cleveland: Frank's Edgewater
    Tackle
Cleveland: The Rodmaker
    Shoppe
Columbus: Dame Juliana
Dayton: Fisherman's Quarters
Maumee: Jann's
Montgomery: Ryan's Streamside
    Outfitters
North Canton: Dave's & Son
Ravenna: TMF Sports Shop
Sheffield Village: Backpackers
    Shop of Ohio Canoe
    Adventures
Toledo: Netcraft
Toledo: The Tackle Box
Youngstown: Boardman Fly
    Fisherman

OKLAHOMA

Cookson: Jimmy Houston
    Outdoors
Lawton: Cache Creek Fly Shop
Oklahoma City: B & B Tackle
Oklahoma City: Backwoods
Oklahoma City: Bass Pro Shops
Oklahoma City: Outdoor
    Sportsman Shop
Oklahoma City: Southwest Tackle
    & Bow
Tulsa: Army Navy Surplus
Tulsa: D & B Outfitters
Tulsa: Enler's Rod & Reel
Tulsa: Okiebug Retail Store
Tulsa: Woody's Bait & Tackle

OREGON

Albany: South Fork Fly Fishing
Ashland: Southern Oregon Fly
    Shop
Bend: The Fly Box
Bend: The Patient Angler
Corvallis: Anderson's Sporting
    Goods
Corvallis: Scarlet Ibis Fly Shop
Elgin: Minan
Enterprise: Wallowa Outdoors
Eugene: The Caddis Fly Angling
    Shop
Eugene: Home Waters Fly Shop
Eugene: McKenzie Outfitters
Gresham: Northwest Flyfishing
    Outfitters
Gresham: Teeny Nymph Co.
Hood River: Gorge Fly Shop
Joseph: Joseph Fly Shop
La Grande: Grande Ronde
    Angler Fly Shop
Lincoln City: B & B Hackle +
    Tackle
McMinnville: Fishing Unlimited
Merlin: Silver Sedge Fly Shoppe
Portland: Countrysport
Portland: Fisherman's Marine
    Supply
Rogue River: Anderson Custom
    Rods & Reels
Salem: Anderson's Sporting
    Goods
Salem: The Valley Fisherman
Sisters: The Fly Fisher's Place
Tighard: Kaufmann's Streamborn
Warrenton: Salmon Republic Fly
    Fishing Outfitters
Welches: Fly Fishing Shop
Wood Village: Stewart's Fly Shop

PENNSYLVANIA

Allentown: Pro-Am Fishing Shop
Altoona: Unkel Joe's Woodshed
Bedford: Laurel Sport Shop
Benton: Benton Sports Center
Benton: Fishing Creek Outfitters
Boiling Springs: Yellow Breeches
    Fly Shop
Broomall: Gordon's Sporting
    Goods Store
Bryn Mawr: Eyler's Fly & Tackle
Carlisle: Cold Spring Anglers
Carlisle: The Olde Fishing
    Station
Chalfont: A & B Fishin' Center
Chalfont: Prestia Lock & Door
    Service
Chalfont: Target World
Chestnut Hill: Orvis
Clairton: Tackle Unlimited
Clearfield: Jim's Sports Center
Coburn: The Feathered Hook
Conneaut Lake: Conneaut Lake
    Tackle
Coundersport: Halloran's
    Hardware & Sporting Goods
Cresco: Fly Fishing Tackle Shop
Denton: Beckie's Fishing Creek
    Outfitters
Doylestown: Dave's Sporting
    Goods
Eagle: Gordon's Sports Supply
Elizabethtown: Top Gun Shop
Emporium: Thunderstick
    Trading Post
Ephrata: Trout Run Sports
Erie: Erie Sports Store
Exton: Brandywine Outfitters
Fredericksburg: The Fly
    Fisherman's Shop

Gordonville: Evening Rise Fly
   Angler's Shop
Grantville: Shelly's Sporting
   Goods
Greensburg: The Fishing Post
Hanover: Byer's Fly & Tackle
   Shop
Harrisburg: The Tackle Shop
Hazelton: Bob's Sporting Goods
Hillsgrove: Renninger's Country
   Store
Honesdale: Northeast Flyfishing
Horsham: Clayton's Hunting &
   Fishing
Indiana: Indiana Angler
Intercourse: Evening Rise Fly
   Angler's Shop
Jamison: Tanner's Sports Center
Jersey Shore: Fred Reese Trout
   Shop
Jersey Shore: National Sporting
   Goods
Johnstown: Hart's Sporting
   Center
Johnstown: Hornick's Sporting
   Goods
Kennett Square: Pete's Outdoor
   Store
Lackawaxen: Angler's Roost &
   Hunter's Rest
Lehighton: Pocono Gateway
   Sporting Outfitters
Lewistown: Dan Pierce Outdoor
   Shop
Lock Haven: Unkel Joe's
   Woodshed
Luzerne: Dick Ackourey & Sons
Mansfield: Cooper's Sporting
   Goods
Media: The Sporting Gentleman

Meyersdale: Laurel Sport Shop
Middletown: Clouser's Fly Shop
Milton: Milton Sports Center
Montgomeryville: Leslie Edelman
   Inc.
New Cumberland: Shelly's
   Sporting Goods
Oakford: Bryant's Gunsmithing
   Inc.
Oil City: Oil Creek Outfitters
Omigsburg: Wilderness Trekker
Osceola Mills: Richardson's
   Sportsman Store
Philadelphia: Bob's Bait & Tackle
Philadelphia: Dee's Bait & Tackle
Philadelphia: Orvis
Philadelphia: Taylor's Bait &
   Tackle
Pittsburgh: International Angler
Pittsburgh: South Hills Rod &
   Reel
Pottstown: French Creek
   Outfitters
Pottsville: Ed's Fly Shop
Reading: Blue Mountain
   Outfitters
Rockwood: S & S Sports Shop
Scotland: Falling Springs Outfitter
Shamokin: Dave's Taxidermy &
   Tackle Shop
Shippenville: J & L Sporting
   Goods
Slate Run: Slate Run Tackle Shop
Souderton: Angler's Pro Shop
Southampton: Robinson's Gun &
   Tackle Shop
Springfield: Wright's Wholesale
   Sportsman's Supplies
Spruce Creek: Spruce Creek
   Outfitters

State College: Flyfisher's Paradise
Stroudsburg: Dunkleberger's
   Sports Outfitters
Stroudsburg: Winsor Fly Shop
Tionesta: Forest County Sports
   Center
Volant: The Outdoor Shop
West Chester: Chip's Bait &
   Tackle
West Kittaning: Transue's Tackle
Westlawn: Tulpehocken Creek
   Outfitters
Whitehall: Nestor's Rod & Bow
   Pro Shop
White Haven: A A Pro Shop
Williamsport: Brown & Waldman
   Bass Pro Shop
Williamsport: Pa. Outdoor
   Warehouse
Willow Grove: Delaware River
   Anglers
York: Chet Patterson & Sons

RHODE ISLAND

Charlestown: Sportsman Cove
Coventry: Angler's Image, Inc.
Cranston: Continental Bait &
   Tackle
East Greenwich: Fin & Feather
   Lodge
Hope: Carr's Rod-N-Gun
Newport: The Saltwater Edge
North Kingston: Quaker Lane Bait
   & Tackle
South Kingston: Gil's Custom
   Tackle
Warwick: Ray's Bait & Tackle
Warwick: Rijo's Sports Shop
Watch Hill: Watch Hill Fly
   Fishing Co.

Woonsocket: Edgar's Sporting
   Goods

SOUTH CAROLINA

Charleston: John's Rod & Reel
Columbia: Barron's Fishing &
   Hunting Center
Greenville: The Carolina Fly
   Fisherman
Greenville: Foothills Fly Fishing
Mt. Pleasant: Haddrelle's Point
   Tackle
Pawley's Island: Sporting Life of
   Pawley's Island
Rock Hill: Carolina Sportsman

SOUTH DAKOTA

Hill City: Mrs. C's
Rapid City: Custom Caster
Rapid City: LaCrosse Bait Shop
Rapid City: Nick's Bait & Tackle
Sioux Falls: M & W Bait & Tackle
Sioux Falls: Four Seasons Bait &
   Tackle
Sioux Falls: J & M Bait & Tackle
Sioux Falls: Scheels All Sports
Sturgis: Westberg's Sporting
   Goods

TENNESSEE

Chattanooga: Choo Choo Fly &
   Tackle
Chattanooga: Dry Fly Outfitters
Cleveland: Outdoor Adventures
Gaitlinburg: Old Smokey
   Outfitters
Henderson: Hunt's Sporting
   Goods

Johnson City: Great Outdoors
   Shop
Knoxville: The Creel
Knoxville: Knoxville Sports
   Unlimited
Memphis: Buck & Bass Sports
   Centre
Memphis: Fisherman's
   Headquarters
Memphis: Sports Unlimited
Memphis: The Sporting Life
Memphis: Tommy Bronson's
   Sporting Goods
Nashville: Cumberland Transit
   Backpacking
Nashville: Friedman's Army-Navy
   Stores
Nashville: Game Fair Ltd.
Nashville: Nashville Sports
Nashville: Starkey's Bait & Tackle
Oak Ridge: Oak Ridge Sporting
   Goods
Reliance: Adams Fly & Tackle
Sevierville: Wynn's

TEXAS

Abeline: Dry Creek Anglers
Austin: The Austin Angler
Bryan: Sullivan's Outfitters
Corpus Christi: Roy's Bait &
   Tackle
Dallas: The Gun & Tackle Store
Dallas: Hunter Bradlee Co.
Dallas: Ray's Hardware &
   Sporting Goods
Dallas: Westbank Anglers
Ft. Worth: Backwoods Equipment
   Co.
Ft. Worth: Texas Outdoors
Houston: The Angler's Edge

Houston: Cut Rate Fishing Tackle
   Unlimited
Houston: Marburger's Sporting
   Goods
Houston: Orvis
Houston: Outdoor Sports Shop
Houston: Tackle Hut
McAllen: Bud Rowland Fly Shop
New Brauenfels: Gruene
   Outfitters
Pasadena: McDowell's Sporting
   Goods
Pottsboro: Texoma Fishing Center
Richardson: Barlow's Tackle Shop
San Antonio: Tackle Box
   Outfitters
Spicewood: Norman's Fish Hook
Victoria: Victoria All-Sports
   Center
Waco: Sports Spectrum

UTAH

Dutch John: Collett's Flaming
   Gorge Lodge
Logan: Al's Sporting Goods
Layton: Eagle Outfitters
Murray: Troutsmen Enterprises
Ogden: Angler's Inn
Ogden: The Fly Line
Ogden: Gart Bros. Sporting
   Goods
Ogden: Smith & Edwards
Orem: Gart Bros. Sporting Goods
Orem: Parks Sporting Goods
Park City: The Fly Shop
Park City: Jan's Mountain
   Outfitters
Payson: Payson Sports & Trophy
Pleasant Grove: The Flyfishers
   Den

Salt Lake City: Angler's Inn
Salt Lake City: Angler's Tackle
  Service
Salt Lake City: Spinner Fall Fly
  Shop
Salt Lake City: Western Rivers
  Flyfisher
Sandy: Angler's Inn
Vernal: Basin Sports

VERMONT

Essex Junction: Knight's Sports
  Center
Killington: Vermont Bound
Manchester: Orvis
Rutland: Lindholm Sports Center
Sharon: Skowronski's Trout &
  Salmon Supplies
Stowe: Classic Outfitters & Fly
  Fishing Shop
Stowe: Fly Fish Vermont
Waitsfield: Streamline
Websterville: Wright Rod
  Company
White River Junction: Briggs, Ltd.
Winooski: Classic Outfitters &
  Flyfishers Shop

VIRGINIA

Annandale: Dawson's
Arlington: The Angler's Lie
Bridgewater: Mossy Creek Fly
  Shop
Charlottesville: Stoney Creek
  Tackle Co.
Edinburg: Murray's Fly Shop
Fairfax: Hundson Trail Outfitters
Glenn Allen: Green Top Sporting
  Goods

Hallieford: Queen's Creek
  Company
Hot Springs: The Outpost
Lynchburg: Timberlake Sporting
  Goods
Martinsville: Bryant's Sport
  Center
Norfolk: Bob's Gun & Tackle
  Shop
Roanoke: Orvis
Vienna (Tysons Corner): Orvis
Waynesboro: Hassett Gun Supply

WASHINGTON

Bellevue: Kaufmann's Streamborn
Bellingham: H & H Outdoor
  Sports
Bothell: Swede's Anglers Retreat
Everett: John's Sporting Goods
Kennewick: Clearwater Fly Shop
Kent: Shoff Tackle
Lacey: The Fly Fisher
Lynden: Turner's Fly & Tackle
Mt. Vernon: Ed's Sports Shop
Richland: B B & M Sporting
  Goods
Seattle: Avid Angler Fly Shoppe
Seattle: Countrysport
Seattle: Kaufmann's Streamborn
Seattle: Patrick's Fly Shop
Seattle: Swallow's Nest
Seattle: Warshal's Sporting Goods
Silverdale: Kitsap Sports
Silverdale: Morning Hatch
Spokane: The Outdoor
  Sportsman
Spokane: Propp's Rod & Fly
  Shop
Spokane: Silverbow Flyfishing
  Adventures

Spokane: The Sport Cove
Sumas: The Selective Angler
Tacoma: The Morning Hatch Fly
  Shoppe
Walla Walla: Drumheller Sports
  Center
Wenatchee: Blue Dun
Woodland: Angler's Workshop
Yakima: Gary's Fly Shop

WEST VIRGINIA

Elkins: Mountaineer Sports
Morgantown: Upstream
West Sulphur: Kate's Mountain
  Outfitters

WISCONSIN

DePere: PX Sports & Fly Shop
Eagle River: Eagle Sports
Green Bay: Bob's Bait & Tackle
Hayward: Pastika's Sports Shop
Janesville: The Sportsman's
  Choice
Madison: Bob's Rod & Reel
Madison: Broadway Bait & Tackle
Madison: Steve Gerhardt's Sport
  Center
Menomonee Falls: Jay's Sports
  Shop
Milwaukee: Laacke & Joys
4Horeb: Lunde's Fly Fishing
  Chalet
Park Falls: Bridge Bait & Tackle
Racine: D.I.Y. Rod & Tackle
Rhineland: Ralley & Helen's
  Musky Shop
Stevens Pt.: Point Surplus Store
West Allis: The Fly Fishers
Wilmot: Gander Mountain

WYOMING

Buffalo: Sports Lure
Casper: Ugly Bug Fly Shop
Cody: North Fork Anglers
DuBois: Whiskey Mountain Tackle
Evanson: Bob's Outdoor
    Adventure
Jackson: High Country Flies
Jackson: Jack Dennis Outdoor
    Shop
Jackson Hole: Orvis Jackson Hole
Laramie: Lou's Sport Shop
Pinedale: Great Outdoor Shop
Rock Spring: Gart Bros. Sporting
    Goods
Saratoga: Great Rocky Mountain
    Outfitters
Sheridan: Bighorn Mountain
    Sports
Sheridan: Fly Shop of the Big
    Horns
Sheridan: Ritz Sport Goods
Teton Village: Westbank Anglers
Worland: Outdoorsman

FOREIGN COUNTRIES

ARGENTINA

Buenos Aires: Buenos Aires
    Angler
Cordoba: Federico Prato Fly Shop
Rosario: Hector D. Trape Fly
    Fishing Supplies

AUSTRALIA

Melbourne: Australian Fly
    Fisherman
Sydney: Australian Fly Fisherman

CANADA

ALBERTA

Bellevue: The Crow's Nest Angler
Calgary: Country Pleasures
Cochrane: Smallman's Fly Shop
Edmonton: The Fishing Hole

BRITISH COLUMBIA

Burnaby: Ruddick's Fly Shop
Colquitlam: Babcock Fly &
    Tackle
North Vancouver: Highway Tackle
Surray: Michael & Young Fly
    Fishing
Vernon: Herby's Surplus &
    Supplies
Vancouver: Hanson's Fishing
    Outfitter
Vancouver: Cowichan Fly &
    Tackle
Whistler: Whistler Backcountry
    Adventures

NEWFOUNDLAND

Gander: Straight Line Sports

ONTARIO

Concord: Angling Specialties
Grimsby: Northeast Anglers &
    Outdoor
Inglewood: The Forks Fly Shop
Thunder Bay: River's Edge Fly
    Shop
Toronto: Skinner Sports (1976)
    Ltd.

QUEBEC

Charlesbourg: La Halte de
    Pêcheur

Montmagny: P.A.S. Sport
Trois-Rivières: L'Ami du
    Moucheur

FRANCE

Paris: Au Martin Pêcheur

GERMANY

Mohnesee-Delecke: Fly Fishing
    Brinhoff
Stuttgart: CPE Flyfishing

ITALY

Florence: Wet & Dry
Modena: Geiorgio Benecchi
    Products
Valle San Nicolo: Alpi Flies

JAPAN

Kawasaki: Pro Shop Haze
Seto City: Inagaki Co., Ltd.
Warabi City: Sasano Corp.

NETHERLANDS

Amsterdam: Peeters Hengelsport

NEW ZEALAND

Lake Taupo/Turangi: Sporting
    Life Fishing Outfitters

NORWAY

Storkvina: Vico Marketing

SOUTH AFRICA

Durban: Fly Anglers
Durban: King Sports (Pty.) Ltd.

Pietermaritzburg: Flyfisherman
   (Pty.) Ltd.

S W E D E N

Enbskede: Royal Coachman
Stockholm: Lennart Bergqvist
   Flugfoske

S W I T Z E R L A N D

Therwil: Rudolf Schuppli
Zurich: A & H Hebeisen

U N I T E D   K I N G D O M

Basingstoke: Fly Dressers Guild
Harrow: Young's of Harrow

Harrowgate: Orvis
London: Farlow's
London: House of Hardy
London: Orvis
Manchester: Leatherbarrows
Stockbridge: Orvis
Winchester: The Rod Box

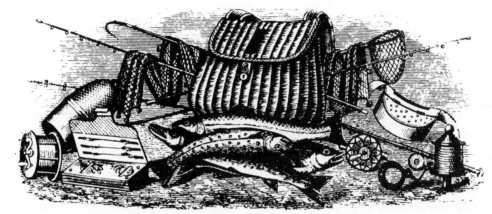

From Great Fishing Tackle Catalogs of the Golden Age.
[courtesy Nick Lyons Books]

A GLOSSARY
OF FISHING TERMS

Aberdeen
a hook shape characterized by a round bend and a wide gap.

action
the flexibility properties of a rod; also, the movement of a lure due to its built-in properties (e.g., the lip of a crankbait).

adipose fin
the fatty fin located between the dorsal and tail fins of some species.

alevin
a freshly hatched fish.

amphidromous
fish that migrate between fresh- and salt water for purposes other than spawning.

anadromous
describes saltwater fish, such as shad and salmon, that migrate to freshwater rivers to spawn.

anal fin
the fin located on the underside of a fish's body just ahead of the tail.

angling
a general synonym for "fishing"; it originally meant fishing with a hook, as distinguished from a net, spear, or any other equipment.

anti-reverse lock
the mechanism on a reel that prevents the crank handle from turning backwards.

aquatic insect
an insect that spends at least a portion of its life underwater.

arbor
the axle or spindle on which a fly reel's spool revolves.

artificial bait
plugs, spoons, flies, and other bait that simulate actual creatures that fish feed on.

attractor
a fly or other artificial bait that is not designed to resemble a specific insect or other live bait, but simply to suggest one that would appeal to a fish.

auger
a drill used to cut holes in the ice, for ice-fishing.

automatic reel
a fly reel with a spring mechanism that retrieves the line without manual winding.

backing
extra line on a fly reel between the fly line and the spool. Backing provides underlying bulk that speeds rewinding the fly line, as well as providing additional line, if needed, to play a fish.

backlash
a tangle of line on a reel caused by the spool's rotating faster than the line is being rewound. Also called Overrun (q.v.) or "bird's nest."

bag
the mesh sack portion of a landing net.

bail pickup
the revolving arm on a spinning reel that picks up the line during the rewinding process.

baitcasting
tackle that involves a baitcasting, or "level-wind," reel.

baitfish
various species of fish, such as minnows, sought as food by larger fish and used as bait by anglers.

barb
a reverse projection at the end of a hook to prevent the hook from sliding out of a fish's mouth. Also, an individual fiber of feather.

bass boat
a boat designed for bass fishing.

belly
the thickest section of a fly line.

bend
the curved portion of a hook.

big game
the largest game fish, such as tuna, sailfish, and sharks.

billfish
species of fish, such as swordfish, sailfish, and marlins, that are characterized by the "swords" that extend from their snouts.

biot
the short leading edge of a goose quill, used in fly-tying.

blank
a bare rod, before guides and other accessories have been attached.

blue-water
describes fishing the deepest areas of ocean (as distinguished from Offshore and Inshore fishing, q.v.).

boat
to bring a fish to a boat after it has been caught. *See also* Land.

bobber
See Float. *also* "bob."

bobbin
the fly-tying tool that holds a spool of thread.

bodkin
a needle used in fly-tying.

boot-foot
a wader with an attached boot (cf. stocking-foot waders).

brackish
describes water having a lower saline content than normal seawater, usually found where a freshwater stream or river meets the ocean.

bucktail
a lure or streamer fly having a tail made of long strands of deer hair.

bump
a fish's investigatory prodding the bait, often before striking.

butt
the rear portion of a rod.

butt cap
the protective device, usually made of metal, plastic, or cork, found at the butt end of a fly rod.

buzzbait
a lure having a propeller that churns the surface during the retrieval in order to attract fish.

caddis
an insect of the order *Trichoptera*, characterized by swept-back wings; also, dry flies or nymphs that imitate such insects.

cane
an entire stalk of bamboo. "Split-cane" describes a rod made of bamboo strips.

cape
(fly-tying) the portion of a bird's feathers from the neck to the base of the back.

Carlisle
a hook shape characterized by a long shank.

cast
to throw a line and its bait onto the water.

catadromous
describes fish that migrate from freshwater to salt water to spawn.

catch-and-release
the philosophy and practice of returning all fish back into the body of water from which they were taken.

Catskill Dry Fly
the traditional dry fly pattern, marked by upright wings, hackle collar, slim body, and long tail.

caudal fin
the fish's tail.

cfs
cubic feet per second, a measurement of water flow.

charter
to hire a boat, or a boat that is available for hire.

chenille
a popular fly-tying material, made from short soft fibers twisted into a cord (French for "caterpillar").

chum
to attract fish by dumping or scattering food in the water.

clevis
the swivel device to which a spinner blade is attached and which allows the blade to rotate.

coarse
a British term for sport fish other than trout and salmon.

cock
the male of the salmon and several other species of fish.

come off
(of an insect hatch) to happen, as in "The dun hatch comes off the stream right before sundown."

conventional
a saltwater fishing term for baitcasting, used to describe a "conventional rod" or "conventional reel."

cover
underwater plant growth in which fish lurk or hide.

coverbait
plugs and other lures designed to be used in heavy cover.

crank
another word for a reel's "handle."

crankbait
a plug designed to dive below the surface as it is retrieved.

creel
a wicker basket or canvas container in which "keeper" fish are stored.

crimp
to squeeze down a hook's barb or split-shot sinker.

cul de canard
the oily waterproof feathers on the rear of a duck, used in fly-tying.

cup
the concave bend of a spinner blade; the deeper the "cup," the more vibration the rotating blade will produce.

Dacron®
a popular polyester synthetic used for fishing line.

dampen
(of a rod) to recover its original position after being flexed during a cast.

dap
to fish by letting the fly or bait fall lightly onto the water surface.

depth-finder
an electronic device on a boat that measures and displays the distance from the boat to the bottom of the water.

disc drag
mechanism that produces resistance on a reel spool by means of a brake-like friction disc.

dorsal fin
one or more fins located on the back of a fish or on its highest part.

double haul
(fly-fishing) to Haul (q.v.) on the line twice, first during the back cast and again during the forward cast.

double-tapered
a fly line that is tapered at both ends (cf. Weight-Forward).

downrigger
a cable-and-weight device that maintains bait at a certain depth and then releases the line when a fish strikes.

drag
to slow the speed with which line leaves the reel by increasing friction on the line. Also, a mechanism on a reel (also called the "drag knob") that regulates such resistance.

drag-free
(of a fly) carried entirely by the current, with no resistance from the line.

dress
to clean line of dirt and other debris; also, to tie a fly.

dropper
a second fly attached to a leader, often a dry fly used as a strike indicator.

dry fly
a fly that is fished floating on the surface (cf. Wet Fly).

dubbing
(fly-tying) fur or fur-like material used to replicate an insect's body.

dun
(fly-tying) one of various shades of gray.

eye
the loop at the end of the shank of a hook, to which the line or leader is tied.

false cast
(fly-fishing) a cast in which the fly does not touch the water. False-casting is used to gain line speed, extend the amount of line, or dry a soaked dry fly.

fast
(of a rod) having an action in which most of the bend is in the tip end (cf. Parabolic).

ferrule
the plug or the socket at the end of a section of a multi-section rod, by which the rod's sections are joined.

fiberglass
rod material made of flexible glass filaments embedded in resin.

fighting butt
an extension to a rod butt designed to provide greater leverage in fighting a large fish; the angler usually presses the butt against his stomach.

fingerling
a young fish that measures just a few inches long (the next stage after Fry, q.v.).

"fish on!"
(as in "a fish is on the line") a shout that indicates the shouter has hooked a fish.

flats
a shallow coastal sandy-bottom expanse, most usually in semitropical waters and a prime area for bonefishing.

flip
to cast a rod in an underhand manner.

float
a bobber used as a strike indicator; also, to fish off a boat or raft while drifting down a river or stream.

float tube
a one-person buoyant chair-like apparatus for lake or pond fishing, in which an angler sits and propels himself by means of flippers on his feet.

floatant
a chemical or another substance used to keep a fly buoyant.

fly
an artificial imitation of an insect or another living bait.

foot
one of two projections on the base of a fly reel that attaches to the rod's seat.

foul-hook
to hook or snag a fish anywhere but in its mouth.

fry
a newly-hatched fish.

gaff
a hook mounted on a long handle, used to land large fish.

gap
(of a hook) the span as measured directly between the shank and the point (sometimes "gape").

ghillie
a Scottish word for a guide or game-keeper. *also* gillie.

gill
one of the pair of breathing-apparatus organs located behind a fish's head.

gink
another word for Floatant, q.v.

"Grand Slam"
a saltwater fly-fishing term for catching a bonefish, a permit, and a tarpon in the same day.

grilse
a mature but undersized male salmon on its first spawning migration.

grip
the handle a rod, usually made cork or synthetic foam.

grizzly
(of a feather) black and white striped.

guide
one of the metal ring devices along the length of a rod through which line is threaded.
  Also, someone hired to escort a fisherman to likely places to fish and render advice with regard to bait, tackle, etc.

handle
the part of the reel that is cranked to retrieve line.

hatch
the simultaneous emergence of a particular species of insect out of a body of water.

haul
to tug on a fly line during a cast to accelerate line speed.

hemostat
surgical pliers used to remove hooks from fish.

hen
the female of several species of fish.

hip waders
waders that cover the angler from the waist down. *also* "hippers."

hog
(often pronounced "hawg") a colloquial term for a large fish, usually a bass.

hold
(of a fish) to remain in one place, usually in moving water.

imago
an insect's adult stage of life, especially when it is in its mating stage. *See also* Spinner.

imitator
a fly or other artificial bait designed to resemble a specific species of insect or other live bait.

inshore
describes saltwater fishing close to land (as distinguished from Offshore and Blue-Water Fishing, q.v.).

jerkbait
plugs that move with no built-in action of their own; any action comes from the fisherman's maneuvering the rod and line.

jig
a lure composed of a metal head to which feathers, a plastic skirt, or another attractor is attached. Also, to fish by jerking bait up and down in a vertical plane.

keel
a hook design characterized by a bent shank, designed to work with its shank down and its point up.

keeper
a fish worth saving, especially one that is not released back into the water. Also, (1) a gamekeeper; (2) a small metal loop mounted above the grip of a rod to hold the hook while the hook is not in use.

Kirby
a hook having its point angled to the right of the shank.

kype
a hook-like growth at the end of the jaw of male salmon during spawning.

land
to capture a fish after it has been played on the line. *See also* Boat.

lateral line
a series of tiny pores running the length of a fish's side that sense sound vibrations.

leader
a length of monofilament, wire, or another material that connects a hook to a line.

level wind
a device on some baitcasting reels that moves back and forth across the spool to distributes the line evening during the rewind.

lie
(of a fish) to rest with little or no movement.

Limerick
a hook type having a much sharper angle from bend to point than from shank to bend.

limit
the maximum number of caught fish that may be legally kept, usually on a daily basis.

limnology
the study of ponds, lakes, and other freshwater bodies with regard to their physical and biological characteristics.

line
(n.) the cord mounted on a reel to which a hook and other terminal tackle are attached.
(v.) to frighten a fish by disturbing the water above it with a badly-cast line.

line pickup pin
the device on a spin-casting reel that rewinds the line.

lip
(n.) the plastic or metal projection on a crankbait that produces its diving action.
(v.) to lift a fish (usually a bass) by its lower lip.

littoral
of or pertaining to the shore of an ocean or other coastal water.

live bait
worms, minnows, and other living creatures used for bait (cf. Artificial Bait).

live-well
a tank or similar receptacle on a boat in which fish can be stored alive.

loading
the process by which a rod takes on the weight of a lure or fly line to a rod during the back cast, thus giving the rod the potential energy ready to propel the lure or line (*see* Unloading).

"long-line release"
a rueful euphemism for losing a fish before it can be landed.

lunker
an especially large fish, most usually applied to bass, pickerel, and muskies.

lure
a general term for any kind of artificial bait.

mandrel
the bar around which fiberglass or graphite is wrapped to form a rod blank.

match the hatch
to select a fly that closely resembles the species of insect that is being hatched.

mayfly
an insect of the order *Ephemeroptera*, characterized by large upright front wings; also, dry flies or nymphs that imitate such insects.

mend
to adjust the position of a fly line on the water in relation to the fly's position and the current's speed(s), in order to allow the fly to float drag-free.

midge
a member of the insect family *Chironomiidae*, or a term for any small fly (size 20 or smaller).

milt
fish sperm.

modified release
a kind of marine fishing tournament in which only fish below a stipulated size are released.

modulus
the stiffness of a graphite rod as expressed per square inch.

m.o.e. fly
(for "mother of epoxy") a fly made of molded epoxy resin glue.

monofilament
a single strand of nylon line used as lines and leaders.

mooching
a technique used primarily for steelhead in the Pacific Northwest, in which live bait is allowed to drift carried by the tidal flow.

muddler
a wet fly having a clipped deer-hair head, designed to resemble the sculpin baitfish.

multiplying reel
a reel having a spool that turns more than once for each revolution of the crank handle, thus producing a faster line retrieval than on a comparable single-action reel.

natural
an artificial fly that replicates a real insect.

neoprene
synthetic rubber used to make waders.

nymph
the underwater stage of an insect's life before it is hatched.

one-foot
a rod guide attached to the rod by a single projection (cf. Two-foot or Snake).

offshore
describing saltwater fishing beyond inshore areas, but closer to land than blue-water areas.

otolith
the hard calcium part of a fish's inner ear, the scales of which can serve as growth rings to determine an individual's age.

outrigger
an apparatus used in trolling that positions one or more rods away from the wake of a boat.

overrun
See Backlash.

pack rod
a rod that can be disassembled into sections short enough to be stowed in a backpack.

palm
to retard the amount of line a fish pulls off a fly reel by pressure from the fisherman's hand against the edge of the reel spool.

palmered
(fly-tying) a hackle feather that is wrapped around the length of a hook's shank.

palming ring
the uncovered edge of a fly reel spool.

panfish
individually or collectively, any of several species of fish (e.g., perch, sunfish, crappie) that are small enough to be fried in a pan.

parabolic
(of a rod) an action that extends the entire length of the rod (cf. Fast).

parachute
(fly-tying) a fly tied with its hackle wrapped parallel to the hook shank.

parr
a young salmon or trout up to the age of two years, identifiable by dark bars on the fish's sides (called "parr marks").

pawl
a pivoting projection that engages with the teeth of a sprocket, part of the drag system of some reels.

pectoral fin
the fin located just behind a fish's head.

PFD
a "personal flotation device," or life jacket.

pH
the measure of the acid/allkaline contents of a section of water. A measurement of 7 indicates a neutral pH. Below 7 shows acidic water, while above 7 (to a maximum of 14) indicates the presence of alkali.

pillar
one of the crossbars on a reel that support the sides of the reel.

piscivorous
of or pertaining to species of fish that eat other fish.

pitch
to cast with an overhand motion.

play
to maneuver a fish in a give-and-take manner prior to landing it.

plug
a lure usually made of plastic or wood and shaped and painted to resemble a baitfish; the category includes crankbaits and stickbaits.

pocket
an indentation on a stream bottom below a run or riffle.

pocket water
a relatively calm area of water, often behind a large rock in a stream or river, where fish are likely to hold.

popper
a lure having a solid body that "pops" through the water, used primarily for bass and bluefish.

potamodromous
describing species of fish that migrate within freshwater.

present
to offer bait to a fish, usually by means of casting.

pressure
an intense amount of fishing activity on a lake, stream, or any other specific area of water.

priest
a short wood or metal club used to dispatch a fish in a humane manner.

pump
to lift a rod toward the angler, then rapidly wind the line that the movement has made slack (a technique used in playing a fish).

put-and-take
the policy of encouraging anglers to keep stocked fish they catch, subject to size and limit restrictions.

quarter cast
(fly-fishing) a cast made directly across a stream and allowed to drift until the fly is as far downstream as the amount of line permits.

quill
a peacock herl stem from which the feathers have been removed, used in tying such flies as the Quill Gordon.

redd
a female fish's breeding nest.

retractor
a spring device that holds small tools on a vest. *also* Zinger, q.v.

retrieve
to reel in a line.

reversed
a hook having its point angled to the left of the shank; the opposite of a Kirby hook.

riffle
a small, usually shallow rapid in a stream or river.

ring
a rod guide in the shape of a circle.

riparian
of or pertaining to river banks.

rip-rap
loose rock, usually on the bottom of a stream.

rise
(of a fish) to move to the surface, almost invariably to inspect or ingest an insect or another prey.

roll cast
(fly-fishing) a cast in which the fly is lifted off the water and rolled forward in a single motion.

run
a mass migration of fish; also, an individual fish's moving away from the angler after a strike.

saddle
(fly-tying) a strip of feathers taken from the center of the Cape (q.v.).

salmonid
belonging to the family of fish that includes trout, salmon, and char.

scale
one of a set of thin bony overlapping skin growth that forms a protective outer body layer on most species of fish.

school
a group of the same species of fish that is traveling together.

sculpin
a small baitfish, which the muddler fly was designed to replicate.

seam
the boundary between contiguous currents moving at different speeds.

season
the period during the year when a species of fish may be legally caught and kept.

seat
the portion of the rod to which the reel is attached.

set
to tug on the line so as to fix the hook in a fish's mouth, as in the phrase "to set the hook."

shank
the long, usually straight, portion of a hook between the eye and the bend.

shock leader
a heavy leader that protects against the line's breaking or being damaged by the impact of a heavy fish.

shooting head
a weighted attachment to a fly line used to achieve greater casting distance.

simulator
an artificial fly that resembles an insect or another bait, but not any specific species.

single-action
a reel on which one revolution of the winder knob produces one revolution of the spool (cf. Multiplying Reel).

sinker
a weight, of lead or another material, attached to a line to make it descend faster and farther.

sinking tip
the front portion of a type of fly line that takes the fly below the water's surface.

smolt
the third stage in the life of a young salmon or trout, when the fish is capable of migrating.

snake
a Two-Foot (q.v.) rod guide made of a single piece of extended spiral metal.

snell
a length of leader that is permanently wound around shank of the hook.

spawn
(of a female fish) to lay eggs.

Spey
(named for a river in Scotland) a long two-handed rod customarily used for salmon and steelheads.

Spey cast
a cast in which the fly does not travel above or behind the fisherman.

spinner
a type of lure having a metal or plastic blade that rotates around a shaft. *See also* Imago.

spinnerbait
a lure composed of one or more spinners on one wire arm and a hook on another arm.

spool
the part of the reel around which the line is wrapped.

spoon
a flat or slightly curved metallic lure with a hook at one end.

sport-fishing
fishing for recreation, as distinguished from commercial reasons.

sproat
a hook shape characterized by a gently-angled bend.

sprocket
a toothed wheel, part of the drag system of some reels.

spud
a long-handled chisel used in ice-fishing to make holes in the ice.

standing part
the main portion of a line (cf. Tag End).

star drag
a five-spoked wheel on some bait-casting reels that controls the drag mechanism.

stickbait
a floating plug with no lip or other attachment that would produce action.

stock
to increase the population of a body of water by introducing (usually hatchery-raised) fish.

stocking-foot waders
waders that do not have attached boots.

stonefly
an insect of the order *Plecoptera*, characterized by wings that fold over its body; also, dry flies or nymphs that imitate such insects.

streamer
a variety of fly characterized by long trailing feathers or hair intended to replicate a baitfish.

strike
the act of a fish's taking the bait, usually in an emphatic manner.

strike indicator
a bobber or similar device that is pulled below the water surface by a striking fish.

stringer
a rope or chain on which fish may be kept alive in water.

strip
to release or retrieve line off a reel by a series of short pulls.

stripping basket
(fly-fishing) an open container worn on an angler's waist to hold unwound line.

structure
the configuration of terrain and other objects (e.g., logs, rocks, piers) above and below the water surface, interpreted by fishermen to determine likely places to find fish.

swivel
a rotating piece of tackle that prevents line from twisting.

tackle
a collective noun for fishing equipment, especially rods and reels.

tag-and-release
a saltwater fishing technique in which an identification tag is attached to the fish before it is released.

tag end
the part of a line in which a knot is tied; also, the small portion of line that remains after a knot is tied and that is normally trimmed.

tail
to lift a fish by its tail. Also (of a fish), to swim in shallow water with only its tail visible.

tailer
a device used to land fish by slipping its noose around the fish's tail.

tailwater
a stream or river formed by runoff from a dam.

take
(of a fish) to seize the bait.

tapered
describing a rod, line, or leader that is thicker at one end than the other.

tensile strength
the maximum stress that a line can withstand before it breaks.

terminal tackle
a term that refers collectively to bobbers, sinkers, leaders, hooks, lures, and other gear that go at the "business end" of a line.

terrestrial
any of the insects that live on land but that often fall into water (such as ants and grasshoppers), or a bait that resembles such a creature.

test
the measure of a line's tensile strength (expressed as "X-pound test").

throat
(fly-tying) a hackle tied only on the underside of a fly.

tie into
a colloquial phrase meaning to hook a fish (as in, "After only 10 minutes, I tied into a lunker").

tip
the topmost portion of a rod.

tip-top
the guide at the end of a rod.

tippet
the thinnest portion of a leader to which the fly is tied; also, a section of monofilament tied on to the leader as a replacement for the original tippet.

tip-up
an ice-fishing indicator that signals a strike by a change of its signal's position.

topbait
describing a plug designed to move along the water surface.

treble hook
a hook composed of three bends and points that share a single shank.

trico
abbreviation of *Trichoptera*, a tiny caddis insect or a fly that represents such an insect.

troll
to fish by towing a plug or another bait behind a moving boat.

trude
a variety of dry fly characterized by a bucktail wing tied parallel to the hook shank and pointing toward the bend.

tube fly
a fly, used primarily for steelhead and salmon, that is tied on a thin tube. The tube, which fits over a hook, slides back toward the line to expose the hook when a fish strikes.

two-foot
a rod guide that is attached to the rod by two projections (cf. One-Foot).

unloading
the process by which the weight of a lure or fly line is released from a rod during the forward cast, so that the rod can propel the lure or line (*see also* Loading).

ventral fin
the fin located on the front of a fish's abdomen.

weedless
describing a lure or fly that contains a "weed guard" device that reduces the chance of snagging on underwater foliage.

weight-forward
the type of fly line that has its heaviest portion at the front end.

well
See Live-Well.

wet fly
a fly that is fished underwater (cf. Dry Fly).

wind knot
an unwanted overhand knot formed by the wind's looping the line during a cast.

window
the supposed parameters within which a fish is able to view activity on or above the water surface.

wrapping
thread or other material wound around the guides of a rod to hold them in place.

zinger
See Retractor.